IRISH

To Manuel:

"Remember Jan 1, 1987 — You are to stop smoking. Remember your new years resolution!"

Howard R. Wagner
Dec 9 86

IRISH

by
DONALD R. WAGNER

Shamrock Press & Publishing Company
P.O. Box 7256
Alexandria, Virginia 22307

First Edition
Design and Production – Irv Garfield
Printed in the United States of America

Library of Congress Cataloging in Publication Data

Wagner, Donald R., 1935–
    Irish

    I. Title
82–62239
ISBN: 0-910583-00-5

To My Daughters
Annie, Mary & Rosie
I LOVE YOU

Acknowledgements

My sincerest and heartfelt thanks to the following people whose help, love and devotion have made my dream come true.

Mrs. Mary Stuart Price Diefenbach
Mr. Irv Garfield
Miss Beth Goodman
Mrs. Elizabeth Hattemer
Mrs. Janet Horwitz
Mrs. Donna Marie Lamy
Mr. and Mrs. Robert H. Langner
Miss Rosemarie Lenahan
Mr. and Mrs. Frank P. Miller
Miss Patricia M. B. Miller
Miss Ann C. O'Connor
Miss Victoria Maria Pappas
Mr. and Mrs. Allen I. Price, Jr.
Mrs. Beatrice M. (Wagner) Spallone
Miss Mara Tryck Sternberg
Mr. and Mrs. James M. Wagner
Ms Anna Louise Wallis

PREFACE

A LOVE FOR ALL SEASONS

If we could choose our time to leave this earth
    How difficult it would be
All our friends and loved ones never again to see
    Then, too, the time of year would be difficult to choose
For no matter what the season, there's so terribly much to lose

Could I choose Autumn as my time to leave
    Remembering how we frolicked in soft Autumn leaves
Running, laughing, doing as we pleased
    Remembering the first time we made love
I'm sure we were blessed by the Lord up above
    It seemed all the world had stopped to pray
As I held you close and heard you say
    "I love you darling, please promise you'll stay"

But what if with God I choose to abide
    I'd no longer be lying by your side
I'd miss Mother Nature's colorful display
    Of beautiful leaves on cool Autumn days
I'd need you to be brave and strong
    For God would be calling before too long

It feels so comforting, the warmth of a sweater
    Against the chill of the cool Autumn weather
It's God's gentle reminder for winter to prepare
    To treat one another with sweet loving care

Perhaps in Winter, the bells I'd toll
    But then who'd protect you from Winter's cold
Yes, I'd stay to share my warmth with you
    I'd try to be comforting all Winter through

The beautiful Winter so hushed and calm
    After the raging storm, its bitter winds gone
To feel the velvety softness of new Winter snow
    Yes, I'd stay to protect you, I never could go

For all this wonderment, there must be a reason
    Yes, right in the middle is the Christmas season
A time for depending on one another
    Of sharing the love we have for each other
Winter's truly magnificent and for what it's worth
    A crowning tribute to the Maker of Earth

How can I explain the peaceful glow
    The loving sensations from head to toe
After loving you in Winter, I could never go
    For a sweeter love, I'll never know

When Winter ends and all seems dead
    Mother Nature pulls, from over her head
Her snowy white blanket, that covered her bed
    Nurturing all living things, she fought the good fight
She protected the Earth, on those bitter cold nights
    Now fulfilling God's promise of life in the Spring
She'll bring life full cycle, in all living things

Things lying dormant all Winter through
    Are suddenly waiting to start life anew
As a baby bird struggles from its shell to live
    So from under the snow Mother Nature forgives
The ravages of Winter and starts to live

Her beautiful crocus and roses in bloom
    All Winter were safe in her warm loving womb
Her sparkling brooks, her crystal clear springs
    They're her breasts that feed all living things
With help from the sun and gentle rain
    Her fabulous colors we'll enjoy again
Such peace and tranquility only God could send
    Yes, of love and nature there's a perfect blend

With winds of March and April showers
    Nature's showing off her pretty flowers
The trees in blossom as Nature displays
    All her precious wonders this month of May

PREFACE

So, how could I leave in the Spring of the year
  That's when you married me, my dear
With oceans of blue skies and soft sweet rain
  There's so much to lose with immeasurable gains
I could never leave in the Spring of the year
  I would have to stay to love you, my dear

But how could I leave in the summertime
  As thoughts of you race across my mind
The hopes and joys and promises of Spring
  The golden days of Summer will bring
Yes, it's nature's song that Summer sings

We walked hand in hand through quiet green meadows
  Admiring a rose with its sweet tender petals
It was there I confessed my love for you
  As I gave you a rosebud impearled with dew

Suddenly all nature was in full swing
  I shouted, "Come, come quickly, let's not miss a thing"
The corn's in the field and the wheat's up too
  God's promise of an abundant life is coming true
The beautiful fruits and the flower gardens
  This wonderful life is truly a bargain
All things conceived in Winter's cold
  Are born in love as Summer unfolds

Lying beside you on a warm summer's eve
  Star-gazing as far as the mind can conceive
There's the Big Dipper and see the North Star
  Like God so near, yet so very far

As far as one can imagine and even beyond
  To float in space with all care gone
Yes, viewing with God all his creations
  Forgetting Hell and all other damnations

Seeing your brown eyes so clear and cool
  Moonbeams quivering in those crystal clear pools
Where tear drops sparkle like precious jewels
  Those tears of joy that leave me weak
As they linger softly on your cheek

Your soft ruby lips, your trembling voice
  Telling me, I was the love of your choice

ix

PREFACE

As we lovingly kissed, my spirits soared
    Love, sweet, sweet love, forever more
For me to leave in Summer, there'd be no reason
    No, my passing would wait for another season

God doesn't tell us to pick the flowers
    And God doesn't want us to pick the hour
It's abundantly clear why the choice is not ours
    Only God will choose our day and the hour
So while we're waiting for God to decide
    Let's love one another and walk side by side

Please promise you'll love me in every season
    And I promise I'll love you for every reason
For after all the years have rushed on by
    Softly, God will be calling me from your side

D. R. WAGNER

1

Irish and the Army get Acquainted

The Chinese say that a journey of a thousand miles starts with that first step. Having just signed up with the army, standing there taking the oath and being asked to take the customary one step forward, I somehow got the feeling that I was making a terrible mistake as I took that one step forward. As it turned out, this journey not only covered a thousand miles, but thousands and thousands of miles filled with every conceivable pitfall and hardship. During this journey I experienced the whole gamut of human emotions.

The army and I got acquainted in Ohio. I was out there looking for work when I met a slick-talking army recruiter who convinced me to join a fancy outfit in something called the "Special Forces." This recruiter fed me the usual bullcrap of how this wasn't like the regular army, and that after basic training most of the men wound up wearing civilian clothes with a .38 revolver and the whole bit. That was the cloak and dagger stuff. I ate it up like a cat lapping cream.

Anyway, I found myself on an airplane with twenty other recruits being shipped down to Kentucky. We arrived about eleven o'clock at night and were herded into receiving barracks.

1

We were given a sheet, two blankets, and told to hit the rack. I was so naive that I left my wallet in my pants that I hung on the wall. Needless to say, the wallet was gone in the morning.

Speaking of morning, it came around 2:00 A.M. with some asshole blowing a whistle in my ear. I instinctively reached out and tried to shove that damned whistle down his throat. We must have wrestled around on the floor for several minutes before they separated us. Everyone was hollering, screaming, and raising hell. When things quieted down, the sergeant chewed us out. He threatened to have us all put in the stockade if we didn't shape up. He left mumbling something about never having encountered such a rowdy bunch of bastards in his twelve years in the army. He warned us that the next time we heard that whistle we had better hit the street on the double.

Soon we were sent to get our hair cut. The barber asked me how I would like it cut. I told him I just wanted a trim. He then cut almost every hair off my head.

From there we were led to the supply house to receive our government issue. We were each given a slip of paper and told to stand in line. As we went through the line, we were measured for various items of clothing and footwear, and the sizes were written on a slip of paper. Then came the fun part, going through the line to pick up your clothing. Those idiots on the other side of the counter took sheer delight in handing out the wrong sizes to everybody. I wound up with a wardrobe that would have fit King Kong: size nine boots when I took size seven, and so on, down to the hat that drooped over my ears. I sure was a sad-looking specimen.

We no sooner got back to the barracks area than this guy called out my name and told me to report to the personnel office about some mix-up in my records or something. He gave me directions and sent me on my way.

I was walking across this big field, kicking rocks, and hating myself and the world for getting mixed up with the army, when this really sharply dressed dude passed me. He started hollering, "Hey Crute."

I didn't pay any attention because that wasn't my name. Be-

2

sides, I didn't know what a "Crute" was anyway. (It wasn't long before I found out it was short for "recruit.")

He came after me, grabbed me by the arm, and started hollering, "Didn't you see this uniform I'm wearing?"

To which I replied, "What the fuck are you bitching about? Look what they gave me."

He asked me if I had had the "Articles of War" read to me yet.

"If you mean have I caught hell yet, that's all I've been catching since I got here," I told him.

He started hollering something about his being an officer and a gentleman and that I was supposed to salute him.

I grimaced. "That sounds horrible. I wouldn't brag about it if I were you." Then I added, "If you guys would treat a guy a little better and stop all this damned hollering, I'm sure we would all get along a lot better."

He asked for my name and barracks number and told me he would see me later on in the day. I said fine and thanked him for the warning.

True to his word, he showed up about six that evening and asked me to go outside with him.

"What for? Do you want to kick the shit out of me or what?"

He said he wanted to read the "Articles of War" to me so that if I screwed up again they could court-martial me.

"Well, that's just dandy. I don't even know what a court-martial is, and you bastards want to give me one."

"It simply means that if you fuck up, you're going to jail."

"Great, simply great! Without any training whatsoever you expect me to know all about your army. What the hell kind of a deal is that, anyway!"

At any rate we wound up outside, where I promptly plunked my ass down under a big shade tree and lit up a cigarette. He began to read the "Articles of War" to me.

It got rather amusing after a while. I wasn't all that dumb, but playing the part of a dumb bastard seemed like the best defense. I interrupted him at every other sentence and made him explain the meaning. By the time he was through, I don't believe I'd ever seen anyone madder in my whole life.

3

He asked me if I had learned anything.

"All that shit you've been pumping out of your mouth for the last two hours is fine, but I don't think I understand. Perhaps if you went over the important parts again, maybe it might make sense to me."

He turned and walked away into the night, mumbling something to himself about resigning his commission.

After several more days of constant harassment, orientations, and lectures, plus the typical experiences with the shots and the likes, we were finally assigned to our training company. I really got off on the right foot there—or the wrong foot, depending on how you want to look at it.

Carrying our duffel bags, AWOL bags, papers, and all kinds of paraphernalia, we were herded off the bus like a bunch of cattle being led to the slaughterhouse. I got to the door of the bus, missed the first step, and fell out onto the street. All my gear scattered everywhere. These guys in shiny helmets were reprimanding me while I was trying to reassemble my stuff and regain my composure.

After a twenty-minute ass-chewing session on what a bunch of dumb people we were, we were herded into barracks, assigned bunk beds, foot and wall lockers. We no sooner caught our breath than a whistle blew again, and we were herded back outside where the top sergeant chewed our asses because we were too slow. He sent us back inside and told us to make it faster the next time he blew his whistle.

Since my bunk was at the top of the stairs on the second floor, I was the first one to get to the door. The only problem was that the screen door opened in. About the tenth time practicing this drill, I missed the door handle. In the rush to get down the steps, thirty-nine guys behind me shoved me right through that screen door, and we all collided with the forty guys coming out the other door from the first floor. You have never seen such a mixture of assholes and elbows in all your life. Eighty guys landed in one big heap, with cuts and bruises galore, but no broken bones. It was complete chaos.

They got us unscrambled and, sure enough, they made us

4

practice again and again for the next thirty minutes, all the while cussing and yelling at us at the top of their voices.

I figured right then and there that I wasn't going to let the bastards get me down. I'd just do what they wanted and get it over with, without a hassle. Unfortunately, it didn't work out that way. The harder I tried, the more I screwed up.

In the chow line we were required to stand at parade rest with our hands behind our backs, come to attention, move forward as the line moved, and move back to parade rest when we stopped. No talking or other movements of any kind were permitted. My balls were itchy, and when I thought no one was looking I scratched them. Sure enough, I got caught, and was taken to the head of the chow line. They told me to holler as loud as I could that I would not scratch my nuts in chow line.

While I'm hollering this for all the world to hear, three or four other guys thought it was funny and were laughing at me.

They were brought to the front of the line and told to stand there and laugh at me. I thought I was in a madhouse. Here I am screaming, "I will not scratch my nuts in chow line," while they were standing there going Ha Ha Ha Ha. From there on out I was a marked man.

The next morning, we were issued our field packs and rifles. Sure enough, I made the classic mistake of calling my rifle a gun. For this I was placed in front of the whole company so that they could make an example of me. I had to hold the rifle in my left hand, above my head, and with my right hand, pat the rifle while saying, "This is my rifle." And then I had to move my right hand down to my pecker and say, "This is my gun." Then move my right hand back up to the rifle and say, "This is for shooting; the other is for fun."

This went on for ten minutes or more, I guess, and by this time I was beyond humiliation. I told them they could do whatever they wanted with me, because I was disgusted with their whole operation by now. This remark got me the rest of the day on KP duty.

So on it went, hour after hour, day after day. They would rat race us everywhere we went. Walking was out of the question.

Double-time here, double-time there. I had forgotten how to walk by now. We were to have a ten-minute break every hour, but it usually worked out something like this: Take ten, expect five, and get two. They were real sweethearts.

We were changing sheets one day. I was about to jump this ditch while holding on to my sheets, which were flying in the breeze. An officer came around the corner of the building. In midair, I tried to throw him a salute, negotiate the ditch, and hold on to my sheets, all at the same time. It didn't work out at all. My foot hit the edge of the ditch, and I fell right into him, knocking him up against the building. There I was lying on the ground with my sheets draped all around me, and there he was standing over me screaming various theories as to the legality of my birth. He told me that as a soldier, I'd make Sad Sack look like a West Pointer. He regained his composure and went on his way, leaving me lying there on the ground. I was thoroughly convinced by this time that as a soldier, I'd make an excellent civilian.

I had another problem that caused me no end of trouble. I was so damned short that I could never seem to keep in line with the guy ahead of or beside me when we were marching. They would say that I marched in a rank and file all my own, and they were right.

I remember one parade in particular. The post commander and everyone who was anyone was there. At the end of the parade, we were standing in formation while he commented on the parade. He called attention to our battalion and company and made a public announcement on my marching ability. He said the whole damned regiment was out of step, except for the man from Company B who marched in a rank and file all his own.

I thought that was extremely nice of him to point me out for special mention; however, our company commander thought differently, and that was the last parade I ever marched in until graduation from basic training. I always wound up with KP duty or some other undesirable detail when it was parade day.

I didn't much care, though, for I managed to screw up at whatever they had me doing.

Those first few weeks were invaluable for helping me plan my strategy and determine the lines of defense. Anyone in a position of authority became the enemy, and anything I could do to screw them up or make them look bad, I did without hesitation, for they were experts at making people hate them.

If you got sick, they called you a goldbrick. If you got blisters, you were a candyass. If you didn't understand something after it was explained only once, you were a dumb ass. And the tone they used when they addressed you made you wonder if perhaps you should kill your mother for having given birth to someone like you.

I learned all about the chain of command. No matter what happened you could always pass the buck up the ladder by simply saying, "He told me to do it." The only defense that guy had would be to pass the buck higher up the chain.

They also had what seemed like half a million regulations, covering everything from shining your shoes to starting a war. Naturally, it was impossible for anyone to know even a fraction of these regulations. It was equally impossible for every company, battalion, or even base to have copies of all of them. I found these regulations very useful throughout my career. Everytime I was in trouble, I'd simply quote an army regulation covering the subject—to my advantage, of course. "According to AR 180-3, I'm right in the present situation." Ninety-nine times out of a hundred, that is as far as it would go. For one reason or another, they would never take time to look it up. Or else they couldn't because it was not available to them. Or by the time that they got an answer as to whether or not I was right, the incident was usually forgotten.

There was also another weapon at my disposal—the rumor. The whole damned army, it seemed, ran on rumors, and I would start some of the damnedest rumors you ever heard. For instance, the Defense Department was closing the base or the whole division was being rotated overseas.

I took advantage of all those details to which I was assigned. When we would be cleaning battalion or post headquarters, I would read everything on everyone's desk. I would even thumb through the files and desk drawers to gather bits of information. Then I would simply make up the balance. In this way most of my rumors had an aura of credibility. As it turns out, most of those fools would have believed anything you told them, anyway; but if you told them the story came from post headquarters, there was no way they could doubt you.

What I remember best about basic training was the nights: lying in our bunks, too damned tired from the day's harassments, drills, details, and what have you, even to sleep. We would bullshit back and forth for hours. We had a real mixture from all walks of life: draftees, those of us dumb enough to enlist, guys with college degrees, high school graduates, and high school dropouts.

The first day in our company the company commander pointed this out in unmistakable terms. We were in formation when he made his announcement.

"All you people with college degrees, step to the front of the ranks. All you people with high school diplomas, step to the rear. Now, all you people with high school diplomas, walk around the company area, pick up every cigarette butt, scrap of paper, and debris. You people with college degrees, supervise. The rest of you dumb bastards, follow them around and see if you can learn something."

I remember we were lying there one night when one old boy from Harlan County, Kentucky, started telling us a tale about his hound dog named "Old Blue." He was in a bar, and as the beer and the bullshit flowed, he got to bragging about Old Blue.

He told this guy that not only would Old Blue flush quail out of the bush, but he would also come back first and tell you how many quail were in there. The two of them finally went into the woods to test Old Blue.

He'd tell Old Blue to flush the bush and Blue would haul his ass into the bush and come back and stomp on the ground with his paw: one, two, three. That meant there were three quail in that bush. The owner told Old Blue to flush them out. Into the bush the dog went, and sure enough, three quail flew out.

Old Blue's owner continued his story. "The stranger still wasn't convinced and made Old Blue do it several more times before he became a believer. He finally talked me into selling him Old Blue. He called me about a week later and told me he had shot Old Blue."

"What in the world did you do that for?"

"He made an ass out of me in front of all my buddies."

"How did he do that?"

"Well, I was bragging on him, how he could flush quail and come back and let you know how many quail were in the bush and all, so we took him out in the woods so that I could prove it. I'd tell him to flush the bush. He'd go running in and come back, jump up, wrap his legs around mine and start humpin' like crazy. Then he'd jump down, pick up a stick and shake it like he was mad. He did it several times, and naturally I was the laughing stock of the whole damned town. I figured he had gone crazy and I shot him."

"Oh, hell, buddy, I sure wish you hadn't shot Old Blue. All he was trying to tell you was that there were more fuckin' quail in that bush than you could shake a stick at."

The roof almost came off the barracks with laughter.

Then there were the poets and the rhyme makers. Every place I was ever stationed, there was at least one. Some of their works were real jewels, and after we had heard them several times and knew them by heart, we would lay there and each guy would take a line.

Someone would holler, "Where's the Queen?" Someone else would say, "In bed with diphtheria." Then another would ask, "What? Hasn't that Greek bastard left yet?" Then you might hear something like, " 'Come forth,' cried the King." "David slipped on a pile of shit and came in fifth."

On and on the jokes would go for hours. If it hadn't been for the humor, I'm sure we would all have gone mad.

I was never one to join in conspiracies, choosing to carry on my vendetta against the army alone. Of course, we all benefited or suffered from my efforts; but rarely did I get caught or squealed on because I never admitted to anyone that I ever did anything. I felt like I was in a big brother organization. Everybody watching everybody else, and I trusted none of them.

I'll never forget the time I got up about 4:00 A.M. and stretched a rope across the barracks approximately six inches off the floor. The sergeant came busting through the door, turned the lights on, and started down the aisle blowing his whistle for all he was worth. He tripped over the rope and knocked both front teeth out on his whistle.

They tried for days to find out who put that rope there. But I never confessed and no one knew about it except me. I think they suspected I did it, but they couldn't prove it. Every time I saw the sergeant after that I would start to whistle, "All I Want for Christmas Is My Two Front Teeth." And he'd threaten, "I'll get you yet, you bastard."

We were out on the rifle range one day and they had me pulling targets and patching holes in them. I'd no sooner start back up with the target than they would start blazing away at it before I even had a chance to get it back up all the way and get clear of it.

I grabbed the field phone and rang it. As soon as someone answered I started raising hell. "Who's the dumb son of a bitch who's firing? We can't even get the targets up. Tell that stupid bastard to wait."

The voice on the other end of the phone asked with authority, "Do you know who you're talking to?"

"I don't give a shit who it is. Just relay my message."

"This is Lieutenant Jones."

"Well, I wouldn't brag about it if I were you. Do you know who this is?"

"No."

I said, "Good!" and hung up.

Then suddenly they ceased firing and converged on the bunkers trying to find out who had been on the phone. After many threats and much questioning of every man to no avail, they decided to go back to business as usual.

I'm not sure if that was a good day or a bad one—several wins and a few losses.

When it was my turn on the firing line, I had a helluva problem hitting the targets. Every time you would miss, they would wave a flag on a pole to indicate that you had missed the target. They called it "Maggie's Drawers." I got so tired of seeing Maggie's Drawers that one time I took a shot at them and knocked them out of the hands of the guy that was waving them. Boy, did I catch hell for that.

As we moved from position to position, we were required to double-time. It was getting late in the day and I was dog tired. I started walking from one position to another. Sure enough, I got caught. Some old sergeant down at the bottom of the hill spotted me walking and started into his routine of name-calling to get my attention and told me to double-time down to where he was.

I started down the hill with my rifle in front of me, and I stumbled. As I was trying to regain my balance, I kept going faster until I finally tripped over a tent rope and dove headlong into three rifle racks, meanwhile clearing out almost every rifle in them.

My punishment for that fiasco was to carry my rifle with me everywhere I went for the next two weeks, even to bed with me. If that wasn't bad enough, I dropped my canteen a few minutes later and was instructed to carry that for two weeks also.

While I was standing there hating myself, the army, and the world in general, a jeep pulled up behind me. I wasn't paying any attention, and sure enough, it was a goddamned officer who started reprimanding me for not saluting him. As he was walking away, I reached in his jeep and put the gear shift in neutral, hurried to the front of the jeep, put my foot on the bumper, and shoved it backwards. As it started rolling down the hill, I hollered at the lieutenant that his jeep was leaving without him. You should have seen the look on his face when he turned around just in time to see the jeep go over a thirty-foot cliff and blow up upon hitting the bottom.

I never did find out for sure, but as best as I could figure, he was court-martialed and had to pay for the jeep. I offered to testify that I saw him put the hand brake on, but he was too proud to become indebted to a lowly private, so I figure he got what he deserved. Come to think of it, I think I came out ahead that day.

The following Thursday afternoon, they pulled six of us out of ranks and sent us on a detail cleaning up the Officers' Club after a bridge party the officers' wives held there weekly. We arrived before the game was over.

I had checked the regulation at battalion headquarters on the use of enlisted personnel for such duties. I discovered they were supposed to hire civilians to work in the Officers' Club and the Officers' Mess Hall. It was expressly forbidden to use enlisted personnel. On my third trip on this detail I decided to get even with the busboys, whose work we were doing.

So, I started picking up the gratuities from the saucers on the tables and dumping the money in my hat. One lady asked me what I was doing. I told her that all these gratuities were going to the Old Soldiers' Home in Washington, D. C., and that I was sure the old soldiers appreciated their generosity. She said, "Well, since it's for such a worthy cause, here are two more dollars."

The word spread up and down the tables like wild fire. Here I was walking through the aisles and all the officers' wives were cramming money into my outstretched hat while I continued to pick up the loose change from the saucers. You see, in the army everything is done by rank. The colonel's wife wouldn't think of donating less than a major's wife. They all gave according to rank. The general's wife put a ten-dollar bill in the hat. I collected over one hundred dollars from all of them.

When no one was looking I slipped outside, crawled under the building, and buried the money. I then walked back in as if nothing had happened.

As soon as the ladies had left, the regular busboys hit those tables like flies on shit. They were looking for their usual tips and when they came up empty, they started bitching that we had stolen their money. They demanded that we come up with it or they were going to rat on us and see that we were court-martialed.

This one little chicken-shit bastard on our detail got scared and put the finger on me. Those bastards jumped me and searched me right down to my shorts. Of course they came up empty.

We no sooner got back to the company area than the commanding officer called me into his office. It seemed that the busboys had called him and told him what I had done. He really let me have it and told me that if I didn't put the money on his desk right away, he would have the clerk draw up court-martial papers and have my ass in the stockade by morning.

I pointed out that there was an army regulation on help in the Officers' Club and accordingly we had no business being there. He replied that the base commander was aware of the situation and condoned it.

"Fine; but he has a boss, too, and I'll get word to him," I retorted.

He told me that the general would be happy to learn that I didn't like the way he was running the base. He said he was also going to charge me with trying to blackmail the general.

"I'm not trying to do any such thing," I insisted, "but if you court-martial me, I'm going to call every officer's wife who was there as a witness in my defense."

"You're crazy, you dumb bastard. If they testify that they gave you money, you've hung yourself."

"Well, that just might be true, but are *you* going to be the one to tell the general that his wife was conned? How do you suppose the general will react to that? And conned by a man from *your* outfit, too! That should fix you up really well with him, don't you think?"

"You're not bluffing me, you common bastard, you," this slick co retorted. He called the company clerk in and told him to prepare court-martial papers against me for theft and attempted blackmail. He dismissed me and told me if I came up with the money by morning, he would consider dropping the charges.

I thanked him, threw him a salute, and left, confident that I

13

had heard the last of that. I was right. I never heard another word about it for the rest of my hitch in the army. Besides, if push had come to shove, all I had to do was to mail a few dollars to the Old Soldiers' Home and I would have been home free anyway.

That co didn't forget about it, though. He tried his damnedest to get me to screw up until one day he figured he really had the goods on me.

He had been chewing my ass out for something or other. As he dismissed me and I turned to leave, I uttered the letters FTA, which meant "Fuck the Army," and he heard me.

With a smile of sheer delight on his face, he said, "This time I got you for sure. I'm having special court-martial papers drawn up against you for making derogatory remarks against the United States Army, an act of total insubordination."

I never uttered a sound in my own defense, choosing instead to let the proceedings take their course.

On the day of the court-martial, the captain came in and told me to turn in all my equipment: sheets, blankets, field gear and all. He ordered me to pack my duffel bag, because after the court-martial, he was sure I would be going to the stockade for at least six months.

I complied with his wishes, still remaining silent. He personally drove me to battalion headquarters, where a full bird colonel and a major were ready to conduct the court-martial.

The proceedings began with the reading of the formal charges against me. Then the captain was called to testify, which he did in eloquent terms. I could tell he was enjoying every minute of it.

I was finally called and told to stand in front of the board. I was asked if I had anything to say in my own defense, or anything to offer in the way of extenuation or mitigation.

I could see the captain sitting there with a big smile on his face. He really and truly believed at this point that he had won and was getting revenge, not only for himself, but for everyone who had ever encountered me. I'm sure he fully expected to hear me say, "No excuse, sir," and throw myself on the mercy of the court.

I started in by saying that I had only been in the army for six weeks and that I was aware of the fact that I was having a little trouble catching on and learning just what was expected of me. I explained that as a result, I had been forced to perform all kinds of special duty and had been sent on numerous details and had been averaging only two hours' sleep a night since I had been there.

"I'm not blaming the captain or his cadre," I continued. "I understand that they are just trying to make a good soldier out of me, and if that's what it takes, then I accept it without question. I believe I try harder than anyone in our company, but the harder I try, the more trouble I seem to get into."

I went into a forty-five minute oration of every incident that had happened to me since I had first arrived there. Clarence Darrow and F. Lee Bailey sure would have been proud of me.

And in conclusion, I reached into my pocket and pulled out a little recruiting poster and unfolded it in front of them. It was a poster of a sergeant instructing a private in the use of a field radio. The caption across the top read "Finest Training Anywhere" (FTA.). Across the bottom it read, "Join the U.S. Army."

"So you see, sir, all I meant by FTA. was 'Finest Training Anywhere.' But the captain never gave me a chance to explain. He just assumed that I meant 'Fuck the Army.' "

They turned to the captain and asked him if he had anything to say. By now his confident smile had been replaced by a look of total disbelief. He really was at a loss for words and just sat there dumbfounded.

The colonel turned to me and said that he was dismissing all the charges against me and would have the record expunged. He told me to report back to my training company, and if I had any more problems to get word to him.

I saluted, did an about-face, and started for the door with the captain dead on my heels.

Just as I reached for the door handle, I heard the colonel say in no uncertain terms, "Just one moment, Captain. I would like a word with you before you leave."

I turned to the captain and politely informed him that I would wait for him in the jeep.

I don't know how he restrained himself. He looked as if he wanted to hit me so badly that he could almost taste it.

I listened at the door for about five minutes. I had never heard such an ass-chewing in all my life. First the colonel would work on him, and then while he was catching his breath the major would start in on him. They started off with, "You should have known that you don't assume *anything* in the army; for if you do, it's what it implies—ASS/U/ME. You make an ass out of you and me, and that's just what you did, Captain."

"Besides, that was a nice young man you had in here, and I'm sure he'll make a fine soldier. No wonder he's always screwing up. I doubt if you could keep up a twenty-hour-a-day pace for six weeks yourself, Captain. And that uniform he was wearing was about six sizes too big for him. How could you permit that to happen? Why didn't you get him a new issue of clothing?"

On and on they went. I can't say that I wasn't delighted with the outcome. I thought to myself, "If you fuck with the bull, you get the horn." I felt he had been fucking with the horn, so I had given him the whole bull.

I went on out to the jeep to wait. The captain showed up about twenty minutes later. He sure looked depressed. He got in and without saying a word we drove away. I figured I had better keep my mouth shut.

He pulled up in front of the main PX and told me to follow him. We went on inside where he bought me a cup of coffee. As we sat there drinking our coffee, he spoke his first words. "What the fuck makes you tick, Irish? I can't figure if you're so dumb that you're brilliant, or so brilliant that you just act dumb."

I said, "That's a start, Captain. At least you know I have a name besides 'Crute' or 'you dumb bastard.' I'm not one damned bit mad at you; I don't see what you're so mad at me for. Besides, I don't care what you say, Captain, I know you like me."

He cut a big fart and said, "That's what I think of you, Irish." I asked him if he would like a piece of bread to sop it up with.

I figured I had better console him, so I told him I had been listening at the door while they gave him hell and that I knew how he felt. His face turned as red as a beet. He nearly choked on his coffee. After regaining his composure, he told me he had been considering his options.

First option: "I could take you off base and tell you to get lost, but I'm sure that you'd only turn up again to torment me."

Second option: "I could take you out in the woods and shoot you, which at this point doesn't sound like a half bad idea."

Third option: "I could take you back to the company area and try to forget that any of this happened. But if I did that, my effectiveness as a leader would be compromised as soon as you started running off at the mouth about what an ass you made of me at that court-martial today. I'd be the laughing stock of the whole damned post by nightfall. I hate to admit it, but you have me beat. In five years of training recruits, I thought I had seen everything. I felt I could handle any of them until now. Like I said, I don't know if you're dumb or brilliant or just plain crazy. You just don't act or react in a normal manner. I'm flat-ass beaten."

Disgusted, the captain continued, "If you were listening at the door, you know that I'm to give you a couple of days off to rest up and also I'm to personally take you over to Supplies for a new issue of clothing. I just wish there were some way I could resign and leave this base and try to forget we ever met."

"Look, Captain," I suggested, "you don't have to take me for a new issue. Let your first sergeant do that. It sure would be nice to have a pair of shoes that fit and a hat that didn't fall down over my ears. As for the time off, well, I can forgo that. Hell, I'm used to that twenty-hour-a-day routine by now. I hope you don't think I was dumb enough to spend my time doing any work while on details. Hell, I spent most of that time sleeping. That's how I survived so long—sleeping under the barracks or on the major's desk. I didn't care, just so no one was looking, and wherever I was I went to sleep."

"As for the court-martial results, I know everyone figures I'm in the stockade by now; but we can always tell them that the colonel postponed it. What the hell, I'll be gone in a couple of weeks, anyway. Just as soon as basic training is over. You have my word, I won't say anything to anyone."

"How the hell can I trust *you* after all that has happened?"

"Well, if you don't take me out and shoot me, you really don't have much choice in the matter now, do you?"

"Details and all?"

"Sure, Captain, no immediate fear of perspiration."

"How's that again?"

"No sweat."

"Oh. . . ."

So back to the company area we went. I kept my word and simply told all my buddies that they had postponed the court-martial. But the guys wouldn't buy it; they wanted to know how I had managed to rob the old man of his day of glory. I just insisted that the proceedings had been postponed until a later date.

Still no sale, for by now my scraps with the army and those in authority had become common knowledge, and I had become somewhat of an unsung hero.

The next two weeks went by rather quickly and life was a little easier for me. I would imagine the captain told them to give me some slack because all he wanted was for me to graduate and get out of his life at all costs.

Two days before graduation I was on a detail at division headquarters. I was doing my usual snooping when I discovered a list of names of trainees to be given awards at graduation. I said to myself, "Self, why not." I sat down and retyped the list. I substituted my name for the name of the top graduate, the most outstanding trainee of over 1,200 men graduating that day. I figured I deserved it for I was "outstanding" most of the time, anyway. "Out standing" in the rain, the mud, the wind, and the cold. Then of course, once the general made the awards, who was going to challenge him? I couldn't lose.

I'll never forget graduation day. There we were, standing in formation with the general giving this big spiel about what it took to be named top trainee and what an honor it was to receive such an award, having distinguished oneself by exceptional and outstanding dedication to duty, training, and so forth.

I'll never forget the look of astonishment and the gasps for breath from everyone who had ever come into contact with me, when the general called out my name and company and ordered me front and center to receive the award.

The general invited me, along with all the other award recipients, up on the reviewing stand to watch the parade with him. Then came the order to "pass in review."

There I was up there with the general while the band was playing and the troops were passing in review. I gave a special salute and a grin from ear to ear when my outfit went by. I felt like thumbing my nose at the captain, but I knew I had better forgo that pleasure.

Everyone in our company had trouble restraining themselves. My buddies could hardly keep from laughing. It was worth it just to see the look of sheer amazement on everyone's faces.

After all the pomp and circumstance, the captain picked me up and took me back to the company area to get my duffel bag and things. He personally drove me to the finance office to get my pay and travel orders. He then drove me to the bus depot and waited until I was on the bus and the bus was on its way.

I think I really drove him bananas. The whole time he was driving me around, he kept saying to himself, "I can't believe it. Why me, God?"

At any rate, I was away from the army for two weeks before I was to report to a specialty training school at a base in Massachusetts.

2

The Civil War Revisited; Irish Meets Moose

After two weeks of becoming reacquainted with the real world I found myself at the main gate of another military installation waiting for a bus to take me to the receiving barracks. You learn to do a lot of that in the army. Hurry up and wait. The bus finally came, and at the next stop a second lieutenant got on and sat down beside me. Several women also got on, and the bus was full.

One lady was standing by our seats. The lieutenant looked over at me and asked, "Why don't you give this lady your seat, Private?"

I looked back at him and said, "Sir, the same act of Congress that made me a private also made you an officer and a gentlemen, so why don't *you* give her *your* seat?" He gave the lady his seat, after threatening to see me later. I made sure that that was the last time I ever laid eyes on him.

I checked in and got to bullshitting with the clerk on duty, trying to find out how things were run there. He was a wealth of information. He told me that the personnel files were forwarded to the processing center, which would send down a list of names of those to be interviewed the next day. He explained that this list was posted on the bulletin board and you should watch for your name to show up on it. He said you were supposed to stay in the barracks until 1700 hours, and then you could pick up your class A pass and go to town or do whatever you wanted to do, just as long as you made roll call in the morning.

He also told me they made up the duty roster (KP, guard duty, and the like) from the class A pass box by pulling the passes from those not scheduled for interviews. Well, I figured, no class A pass in the box, no details for me. After I picked the pass up the first night, I simply kept it in my pocket.

With a class A pass in my pocket I could go anywhere I wanted on or off post without question. And if I would get stopped, I'd simply tell them I was on my way to personnel; but that rarely happened.

There were a few more little tricks I learned. One was to act like you owned the place and the other was to carry a clipboard with you wherever you went. It seemed a clipboard was synonymous with authority. If someone really glared at you, you would just raise your clipboard, pull out your pen, make believe you were writing, or ask him for his name. He wouldn't hesitate to give it to you and if they found the courage to ask what it was for, you'd simply tell him that he would know soon enough. Leave it at that and walk away. It would work like magic. Like I said, it was like a big brother organization with everyone spying on everyone else.

I had made the transition very nicely, I thought. From the biggest fuck-up in basic training to the biggest fuck-off for the remainder of my career.

The Civil War was relived on every post I was ever stationed at, but it was especially prevalent up here. There was almost an equal division between Yankees and Rebels, and it was usually the Rebels who would start the ball rolling. A couple of them would come in drunk at night and start giving the Rebel Yell. They would wake the whole damned barracks up and start hollering, "Save your Confederate money, boys, the South shall rise again!" Some Yankee would holler back, "See you at Gettysburg!"

The Rebels would start to sing "Dixie" and the Yankees would try to drown them out with their own version of "Dixie." It went something like this: "I'm glad I'm not from the land of cotton, where everything smells so goddamned rotten, run away, run away, run away from it all."

The Rebels would start to get rowdy and want to fight, but it seldom went that far. Most of it was in good fun and just for laughs. Someone would holler, "What's the Mason Dixon line?" Someone would holler back, "That's where the Rebels come to shit and the Yankees come to eat."

Usually the Yankees would retaliate by singing about the Rebel flag: "Oh the Rebel flag was a dirty pussy rag, and General Lee was a bastard."

On and on it would go for hours at a time. I really enjoyed the ruckus and would do my best to keep things rolling. Like the day I stole a can of white paint and painted a white line down the middle of the barracks. I even painted a white line down the middle of the shit house. When everyone returned that evening and inquired about the line, I told them it was the Mason Dixon line—The Yankees sleep on the North and the Rebels on the South. Same thing for the shit house. Johns on the North were for the Yankees and those on the South belonged to the Rebels. Same for the sinks and showers.

This caught on like wildfire with bunks, foot and wall lockers being moved around to conform to individual preferences. The idea was a big success, especially when the name-calling started. You knew where it was coming from and could respond in kind.

We would even line up to piss and shave on our appropriate sides. Any self-respecting Rebel wouldn't think of pissing in the Yankee side of the urinal, and vice versa.

The Brass raised hell and ordered the line removed; but it still remained, real or imaginary. Yankees and Rebels alike respected it and wouldn't step over it, even on police call in the morning.

22

The Rebels would police the southern half of the area and the Yankees the northern half.

The Rebels seemed to take things more seriously than the Yankees, for after all was said and done, the Yankees had won the war and could always throw that up in their faces to get them into a rage. Or they could tell them they were just pissed off because they were conceived in the North and only born in the South. That would always go over big.

I was there for about two weeks when they decided to ship me to a training school down in Georgia. "Jesus Christ!" cried the Rebels. "A fuckin' half-blind Catholic Yankee going down to tread on such hallowed ground! Why it's sacrilegious, that's what it is. The pure and sacred sands of Georgia will never be the same."

"I'll do my best, Rebs, and when I get there I'll pour a fifth of whiskey on the Rebel flag for you."

They all gave a big Rebel yell, for that was a sign of reverence and respect for their flag.

"You-all don't mind if I drink it first, though, do you?"

It was a good thing I was on my way out, for they chased me all the way to the bus stop. Lucky for me, the bus was ready to pull out. I'm sure that if they had caught up with me, they would have killed me on the spot.

I heard later from a couple of guys who were shipped down to Georgia that when the Rebels got back to the barracks, the Yankees began ribbing them so much about me pissing on their flag that they started a riot. They completely destroyed two barracks. Six guys wound up in the hospital and four others wound up in the stockade. Too bad I had to miss all that excitement.

As soon as I reached my new post in Georgia, I was assigned to a trainee company with training to commence the following Monday.

Life was a little easier down there. There were the customary duty rosters for KP duty and the likes, but usually you had your evenings and weekends free. With a class A pass you could go to town or to the PX, drink 3.2 beer, and bullshit with your buddies.

It was in Georgia that I met Moose. He was from West Virginia and weighed in at 260 pounds and stood six feet five inches. Under normal circumstances he was as gentle as a kitten. He was a little on the slow side and had trouble catching on to things. Probably he would have flunked out of school and been sent to the infantry or some other undesirable outfit, but I didn't let that happen. I covered him every step of the way. I even gave him all the answers to the exams. It wasn't that I was so smart. I simply stole copies of the exams along with the answers. I figured that was easier than studying.

It wasn't really necessary, for everything was so elementary and was taught from the most minute detail on. Like learning to drive a jeep. They would start with the ignition switch and show you how to turn it on and off. Then the brake, and how to apply it. And then the clutch, and so on.

Everyone called him "Moose" because of his size, and no one bothered him—or me either, for that matter. They knew if they messed with me, they had Moose to contend with and nobody would take that chance.

Moose had his own car, and every opportunity we had we went to town to hit the bars or stand around the street corners watching girls. I was unique and considered somewhat of an oddball because I didn't drink. I had just as much fun, and perhaps more, because I always knew what was happening and where I was—which is more than I can say for Moose. When he would get drunk, he wouldn't know his ass from his elbow. The more he drank, the louder he got, and the next thing you knew he wanted to fight.

He'd stand up at the bar and holler as loudly as he could (that was pretty loud), "Me and my little buddy here can whip any two of you bastards in the house."

I'd say, "Moose, you crazy bastard you, you had better be able to whip them both, because if we get any takers, you're on your own."

He'd say, "All right then, Irish, if you don't want to fight, let's get the hell out of this place. I don't like it anyhow."

Then he'd turn around and say, "Drinks on the house, I mean the Moose. When Moose drinks, everybody drinks. Everybody to the bar."

Man, for a free drink most of those guys would have murdered their own mother. They would all flock to the bar and at Moose's urging the bartender would pour everybody a drink.

The first time he pulled that, I didn't know what was coming off. I knew Moose didn't have enough money to pay for all those drinks and I sure as hell didn't. I begged Moose to clear out fast before the fur started flying.

He told me not to worry and to give him half a buck. I did and he threw it on the bar as he cried out, "When the Moose pays, everybody pays."

At that we beat a hasty retreat for the car. He must have pulled that stunt half a dozen times while we were stationed down there. Sure did piss a lot of people off!

Moose liked the idea of having me along. He could get as drunk as he wanted to and always have someone sober to drive him back on post so that they couldn't nail him for drunk driving when he returned to base. It worked out fine for me too. I always had a ride to town and I didn't need my money as long as Moose's money held out.

Our friendship grew and we became inseparable. Moose and I went everywhere together. They would refer to us as Mutt and Jeff, for I was only five foot three inches and weighed 130 pounds. I guess another reason Moose and I hit it off so well was that, for one reason or another, he thought everything I said was funny and he would laugh like a seal, which would crack me up. So we got on really well together.

Moose and I and a couple of other guys were standing on a street corner in town one night watching the girls and trying to decide what to do next when this real pretty little filly came waltzing by. Our eyes were glued on her. One guy in our group called out to her, "I sure would like to get into your pants." Just that quickly, she turned and hollered back at him, "Why? What's wrong with yours? Did you shit in them?" I looked at him and remarked that that should cool his heels for a while.

The townspeople really hated GIs and not without cause, I'm sure. You got the feeling GIs weren't welcome when you walked down the residential streets and saw such signs as "DOGS AND SOLDIERS KEEP OFF THE GRASS." It made us feel unwanted.

On the other side of the coin, though, these guys were always getting drunk and raising hell or trying to seduce their daughters. I guess you couldn't much blame them for hating us.

We finally wandered into a piano bar with the usual sleazy-looking bar maids and prostitutes. I'm not saying they were loose or anything like that; but when Moose asked one of them, "Look, I'm a man of few words—will you or won't you?" Her reply was "Your place or mine?" Moose came back with, "Well, if you're going to argue about it, just forget it." She tried to slap his face and Moose grabbed her arm and told her to get lost. She told him to go to hell and sauntered off looking for some other suckers.

We were in there for an hour or so when a cop came through the front door wanting to know who owned the dog tied up out front.

Some drunk at the bar turned around and replied, "That's my dog."

"Well you had better move her, buddy, that dog's in heat."

"Can't be, I tied her in the shade."

"No! No! Look, the dog wants to get bred."

"She can't be hungry. I fed her right before we left the house."

"Look, buddy, in plain words, that dog wants to be screwed."

"Well, go ahead, I always wanted a part police dog anyway."

The cop just turned and disappeared back through the door.

Our group was getting pretty drunk and started to heckle the piano player. I don't know where they found him, but he couldn't play worth a damn. Every time he would stumble through a song, Moose would holler at him, "Play it again, Sam." He finally got tired of it and hollered back, "My name ain't Sam and I won't play it again."

Someone hollered out, "The piano player is a mother fucker."
The manager came running over to our table and wanted to know if we had called his piano player a mother fucker.

"Hell no, what I want to know is who called the mother fucker a piano player?"

"Do you think you can do better?" the manager asked.

"Hell yes, just get that drunk away from those ivories and I'll show you."

He went over and told the guy to take a break and hollered back at me, "Okay, smart ass, it's all yours."

I told everyone to follow me and we would have a sing-along. So all six of us crowded around the piano. I played and we all sang. Moose wanted me to play "Dixie," so I did, and soon everybody in the place was singing along.

We spent the rest of the night there and never did let the regular piano player back at the keyboard. We sure had a good time. Finally we all loaded into Moose's car and headed back to the post, still singing at the top of our voices: "Lady of Spain, you old whore, you; pull down your pants and I'll floor you."

When we reached the main gate of the post, the MPs stopped us and made us all get out of the car. I had one helluva time convincing them that I was sober, for one look at that bunch of drunks with me was enough to put doubt in anyone's mind.

They made me take several sobriety tests before they were convinced. That was something else! Here I was, trying to walk a straight line, with this crazy bunch of bastards standing there hollering and cheering for me. When I finished, they all gave me a round of applause. Finally the MP let us go, and on to the post we drove, still singing and raising hell.

I would always start off with an ethnic joke, and that was sure to piss someone off and they would have to respond in kind. Something like, "What's faster than a rolling bagel and able to leap tall synagogues in a single bound? It's a bird . . . It's a plane . . . No, it's Super Jew!"

The Jews would come back with something like, "Go soak your head in a bucket of shit, you mackerel-snapping Irishman, you" (referring to the fact that I was Catholic).

27

Then things would really get rolling. Moose and I would lay down on our bunks and listen to them cut each other to ribbons.

Someone would holler, "What does shit say when it hits the wall?" Then you'd hear, "Wop."

The Italians would take offense to this and would strike back with something like "That's about as funny as a screen door on a submarine," or they'd remind the Jews of the story of the Rabbi who cut a piece off the tail pipe of his car because he was trying to circumcise it.

The Catholics really caught hell for one reason or another. The Protestants would say that the Catholics were freezing holy water and selling it as "Pope cicles."

Moose and I would just lay there and laugh at them. Every once in a while, when things would get slack or someone was taking too much abuse, I would interject a wisecrack or two of my own to keep the ball rolling or get some guy off the hook. I could match wits with the best of them and was never at a loss for something to say.

We finished our training there in Georgia and were being shipped to Fort Lewis for processing to the Far East Command.

I'm not sure how we made it, for Moose was afraid to fly and flat-ass refused even to go to the airport with me. He said, "Fuck it, we'll drive up in my car."

"What if they want to fly us from there to Japan, what are you going to do then?"

"Well, they will just have to find some other way to get us there."

"What about your car, Moose? You can't take that to Japan."

"We'll park it up there so we'll have a way home when we get back."

"It's your car, Moose, but I don't think it will be there when we get back. We might be gone a long time."

"Don't worry about it, Irish. Come on, let's get the hell out of this place."

So off we went, heading for his home in West Virginia first. I know now where they got the idea for the Lil' Abner comic strip. As we were traveling along those old country roads and through the hollows between the hills, you could almost see the characters coming alive, with all the old junk cars, tarpaper shacks, chickens and pigs, and stovepipe hats.

We pulled up in front of this old country store that served as the post office and the town meeting hall. There were several other old dilapidated buildings nearby.

Moose wanted to go into the general store. I had to piss, so he directed me to an old run-down building across the road that served as the local gin mill. He told me he'd join me in a few minutes, for he wanted a beer before going on home.

I walked in. It was so dark in there you could hardly see your hand in front of your face. I made my way to the bar and asked this old guy where the men's room was.

He asked me, "Who wants to know?"

I said, "I do."

"What for?"

"I have to take a leak."

"I don't think these boys would like you pissing in their toilet. They don't cotton to strangers much, anyway. How about it, boys?"

I turned around and there were eight or ten big old hillbillies sitting around a table, just staring right through me. They must have just come back from hunting, because there were several shotguns and rifles leaning against the table. Finally this one old boy said, "Go ahead. But stay away from the door once you get in there."

I didn't know what the hell he meant by that, and I sure as hell wasn't going to ask for an explanation. I went on in, and no sooner had I started relieving myself than a rifle went off and a bullet came zinging right through the door.

I jumped right up on the toilet, grabbed onto the pipes, and hung on for all I was worth. I didn't have to piss any longer. I must have held on for at least ten minutes, contemplating my fate. I could hear them out there laughing their asses off, but I was too scared to move for fear they would shoot again and I figured I was much too young to die.

Then I heard old Moose out there inquiring about me. It was

like the sound of sweet music to my ears to hear that big hill-billy's voice, and when he came busting through that door looking for me, I could have cried. I don't think I've ever been happier to see anyone in my whole life.

I guess I was a sorry-looking somebody hanging onto those pipes and standing up on that toilet. Old Moose started laughing at me and couldn't stop. I failed to see the humor myself and told Moose so. He said, "Shucks, the boys were just having some fun."

Moose only lived a few miles from there and knew them all. They offered to buy me a drink, but I respectfully declined, saying I'd had about all the West Virginia hospitality I could use for one day.

We went on out to Moose's place. It was an old run-down farm set back in a hollow. I asked Moose if they had to pipe sunlight in. Moose just laughed and said "No," but added that some years the snow could still be found back there as late as July.

Moose and I were still talking as if we were in the barracks and were using one four-letter word after another without realizing it. His old man took us aside and told us he understood, but requested us to watch the language around his wife and the kids. Moose assured him, "No sweat, Dad," but that very evening at the supper table old Moose screwed up again. "Dad, pass me the fu. . . ." He caught himself, laughed, and said, "Ha! Ha!, Dad, you thought I was going to fuck up, didn't you?" The old man picked up a baked potato and threw it at him. Moose ducked and it splattered off the wall.

Moose had eight brothers and sisters, and they were as poor as church mice. You got the feeling you had it pretty damned good by comparison. When you see a kid combing his hair with a fork, you know things must be pretty tight.

He had one sister who was about eighteen. For some reason she really took a fancy to me. She would call me "Soldier Boy" and constantly follow me around. Every time we were alone, she would ask me if I wanted to go down to the barn and have some fun. It took a lot of will power to turn her down, but I sure didn't want to get Moose pissed off at me. Besides that, I had heard how they conducted marriage ceremonies up there with a shotgun at your neck. I figured I was too young to get married, and especially under those circumstances.

His parents were real down-to-earth people, and I don't believe I have ever eaten better home cooking in my life. They treated me just like one of the family. They sure had a way of making you feel welcome. We spent two and one-half days there and headed for Pennsylvania to see my mother before heading west for the state of Washington.

We were somewhere around Minnesota when the car blew up and we had to hitchhike the rest of the way. It was a good thing we had ten days to get there, for we needed every one of them. As it turned out, we made it with only forty-five minutes to spare.

It took three days to process through there. Then they sent us to a nearby air force base for transportation to San Francisco. Meanwhile, old Moose was still steadfastly refusing to fly anywhere. I snuck off base and bought a fifth of whiskey. About an hour before takeoff time, I started pouring it into Moose. When we boarded the plane, Moose didn't know where he was or what he was doing. I told him we were getting on a Greyhound bus and he bought it. He wanted to know how come there were so many steps, and I told him it was one of those new two-story jobs they had just put on the road. He believed me until we were under way for about half an hour, and he suddenly leaned over me and looked out the window. I thought he was going to faint. He never spoke another word until we were on the ground again. However, that flight did manage to get him over his fear of flying. From there on out I had little trouble getting him aboard a plane.

Our next stop after San Francisco was Hawaii. We spent two glorious days and nights there. Moose and I teamed up with three other guys and rented a car and took our own tour of the island. We hit every bar and after-hours place we could find. Our first night there we invited ourselves to a beach party simply by mingling with the guests and acting as if we had been invited. No one even bothered to ask us who we were or who invited us, and before long we were singing and dancing, making jokes and having a ball.

Moose got lost and we never did find him until ten o'clock the following morning. He was sitting on a park bench down by the beach. It turned out that a broad Moose had taken a shine to lured him away from the party with the promise of something better up at her apartment. Moose was three sheets to the wind and went with her. He said he no sooner stepped through the door than someone hit him over the head and the lights went out. He woke up in an alley several hours later minus his wallet, watch, ring, and shoes.

We took him back to the barracks and got him to shave, shower, and settle down. All he wanted to do was go out and find that broad and break her neck. I'm sure if he had found her, that's just what would have happened. We finally talked him out of it.

We spent the rest of the day on the beach watching girls and hitting the surf. We were finally on our way again the following day.

3

Moose and Irish in Japan

After a slam, bam, thank you ma'am, one-hour refueling stop on Wake Island, we next stopped in Japan. We checked in at the airport and were assigned to a bus to take us to our processing center there.

We were riding through downtown Tokyo when old Moose looked out the window of the bus and confided in me that he had never seen so many foreigners in all his life. I agreed with him.

I pointed out a little old man standing along the curb taking a piss into the gutter. There were hundreds of people all around with no one paying any attention to him, and he seemed undisturbed by their presence. I thought that was the funniest thing I had seen in a long time. I thought Moose was going to have convulsions, he was laughing so hard. It was perfectly natural and acceptable over there, but to we "natives" (as Moose put it), it was something else. That was our introduction to Japan.

Our stay in Japan was only to last five days before we were shipped out to Korea; but, as you'll see, we managed to extend our time there.

First chance we had to get off post we headed for the bright lights of Tokyo. We didn't know where to go or what to do if we got in a jam. And, of course, the language barrier was something else. Somehow, we made it into Tokyo and started looking for the action. There must have been half a million of these little foreigners all over the place, pulling rickshaws, riding bikes, driving kamikaze style in what looked to me like miniature samples of American automobiles. I remember telling Moose that he would need one for each foot like a pair of roller skates.

We finally commandeered a rickshaw and told the driver who spoke a little English that we wanted to go where the good times were. He had a hell of a time pulling us. When we would sit back, his feet would come off the ground. As long as we leaned forward, the rickshaw would balance itself to the point where he could pull it. He managed to pull us into a brightly lit section of town where he dropped us off.

Bars, nightclubs, and gift stores were everywhere, and pimps seemed to be hanging from every lamp post. Before we hit the first bar, we must have shooed ten of those persistent little bastards away. "You catchie short time, GI. Nice girls. No VD."

Moose told this one pimp that he was looking for a cherry girl and the pimp said, "Ah, so, Mommy Sun a cherry girl."

Moose slugged him and sent him reeling down the street. I asked Moose why he hit him, and he said, "I didn't mind when he tried to tell me his mother was a cherry girl, but to call her an asshole was more than I could stand. That guy should have more respect for his mother."

I tried to explain to Moose that "Ah, so" was their way of saying that they understood what you were trying to tell them, but Moose remained convinced that it was their way of saying asshole.

We went into the next nightclub we saw. It was so dark in there that we couldn't see a thing. A little Japanese girl took us by the hand and led us to a booth in the back of the place and took our order. I had my usual 7-up on the rocks and Moose was just dying to try some of that Japanese sake.

It wasn't long before we were joined by two little slant-eyed girls who offered to keep us company. We obliged them, and the next thing you knew they were pestering the hell out of us to

34

buy them drinks. Moose said they were just like the hustlers back in the States. We bought them several drinks, and they started hanging all over us, getting us all bothered. This went on for an hour or so and then they suddenly excused themselves. I asked Moose if he was ready to leave, and when we reached for our wallets to pay the check, we discovered that we had been rolled. Moose was furious, and I wasn't too happy either. Moose had already consumed about a quart of sake and was feeling no pain.

We headed for the cashier. Moose grabbed him and demanded that he produce the broads that had rolled us. Moose had him clear off the ground and the cashier was hollering, "No speaka the English, No speaka the English."

From out of nowhere came six of the biggest Japs you ever laid eyes on. After much hollering and pushing and shoving, Moose and I wound up out on the street. Moose wanted to go back in and destroy the place, but I convinced him that we would get even with them later.

So there we were, no money, no wallets. Even our class A passes along with our ID cards were gone. We had no idea how we were even going to get back to the post.

"Wait a minute, Moose, I still have my watch," I realized, "and there must be a hock shop around here somewhere. Let's see if we can find one." We started asking everybody where we could find a hock shop. Hell, they didn't even know what a hock shop was. I finally got through to this one little Jap who spoke a little English and he told me he knew someone who would buy my watch if I would follow him.

Off we went down this deserted side street and into an alley. He told Moose to wait there and for me to follow him and he would take me to the man. We agreed and no sooner had I gone ten feet into the alley than someone stepped up behind me and put a knife to my throat. This other little bastard turned around and announced that this was a stickup and demanded that I give him my watch, money, and whatever else I might have on me.

I was so scared that I thought my bowels were going to let go at any second. Suddenly the knife was gone from my throat. I instinctively reached out and grabbed at the little bastard in front of me. Moose had followed us into the alley and had come up behind the guy who was holding the knife on me. Using his arm and fist like a twenty-pound sledgehammer, Moose hit that son of a bitch right on top of the head. I swear he must have driven him two feet into the ground. He then grabbed the asshole I was holding and hit him so hard in the stomach that the guy threw up.

"What the hell are we going to do now, Moose?" I asked. In response Moose started rifling their pockets, explaining that since the bastards were going to rob us, turnabout was fair play. We stripped them naked and threw their clothes up on a roof. I went over to the guy who had held the knife on me and I stomped on his hand with the heel of my boot. I know I must have broken every bone in his hand. I said with satisfaction, "I'll bet it's a long time before he'll pull a knife on anyone else."

We headed for the nearest bar and went into the toilet to count our loot. As we walked in, I spotted a woman sitting there on a toilet. There were no partitions or anything. I told Moose we must be in the ladies' room. We beat a hasty retreat.

We asked the bartender where the men's room was, and he pointed out the same door. I explained to him that there was a woman in there and he said, "No matter, GI, she see before. Besides, we only have one room for men and women."

We waited until she came out and then went in. We had done better than we had ever dreamed of. Seven hundred dollars in American money, four watches, two rings, three wallets, and one camera. All belonging to GIs held up by those no-good bastards. Plus several thousand yen.

We went back out to the bar and sat down. Moose had several more sakes and I had another 7-up on the rocks while we discussed our good fortune and tried to decide how to spend it. A couple of Japanese broads came over and invited themselves to sit with us. Moose gave the one who was trying to sit down beside him a shove with his foot.

She went flying into the next table, spilling drinks and food over the people sitting there. They started hollering and screaming at her, while she was trying to explain to them what had happened.

Amidst all the confusion, I convinced Moose we should get the hell out of there, so we hit the street again. We didn't feel like walking, so we flagged down a rickshaw. The little guy pulling it couldn't get his feet back on the ground. Those rickshaws are pretty well balanced, but with Moose and me both in there, it was more than he could handle. I can still see him laying across that bar, trying to get his feet on the ground while his legs were going ninety miles an hour in midair.

Finally Moose got out and ordered the driver onto the seat with me and Moose proceeded to navigate the rickshaw down the road singing at the top of his voice, "Lord, I'm a truck-driving man." We had gone about two blocks when we started down a hill. We really began to pick up speed, so I hollered to Moose to slow it down. He hollered back that he couldn't stop. There was no way for him to get out on account of the bar. He was penned in like a horse in a harness. He finally ran up over a curb and fell flat on his face as we ran right over him. Lucky for Moose the rickshaw sat high off the ground and cleared him; otherwise, he might have been killed.

The driver and I leaned forward, trying to figure out some way to stop this damned thing. We must have knocked down two dozen people, as well as half a dozen sidewalk stands, until finally we crashed right through the front of a restaurant. We both went flying through the air and I wound up about thirty feet inside the place.

I was stone-sober, and I knew we were in trouble, so I got to my feet and ran back up the hill looking for Moose. There he was leaning up against a building, nursing all his cuts and bruises.

I grabbed him by the arm, and with about twenty little Japs on our asses, we managed to escape with our lives.

We wandered around looking for someplace to sit down a while. We walked into this hole in the wall with no one but British and Australian soldiers. They let us know in no uncertain terms that they didn't fancy any damned Yanks hanging around in there. Of course Moose, being a self-respecting Rebel, took exception to being called a "damned Yank" and wanted to fight. I convinced him it would be better if we left, saying, "Who wants to drink with a bunch of foreigners, anyway?"

We hit the street again, and Moose and I had to answer nature's call. We went into this alley to relieve ourselves and were standing by this open window. I happened to look in and said to Moose, "That's the place we just got put out of. Let's get even with those Limey and Aussie bastards."

Moose wanted to know how.

"Leave it to me."

I hollered in the window in my best Aussie accent, "God fuck the Queen."

A big British soldier jumped up and demanded "Who said that?"

In my best English imitation I hollered, "That bloomin' red-bearded Aussie over here. Go get him, guv'nor."

At that he walked over to where the Aussie was sitting and smashed him in the nose. The blood and snot flew everywhere and the brawl was on. Moose and I had a ringside seat from the window and watched the proceedings until we heard the sirens of the MPs and Japanese police. We then decided it was time to move on.

By this time we were trying to figure out how to get back to the post, for we had no idea where we were or where we were heading.

We were finally picked up by the MPs and taken to their headquarters. They took us in to see the officer of the day. He searched us and put all the goodies we had collected on his desk. Moose was out of it by this time, and all he wanted to do was sleep; but I was stone-sober and wasn't quite sure whether or not I could talk us out of being court-martialed.

As it turned out, the officer in charge wasn't such a bad guy. I explained to him just exactly what had happened and how we had managed to come up with three wallets, none of which belonged to us, as well as the watches and the rings. I told him how we had been rolled and mistreated, and I promised him if he would just get us back to our post, we wouldn't come back to town anymore (we were being shipped to Korea in a day or so anyway).

He told me he was due to rotate back to the States in a couple of days and that if he preferred charges against us, he'd have to stay there for our court-martial. So he was going to give us a break this time. In return he made us promise not to come back to town anymore.

"You got it, Lieutenant."

He gave us back the money, telling us we had earned it, and said he would try to locate the owners of the other things.

He called in his MPs and told them to drive us back to our post and see that we were allowed to go to our barracks without a hassle. By the time we reached the barracks, we were so beat that we didn't bother to get undressed. We just flopped down on our bunks and fell asleep.

When we hit the showers the following morning, we were two sorry-looking somebodies.

We had an assortment of lumps, bruises, and minor cuts on our faces, arms, legs, and everywhere else. Plus I had a neat little red line across my neck from where that Jap held the knife to my throat and had barely broken the skin. Everyone was asking us if we had run into a meat grinder. I replied, "No, only a buzz saw." I thought to myself, "Never, never again."

After breakfast, we went into the orderly room to report the loss of our class A passes and ID cards. We were trying to talk the clerk into letting us go to the personnel office to get new IDs when the company commander came in. He took one look at us and ordered us into his office.

I guess we looked pretty bad, with Moose and me bruised from one end to the other. Moose's hands were so sore that he couldn't close them, and his knees hurt so bad that he couldn't bend them. I was sore all over and had trouble moving without pain. Moose walked like a big gorilla—stiff-legged with his hands in front of him, palms up. He couldn't even open a door.

The Captain sat down behind his desk and asked us how long we had been there. "This is our second day, sir."

"I don't suppose you want to tell me what happened to you, do you?" "No, sir."

"Well, try anyway. I'm a good listener."

"We got rolled in town last night, sir."

"Is that all there is to it?" "Yes, sir, except they got our ID and class A passes."

"Just what part of town were you in?" "I don't know, sir."

"Describe some of the dives to me."

So I told him about the British and Aussie bar we happened into. His face got red and he got up and walked over to a map hanging on the wall which had all kinds of areas marked in red. He pointed them out to us and told us they were off limits areas and wanted to know what we were doing in one of them.

I told him we didn't know it was an off limits area, to which he replied, "Well, weren't you given an orientation when you arrived?"

"No, sir."

"No one gets a pass until they have had an orientation as to the dos and don'ts around here. It's a standing order."

"Well, sir, our passes were in the box, so we figured it was all right to go to town after 1700 hours."

"It's not your fault. Your passes shouldn't have been in the box. Someone in this outfit has some explaining to do. We had two GIs from this post killed in that area last month. They were found in an alley with their throats cut wide open. (I gulped and clutched my throat.) I'd like to take a battalion of men down there and clean that place out myself."

Old Moose chimed in with, "Me and Irish got a couple of them for you last night, sir." I nudged Moose and told him to be quiet.

"You guys did what?" he demanded. We had no choice but to tell him the whole story.

After we described our adventures, he just shook his head and said, "Both you bastards are lucky to be alive."

"I know, sir. Being off limits and all explains the absence of other GIs in the area."

He just couldn't believe it. He told us to get passes off the clerk and report for sick call down at the hospital. They admitted both of us for observation, so we had three days in the hospital to goof off and lick our wounds.

Our second day there, we were visited by a chaplain who was making his rounds. He was quite a guy and had a really marvelous sense of humor. After talking to him for a few minutes, Moose forgot he was a chaplain, and he started talking to him like one of the boys.

Moose kept quoting the Bible and Bible stories that interested him. He was getting his facts all mixed up, but the chaplain tried to straighten him out.

Such inconsistencies as "There are only ten commandments, not twelve, Moose. There were twelve disciples, not ten, and they were referred to as 'The Lord and His Twelve Disciples,' not 'J.C. and his gang.' "David slew Goliath; he did not kick the shit out of the big SOB."

"The Holy Trinity is referred to as 'the Father, the Son and the Holy Ghost,' not 'the Daddy, Junior and the Holy Spook.' "

"Yes, Moose, I did see that advertisement in the San Francisco paper for a taffy-pulling contest at St. Peter's, but it wasn't a peter-pulling contest at St. Taffy's."

We kept the chaplain busy for over an hour, and he told us that we looked like a couple of goldbricks waiting for our ship to come in. I added that if we waited around there long enough, we'd be nothing more than wrecks on the shores of time. He said he would have to remember that one.

He was kind enough not to ask us how we wound up there in the first place. Come to think of it, he probably just assumed we were flown in from Korea with combat wounds. He asked us if there was anything he could do for us. I informed him that we were being shipped back to Korea in a couple of days and could use some more time to recuperate before returning to the war. I felt funny lying to him like that. But on the other hand, part of what I said was true: We were on our way to Korea; it was just that we hadn't been there before.

When we were discharged from the hospital the following day, there were two sets of orders waiting for us—one for Moose and one for me. Two weeks' convalescent leave signed by a full bird colonel in charge of the hospital.

We were both ecstatic, and Moose said, "The chaplain came through. He sure believed you, Irish."

We reported back to post just long enough to check in at the orderly room and present our leave orders to the captain, who was very upset. He told us he had seen combat veterans shipped in, patched up, and returned to Korea the following day, and that they sure as hell deserved leave more than a couple of fuck-ups like us.

"Well, we never look a gift horse in the mouth, Captain."

"Yeah, sure, I know. Why do I get the feeling that trying to mix you two with military life and discipline is like trying to mix oil with water? Before you two bastards go anywhere, you're going to get new IDs and an orientation to Japan. A word to the wise should be sufficient—stay out of trouble. Next time you may not be so lucky."

Luck was still with us though. We had our new IDs within one hour and were able to catch an orientation class that same morning.

In the class they outlined the off limits areas and told us how to watch out for "Slicky Boys" (robbers), prostitutes, pimps, bar flies, and the likes. They told us VD was rampant there and that Pro Kits and prophylactics were available at the main gate for all who wanted them. Why hell, Moose and I could have told them a few dos and don'ts ourselves. They weren't telling us anything we hadn't already found out the hard way.

We checked back with the captain after we were through, and he cut us loose on Japan. Downtown we checked into a hotel.

We were sitting in the hotel bar bullshitting when an unescorted American woman, about forty, came in and sat down at a table next to ours. Seeing an American woman after all those Japanese was a sight for sore eyes. We were already getting homesick and sat there staring at her. After a while, we got up courage enough to say hello to her and start a conversation.

She was very friendly and, like a couple of lovesick puppies, we hung onto every word she spoke. She matched drinks with us and even bought a few rounds herself. She was a widow from Los Angeles and was over there on a two-week vacation. She said she wanted to get away from it all and do something different.

The evening wore on and she was getting pretty well-lit herself. After we told her some of the things that had happened to us since we arrived, she began to open up and tell us about her first night there.

She started out drinking sake and after the first two hours, she remembered nothing until she woke up the next morning in her hotel room with a little Japanese guy sitting at the bottom of her bed. She said she was startled, grabbed a sheet to cover herself, and asked where she was.

"You in hotel room, ma'am. Okee-dokee?"

"How did I get here?"

"I bring you, ma-am. Okee-dokee?"

"Well who undressed me?"

"I undressed you, ma-am. Okee-dokee?"

She said, "Man, I must have really been tight."

He replied, "First time, pretty tight. Second time, okee-dokee."

We must have laughed for twenty minutes.

We sat there and swapped stories with her until about three in the morning. She was going home the next day and gave us her address, along with an invitation to visit her if we ever got to Los Angeles. It was like two ships passing in the night, each giving greeting and a warm feeling of someone caring and then going on alone.

I never knew what being homesick meant until that night. There is no cure for it, no medicine, no magic potions, just an empty hollow feeling in the bottom of your guts that gets worse with the passing of time. Moose felt the same way I did. I guess that's why we were so good for each other. We could talk, laugh, raise hell, and at least take our minds off of home for a while anyway. But those nights in bed trying to get to sleep were rough, and that is when it would hit the hardest.

Moose and I spent the rest of our leave sightseeing, taking hot baths, and raising a little hell now and then until our time finally ran out.

We reported back to post and started processing out. Before we knew it, we were at the airport being loaded aboard a giant cargo plane that had been converted into a troop carrier. The whole ass end of this monster opened up, and you had to walk up a big ramp to get inside. The ramp was normally used for loading jeeps and trucks, but this trip it was strictly for troops. Moose took one look at that contraption and said, "I'd rather swim than fly in that fuckin' thing."

We hung around outside the plane until everyone was aboard, hoping it would fill up and they wouldn't have room for us. No such luck. We were ordered aboard. We went reluctantly.

The seats faced the rear of the plane, and Moose and I had the last seats next to the door. When they took down the ramp and those huge doors started to close, sealing off our only route of escape, I thought Moose was going to pass out. I said, "Cheer up, Moose, now you know how Jonah felt being swallowed in the belly of a whale." That didn't help Moose. He was sure we were all going to be killed.

He wasn't far from wrong. As that big old giant went rumbling down the runway, it didn't sound right to me. They managed, however, to get it in the air and headed out over the water toward Korea.

We were in the air for half an hour when one of the engines started to sputter. The pilot came on over the loudspeaker and assured us that everything was okay and we would make it. However, as a precautionary measure, he was instructing the flight attendants to conduct a drill in case we had to ditch in the water.

They popped the Mae West life jackets out from overhead, told us to put them on, and instructed us on how to inflate them, should we hit the water. They gave us ditching instructions, and we even had time for rehearsals.

They told us to fasten our seat belts, put our heads between our knees and our hands behind our heads with fingers locked together, and pull down as hard as we could. Moose asked me what they wanted us to do that for. "I don't know Moose. I guess they want us to kiss our ass good-bye or something."

The siutation began to deteriorate rapidly from there on. A second engine and then a third went out. The pilot made the announcement that we were going to ditch the plane. By now we were all petrified. We could feel the plane losing altitude, and when we were about one hundred feet above the water, they opened the rear door. As the cold night air came rushing in I kept looking for the water, but it was pitch-black out there.

Then I heard the pilot say, "Prepare yourselves. We're going in."

It felt like we hit a brick wall, for we went flying against those seats with such force that they broke loose from their anchor bolts.

As soon as we stopped going forward, I snapped my safety belt and popped my Mae West. I hollered to Moose, "Let's get the hell out of here."

Moose wasn't moving. He had hit his head on the side of the plane and was out cold. I got his safety belt loose and pulled the cord on his Mae West. The plane was already sinking and the water was knee-deep.

I managed somehow to roll Moose over on his back and float him through the door. I swam as hard as I could, while hanging on to Moose and trying to keep his head above the water. We must have been a hundred yards or so from the plane, in two-foot waves, when the plane disappeared under the water.

It had been about fifteen minutes since the plane had started having trouble, so there had been plenty of time to send out Mayday calls. Although it seemed like an eternity in that cold water, it was only twenty minutes or so until we were picked up by a Navy destroyer. Out of the one hundred fifty guys on the plane, only fifty of us got out. The rest were either killed on impact or went down with the plane.

They took us to their sick bay where they treated the injured, gave us some dry clothes and some hot food. I stayed with Moose until he woke up. He had a slight concussion, but other than that, he had come through our ordeal in good shape.

As soon as he regained consciousness, he wanted to play twenty questions. "Where are we? How did we get here? Where is the airplane? Did everybody get out?"

I knew the only way to shut him up and have him relax was to answer all his questions. He couldn't tell me often enough how grateful he was to me for saving his life. I told him I owed it to him for the time he saved me from getting my throat cut back in Japan, "So we're even now, you big bastard, and I don't want to hear any more about it."

"Hell, we were just having fun that night in Japan. This plane crash was serious. I knew I was going to die and you saved my life."

"Forget it, Moose."

"Well, all I know is nobody had better ever fuck with you or they got me to answer to. I don't care who it is, either."

The following morning they transferred us onto a hospital ship and we spent the next ten days floating around on the Sea of Japan. By this time Moose had recovered from his concussion, and they landed us all in Pusan, South Korea.

4

Moose and Irish Land in Korea

Things were pretty well fouled up there because of the war
going on north of us.

They assigned us to receiving quarters and processed and
transferred everyone but Moose and me out to different outfits
heading north. Moose and I were in something called the "Special Forces." By its very nature, its whereabouts was not common knowledge for any other segment of the army. Our closest
counterpart was the Signal Corps, and even they had no juris-
diction over our whereabouts or how we conducted our operations. We were a wholly self-contained operation, not responsible to anyone but our headquarters in Japan and, of course, in
Washington, D.C.

As a result no one wanted to fool with us. We could have told
them to send us to Seoul and we could have made contact with
our liaison officer there, like we were supposed to do in the first
place. But they never asked us, and we were too smart to volunteer any information. Therefore, we were in limbo for the next
two months, playing cards with the new arrivals, bullshitting,
looking for someone from home, and stealing whiskey from the
BOQ (bachelor officers' quarters).

47

They had a nice bar set up in the BOQ. The bar was in front of a window near a fence. All we had to do was wait until all the officers were out, and Moose would boost me up to the window. I would reach in and grab a bottle that was almost full and replace it with one that was empty. They never did catch on to what was happening to their whiskey and kept accusing each other of drinking it.

We were sitting in our quonset hut one evening playing cards when we heard something scrape against the side of the building. This was followed a few seconds later by a deafening noise; it sounded as if all hell had broken loose. We all ran outside to see what was happening. A few hundred feet away sat a second lieutenant in a badly mangled jeep. We all crowded around as he crawled out of it and started staggering around. You could tell he was dead drunk. He started to survey the damage and said in a slurred voice, "Some of you men give me a hand here."

I started to clap and everyone else picked up on it and began clapping, hollering, and cheering wildly. It was so seldom that you caught an officer fucking up that when you did you made the most of it.

It wasn't long before a major arrived on the scene, pushed his way through the crowd, placed the drunk officer under house arrest, and ordered him back to the BOQ.

What he had hit was a mountain of empty fifty-five-gallon drums stacked in rows of twenty high. After he knocked the wedges out from under the first couple of rows, the drums started falling and rolling, knocking other rows down. You would have sworn we were being bombed. We laughed about it for weeks.

Moose and I were wandering around camp one night for want of something better to do, when we happened upon a crap game. We watched for a while when I noticed this one sergeant who seemed to have the game pretty well in hand. He wouldn't face anyone or take any side bets. He'd wait for the dice to come around to him, make four passes, letting the money ride. Then he'd take it all except ten or twenty dollars and roll until he crapped out. I watched him do it three more times around and took Moose aside and voiced my suspicion.

"Notice how every time he gets the dice he puts them to his mouth like he's blowing on them?"

Moose said "Lots of guys do that for luck. That ain't nothin'."

"True, but I think he's got another set of dice in his mouth. Notice how he rolls the dice around in his hands and on his pants leg like he's trying to dry them off?"

"Well, if he's cheating, it's none of our business."

I agreed, but told Moose we could cash in on it.

"How?"

"Give me your money and back me up."

Moose had only ten dollars and I was broke, but back to the game we went. I waited for this guy to get the dice, threw my ten down, and bet he'd make his point. I was covered and after his fourth roll, letting it ride, betting he would make his point, I picked up my money. Sure enough, he crapped out on the next roll. It went around five or six times and we were really starting to cut into his action.

He was no dummy, though, and by now I'm sure he suspected what was going on, for he started to get nervous and sweaty. He was afraid to break the pattern for fear of being accused of cheating, so he kept up the same pattern.

He kept saying he was going to have to leave soon. Moose kept telling him to keep on playing. He was really getting shook up. When he threw the dice for what was to be his last time, three dice popped out of his mouth. You could have heard a pin drop in there.

Moose reached over and picked up one of the dice and said, "Fifteen's your point, Buddy." The guy was kneeling there looking like Yoo Dee Kiotee after he had just fucked up.

Moose told him to leave. This cheater had nerve, though. Before leaving, he reached for this huge pile of money in front of him. Moose told him that if he touched the money, he would personally break his goddamned neck. At that, the guy got up and left. Moose grabbed the money and threw it in the pot saying, "Here's your money back, boys." Moose and I left, about four hundred dollars richer.

The guys in the game had just landed the day before and were not even aware that they were being cheated. This hustler was taking advantage of their ignorance. I think guys like him joined up just to gamble and take advantage of all the suckers. They never had any trouble finding a little action, for as long as the money held out, there would be guys willing to gamble. Some gambled because there was nothing else to do; some because they had gambler's fever; but for most, it was their first time away from home and they thought they could play with the big boys now.

I heard it said that the services will either make or break a man, and if you wanted to see human nature in the raw, joining the services was the thing to do. No one has any peers or siblings to look up to. No one has to worry about being kicked out of the family if he gets drunk, shacks up, or gambles his money away. As a result, I believe the services are responsible for making more alcoholics, more gamblers, and more screwed-up people than any other organization in the world.

By this time I was beginning to believe that the army was made up of nothing more than the unwilling run by the incompetent to do the unnecessary. As far as I was concerned, I was ready to go home and let these people settle their own differences. Of course, you had to consider all the big businessmen in the States who were making huge fortunes out of this police action. They weren't horseshitting me. They were getting rich at my expense, for I was only getting seventy-two dollars a month for dispensing their goods—wasting them if you will, so they could sell more to the government.

It was even rumored that the British were selling guns and ammunition in Shanghai to the Red Chinese. They were being shipped north up through Manchuria and into North Korea to be used against their own troops. When they say, "War is hell," they only mean for the people stuck fighting it, or for the poor innocent bystanders who were unfortunate enough to have their country invaded by outsiders. And meanwhile the big businessmen were making big bucks because of the war.

As far as I could see, the Korean people couldn't have cared less who was running their country. All they were interested in was a patch of ground for a rice paddy and a roof over their heads. Life had gone on that way for centuries, so who the hell were we to impose our way of life on them?

But then again, who the hell was I to say what was right or wrong? After all, Uncle Sam had fed me all that propaganda about what a good and noble cause we represented, and how these people wanted freedom and a democratic government just like ours, and it was our duty to see that they got it. From where I stood, they couldn't have cared less. We'd be in town; they would fly our flag. The Reds would be in town; and they would fly their flag. Survival was the name of the game. Self-preservation in the final analysis was their main goal, regardless of the outcome of the war.

They looked at life a lot differently than we did, and our ways didn't seem to fit into their scheme of things at all. In the first place, the Americans would try to drink the country dry and impregnate every woman they could get their hands on, not to mention the havoc they wreaked on the countryside with their holier-than-thou attitude and all their hell-raising.

There was no doubt in my mind as to why they hated our guts, set us up as targets for every dirty trick they could think of, and tried to steal everything of ours they could get their hands on. The GIs were fair game for one and all. The only ones who would be nice were those who wanted to sell you something, beg something from you, or offer you a piece of ass.

The pimps and prostitutes ran rampant, absolutely out of control. The easiest way to separate a GI from his money seemed to be by offering him a piece of ass. I don't believe a hornier army ever went to war. Most guys would get drunk before they went out looking and then use that as an excuse: "Well, I was drunk; otherwise I wouldn't have gone."

And the aftereffects they suffered! They came down with such nice things as the clap, gonorrhea, syphilis and a few that hadn't even made the medical journals yet. Some of the cures and treatments must have come out of a horror book—for example, the one used for clap and sometimes for gonorrhea. A long, slender steel rod with a knob on the end of it was inserted in the guy's penis. The knob was turned and little wing-like projectiles

51

came out of the rod. The blister-like sores inside the penis broke as the rod was yanked out. The poor guys howled in sheer agony.

Then of course, there was the series of shots—plus no booze or even coffee for at least two weeks, if they were lucky enough to get rid of it in that time.

If that wasn't bad enough, they became fair game for all the bad jokes that everyone threw at them. "Andy got the . . ." (then clap your hands), or they'd sing little ditties like "I am a raunchy cowboy, I got the gonorrhea, I got it from Maria, she gave it to me freea, and it hurts me when I peeeaaah."

I remember one day the chaplain gave our outfit a lecture on prostitutes, VD, and the aftereffects. He was summing it all up by telling us that an hour's pleasure wasn't worth a lifetime of shame. I had a beautiful line for that one and couldn't resist interjecting it into the discussion. I raised my hand, which he acknowledged with "Yes, do you have a question?" "Just one. How do you make it last for an hour?" That broke the place up, and the chaplain folded his papers and went off into the night mumbling something about how we were all going to burn in hell.

Those MASH hospitals depicted on TV are more like Johns Hopkins Medical Centers than what we ran into over there. The medics and doctors were a sadistic bunch, especially when it came to giving shots or treating someone dumb enough to get VD. It was necessary to take the whole series of shots every four months. I swear that every time these doctors gave shots, they would aim for a muscle and wriggle the needle up and down while it was still in your arm, trying to get an unfavorable reaction from you.

One of the most pitiful sights was watching someone with gonorrhea trying to take a piss. Sheer agony. He would stand on one foot and then the other, put his hands behind his head, grit his teeth, crouch down, grab at anything in sight. Something else! Of course, there was usually someone there to rub salt on the wounds by saying something like, "Sure must have been a good piece of ass to go through all that for." Or imitate a Korean pimp: "Catchie short time, GI . . . clean pussy . . . no VD." If you didn't especially like the guy, you might say, "Couldn't happen to a nicer guy." For some reason this would really make him mad.

Moose and I had figured out that we were going to spend the remainder of our tour right there in Pusan. We didn't much care. We weren't all that gung-ho to get our asses shot at, so we kept out of the way and let the army and the war pass us by. But our luck ran out!

One day the post locator came looking for us and told us to report to headquarters. We checked in and this little red-headed captain jumped all over us. He accused us of malingering and a whole list of other things. We explained our position to him and told him that as good soldiers we were not obligated to volunteer any information. We explained that it wasn't our responsibility if they didn't do their job or weren't able to keep track of us and process us out as they were supposed to do. We were simply following orders by waiting for someone to tell us what was going on.

It seems they had been looking all over the Far East for us. The last word they had on us was that we were picked up by a Navy destroyer after the plane went down. But when we didn't report to our liaison officer in Seoul for assignment to a reconnaissance unit, they thought perhaps we were missing in the crash. And yet they didn't want to report us as dead until they had exhausted all possibilities.

We stood there and took his ass-chewing for about ten minutes, I guess. I finally had enough and told him that our asses had been chewed out by experts and that he could eat all he wanted, sir. (You could say anything you wanted to them as long as you said "sir" or addressed them by their rank at the end.) He was finally convinced that we were just victims of the system and sent us to personnel to have orders cut for assignment to the next convoy heading north to Seoul. Even though we weren't too anxious to go north, we were bored to death with this place, and I guess we welcomed the change of pace.

We were temporarily assigned to an infantry outfit heading

north and had to draw full field gear, rifles, ammunition, and the whole bit. They loaded us up on deuce-and-a-halfs (two and one-half ton trucks) and the trip began.

The first day was uneventful, just bouncing around in that damned truck, up one mountain and down another. Suddenly on the second day we came to an unscheduled stop—there was a train blocking the road. We soon discovered that the train had been abandoned. All the coal was gone from the tender, even the water from the boiler. It had been pulling twelve flat cars that were also without cargo.

We grabbed a couple of gooks who were standing nearby and made them tell us what had happened. They were a little reluctant to talk, but with a bayonet held to their throats, they opened up. It seemed that the train had left Pusan with its cargo of telephone poles and an all-Korean crew heading north for Taegu. Along the way, the crew stopped at every little nook and cranny and sold the coal, hot water, and telephone poles for whatever they could get. When they finally ran out of merchandise to sell, they abandoned the train and headed for the hills. The officer in charge of the convoy radioed back to Pusan to let them know where their train was. We uncoupled the cars, and using a deuce-and-a-half we pushed the cars down the track just far enough to clear the road. We loaded back up and were on our way again.

This was a pretty good bunch of GIs we were traveling with. They were not your ordinary infantry outfit with an average IQ just high enough to be accepted in the army in the first place. Most of these guys were draftees, and a lot of them had college degrees. They were an unhappy lot, just wanting to serve their time and get as far away from the military as possible. Moose and I shared their sentiments exactly. In fact, that is all that kept us going, the thought that it couldn't last forever. We would tell ourselves that some day we would all look back on this and laugh, or perhaps cry.

The average infantry men wanted only to talk about drinking and getting drunk, how many pieces of ass they had got, or if anyone had a copy of their favorite comic book. Perhaps they might even venture to read a copy of such classics as *Dick Tracy* or *Little Orphan Annie.* The conversation of these men was on a little higher level of thought than that of the average GI. They discussed such topics as religion, politics, economics, and philosophy.

The army figured it only had these guys for two years, so why teach them anything beyond the basic skills of marching and firing a rifle, or so it seemed. There was absolutely no incentive to do a good job or get ahead. Just do what you were told and nothing more. Stay out of trouble and time in grade would automatically bring you promotions. As a result, you had such shit as sergeants (our "fearless leaders") with fourth-grade educations, ordering a guy with a master's degree in business management to pick up papers and trash off the ground. Beautiful setup, if you were a zombie and had no self-respect.

If you stayed with them long enough, you became childish and lost all sense of responsibility. They told you when to eat, when to sleep, and when to go to the bathroom. They paid you once a month, but that only lasted for one week or less. The other three weeks you would bum everything from cigarettes to a squirt of toothpaste. If you stayed with them for twenty years until retirement, you would wind up with a stomach full of ulcers and a pension just big enough to support your bad habits for perhaps two weeks out of every month for the rest of your life. The average life of a military retiree at that time was only five years. Some career to look forward to! I figured they had my body for thirty-six months, but my mind and soul they could never have. Maybe that's why I fought them every step of the way; my heart wasn't in it.

Anyway, on and on up the road we traveled, making our way towards Seoul. A couple of guys began discussing politics. I listened to them and every once in a while I interjected a thought or two of my own—something I thought was funny, or something to piss one or the other off. Kind of like agitating, never taking sides, but trying to help the guy who seemed to be losing. The Republican had it all together and was cutting the guy defending the Democrats to ribbons. I said, "Hold it! As a good Democrat myself, I propose a truce. We'll kiss your elephant if you'll kiss our ass." That broke everybody up and ended that discussion.

The convoy came to a sudden halt and someone hollered, "Hit the ditch!" We jumped out and ran for the cover of a nearby woods. We heard jets and gunfire. The Russian MIGs had decided to use our convoy for target practice. They made about three passes at us and just as quickly as they had appeared, were gone. We were lucky that we lost only six vehicles and suffered only one casualty.

When we were running for cover he dove in a ditch. There were two dead Red Chinese in there. God only knows how long they had been there, but they were all bloated up, and when he landed on top of them they exploded all over him. Such a horrible stench and odor you couldn't imagine in your wildest dreams.

He jumped up hollering and screaming as loudly as he possibly could while tugging at his clothes, trying to get them off. He was running around like a madman, clear out of his mind from the smell. He came running at Moose and I hit him right in the jaw with the butt of my rifle, knocking him out cold. He no sooner hit the ground than I threw up all over him. I thought I had a strong stomach up until then, but that was more than I could take.

We hollered for the medics, and even they had to put masks on before they could work on him. They cut his clothes off and kept washing him down with alcohol, but the smell was still there; I guess it would always be there for the rest of his life, at least in his mind. They finally loaded him up in the ambulance and hauled him away to a helicopter evacuation point several miles from our location.

We loaded back up in the remaining vehicles and made our way into Seoul where Moose and I parted company with the infantry. Just as well, I thought, for they were on their way to the front lines, and we were still not too anxious to find out what it was like up there.

We made our way to the Eighth Army Headquarters and were put in touch with our liaison officer. He loaded us up in a jeep and we headed further north to an encampment high on a mountaintop. This was a self-contained outfit whose mission was communication reconnaissance, and every GI there had to have a top secret clearance.

Moose and I had enlisted for this bullshit, so we already had our credentials. The company commander was a major and welcomed us to the outfit. He told us that it was a real blood and guts outfit and if we were attacked, we would be evacuated first, then the women and children, then the troops. We were a highly mobile operation, with 500 vehicles and 250 men, and if we had to evacuate, every man was expected to take two vehicles with him.

He asked where we were from and when Moose told him he was from West Virginia, we were in like Flynn, for that was the major's home state. He told us we had arrived just in time and there were a couple of good jobs for us if we wanted them. He wanted Moose to be his driver and me to be his company clerk. We jumped at the offer. Our duties would also require us to be couriers. We would have to make at least one trip a day into Seoul with the radio transmissions that had been intercepted and recorded. There we would turn them over to our liaison officer to be forwarded to Japan, where they would try to break the codes and find out what was going on.

Moose and I were in clover; for with me as company clerk and Moose as the old man's driver, we were both ED (exempt from duty). The courier runs meant we were in Seoul at least once a day.

It didn't take us long to learn all the ins and outs of the black market—where to go and not to go, where we could buy good whiskey, how to tell if it was resealed, what to pay for it, and who we could sell it to. It was only a matter of weeks before Moose and I had more business than we could handle. We were even selling to the officers. We would never deliver directly. We would tell them what we had for sale, collect the money, and then tell them where they might find a bottle if they were to look.

Of course, the major was a special case. We would always put a fifth or two in his desk drawer every few days. The first time he found it he came out and asked me if I knew where it came from. I feigned innocence and told him I had no idea and with a smile kept right on typing. He was pretty cool, though, for he asked, "How much do I owe you and Moose for it?" I assured him, "Nothing. There is plenty more where that came from." He smiled his knowing smile and went back into his office. From then on, Moose and I could do no wrong.

As in all outfits, there was one jealous bastard who blew the whistle on Moose and me by telling the MPs we were running whiskey up from Seoul. Moose and I were returning to camp with two cases of Canadian Mist when we saw their trap about five miles down the road. They had set up a roadblock, and we had no choice but to stop or run right into them.

They were not too bright, for all three of them started walking towards our jeep and they hadn't even pulled their .45s out of the holsters. I told Moose to let me handle it. I stood up, leveled my carbine at them, and told them to halt.

They looked at me with disbelief. One reached for his .45, and I let one round go at his feet with the warning that the next one was going through his head. Moose took their guns and then ordered them to start running back down the road. We moved one of their jeeps out of the road and we flattened a tire on each jeep. We then jumped back in our jeep and tore back to our compound.

We went straight in to the major, told him exactly what had happened, and gave their .45s to him. We had decided not to try to bullshit him, and we just hoped he would help us out, for we both knew we were in big trouble. He said to let him handle it and not to say a word about it to anyone.

About an hour later there were five jeep loads of MPs at the main gate wanting to get on post to look for Moose and me. Of course, no one was allowed on, regardless of who they were or what they wanted, without prior clearance. They threatened to storm the gate; at that the guard fired three shots in the air. This brought everyone on post running with rifles in hand.

I remember thinking to myself, "I thought we were supposed to be fighting with the North Koreans not each other."

The MPs sure were a mad bunch of bastards. They wanted Moose and me in the worst kind of way. We had made complete fools out of them and they wanted revenge, and they meant to have it at all costs.

The major came out and took their second lieutenant aside. He returned the weapons to them with the explanation that Moose and I were special couriers with top secret material in our jeep, and we had strict orders from him not to stop for anyone, not even our own troops.

He confided, "If they had let your men search their jeep, they would have been court-martialed and the material they were carrying compromised, because your men don't have a clearance or a need to know." He pointed out to them that he was proud of our actions and might even recommend us for an award, or at least a letter of recognition. He also told them that if they stopped any of our jeeps in the future, some heads would roll.

They all loaded up and left, still boiling mad. They had come for satisfaction and wound up getting their asses chewed out for their trouble and their stupidity. I'm sure when they got back to their post, the original three had some tall explaining to do —how two Special Forces assholes managed to disarm them and render their vehicles useless. I sure would have liked to have heard that.

The major took Moose and me into his office and told us he wasn't sure that we had heard the last of it. He was sure that they would be waiting for us when we left post again. As a precaution, he was going to call for a helicopter to transport the courier materials, at least for a month or so until this thing blew over. Moose and I had to ride the chopper back and forth every day, and I don't mind telling you it was a bit much—for the first few trips, anyway. Moose wasn't especially fond of flying in the first place and couldn't shake the memories of the plane crash in the Sea of Japan.

The pilots were all highly skilled, and after the first few flights Moose and I were transporting our whiskey by air. We would always give each pilot one fifth and before long they became our best customers, buying up to a case at a time to take back to their air base for resale.

5

The Copter Crash and the Ordeal
in the Jungle

Moose and I couldn't miss until one day a MIG got on our ass and shot at our chopper. The pilot was forced to crash-land in a rice paddy.

We got out of the helicopter without a scratch; but our trouble was only beginning. We were behind enemy lines and had two packages of top secret intercepted radio transmissions with us. If we were caught by the gooks with that stuff, they would have shot us on the spot as spies. We made it to the woods a few hundred yards away, sat down and contemplated our fate, and tried to decide what to do next.

We agreed to ditch the packages and buried them in a hollow stump along with our dog tags, wallets, and anything else that might give us away as enlisted men in case we were captured. Since the pilot was a first lieutenant, we decided that if we were captured we would all pretend to be officers. Officers got better treatment and were kept in separate quarters. Anyway, we took the silver bars from his jacket and each put one of them on our hats so we would all look alike.

We stayed in the woods until nightfall and then tried to make our way out. We literally stank like shit after waddling out of that rice paddy; for that's all they use for fertilizer—pure, unadulterated human waste, along with horse, cow, donkey, or any other kind of shit available. The paddies became breeding grounds for mosquitoes and twenty thousand other bugs and insects of all makes and descriptions. They all seemed to have one thing in common, and that was to bite and harass us. At daybreak we got a look at one another and saw that we were bitten from head to toe. The gnats and fleas had infiltrated every part of our bodies.

We were all starving by this time. It seemed like our belly buttons were rubbing our backbones. I can't recall ever being so hungry in all my life. It was getting to Moose too; he said he was so hungry that he could eat the asshole out of a skunk. I wasn't that hungry, at least not yet.

We holed up in an abandoned shack for the remainder of the day. After dark we started out to find our way back to our own lines, or at least to find something to eat. We saw a village; we contemplated taking a chance of going in. Driven by hunger, we decided to sneak into one of the huts near the edge of the village. As we went through the front door, we were confronted by a Korean man and woman. We grabbed them both so they couldn't run and sound the alarm.

We tried to tell them all we wanted was food, but either they were too scared or they didn't understand us. Moose and the lieutenant held them while I rifled the house. I came up with several eggs and about two pounds of rice. We shoved the couple into the next room and beat a hasty retreat for the woods to eat our rice and eggs. We cracked the top off the eggs, sucked the eggs out, and consumed as much rice as we could dry. Our stomachs had shrunk to the point where they wouldn't hold much anyway.

We traveled as best we could for the rest of the night and by daybreak had made the coast. It was pathetic—all that water and not a drop to drink. We figured we were on the west coast of Korea—or at least we hoped we were. It was so overcast, that we couldn't get our bearings from the sun. We decided to hole up there for the day, figuring it was still too dangerous to travel in daylight, so we spent the day bullshitting and trying to sleep. Under those conditions, you really can get to know somebody. It turned out the lieutenant was quite a character and had a great sense of humor.

He started telling us about his home in Ohio and about his old man who was a plumbing contractor. He said he used to work for the old man before he joined the service. He said he had a crew out at a Catholic convent one day replacing a sewer line and after a few hours on the job, the Mother Superior came out and told him that the language his men were using was really starting to upset some of the nuns and could he please tell them to watch it. He told her that they were a good bunch of men and gave him a fair day's work for a fair day's pay. "Of course, I'll have to admit that they call a spade a spade." She shot back, "They do not; they call it a fuckin' shovel!"

Moose and I were laughing so hard that if there had been any gooks around, they wouldn't have had any trouble finding us, that's for sure.

I remember thinking to myself while I was sitting there looking out over the water on the rocky coastline that I would give anything if I were sitting on the sands of Malibu looking out over the Pacific Ocean. It was cold and overcast, gray and miserable, depressing enough under any circumstances. But to be caught up in a war that I didn't even believe in was almost incomprehensible.

Of course, I couldn't let my feelings be known to anyone, even Moose. I didn't want to depress the rest of the men any more than they already were. Thoughts like not believing in the war translated into words that were considered treasonous. The officers talked about the brainwashing the Red Chinese were doing on our captured troops. I couldn't help thinking what a bill of goods *we* had been sold.

The lieutenant brought me out of my reverie when he asked me what I was going to do when I got out.

"Jump up and down!" I replied. "What about you, Moose?"

"I'm with Irish. Irish and I are going to pool our money and invest it in lots and houses. Lots of booze and plenty of whorehouses."

We sat there chuckling to ourselves, meanwhile trying to take stock of the situation. If we were on the west coast, we shouldn't be too far above Inchon, the northernmost post of the Allies. If we made it there, we were home free.

We had no more than a pound of rice left, and no water. I would have given my place in hell for a cigarette.

The temperature was hovering around fifty degrees and it was misting. We were soaked to our bones, covered with insect bites. To top it off, we had come down with dysentery; (probably from drinking water from those not-so-pure streams we had crossed during the night.) We decided it was still too dangerous to travel in daylight, so we crawled into some thick underbrush to try to sleep until nightfall and then make our way down the coastline.

Our rest didn't last long. I peered out from the underbrush and saw about ten sampans (flat-bottomed boats) making their way to shore. I alerted Moose and the lieutenant. We decided not to run, but to stay put and wait.

A mixture of Red Chinese soldiers and North Korean civilians formed a line and proceeded to unload their cargo about a quarter of a mile up the coast from us. It must have taken them four hours to unload all those boats. From our vantage point we couldn't see where they were storing it. When they finished, they got back aboard and headed north. We decided the area was now safe to investigate and see what they were bringing in. Those sneaky little bastards had that stuff so well camouflaged, that it took us a long time to locate it. It was in a cave in the rocks and was almost impossible to detect. As I said, we watched them unload it and still had trouble finding it.

We crawled inside. To our utter amazement, we found a cache of weapons big enough to keep ten thousand soldiers supplied for weeks. Tons and tons of rice and at least two thousand five-gallon cans of gasoline, medical supplies, hand grenades, and radios. They must have been hauling that stuff in for weeks.

DONALD R. WAGNER

As best we could figure, they were storing up for their expected spring offensive.

We knew we had to destroy it, but we didn't quite know how to go about it. We grabbed a couple of canvas bags and filled them with rice, and then took a few hand grenades, and some boxes of gauze. We decided to burn everything, but we didn't even have a match. Instead, we each took two cans of gasoline and poured them over everything we could, working our way back to the entrance.

The lieutenant told us to head toward the beach and keep on going. We protested and told him we would wait for him. He ordered us, so we went down the beach about five hundred yards and waited for him. At first all we heard was a hand grenade going off and then the smoke started billowing skyward. About that time, the lieutenant passed us on a dead run and we fell in behind him. We must have been a quarter of a mile down the beach before we heard this tremendous explosion.

After the initial explosion, we kept hearing explosions for the next hour or so. Another half mile down the beach we decided we had better hole up in case the explosions drew a crowd of unfriendly gooks.

As we sat there congratulating ourselves on our success, we deliberated on how the gooks would react when they returned. "Do you suppose they will figure it was sabotage or what?" Moose was asking when the lieutenant told us to be quiet. He thought he heard a noise.

We started to hear a lot of Chinese chatter and hid ourselves as well as we could. The explosions and smoke had drawn a crowd after all. I don't know how many of them there were, but it sounded like hundreds of them passing on either side of our hideout. At one point they were so close I could have reached out and tripped them, but the thought never entered my mind. I was too frightened to move a muscle. I don't think I was even breathing, and it felt as if my heart had stopped beating.

A big red ant who was crawling around in front of my face suddenly sensed the helplessness of my plight and decided to take advantage of me. He climbed up on my nose and defied me

65

to swat him off. I could see him standing up on his back legs and sticking his tongue out at me while holding his front leg to his nose as if to thumb it at me. I remember thinking to myself, "This bastard has got to be a communist ant." He certainly was the right color. When he didn't get any reaction from me, he really got brazen and bit me. Still no response, so he whistled for all his friends and relatives to join him on my face. They did, and held old homecoming week right then and there.

Such dancing and carryings on you never heard tell. I believe they were doing the Virginia reel, or perhaps it was an Irish jig. They carried on like a bunch of nuts for a while, having a good ole time at my expense.

Suddenly I felt one of them run down my neck and under my shirt. He soon came back out and hollered for everybody to join him. Within a few seconds they all went running down my back —except for the original little bastard that had started all the trouble in the first place. He stayed perched on my nose as if to keep an eye on me. Thinking of them as people was the only way I could keep from screaming out in agony, for they were really doing a job on me.

Anyway, the rest of them had chosen sides and had decided to hold a game of tag football, or perhaps it was soccer, on my back. They were running, kicking, biting, and scratching me— really tearing up the turf! I remember thinking, "I must be going mad thinking of ants like people." I was sure of it when I heard the one on my nose say to me, "What are you going to do about it, fucker?" I remember saying to him under my breath, "If you don't get your friends and relatives off my back, I'm going to roll over and crush every fuckin' one of them, and I'm going to kill you inch by inch, you communist bastard you."

We lay there motionless for almost two hours. By now it was night. I had all I could stand of this little fucker on my nose and all his friends. I quickly reached up and snatched him off my nose and got him between my thumb and forefinger. I squeezed him as hard as I could while saying, "Now, you bastard, you'll torment me no more." I rolled over on my back in an attempt to break up the soccer game being held there while saying out loud, "The game is over. Now I'm going to even up the score." I must have crushed four dozen of them on my back, participants and spectators alike. As far as I was concerned, the stadium was closed and being torn down to make room for something much better, like a pair of warm titties against my back.

I finally managed to either kill or otherwise eliminate them all. I could almost hear those who escaped take their parting shots at me as they were running away. "Sore ass, spoilsport, you Yankee mother fucker you." I just stomped at them with my feet and told them to get lost.

Moose and the lieutenant looked at me strangely and asked me if I was all right.

I said, "Yeah. Now that I got that regiment of communist ants off me, I'll be all right."

The lieutenant wanted to know how I knew they were communist ants. I replied, "They were red, weren't they?"

We discussed strategy. If we knew anything, it was that we were in enemy territory, most likely on the west coast. We knew we couldn't stay there. However, we were still too scared to take a chance of heading south and risking capture; for after the day's events, they would have killed us on the spot.

There was a peaceful calm in the air. The rain had stopped and there was a warm breeze coming in from the sea. Our clothes were even starting to dry out and I felt almost warm for the first time since we had hit the rice paddy. The sky had cleared, exposing a full moon and a billion stars. We sat there listening to the waves crash against the rock.

I thought to myself, "What's a nice guy like me doing in a place like this?" I could have beaten this rap very easily. But me, I had decided to enlist at all costs, mainly because everyone had told me the army wouldn't take me because of my bad eyes. I had to prove them all wrong. "What a fool I was," I kept thinking. "They're all back home, nice and comfortable with a full belly and a nice warm bed to crawl into. Here I am, in the middle of nowhere, cold, hungry, not knowing if I'll be alive tomorrow. Hell of a way to prove a point," I chided myself.

We were all suffering from fits of depression. At one point we were so low that we even considered surrendering. After going over all the pros and cons, we had decided to take our chances and try to get back to our own lines. As we sat there in the underbrush, keeping one ear open for any unusual noises, the conversation turned to home.

The lieutenant said, "Wonder what my wife is doing tonight? Probably shacking up with some civilian. We don't get along too well. I caught her shacking up with some guy before I left the States." Moose asked him if he beat the shit out of the guy. "No. I just threw him a five-dollar bill and told him to go down to a whorehouse and get a decent piece of ass."

The lieutenant continued, "I probably would have divorced her before I left the States, but I didn't have time. She doesn't write anymore. Just as well. I wouldn't answer anyhow." He paused to reflect and then wondered aloud, "I don't know why I married her in the first place."

"Well, probably because you loved her," I said.

"Perhaps, but it sure wore off in a hurry after the honeymoon was over. Did I tell you I sent her a washer and dryer for last Christmas from California?"

"Damn, that sure is an unusual gift to send someone you hate. Expensive, too. The freight alone must have cost you a bundle," I said.

"No, it doesn't cost much to send a douche bag and a towel to Ohio."

Moose and I couldn't stop laughing. It took our minds off our predicament for the moment anyway.

"With a little luck, perhaps God will look with sympathy on our plight and help us out," I suggested.

The lieutenant replied, "If you're looking for sympathy, it's between shit and syphilis in the dictionary." He wasn't a true atheist, just an agnostic. He said he would believe in God if he could see him. Well, Moose and I sure as hell couldn't show him. In fact, we were beginning to wonder about his existence ourselves.

"How could anyone with an ounce of sense," we wondered, "let a war like this go on, causing so much death, destruction, pain, and misery on thousands and thousands of people—willing and unwilling participants—just to make a few people rich and get a chosen few listed in the history books?"

The lieutenant said we were defending the right of the Koreans to freedom. From where we stood, they didn't seem to want it. Anyway, you couldn't tell a North Korean from a South Korean and so you had to treat them all as the enemy. Many a dead GI had made the mistake of trusting a Korean, thinking he was friendly, only to wind up with a knife in his back for his trouble.

I believe the official reason for our being there was to stop the Communists from taking over the world. Well, this was the asshole of the world as far as I was concerned, so why not let them have it. "Who wants an asshole anyway," I wondered.

We decided it was time to make our way south. We headed out ever so cautiously for we knew our next mistake would most likely be our last. That's the way it worked out for the lieutenant. We had made our way for about five miles down the coast, staying under cover as best we could, with the lieutenant leading the way when it happened.

He stepped on an antipersonnel mine. It blew both his legs off and riddled him with shrapnel. We ran up, but there was little we could do for him. Moose was practically in a state of shock. We knelt down on either side of him. He was still conscious, but in mortal agony.

He reached out for my hand and said, "Tell me about this God you seem to know, Irish. Do you figure he'll have a place for me?"

I reassured him that he would be welcomed with open arms and that when he got there, he should make room for Moose and me. He told me he wanted to pray, but didn't know how, and he asked me to say one for him.

Being Catholic, I said the "Act of Contrition," pausing after every line to let him repeat it. When I had finished, I assured him that it was a one-way ticket to heaven.

He looked at Moose and then back at me and made one last request. "When you guys get back to the States, how about drinking a fifth of whiskey and doing up San Francisco for me, just like we planned?" We assured him we would. His hand went limp in mine, his eyes closed, and his head rolled slowly to the side. I looked at Moose and said, "He's gone, Moose."

We sat there with him for several minutes. I finally said to Moose, "We had better bury him." Moose refused, saying, "We'll carry him back to our lines. We can't bury him here."

"Moose, he's gone, and we're in no condition to carry him, for God only knows how long."

Finally Moose said, "We can't bury him; we don't even have a shovel. Let's put him over there in the brush, and as soon as we can get back to the post we can tell them where he is so that they can come and get his body."

We moved him to the underbrush and covered him as best we could. We were both heartbroken at our loss. We realized that it could have been one of us lying back there dead. We had seen lots of dead people in the war, but none that we had known personally. Dead bodies hadn't had much effect on us before. This was different, however, and very difficult to accept.

We never spoke a word to each other the rest of the night. At daybreak, we stopped to rest on top of a cliff. Moose broke the silence. "Why did it have to happen, Irish?"

"I don't know, Moose. I guess only God can provide answers to that one. One thing for sure, though; when he rings your bell you're gone. All the money and caring in the world won't help or keep it from happening."

"Why the hell are people born in the first place if this is all they have to look forward to?"

"Hell, Moose, I don't know. I would like to believe that death is not the end, but only the beginning of something warm and beautiful. I guess the only way to prove it is to die. But once you do that, there is no coming back to tell about it. At least I never met anyone who had died and returned to life to tell about what it's like on the other side."

Moose and I were so depressed at this point that we didn't care if we lived or died. Then we spotted a helicopter out over the water. We figured we couldn't be too far from our own lines.

We decided to be extremely cautious now that there was a chance our ordeal was coming to an end.

As we sat there in the underbrush, munching on dry rice, trying to take the edge off our hunger, Moose started to say something. His voice kept getting softer, or so it seemed to me. I started to see brilliant circles of fluorescent lights shooting out from my eyes, every color in the rainbow in a never-ending pattern. Then I blacked out.

6

Recuperating in Japan

I woke up in a hospital in Japan with old Moose sitting there by my bed ordering me to get better or he was going to kick the shit out of me. I remember asking Moose where the hell we were. When he told me we were in a hospital back in Japan, I could have cried, I was so happy.

"How did we get here, Moose?"

"Never mind that, Irish. You tried to die on me, and I wouldn't let you."

I said, "Thanks, Moose," and blacked out again. I regained consciousness again the next day, this time for good. Old Moose was still there by my side. I found out later that he had been there by my side the whole time.

I asked the Doc how long I had been there, and he told me it had been eight days. He told me I had contracted malaria. "But you're going to be just fine now," he assured me. It took several weeks to get the full story out of Moose, but little by little, I managed to piece it all together.

It seemed he had carried me on his back for over fifteen miles before he happened upon an air force base, where he practically commandeered a hospital plane to take me back to Japan. He

72

raised so much hell that they moved their regular scheduled flight up by some four hours just to shut him up.

Old Moose was in pretty bad shape himself. Half out of his mind already from losing the lieutenant and then faced with the prospect of losing me too was almost more than he could handle. When Moose said he would look after me, he really meant it. I couldn't help thinking how much better off the world would be if everybody had a friend like Moose to look after him.

I spent the next three weeks in bed. I think the worst part of it was the daily baths given by this old battle-ax I had for a nurse. All those beautiful nurses running around, and I got stuck with this battle-ax five days out of seven. She was so big and masculine that she wouldn't have had any trouble wrestling a six hundred-pound alligator. In fact, I would have put my money on her to win.

I used to dread her coming in the morning. I was bashful and shy anyway, and somehow I could never get used to her scrubbing me down. I can still hear her coming through the door in the morning calling, "Bath time, fellows." Everybody ducked under the covers.

She would walk up to the bed, and in what seemed like two seconds flat she would have you stripped naked. Then she would just smile and methodically go about giving you a bath. You didn't dare get an erection, for that was her specialty. She would flick her wrist, catching the tip of your penis with her fingernails. It was like popping a balloon with a needle. It would deflate instantly. Then she'd say in her gravelly voice, "You naughty boy, you."

She was good at dispensing medicine also. She would bring it in and tell you to open wide. Then she'd throw it in your mouth. I asked her one day what she would do if I didn't take it. She replied, "I'll break your neck if you don't." At that she pinched my nose and jerked my head back so quickly that I thought it was coming off my shoulders. My mouth flew open. With her free hand she threw the medicine in and with the same motion she clapped me under the chin, closing my mouth and ordering me to swallow it. I did, and when she let me up for air,

73

I suggested she take a trip to the Thousand Islands and spend a year on each one.

I sure was glad when they finally let me out of bed. Then I could go to the showers and not have that half-beast half-woman manhandle me any more.

I guess they figured Moose and I had flipped out; for they had this shrink come around every day and talk to us. They insisted it was just standard procedure for all prisoners of war or those missing in action, which was how Moose and I had been listed.

Moose and I conspired to see if we could drive the shrink crazy. The first thing we did was refuse to talk to him about anything. Every time he would come in, we would simply clam up. We gave him the silent treatment for four days. It wasn't that we didn't want to talk to him, it was just so funny seeing him so frustrated and watching him use various approaches to get us to loosen our tongues. Finally, he threatened to put us both in the psycho ward. That did it!

Moose and I wandered through the psycho ward one day while roaming around the hospital. What we saw there was enough to make us know that we didn't want to spend any time there.

As we walked through the door, this guy jumped up and asked Moose for a cigarette. Moose said he didn't smoke and the guy hauled off and hit him on the jaw. Moose swung back and knocked him out cold.

"Friendly bunch of bastards in here, ain't they, Moose?"

Moose was mumbling something about the no-good SOB or some other descriptive term when another guy started hollering as loudly as he could, "FIRE! FIRE! FIRE!" and the guy in the bunk next to him, showing no emotion at all, was asking "WHERE? WHERE? WHERE?" while calmly rolling his head from side to side.

Moose looked at me and said, "Let's get the hell out of here."

"I'm with you."

As we headed for the door, two guys in white jackets beat us to the door and locked it. Moose demanded that they open the door. They refused, saying patients were not permitted out of the ward area.

Moose said, "Look man, we wandered in here by mistake and ain't looking for any trouble."

"Sure. Sure. No one belongs in here. Now just settle down and go back to your bunks before we have to restrain you both."

Moose told him, "I am finding it hard to restrain myself from breaking your goddamned neck. Now just open the door and we'll be gone."

The guards refused, and at that, the fight was on. Moose smacked one of them and sent him flying and the other guy jumped on his back. I picked up a chair and hit him across the back with it. He let go of Moose and swung at me. I ducked, and by that time, Moose had turned around. He picked up the guy and threw him across the ward. He wound up in some nut's bed with the nut trying to pull his hair out with one hand and beating him on the back with his free fist, meanwhile screaming something about being attacked by a giant insect.

By now someone had sounded the alarm, and I think every orderly and MP in the place was on his way.

As the fight broke out, all the yelling and commotion started to excite the other patients. And believe me, it didn't take much to get them started. They were throwing everything they could get their hands on, including each other.

Moose grabbed the keys off this first bastard he had decked and amid all the confusion, he unlocked the door and hollered for me to come on.

We went running down the hall. The only trouble was just about every nut locked up in there left also. Moose and I made it to our ward, jumped in bed, and covered up. The PA system kept repeating "CODE NINE, CODE NINE" which meant "Mental patient loose in the hospital."

Havoc spread throughout. The mental patients upset trash cans, set off fire alarms, and sprayed fire extinguishers all over the place. They wrecked a kitchen and the mess hall. There was a first-class riot.

The hospital authorities called in reinforcements, barricaded the doors, and methodically swept through the halls and wards rounding up those guys one at a time. It took them almost six hours, for they were hiding in every little nook and cranny they could find. They finally found the last one perched on top of a 150-foot water tower threatening to jump off. Through it all, Moose and I just lay there in bed staying out of trouble.

The reports said it was started by a couple of mental patients, and that's all we ever heard about it.

We saw one of the orderlies in the cafeteria one day, and he started to question us. I asked him if he was writing a book or something. He said, "No, but I could swear that you two started all the trouble down at the psycho ward last week." We told him he was full of shit because we had just gotten there three days ago.

One day we had a visitor from our headquarters in Japan. Since there had been no word on us other than we were shot down over enemy territory, it was assumed that we were prisoners of war, although we were officially listed as MIA (missing in action). Our visitor couldn't understand how we had wound up in Japan and was particularly interested in the material we had been carrying. We told him the whole story, with Moose filling him in from the time I blacked out back in Korea.

He told us that the area we went down in, according to their intelligence reports, was infested with at least ten thousand Red Chinese. He was simply amazed that we were able to avoid capture and even more amazed at how we reached Japan. We told him we were traveling as officers and he knew what preferential treatment they get. Moose didn't tell him how he threatened to blow the whole place up if they didn't get that plane in the air and headed for Japan.

He told us they would send a chopper and a squad of men to try to retrieve the material we had been carrying. I told him not to forget our wallets. After checking with the doctors and the shrink as to when we would be released, he told us that counterintelligence would probably want to debrief us on our ordeal behind enemy lines. The doctor said we could be released, but the shrink wanted another shot at us and wasn't sure when he'd let us go.

The shrink took another shot at me the following day. I was in a particularly ornery mood and decided to see how far I could push him. Our conversation started off something like this:

"Good morning, Private."

"That's just your opinion, Doc."

"Oh. Well, how are you today?"

"As compared to what?"

"Think you're pretty bright, don't you, Private?"

"I'm so bright my mother calls me 'Sun.'"

"I thought you told me you didn't have a mother."

"Well, we didn't for a long time. We were too poor to afford one. Why are you asking me all these stupid questions, anyway, Doc?"

"I want to make you better, Private."

"Better! Hell, I think I'm pretty good now. In fact, some of them even said I was terrific."

"Who are you talking about? Girls you've been out with?"

"I don't care, Doc. Name something."

"What the hell does all this have to do with what we're talking about, anyway?" He was starting to get mad now.

"You brought me, Doc. I guess you'll have to dance with me."

"I'll dance you right out the goddamned door."

"You're just jealous because I can read and write, and you can't, Doc."

"I can so."

"Can so what, Doc?"

"Read and write."

"What does that have to do with me, Doc? I don't care if you *can* read and write."

"You brought it up, didn't you?"

"The only time I bring it up is when I'm with a girl, Doc."

"Your pecker?"

"Getting kinda personal, aren't you, Doc?"

He broke his pencil in half and demanded, "You're just fuckin' with me, aren't you, Private? Why won't you give me a straight answer to my questions without all this double-talk?"

"Sure, Doc. Just tell me what you want to know, and I'll straighten you out if I can."

"Let me get *you* straight, Private."

"Oh, no, you don't Doc. You stay behind your desk and I'll just sit here."

"You seem to have sex on your mind this morning, Private."

"You brought the subject up, Doc, not me. I think I know what's wrong with me, Doc. It's a rare Hawaiian disease called 'Lack of Nooky.' "

"Lack of Nooky? What's that?"

"You have led a sheltered life, haven't you, Doc?"

"Why do you say that?"

"Well, anyone who doesn't know what nooky is sure hasn't been around much."

"Go to hell, Private."

"Do I get to pass Go and collect two hundred dollars?"

"Would you mind explaining that one?"

"We're playing games here, aren't we? Well, in Monopoly, if you . . ." He cut me off short and snapped, "Never mind."

I said "Okay, you don't have to get sore about it, Doc. I'm not one damned bit mad at you. I don't see what you're so mad at me for."

"I'm not mad at you."

"Well, why is your face all red and why are your hands shaking? If you have problems, Doc, sometimes it helps to talk about them. And if you want someone to talk to, I'll be more than glad to listen."

He said, "You listen and you listen good. This is serious business."

"You could have fooled me, Doc. I don't see what's so serious about it."

"Well, from here on out I'm not going to be so easy on you, do you understand?"

"Okay, Doc. What do you want to know?"

"What the fuck makes you tick?"

"What are you asking me for? You're the doctor, not me. Hell, if I knew that, I'd be where you are sitting and perhaps you'd be my patient."

"Heaven forbid! I'll say one thing for you, though, Private. You have to be one of the biggest optimists I've ever run across. Do you know that?"

"Well, no, Doc. Not until you just told me.

"Do you know the difference between an optimist and a pessimist, Irish?"

We were suddenly on a nickname basis and the doctor/patient relationship had deteriorated into a bullshit session.

"Well, Bob, the way I see it, an optimist gets up in the morning, opens the window and says, 'Good morning, God!' Whereas a pessimist gets up in the morning, opens the window, and says, 'Good God, it's morning!' "

He showed me a glass of water and asked me what was wrong with it.

I said, "It's only half full."

"You're an optimist, Irish. A pessimist would have said it was half empty."

Then I thought I'd throw him a curve. "Hell, Bob, I'm no optimist. I belong to the Loyal Order of Sad Sacks and Crepe Hangers. Everything that happens is bad or is going to be bad. Just like now, I feel okay, but that doesn't mean anything. I'll probably feel like hell an hour from now."

He sat there in total silence for the longest time. Then he said, "I think I've got it, Irish. You're just putting me on and have been ever since we first met."

I started to say something, but he cut me off again and said, "Don't interrupt. There isn't a damned thing wrong with you physically or mentally, is there?"

"You tell me. You're the doctor, Bob. I never did say there was anything wrong with my head. You came to see me. I didn't come to see you. Personally, I think any guy who goes to see a psychiatrist ought to have his head examined. I love life too much to get my head all fucked up worrying about things I have no control over."

I sat there bullshitting with him, meanwhile smoking one cigarette after another. He advised me, "You know, Irish, you should quit smoking. You smoke too damned much."

"Hell, Bob, any damned fool can quit smoking. But it takes a real man to die of lung cancer."

He just shook his head and mumbled in resignation, "I should have known better."

"Like I was saying, Bob, I feel time heals all wounds. When an unpleasant memory comes to mind, I simply cancel it out by thinking of happier times. I don't plan things that happen to me. They just happen, and I try to accept them and make the most of them or turn them to my advantage."

"Give me an example of that, Irish."

"Well, just like these sessions with you, Doc. I didn't ask for them and didn't particularly want them. But since I didn't have a choice, I figured I'd at least have some fun out of them."

"How about Moose, Irish? Do you think he's got his head on straight? He drinks quite a bit. Do you think he tries to drown his troubles in booze?"

"Fuck, no, Bob. He just takes them for a swim once in a while, that's all. Moose has his head on straight. Don't worry about that. Like I said, we've just been putting you on for want of something better to do. Moose figured it was a case of mind over matter. You know. If you didn't mind, it didn't matter."

He said, "You two bastards are something else. Tell me, though, didn't all that time you guys spent behind enemy lines bother you, especially when the lieutenant got killed?"

"You bet your ass it did. It bothered the hell out of us especially when the lieutenant got killed. That was a very depressing experience. But we figured that life has to go on, and every time we think about it, we simply dismiss it and try to think about something else. Moose and I are a team. It's almost like one can't function without the other."

"You mean, your brains and his brawn?"

"Not quite, Bob. But he saved my life on more than one occasion, and anything I can do to help Moose will be done without hesitation."

"I understand you saved Moose's life in the plane crash on your way to Korea. Don't you think that evens up the score? And why did you bother? I mean it would have been a lot easier just to save yourself, wouldn't it?"

"Well, Bob, the same goes for Moose. It would have been a lot easier for him to walk that last fifteen miles without me on his back now, wouldn't it? I don't know what you're getting at, but if I couldn't have gotten Moose out of that plane, we both would have gone down with it. Simple as that."

"Moose is my very best friend, Doc. Before he came along, the only thing I could count on was my fingers. People would always let me down or disappoint me in one way or another. As you can see by my size, I could never stand up for myself very well. I had to eat a lot of shit from a lot of bullies and could only retaliate in sneaky ways, like waiting outside for them and busting their heads open with a two-by-four when they weren't looking. With Moose and me as a team, nobody gives me any shit, and I like that feeling."

"What will you do if you and Moose get transferred to different duty posts? How will you react to that?"

"That's simple enough, Doc. If we both can't have the same duty posts, then we both go AWOL. What the hell are you driving at, anyway, Doc? Do you think Moose and I have an unhealthy relationship or something?"

"No. The thought never entered my mind. It's just unusual for two people to build up a friendship such as you and Moose have and be so unwilling to let go under any circumstances— even to the point of going to jail. What would you do if Moose got killed or what would he do if you got killed?"

"Well, I'm sure neither one of us would rest until the killer was in his grave. Although it would be a tragic loss to one of us, I'm sure the one who survived would be able to cope with it, for we would know that's the way the other would have wanted it. Of course, we'd grieve, but we'd get over it."

"Now that's a healthy attitude to have."

"What the hell are you driving at, anyway, Doc?"

"I like you, Irish, and I would like to keep you here to work with me in the hospital as my clerk."

"What about Moose?"

"Well, Moose doesn't fit into the scheme of things right now, Irish."

"Wait a minute, Doc. You can forget it. We're a team, remember?"

"Tell you what I'll do, Irish. Don't give me an answer right now. I'll arrange a thirty-day leave for you and Moose back in the States. That will give you time to discuss it with Moose and give me your answer when you get back."

I already knew what the answer would be, but I decided not to jump up in his face at this point. The prospect of a thirty-day convalescent leave in the States was much too appealing to say anything stupid and perhaps queer the whole deal.

I said, "Fair enough, Doc. When do we leave?"

"I'll have your orders cut—probably two days."

"See if you can get us paid, too, will you, Doc? We've only received ten dollars a month since we left Georgia. Our records never caught up with us."

He said he'd do his best.

I hurried back to the ward to tell Moose of our good fortune. He simply came unglued. "Thirty days stateside. How in the fuck were you ever able to swing that, Irish?"

"I'll tell you when we're flying over the Golden Gate Bridge, Moose."

"Wow! You must have caught the Doc beating his meat to get him to agree to that."

"Not quite, Moose. But don't look up a gift horse's ass."

"Don't look a gift horse in the mouth, you mean."

"Whatever, Moose. I stand corrected. Now let's make plans for our trip stateside. We're going to need lots of money, that's for sure. The Doc said he would try to get us paid, but I wouldn't count on it."

"Thirty days stateside without any money would be like

being in bed with Marilyn Monroe and not being able to get a hard-on."

"We'll have to make some money here," I said.

"Got any ideas, Irish?"

"I sure do. How about a raffle? We'll raffle off one thousand dollars."

"How we gonna do that, Irish? We don't even have one thousand cents. All our money is still back in the old man's safe in Korea."

"Don't worry about the prize money, Moose. We'll win it ourselves. I'll go down to the Doc's office and use his typewriter to cut a couple of stencils for the tickets and then use his mimeograph machine to run them on."

"How much should we charge for them and what's the cause? You have to have a cause."

"We'll charge two dollars apiece for them, and I'll print up a thousand of them on the first stencil. I'll include my name as the purchaser on the second stencil and run a thousand of them. We'll use the tickets from the second stencil when we hold the drawing. As for the cause, well, let's say it's for the hospital recreation fund."

"What happens to the stubs of the ones we sell?"

"Hell, we'll just throw them in the incinerator. And we only have two days so we had better get started."

I went back to the Doc's office and talked him into letting me use his facilities. By 1600 hours everything was ready to roll.

Moose got a big box which we folded, tore, and crumpled to make into an official-looking drawing box for the ticket stubs with my name on them. Then Moose and I split the one thousand tickets between us and took off in different directions to unload them at two dollars each.

We made up a story about how the proceeds were going to the hospital recreation fund. In addition, each participant had a chance to win one thousand dollars from a two-dollar investment.

There were over fifteen hundred patients in that hospital and perhaps as many as one thousand support personnel, doctors, nurses, orderlies, and the like. We managed to unload over five hundred tickets that night. We worked diligently all the next day and by nightfall we had only fifty tickets left.

I talked the Doc into taking them to the Officers' Club that evening and selling them for us. We told him the drawing was being held the next morning and we wanted him to pick the winner. In this way everybody would think everything was on the up-and-up.

He agreed, and word about the drawing spread throughout the hospital. The Doc had sold the rest of the tickets and turned the money and stubs over to Moose and me. We headed for the incinerator, where we burned all the legitimate stubs before returning to the ward for the big drawing. Moose pulled out the big box of stubs, and I asked the Doc to come forward and draw the winner.

There must have been two hundred people gathered for the drawing. We shook the box and when the Doc pulled my name and read it out loud, I was greeted with boos and hisses and cries of a fix. So I settled everyone down and told them if they felt that way about it, I'd put my name back in and we'd hold another drawing.

Most of them said "Never mind. We believe it was fair and square." But there were still those who needed to be silenced, so I put my name back in and asked the Doc to draw another name. When he pulled my name out for a second time, I pretended surprise and by now had made a believer out of ninety-nine percent of those present. After all, if they couldn't trust Doc, who could they trust? The other one percent would only have been satisfied if they had won.

Everyone wandered off, leaving only Moose, the Doc and me there. The Doc asked us how much money we had made from the lottery.

"Not a dime, Doc. We only printed five hundred tickets and at two bucks apiece, it all went for prize money."

"Yes, yes. I get the picture. You and Moose were running a con."

"Who, us? Why we never . . . If you feel that way about it, we'll give a hundred bucks to the recreation fund."

"Well, that's better than nothing." Then, for some unexplainable reason, he reached into the raffle box and started examining the stubs. When he discovered they all had my name on them, he was flabbergasted. He threatened to spill the beans on us, saying that was a dishonest and despicable thing to do.

"I get the dishonest part, Doc, but could you run the other one by me again?"

"I've got no choice but to turn you guys in."

"What in the world would you want to do that for, Doc? Nobody got hurt, and besides, it was the most exciting thing that has happened around here since those nuts went on a rampage through the hospital. And furthermore, aren't lotteries illegal in the service?"

"Yes, they are."

"Well, if it's illegal to sell lottery tickets, then it's illegal to buy them, right?"

"Yes, I guess it is."

"Who did you sell that last bunch of tickets to, Doc?"

"The officers at the Officers' Club."

"Then, they broke the law, too. Right?"

"Yes, I suppose so."

"Well, Moose and I still have the stubs, and if you turn us in for running a lottery, then we'll have no choice but to turn in everyone who bought tickets."

"You can't turn all those officers in. Besides that, I bought some tickets myself."

I said, "Right, Doc."

He said, "Let's compromise. We hold a legitimate drawing and determine a legitimate winner."

"Can't do that, Doc."

"Why not?"

"Moose and I burned all the stubs."

"But you just said you have them."

"I know, Doc. It was worth a shot, wasn't it? Besides, you

85

drew the winner yourself, and if you turn us in, everyone is going to think you were in on it and just trying to save face at our expense."

"What do you suggest, Irish?"

"Tell you what, Doc. Why don't we all take an hour or so and think things over? Then we'll all meet in your office and whatever you decide, Moose and I will go along with it."

He was in a tight spot. His conscience was bothering the hell out of him; at the same time, however, he didn't want to appear to have had any part in it.

As soon as he left Moose and I grabbed the box and headed out the other door for the incinerator. We even burned the stencil used to make the tickets. As far as we were concerned at this point, there never was a lottery. As we stood there watching the evidence go up in smoke, Moose and I shook hands and congratulated each other on a job well-done.

Just about then the Doc walked up behind us and asked if he was too late.

"You sure are, Doc."

"I knew I should have taken those damned things with me. Oh well, probably just as well. You guys would have found some way to wiggle out of it, anyhow. Your orders are ready to be picked up for your leave, but I wasn't able to get your pay."

"Don't worry about it, Doc. We'll manage somehow."

"Yeah, I guess you will with a grand to blow."

"Yeah. We'll make out, Doc."

What he didn't know was that we had a grand apiece.

Moose and I had one more hurdle to clear before we could leave. We didn't have any clothes. All we had were our hospital blues and they sure as hell weren't going to let us off the grounds with them on. So we went to the storage area where they kept the clothing, duffel bags and all. We broke the lock off the door and went to work trying to find some clothes to fit us.

I found a sergeant's duffel bag with a uniform that fit me to a tee. I simply demoted him by tearing the stripes off the sleeves but left the fruit salad on the front and the hash marks on the sleeves. Moose had a little more trouble, being so big and all, but finally found a uniform that almost fit him. He said, "Good enough to get us to the States where we'll buy civies."

We went down to personnel, picked up our orders, and headed for the main gate. We caught a taxi and headed for the airport.

Luck was with us for we only had to wait two hours at the airport before a MATS (Military Air Transportation Service) plane was leaving for the States with stops in Wake and Hawaii. We would have discarded our uniforms in Japan, but we had to be in uniform to ride aboard military aircraft. Including stopovers for fuel and all, we arrived in the States in thirty-six hours.

7

Stateside Leave; Irish meets Pam

We got off base and headed for San Francisco and the best hotel we could find. We checked in and then headed out to get something to eat and buy some civies.

We stopped in a restaurant for a bite to eat. While we were sitting there, an old sergeant came over and asked if he could join us. We got to bullshitting when he noticed the uniform I was wearing had a purple heart on it. He asked me if I got it in Korea. I said, "No, I got it off Moose here. He bought it from some sergeant for two bucks. I guess that guy needed a drink real bad or something."

He remarked that I looked rather young to have all those hash marks on my sleeves and I replied, "Would you believe I'm older than I look?"

The sergeant didn't believe me. I tried again. "Well, I'll tell you the truth, then. When Moose and I hit town, we decided that my uniform looked drab and needed to be dressed up a little. So we went in an army and navy store and I asked for ten dollars' worth of ribbons and told them to mix 'em up."

He said, "It's guys like you that give the army a bad name."

I shot back, "It's bastards like you that make us want to."
"You guys can be court-martialed for wearing those ribbons."
"I'll sell them to you if you want them and at a special discount. I'm planning on throwing them away shortly anyway."
He threatened to turn us in to the MPs. Moose told him he had better get the hell out of there and leave us alone. He got up and walked out.
Moose just shook his head and asked, "Do you believe that shit?"
"Come on, Moose, let's get the hell out of here and go buy some civies. The sooner I get out of this uniform the better I'll feel."
"I'm with you, Irish."
As we were walking around looking for a clothing store, I reminded Moose we had to drink a fifth for the lieutenant.
"You gonna get drunk, Irish?" he asked, a little surprised for he had never seen me take a drink.
"Just one drink for the lieutenant, and you can finish the bottle, Moose. Okay?"
"Fine with me, Irish."
We finally found a store that had clothes small enough for me and big enough for Moose. We bought slacks, sport shirts, shoes, socks, and underwear. We even bought new shaving gear and some fancy after-shave lotion. We didn't want anything that even remotely reminded us of the military.
After we got back to the hotel, we shed our army rags, showered, shaved, and got all dressed up, ready for a night on the town. Hell, we were even starting to feel like human beings again. On the way out I picked up the uniforms, boots and all, and shoved them down the trash chute out in the hall.
We were standing on the sidewalk trying to hail a taxi. We figured a taxi driver would know where all the action was, and we were ready for some.
I felt someone tap me on the shoulder. I turned around and there stood two MPs and the sergeant we had the run-in with at the restaurant.

I don't know what the hell he told them or how they found us, but there they were. I guess he must have spotted us going into the hotel and called them.

One MP asked us where we were stationed, I informed him in no uncertain terms that we were civilians.

He asked, "Can I see your passes?"

I replied, "Can I shoot your gun?"

"You guys sure look like GIs to us, and the sergeant here said he can testify you two were parading around in army uniforms a coupla hours ago."

"Well, you know what a bunch of goddamned liars those soldiers are, especially when they have been drinking."

The sergeant protested that he was stone-sober and that we were wearing unearned and unauthorized decorations.

I said, "Fuck you, buddy. I've had about all the horseshit I can use for one day. Now get the hell out of our way before there is some real trouble here."

The one MP announced, "I'm placing you both under arrest."

As they reached behind them for their handcuffs, Moose hit the one at least four times before he even had a chance to fall to the sidewalk. I kicked the other one right in the nuts, and he went rolling and moaning around the ground as if in mortal agony.

Moose grabbed the sergeant by his jacket and said, "I should break your goddamned neck."

I hollered, "Let him go, Moose! Let's get the hell out of here."

Moose threw him up in the air, like a baseball. As he was coming down, Moose swung like he was trying to hit a home run, hitting him dead in the midsection, and driving him into the crowd that had assembled there.

We ran down the next block and got there just as one of those little cable cars was making its way up the hill. We jumped aboard and rode it to the top of the world, or so it seemed. The view was spectacular. The air was fresh and clean—quite a contrast between this and that putrid-smelling Korea, I thought to myself. Just the thought was enough to make you sick. Then to come back to the States to get away from the military and be hassled by the military on our first day back was both aggravating and humiliating.

Moose and I took in the picturesque view for about twenty minutes and then went looking for a liquor store. Once we found one Moose asked, "What kind of liquor do you suppose the lieutenant would have wanted?"

"Suit yourself, Moose."

He bought a fifth and we headed back out, caught a cab and told the driver to take us where the action was. He drove us to Fisherman's Wharf.

We wandered out on the docks, sitting there watching the water and the boats, not saying much of anything to each other when Moose broke open the bottle and handed it to me.

I had never drank any hard liquor. The strongest thing I had ever tasted was 3.2 beer and that had been enough to gag me.

"Here's to the lieutenant, wherever he may be, and may God rest his soul." I put the bottle to my lips like it was a quart of milk, took a big gulp, and swallowed it. I imagined I was on fire and I started coughing and gagging. That stuff even went up my nose; my eyes were watering and my nose was running. I just knew I was going to die!

After I calmed down and regained my composure, I handed the bottle to Moose, who was laughing his ass off at me. He took the bottle and put it to his lips and must have drank a third of it before he came up for air. He just went, "Ahhh, that sure is smooth stuff."

I shook my head and said, "I don't see how you can drink that rotgut."

"Hell, compared to that moonshine I've been drinking all my life, this stuff is like water."

We spent a couple of hours there, reliving the past and wondering what the future had in store for us. All the while Moose kept nursing his bottle. Finally, when he had finished the last of it, we got up and headed for the bars. There didn't seem to be any law and order at all there. The pimps and prostitutes were everywhere. The hustlers were selling everything from stolen cars to wristwatches to booze at cut-rate prices.

We wandered into a bar and were sitting there in a booth trying to decide how to spend our next thirty days when an old haybag of a prostitute came over and sat down beside Moose and asked him, "Hey, big fellow, would you like a little hay for your goose?"

I asked her, "You want a little mud for your turtle?"

"I wasn't talking to you, Sonny."

"Oh well, are you a prostitute?"

"No honey, I'm only a substitute. I only work three days a week."

"Oh, that's good, because we wouldn't want to get involved with a prostitute."

"What about it, big fellow, do you want to go with me? I'll give you something you've never had before."

I asked, "What's that—leprosy?"

"You're a wise little son of a bitch, aren't you?"

"No wait a minute. Let's keep personalities out of this."

Moose told her he would go with her on one condition. She asked what that was.

"Only if you do it my way."

"What's your way?"

"On credit!"

"I'd call you something, you dizzy little bastard, but what I was going to call you had a head on it, so I guess I can't call you one, can I?"

"You know, sweetheart, your eyes look like two piss holes in the snow, all bloodshot and all. Why don't you cram a couple of Kotex in them so you don't bleed to death?"

"You have something against sex, Sonny?"

"On the contrary, out of all my relations, I like sex the best. It's just that I'm fussy about who I go to bed with. I don't want sloppy fifths or sixths. Besides that Moose couldn't go with you if he wanted to."

"Why not?"

"He's got something wrong with his ear."

"What does that have to do with it?"

"He can't piss out of it, sweetheart."

She finally gave up. Before sauntering off she asked Moose if he was coming or not. Moose said, "No, I ain't even breathing hard yet."

A little later a drunk came staggering by our table and went into the men's room next to our booth. He was in there for five minutes or so when we heard a bloodcurdling scream come out of there. I hollered to the barkeeper that he had better check in there. He said, "It's just some old drunk in there."

Then we heard it again. I repeated, "Man, you better check on him."

"Okay, okay," he said as he flung open the door and shouted, "What's all the commotion in here?"

We could hear this old drunk say, "Man, I'm sitting here taking a shit and every time I go to flush this damned thing, something comes up and squeezes my balls."

"Well, if you would get your ass off that janitor's bucket and over there on the toilet, that wouldn't happen."

It wasn't long before another whore came over and plunked her ass down beside me and asked me to buy her a drink.

"What do I look like, your old man or something?"

She said, "Come on, sweetheart, buy me a drink; then we'll go up to my place and have some fun."

"Doing what?"

She said, "Come on, honey, you've been around, haven't you? Or do you still go to bed with Rosie Palm and her four daughters?"

"Hey, don't forget Madam Thumb. She helps keep it all together."

She decided to change strategy and flatter me a little.

"What do you have on that smells so good?"

"I got a hard-on. I didn't think it smelled that good."

"You're a clever little son of a bitch, aren't you?"

"Well, sweetheart, all I can say to you is that if Cleopatra had the face that could launch a thousand ships, you sure as hell have the face that could sink 'em."

"Okay, dearie, you had your little jokes. Now do you want to get your rocks off or not?"

I had about all of her I could stand so I figured I better get rid of her once and for all. "Well, I'll tell you, sweetie, I don't know if it's instinct or some other kind of stink, but something tells me not to go with you. Besides, I was just circumsized this morning."

"Okay, you little bastard, you made your point," and at that she left.

Moose and I decided to leave that place. It was not quite what we had in mind for a night's excitement. We wandered a little farther uptown to a little higher class bar and went on in. We saddled up on a couple of bar stools to look the place over. It wasn't much better than the place we had just left, but we figured since we were there, we might as well get a sandwich and something to drink before heading back out again. Moose looked across and bar and spotted an old haybag sitting there drunk out of her mind.

She had a stuffed animal under her arm. It looked like a duck but you really couldn't tell; because it was so dark in there.

Anyway, Moose kept hollering over to her until he got her attention. "Hey, lady. What are you doing with that pig in here?"

She hollered back in her slurred voice, "That's not a pig; that's a duck."

I hollered back, "He was talking to a duck lady."

She picked up a beer bottle and threw it at me. I ducked and it hit the head of a merchant seaman sitting at a table behind us.

He jumped up and demanded, "Who threw that bottle?"

Of course, I put the finger on her.

He was pretty drunk himself and walked over to where she was sitting, grabbed her by the hair, pulled her off the bar stool, and threatened to beat the shit out of her.

A couple of guys sitting on that side of the room took exception to a lady being treated that way and told him to let her alone. He cut her loose and took up their challenge. The next thing you knew the whole place was in an uproar. Moose and I just sat there watching the action, occasionally ducking a flying bottle.

Then we decided to leave. Moose led the way, clearing a path over broken tables and chairs, pushing or slugging anyone who got in our way, depending on how much resistance they put up.

We finally made it out to the sidewalk. Moose turned to me and said, "Let's see if we can find some quiet place this time. That sure was a rowdy bunch of bastards in there."

"Yeah; they sure were, Moose," I added.

We grabbed a cab and told the driver to take us to a nice respectable nightclub with lots of broads and good music. The cabbie took us uptown to a nightclub that looked like it was doing a thriving business. We told each other, "This is more like it."

There was a live band playing dance music and the room was filled wall-to-wall with people. Moose and I wandered around inside until we finally found an empty table over in the corner. We called the waitress over and ordered drinks. The prices were a little steep, but the atmosphere was terrific.

As we sat there listening to the band play and watching people dance, Moose said, "Something is missing, Irish."

"I know, Moose. We need some female companionship to help us enjoy ourselves."

"Yeah, Irish. But I never was very good at meeting girls."

"Neither was I, Moose, but I'm sure in a crowd this size there must be a couple of girls who wouldn't mind sharing our hospitality for the evening."

The waitress came over to see if we wanted anything. I got to talking to her and told her of our plight. She said, "I think you're in luck tonight. There are two lovely young ladies over there by the door. They're unattached. Why don't you ask them to dance and see where it goes from there?"

Moose confided "I can't dance."

I said, "I can—a little. Maybe enough to get by. What the hell, Moose, it's worth a try. I'll go ask one of them to dance and then invite them both back to our table."

"If you can swing that, Irish, I swear you should run for President."

Neither one of us wanted to admit it, but we were both ex-

95

tremely homesick and lonely. We craved female companionship, other than the two-bit whore variety, and we would have moved heaven and earth just to hold a decent conversation with a decent girl.

"Well, here goes nothing, Moose." As I approached their table, I could feel the butterflies start to churn in my stomach. The girls looked up as they saw me coming and I said to myself, "Don't give up now. Take a shot at it. She can only say no."

When I finally reached their table, I looked this pretty little ponytailed girl right in the eyes and asked, "Pardon me, ma'am, may I have the pleasure of this dance with you?"

When she said, "Sure, why not," and smiled at me with those big brown cow eyes, I thought for sure I was going to pass out on the spot. My heart was pounding so fast that I feared it was going to stop beating at any moment.

We made our way to the dance floor. They started playing a rock and roll number and she started dancing. After stumbling around for the first minute I got the beat and found out all I had to do was shuffle my feet while she went through the spinning and turning. By the time the dance was over, the initial fear was wearing off, and I was getting a little braver.

I escorted her back to her table. As she was sitting down, I said, "Listen, I have a great idea. I have a friend across the room, and I was wondering if you girls would like to join us at our table. I mean, if you don't want to, I'll understand and all. Well, you know what I mean, don't you?"

The little girl I had been dancing with said, "Don't be silly," (I knew I was a goner then) "we'd love to join you." You could have knocked me over with a feather.

We made our way across the room to where Moose was sitting. When that big rebel saw me coming with those two fillies in tow, he lit up like a Christmas tree. I introduced them to Moose as "the two prettiest girls this side of the Mississippi River."

Moose said, "Hi, my name is Moose—or at least that's what Irish here calls me."

They introduced themselves as Pam and Carol, and we all sat

down. We ordered drinks and were trying to break the ice with small talk. It was like the sound of sweet music to sit there and listen to them talk in fluent English after listening to all that gibberish and broken English in Japan and Korea. I was amazed at the big words they were using. It had seemed that the Japs and Koreans had trouble with anything over four letters.

When they asked us what we did for a living, I took the initiative.

"Moose and I are cattle ranchers from Oklahoma. We're here on vacation."

Pam, the one I had taken a fancy to, said, "Don't try to kid us. You two are GIs on leave, aren't you?"

I was a little shocked and embarrassed at being caught in a lie so early in the conversation, and I guess it must have shown, for she asked, "Why is your face so red?"

"Oh, I didn't think it showed. You're right, and I'm sorry I lied to you. But how in the world did you know? Is it that obvious or is GI stamped on our foreheads?"

She said, "It doesn't matter, Irish." (When she called me Irish, I knew I was in love.) "Some of the nicest boys we meet are in the service. Of course, some of them are a bit much."

"Yes, I know. But seriously, how in the world did you spot us as GIs? We didn't want anyone to know."

"Well, first of all, your hair is cut above your ears. Second, you guys are always so neat and clean-shaven. And third, usually you are from a different part of the country."

"I'll make a note of that. Don't shave, let hair grow, dress sloppy, and do as the natives do."

Moose asked them what they did. They were students at a local college in San Francisco. They usually came to this night-club every Friday and Saturday night to dance and listen to the music.

We sat there for the next three hours and did nothing but talk, eat, and drink—with the usual trips to the men's and ladies' rooms. Finally, as with all good times, this one was coming to an end. They were getting ready to close the place down.

Moose and I offered to get a cab and see them home, but they said they had their own car and offered to drop us off where we were staying. We told them that might be a problem because we had had a little trouble at the place we were staying and didn't wish to go back there to stay.

They suggested a rooming house out by the college they were attending.

"Great! Lead the way."

They dropped us off there and told us the name of the person who ran it.

I said, "Pam, I hope you don't think me too forward, but I was wondering what you girls are doing tomorrow night?"

They said they would probably go dancing at the same place. I asked if Moose and I could take them.

They agreed and even offered to pick us up there at the rooming house.

We said goodnight, and they drove off, leaving Moose and me standing there all dreamy and starry-eyed. We both thought we had died and gone to heaven! I remember asking myself, "If I'm dead, how come I have to go to the bathroom?"

We floated up the steps and rang the bell. An elderly man answered the door. We told him we were told he had rooms for rent. He invited us in and showed us a room with twin beds and a shower. Perfect. We paid him and hit the sack.

Neither one of us was saying much; we just lay there savoring every luscious moment of the perfect evening until we finally drifted off to sleep.

We slept until noon the next day and had just finished taking a shower and getting dressed when we heard a horn blowing out front. I went to look out the window. It was Pam and Carol. I couldn't believe my eyes! I flung open the window, crawled out on the porch roof, jumped ten feet to the ground and hurried over to their car.

They were both laughing hysterically at my movements. For want to something better to say, I said, "I thought I'd drop in to see you."

Just about then Moose came busting through the front door and joined us.

"What's up, girls?"

"We're on our way to the beach and thought that if you guys weren't doing anything you might like to join us."

Would we ever! I guess our enthusiasm overwhelmed us as Moose and I kept trying to get through the car door at the same time.

We finally paired off, with Moose and Carol in the front seat and Pam and me in the back. Off to the beach we drove.

About half way there, I remembered we didn't have any bathing trunks. I told them that unless we planned to go skinny-dipping, we had better stop and buy some.

They took us to a department store where Moose and I bought everything we needed—trunks, towels, and suntan lotion. Soon we were on our way again.

We spent the afternoon hitting the surf, playing volleyball on the beach, and having a ball in general. I don't recall ever being happier in all my life. I was doing my best—and so was Moose—to watch my language. In the service, those four-letter words are just part of your everyday vocabulary and after a while you say them without even realizing you're saying them.

Pam and I were lying there on the sand. I was so happy just to be with her. Then I made what I felt was the biggest blunder of my life.

I said, "Fuck me, mamma, I can't dance."

As soon as I said it, I realized what an awful slip of the tongue I had made. I could tell by the look in her eyes that Pam was really hurt.

"I'm really sorry for saying that, Pam. If I could, I'd cut my tongue out."

She didn't say anything. She just sat there staring at the sand.

"Pam, look at me."

I guess she was too embarrassed or didn't want to.

I got up and started slowly walking down the beach thinking to myself, "God, how could I have been so stupid? I know I've lost her, and I hardly had time to get to know her."

I never felt lower or more depressed in my life. I walked half a mile down the beach and sat down on a big rock, staring out at the ocean with big tears in my eyes, thinking, "Lord, what am I?" This goddamned army has my head so screwed up, I'm not even a decent human being any longer. How could I hurt that sweet little girl like that with my foul mouth?

I don't know if it was because I was so homesick and lonely that it hit me so hard, or was I really in love with her?

I knew in my heart that I had really blown it. I was so lost and lonely. I felt a hand on my shoulder. I turned and it was Pam.

"Pam, I'm so sorry."

"Don't worry about it, Irish. I know you didn't mean it. Sometimes things just come out. It's just that I wasn't expecting it and it took me off guard."

"Pam, what can I do to make it up to you?"

"Just come on back and join the group and stop being an old party-pooper."

I stood up and took her hands in mine and said, "Pam, you're the sweetest person I've ever met in my life. God strike me dead if I ever say anything like that around you again."

"I understand, Irish."

I put my hands around her waist and pulled her ever so gently to me. As our lips met for the first time, my heart started pounding. I had a tingling sensation from head to toe. I wished that kiss could last forever. I knew she was enjoying it, too, for she shared my embrace and kissed me in return.

"Oh, Pam, I wish this day could last forever."

She gave me a loving smile and said, "Come on. Let's catch up with the others."

When we got back, Moose was sitting there with Carol. They were getting along really well together. She was almost six feet tall, and they looked so natural together.

Moose hollered, "Where've you been, Irish?"

"In heaven, Moose."

We decided not to go dancing that evening, choosing instead to have our own party there on the beach. Moose and Carol took the car and went shopping for all the goodies—hot dogs, marshmallows, beer, Coke, chips, and all the trimmings.

It was getting dark by now and several other couples that the girls knew had joined our party. We built a fire, turned on the portable radio, and soon the party was in full swing. Pam and Carol were even trying to teach Moose and me how to rock and roll. That was something else!

Everything was just perfect, like a dream come true.

Along about eleven that evening, I asked Pam to go for a walk with me on the beach. We must have walked for half an hour or so before we came upon a secluded little cove. We sat down, not saying much of anything to each other, just watching the ocean roll in and out. The moon was reflecting on the water—everything was perfectly peaceful and calm.

I couldn't help thinking about that night back in Korea, sitting on that cliff, listening to the ocean and daydreaming that I was on the sands of Malibu. I asked Pam if she believed in dreams come true. She said she wasn't sure. I shared my innermost thoughts with her and told her all there was to know about me, from my humble beginnings up to quitting high school. I told her things I had never told another human being before.

She asked, "Why are you telling me all these things, Irish?"

"I want you to know all there is to know about me, Pam—all the good things and the bad. I want you to hear them all from me."

We talked for better than two hours. Then I told her I was in love with her.

She was flabbergasted.

"Wait, Irish! It's probably just infatuation, you being so lonely and all. You'll probably forget all about me once you go back to the army."

"I'll never forget you, Pam. I realize it's very sudden, but I just want you to think about it. Moose and I still have twenty-eight days left, so why can't we just play it by ear and see where it leads us? If you want, I won't mention my feelings for you again until you decide how you feel about me."

Pam was twenty years old, a junior in college, and a real level-headed girl. She said, "Look, Irish. I like you. I really do. But love means different things to different people. And right now you're just looking for someone to fill a void in your life."

"True."

"But you're just grasping at straws like a drowning man. If I said I loved you and filled the void, it would only be a temporary cure. Once you get back home and away from the army, you'll see things differently and then you probably won't want to be obligated to anyone until you get your own life straightened out."

"Pam, the only one who can give any meaning and direction to my life is you. I know you're the one I've waited for all my life. I knew for sure when we kissed this afternoon. I'll always love you, no matter what happens."

"Irish, you don't know anything about me. All you know is that Carol and I were nice to you and Moose and gave you a ride home last night and invited you to the beach today. We shared an embrace and a kiss this afternoon and this evening is simply beautiful. But to say it's love is an entirely different matter."

"Kiss me, Pam."

We kissed and clung to each other. I asked her if she felt a tingling sensation. She confessed that she did.

"Okay, Pam. I don't want to rush you or ask for any commitments. But will you promise me you will think about it? I promise not to crowd you until you are sure one way or the other."

"I have a feeling you will not let go easily, Irish. I would hate to be the one to break your heart. I care too much for you. Perhaps that is why I don't want any commitments."

"See there, you do care for me. So let's just let our feelings grow and see where they lead us."

She agreed.

We lay back on the warm sand and I kissed her for all I was worth.

"Oh, Pam, I wish there were some profound statement or some earth-shattering remark I could make at this time. Words escape me to describe how I'm feeling at this very moment. The only thing that comes to mind is a short little poem by Shelley called 'Love's Philosophy.' Are you familiar with it?"

"Yes, I am, Irish."

The fountains mingle with the river,
    And the rivers with the ocean;
The winds of heaven mix forever
    With a sweet emotion;
Nothing in the world is single;
    All things by a law divine
In one another's being mingle:
    Why not I with thine?
See the mountains kiss high heaven,
    And the waves clasp one another;
No sister flower would be forgiven;
    If it disdained its brother;
And the sunlight clasps the earth,
    And the moonbeams kiss the sea:
What are all these kissings worth,
    If thou kiss not me?

"Beautiful, Irish, simply beautiful. Do you read much poetry?"

"Well, study would be closer to the truth. But few people know that."

"Why?"

"In the circles I have traveled in, if you liked poetry or classical music you were considered weird, a fairy, or otherwise not with it. Things like that had to be enjoyed in the privacy of your bedroom at home with the door closed tightly and the radio turned down low in case one of your buddies happened by and caught you."

"I think that's terrible, Irish. Why do they feel that way about the beautiful things in life?"

"I don't know, honey. Perhaps it was that they never took the time to try to understand. Poetry is a very personal thing. It has to create a mood or arouse certain emotions in you. You have to decide what mood you want to be in or what emotions you're feeling before you can find a poem to fit the situation or mood you are trying to attain."

"No one poet in the world is right for everyone every time. You have to read and reread the works that seem to capture your moods and then study these works until you understand them. It's hard to explain, but to say I'm going to go to the library and check out a book of poetry and sit down and thoroughly enjoy myself reading it is nonsense. In the first place, it's hard to understand what the poet is trying to say and what mood he is trying to capture. I've read and reread hundreds of them and have only come up with a handful that I thoroughly enjoy and can capture the exact emotions or moods I want them to. Does any of this make sense to you, honey?"

"Yes, it does, Irish. I've never heard it explained that way; but perhaps you're right. People do not enjoy things they do not or cannot understand. It's human nature, I guess."

"Well, let's get back to Shelley and take advantage of those lines." *What are all these kissings worth, If thou kiss not me?*

We melted into each other's arms and spent the next hour or so doing just that.

By now it was almost three in the morning, so we decided to call it a night. As we were driving back to the rooming house, Pam fell asleep in my arms with her head resting on my shoulder. There wasn't a single doubt in my mind that this was the girl I had waited all my life for. I intended to make her my wife and spend the rest of my life making her happy.

Carol dropped us off at the rooming house. We made a date to see them the next day. We kissed them good-night and watched them drive off. Moose and I wandered on in and were lying there in bed still pinching ourselves to make sure what was happening was real when Moose asked me what it was like to be in love.

"It's impossible to describe, Moose. But believe me, you'll know when it happens."

"I think I'm in love with Carol, Irish, and I don't know what to do about it."

"You, too, Moose? Christ, old Cupid is slinging those arrows everywhere isn't he? I'm in love with Pam and told her so tonight."

"Good for you, Irish. What did she say?"

I went on to tell Moose the whole story. He said he was real glad and hoped it worked out for us.

"Do you think I should tell Carol, Irish? I'd hate to scare her off."

"I don't know, Moose. First you'll have to decide if you really love her. And if she feels the same as you, then just play it by ear and see what happens."

The next two and a half weeks in Camelot flew by so fast we hardly noticed. We did just about everything there was to do. Dancing, bowling, sight-seeing, beautiful nights on the beach, rides on cable cars for hours on end. It was all too good to be true, but true it was.

Then, on Thursday night, Pam and I were walking on the beach. She seemed a little depressed. I asked her what was wrong and she told me she was going home that weekend.

"You know, Pam, I don't even know where your home is."

"I know, Irish. There are a lot of things you don't know about me. I'm afraid when you find out, you'll be disappointed."

"I don't think you could ever disappoint me honey. Only if you told me there was no chance for us to see each other again would I ever be disappointed."

"You really don't know very much about me, Irish. I've been trying to tell you—I really have. But I was afraid of hurting you and now I don't know what to do."

"Well, let's sit down and we'll talk about it, okay?"

I took advantage of the opportunity to kiss her and when we came up for air, she asked me if I would consider going home with her that weekend.

"I'd be delighted, Pam. It will give me an opportunity to meet your parents. I hope I can measure up and not disappoint you or make any stupid blunders."

"You won't, Irish. I'm sure of that."

She never did get around to telling me what was on her mind, and I didn't press her. I figured she'd tell me in due time and in her own way.

The evening and next day flew by quickly. Before we knew it, we were saying good-bye to Carol and Moose and were on our way.

Pam was driving. I said, "Okay, honey, now you can tell me where home is."

"Outside Sacramento, Irish."

"What about your parents, Pam? Do they know I'm coming home with you?"

"I phoned Daddy on Wednesday and told him we were coming."

I laughed. "How did you know I'd agree to come with you?"

She smiled. "I'm getting to know you pretty well by now, Irish."

"Tell me about your parents, Pam, so I'll know what to expect. You know what I mean, so I won't make an ass—I mean a fool—out of myself."

She laughed and then suddenly turned serious. She asked me what I would have done if I had known the following before we met: (1) that her father was one of the richest men in the Sacramento Valley—a big man in politics and public affairs; (2) that her mother was a socialite; and (3) that she was an only child, whose parents tried to protect her from the world by sending her to one private school after another and by choosing her friends for her and so on right down the line.

I was at a loss for words, but did manage to come up with, "Well, if all that were true, I'm sure we wouldn't be driving down the road right now on our way to meet these pillars of society, would we?" I was half hoping it wasn't true, but something told me that that was what had been bothering Pam. "You wouldn't have given a GI like me a second glance if it were all true. And if I had known before I asked you to dance, chances are I would never have asked you, figuring there wasn't a chance in the world for a guy like me with a girl such as the one you just described."

"You're wrong, Irish. It's all true. I wanted so desperately to tell you all this before, but you swept me off my feet on the beach and really threw me a curve by telling me you loved me. I knew you were lonely, and I didn't want to hurt you. I thought if I told you, you would think unkindly of me, thinking I was just a poor little rich girl out looking for kicks or something. I'm so sorry that I'd didn't tell you sooner, Irish. I truly am. I've had several offers of marriage from prominent boys, but they all knew my family and none of them were sincere. All they were after was the money and prestige of my family, and love was the farthest thing from their minds."

"Then you came along, fell in love with me, without knowing anything about me. You accepted me as a person who you said you cared for very much. You are the first boy to respect me just for being myself. You are the first who didn't want anything or expect anything in return except my love. It was beautiful, Irish. Plus you could have taken advantage of me any time you chose on the beach, and you didn't. Most boys would have, I'm sure."

"Oh, Pam! I love you much too much and have too much respect for you to ever jeopardize our relationship that way. It would be hard to explain our pure and simple love if you suddenly came up pregnant. If you decide you love me—and I pray to God that you do—then we can consummate our love with a more meaningful relationship."

"Oh, Irish, I do love you. I can't expect you to forgive me for leading you on like I did without telling you about my folks and all. I hope you're not too disappointed in me for not telling you all this sooner."

"Darling, I'm overjoyed that you decided to return my love. Little else matters to me at this point. I just want to know what made you decide—are you sure it's not just out of gratitude or because I'm different from those other guys who proposed to you?"

"Irish, I've had almost three weeks to get to know you. You are the warmest, most sincere person I've ever met in my life. I feel I can trust you and feel safe and secure with you. I want to share my life with you and make you the happiest person in the world."

She pulled off the road and we sealed our love with a kiss. We sat there starry-eyed and in a daze. It was as if someone had opened the flood gates and peace and tranquillity had overwhelmed us. There was no more tension or apprehension. All our fears and doubts were gone. We were truly at peace with ourselves and the world. This was precisely the moment when it all came together for us. Two hearts with one accord. As Shelley so ably had phrased it,

> In one another's being mingle:
> Why not I with thine?

We would probably still be sitting in the car spellbound were it not for a highway patrolman who stopped to ask us if everything was all right.

I said, "Yes sir. All is right with the world today. We just sealed our love with a kiss and are on our way to tell the good news to her parents."

To which he replied, "Well, that's fine. But if you'll take my advice, don't get married."

"We can't accept your advice and will have to find out for ourselves."

"Lots of luck. You'll need it."

We got under way again. The shock of all that had transpired was beginning to wear off and I was getting concerned.

"Pam, what if your parents don't like me? I'm sure if your father is as protective of you as you say he is, he's going to turn thumbs down on me. He's going to think I'm just a gold digger or something. I'll have to let him know right from the start that we are going to live our own lives, independent of his wealth and influence, and that we can make it on our own."

"To tell you the truth, Irish, I'm not sure how he will react to you. I only know that I love you and don't want to let you go."

"Would you give me up if he asked you to?"

"Oh Irish, I'm a big girl now. The days of Daddy telling me who I can see and what I'm to do are over."

"I'm glad, Pam. But if he tells me to take a hike or refuses to let me see you anymore, how will you handle that?"

"I hope it doesn't come to that, Irish. But if for some reason you two don't hit it off, I'll go with you, Irish, wherever you take me. We'll just have to make him understand that we didn't plan to fall in love. It just happened, and there is nothing he can do to stop it."

"I love you with all my heart, Pam, and I don't want to come between you and your parents. I'm sure they love you and want what's best for you. The only trouble with parents is that they don't always know what's best for their children, and sometimes there's trouble when they try to impose their will on them."

"I understand what you're saying, Irish. Let's stop worrying. I'm sure everything will turn out just fine for us."

As we drove along, I had her fill me in on all the dos and dont's and what her mother and father liked and disliked. Besides me, that is, for I was certain they wouldn't like me.

She kept telling me not to worry. But the closer we got to Sacramento, the more I worried.

Finally, she parked the car in the driveway of an immense mansion, the likes of which I had seen only in the movies and the magazines. I turned to Pam and asked her if she was sure she wanted me to go through with it.

"Don't be silly, love of my life. Of course I want to show you off to my parents."

"I'm not being silly, honey; I'm just chicken. Hell, the highest class place I've ever been in was the night club where we first met."

"Come on, Irish," she said with a bright confident smile on her face, so hand in hand we walked up to the front door.

As we approached, her father opened the door. She gave him a big hug and a kiss and introduced me.

He said, "Hello," and I said, "Pleased to meet you, sir." I reached to shake his hand. I knew I was in trouble when he didn't reach for mine, so I just kept my hand and arm moving as if to scratch my shoulder and give the impression that I didn't want to shake hands in the first place.

He told us to come on in. No sooner were we in the house then he told Pam he would like a word with her alone. He told me to wait there while he took her off into another room, leaving me standing there in the hallway.

I wanted a cigarette so badly to calm my nerves, but I was afraid to light one up for fear he wouldn't approve.

I only had one thought in my mind and that was my love for Pam. I made up my mind right then that this stuffed shirt was not going to deny us our love and happiness, even if he was her father.

8

Moose is Killed

Mr. Taylor reappeared and asked me to step in. As I walked through the door, I saw Pam sitting there sobbing her heart out. I walked over and knelt down beside her. She reached out for me and put her arms around me and sighed, "Oh, Irish."

"What's wrong, Pam?" She couldn't speak another word. She kept sobbing uncontrollably. It was her father who said, "There has been an accident."

"I'm sorry to hear that. What happened?"

"Carol, Pam's best girl friend, has been killed in an auto accident."

I was stunned. Poor Carol. Then it hit me. "Moose, what about Moose? He was with her, wasn't he?"

Pam managed to mumble, "Yes," and then she started sobbing again.

Her father said, "The young man is dead also."

"Well, what happened? I mean where? How?"

Her father began describing how a truck had lost its brakes and went speeding down a hill until it smashed broadside into the cab that Moose and Carol were riding in. The driver, Moose, and Carol were all killed.

I must have gone into a state of shock. I couldn't accept what I was hearing as the truth. I kept repeating, "There must be some mistake."

Her father assured me there was no mistake. He told me they were looking for someone to identify the young man.

I couldn't speak a word. I knelt there holding Pam in my arms as I asked myself how Moose would want me to react to a situation like this. I realized that he would want me to act strong and not show my emotions. So I decided to do just that—act brave and strong and keep my emotions under control.

After a while, her father put his hand on my shoulder and told me if I were going back to San Francisco, he'd have his chauffeur drive me there. I regained my composure, stood up and told Pam, "I must go, honey."

She got up and said, "I'm going with you, Irish."

Her father protested, saying he would not permit it.

"I'm sorry, Daddy; but you couldn't possibly understand how close Moose and Irish were. Irish needs me now to be with him. We'll call you from San Francisco."

We went outside and got in the car. Her father was still behind us, protesting vehemently. "Pam, I wish you wouldn't. What am I going to tell our friends? And what about Carol's parents? What am I going to tell them?"

"I'm sorry, Daddy, but I must go."

At that he gave up and told the driver to go ahead.

I don't remember much about that trip back to San Francisco except that Pam and I tried to console each other and rationalize the magnitude of our losses. Our two best friends, dead. It was almost more than we could comprehend. We kept hoping, somehow, someway, there had been a mistake.

We arrived at police headquarters and went in to talk to the desk clerk. We told him who we were and what we wanted. I'll never forget how cold and callous he was.

"Oh yeah. Three got hit last night, and you can identify two of them?"

I was disgusted with his lack of sensitivity, but I managed to answer, "Yes."

He gave us directions to the city morgue and told us who to see. We got back in the car and instructed the chauffeur to drive us to the morgue. We walked up to the desk in the lobby of the morgue and told the guy on duty what we wanted. He directed us to a room and told us to wait there for the coroner. Carol's parents arrived a few minutes later. Pam introduced them to me, and we all waited another ten minutes for the coroner to arrive.

"Are you here to identify the accident victims?"

"Yes, we are."

He directed us to a window and went on inside and pulled the curtain open. He pushed a stretcher over to the window and drew back the sheet, revealing Carol's face. Her mother almost passed out in her husband's arms. Her father shook his head to acknowledge that it was his daughter.

Pam was holding on to me for dear life.

The coroner pulled the stretcher away and pulled another into place. Pulling back the sheet he revealed Moose's face. I acknowledged with a nod that I knew him.

He pushed the stretcher back, pulled the curtains closed, and joined us. He began asking for all the information on Moose, and I told him to look after the girl's parents first, which he did. Pam then saw them to the door while I gave him all the information on Moose.

The coroner was abrupt and businesslike. "Well, I guess that about does it."

I asked him, "What happens now?"

"I'll call the army, turn the body over to them, and it will be returned home for burial."

"Just like that, huh? Like it was a parcel post package or something?"

"I don't mean to sound callous, son. I'm just trying to give you the facts."

Disgusted, I walked back out to the hall where Pam was waiting with Carol's parents. Pam suggested we go to a restaurant, since they wanted to talk to us. I agreed, even though I wasn't interested in talking to anyone about anything.

After telling the chauffeur where to meet us later, we rode

with them to a fancy restaurant up on Nob Hill. We all sat down and the waitress came over and took our order. Pam only wanted a glass of orange juice and I had a cup of coffee.

They were all full of questions about Moose. Who was he? How had Carol met him? What was she doing in a cab with him, anyway? Where he was from? Who were his parents? On and on and on they went.

I fielded all their questions, and was really getting upset. Pam could see it coming, too, for she took hold of my arm and said, "It's all right, Irish."

"I'm sorry, Pam; but I can't help myself. I hope you can forgive me." Then I lit into them.

"You know, it seems to me that you're more concerned about the social status of the man your daughter was with than you are with the fact that your daughter is dead. I know, I know. How will it look in the newspaper? Daughter of prominent Sacramento couple killed in taxi accident while out on a date with a common dogface. It doesn't make for a very good epitaph, does it?"

I really let them have it. "Let me tell you about the man your daughter had been dating, if you're so worried that your daughter might have been out with an unsavory character or that he didn't measure up to your social standards. Moose was plain mountain folk from West Virginia with a heart as big as all outdoors. He was a gentle giant and once he became your friend, he was your friend through the good times and the bad. Not like your so-called friends who never come around if you're tainted with a slight scandal or drop out of the social register."

"What kind of man was Moose? He saved me from getting my throat cut in Japan. He carried me over fifteen miles through the jungle on his back when I was stricken with malaria. Could you expect as much from your friends? I think not. I pulled Moose out of a sinking airplane in the Sea of Japan when he was out cold and he figured, rightly or wrongly, that he owed me his life. But the opposite was true."

"You think your daughter was keeping bad company, don't you? Well, people like Moose are the salt of the earth and the world would be a better place if more people were just like he was. As for your daughter being with him, I can't speak for Carol, but I know that Moose was in love with her."

Pam added that Carol was in love with Moose also.

"So, you see, she died with someone she loved. You lost a daughter; Pam and I lost our dearest friends. We are all very sorry it happened. But nothing we say or do will change a single element of what happened. Perhaps Moose wasn't of the proper social status to suit you. But he was honest, sincere and, above all, he loved Carol. If I were you, I would thank God that she at least had what time and happiness with him that she did before she died."

"I'm truly sorry if I hurt you any more than I know you have already been hurt, but I suffered a tragic loss myself today, and I'll not stand by and see his name or reputation diminished by one degree."

I stood up. "Pam, if you're ready to go . . . I'm sure I've said too much already, and I apologize if I added to your pain and suffering. Sometimes it's better to get hit between the eyes with the truth than to wander through life full of doubts and half-truths."

"Let me assure you, your daughter was in the finest company when she died. You have nothing to be ashamed of and those who would try to make more of it are the ones with the problems and the hang-ups. As for me, I don't worry about people like that."

They thanked me for my candor and reassurances. I told them I'd do the same for them if they were my friends.

Pam and I made our exit and had the chauffeur drive us to the army depot in town so that I could check on what arrangements were being made for Moose. After going through all the red tape and proper channels, I was assured that Moose's body would arrive in West Virginia on Monday morning. They had already sent a telegram to his parents.

Pam and I returned to her home in Sacramento, still not believing the events of the past few hours. All we knew was we needed each other more now than ever before.

Pam tried to comfort me. "Everyone has a burden to carry, Irish, and it's not the burden that's important, but the way you carry it. We both lost part of our lives today, but it is also a new beginning for us. I'm sure Carol and Moose wouldn't want us to spend our time grieving for them."

"You're right, Pam, darling. We'll always cherish their memory and lead our lives in a way that will make them proud of us."

"Yes, Irish, and you know, since we are both Catholic, we can draw upon our faith in God and the hereafter. I'm sure God meant it to be for us and will help us share our loss. I'm equally sure Moose and Carol are in heaven now."

This tragedy had somehow added still another dimension to our love, one of need and dependency. And the fact that we were both Catholic was in our favor should the religious issue come up. It was one more point in our favor in winning the approval of her parents.

We had the chauffeur stop in Sacramento, and Pam and I went shopping for a new suit for me. We found a dark blue one that she liked, so I bought it along with several white shirts, ties, and new shoes.

We arrived back at Pam's home. By now we were very tired so Pam showed me to the guest room. I kissed her and told her to wake me when she got up, for I couldn't make it here without her by my side. She left the room, closing the door behind her and telling me to get some rest.

I lay there in the bed thinking of all the hell Moose and I had raised. The realization that he was gone was beginning to set in. I knew he was a once-in-a-lifetime friend, and I would miss him terribly. There was no way I thought life could ever be the same.

My thoughts then turned to Pam and how wonderful she was. I was overjoyed that she was in love with me and only hoped we would be able to overcome any resistance her family might put up. I could feel it in my bones; it was going to be an uphill fight. I dropped off to sleep from sheer exhaustion.

It was early the next morning when Pam came in and awakened me with a kiss.

116

I reached for her hand and pulled her gently to me saying, "Good morning, sweetheart. Did you sleep well?"

"Yes, Irish, how about you?"

"Like a babe in arms."

We kissed and shared a tender embrace. As I held her ever so tightly to me, I told her once again that I loved her.

"I love you, too, Irish. Time will heal our wounds, and God will see us through."

She asked me if I wanted to go to mass with her. I agreed and told her half-kidding that she had better get out before her father caught us together like this. "Besides that," I teased, "this yearning I have for you might cry out for satisfaction!"

She laughed and flirted, "You wouldn't take advantage of my weakened position, would you, honey?" She smiled her knowing smile, showing off the most perfect set of teeth you ever laid eyes on, accented by two of the cutest little dimples and a tiny little cleft on her chin. All this was highlighted by the kindest, biggest, brightest brown eyes in the world. I gave her another hug and a big kiss and said, "I'll see you in twenty minutes, sweetheart."

I got up, shaved, showered, and put on my new blue suit and tie. I was just putting the finishing touches on my shoes when she knocked on the door.

"It's open, but enter at your own risk!"

She opened the door and right behind her was her father, who didn't look too pleased at my remark.

Pam told me breakfast was ready, but her father asked her if she would go on ahead, because he wanted to talk to me alone for a moment. I told him that Pam and I had no secrets from each other, so he could feel free to talk in front of her. He insisted, so I told Pam I would join her shortly.

As she left, he closed the door, turned to me and asked, "What are your intentions toward my daughter?"

"Please, sir. This doesn't seem like the right time to discuss it."

He got a little surly and asked, "Well, when will be a good time?"

117

"Perhaps after the funeral we can talk."

"Yes. I'm sorry, but I didn't think you would be staying for the funeral."

"I couldn't let Pam face that alone, sir."

"She won't be alone, she'll have her family and friends there to console her."

"I know, sir, but I feel I should be there also. I did know Carol and I've met her parents. After all, she was killed with my best friend. It's the least I can do."

"Have they made the funeral arrangements yet?"

"They're not complete, but I would imagine she will be laid out today and buried tomorrow. That should give me time to catch a plane back to West Virginia for Moose's funeral."

"Moose? What kind of a name is that for anybody?"

"You wouldn't understand, sir. It's a long story, and I don't have time to get into it right now."

"All right. Perhaps we can talk later on in the day." I agreed that would be fine.

We went downstairs and joined Pam and her mother for breakfast.

Pam introduced me, and we exchanged niceties. Mrs. Taylor seemed like a warm and friendly person and gave off good vibrations, not at all like Mr. Taylor. I sensed she could feel the electricity between Pam and me. She spoke very little and never asked a direct question. This only added to her charm, for by now I was beginning to feel as welcome as a person with leprosy or something.

The old man kept up a steady stream of chatter though, directed mostly at me. He kept pumping out the questions. I tried to be as polite as I knew how, keeping my answers as brief as possible.

"Where are you from? How old are you? How long have you been in the service? Where are you stationed? What college did you attend before you entered the service?"

He kept trying to downgrade me and make a fool out of me; but I kept my cool through it all and sure was thankful when Pam said, "Are you ready to go, Irish?"

"Yes. If you'll please excuse us."

"Where in the world are you heading so early in the morning, Pam?" he asked.

"To mass, Daddy."

"Oh, I didn't think soldiers went to church, or is this just . . ." Pam cut him short, saying, "Come on now, Daddy."

"No. It's all right, Pam. Let your father finish."

"Oh. I didn't mean anything by that remark, young man."

"Well, just for the record, I was born and raised Catholic, attended parochial schools, and have the flat knuckles to prove it. I seldom, if ever, miss mass. So you see, it's possible you don't have all the answers."

"I stand corrected, young man."

At that Pam and I departed.

On the way, I asked Pam how she thought I handled myself.

"Remarkably well, Irish. I want to thank you for not losing your cool with him."

"As Bogie would say, 'I would walk to the ends of the earth for you, sweetheart.' "

After mass we drove out in the country where we could be alone to try and pick up the pieces. Our worlds were turned upside down, and we were both very depressed. We needed some time to be alone to take stock of our situation and plan the best way to deal with it. We stopped on a wind-swept hill overlooking the valley below. We walked hand in hand through the trees until we came to a small clearing. It felt like we were on top of the world, and all the cares and troubles of all those below us were small and insignificant. As we stood there with the wind blowing in our faces, Pam turned to me, "Oh, Irish, please reassure me that everything is going to be all right!"

I took her in my arms and told her that as long as we had each other we would be able to see it through.

"Irish, I don't want to appear solicitous, but I need your love and understanding to see me through. You once told me you took solace in poetry. I came across a poem by Longfellow last evening when I was trying to go to sleep. It's called "A Psalm of Life." Are you familiar with it, Irish?"

"Yes, I am honey. It's what the heart of a young man said to a psalmist. Do you have it with you?"

"Yes I do, Irish," she said, reaching in her pocket and unfolding it as we sat down on a fallen tree trunk.

"Would you read it to me, Pam? Longfellow also wrote in another poem of his, and I quote:

> Then read from the treasured volume
>   The poem of thy choice,
> And lend to the rhyme of the poet
>   The beauty of thy voice.
> And the night shall be filled with music,
>   And the cares that infest the day
> Shall fold their tents like the Arabs,
>   And as silently steal away.

"Thank you, Irish. I feel better already."

"I'm glad, honey. Now, if you'll lend to the rhyme of the poet the beauty of thy voice, we'll try to analyze it together."

She kissed me and began reading aloud.

> Tell me not in mournful numbers,
>   "Life is but an empty dream!"
> For the soul is dead that slumbers,
>   And things are not what they seem.
>
> Life is real, life is earnest!
>   And the grave is not its goal;
> "Dust thou art, to dust returnest,"
>   Was not spoken of the soul.
>
> Not enjoyment, and not sorrow,
>   Is our destined end or way;
> But to act, that each tomorrow
>   Find us farther than today.
>
> Art is long, and Time is fleeting,
>   And our hearts, though stout and brave,
> Still like muffled drums, are beating
>   Funeral marches to the grave.
>
> In the world's broad field of battle,
>   In the bivouac of Life,
> Be not like dumb, driven cattle!
>   Be a hero in the strife!

Trust no future howe'er pleasant!
    Let the dead Past bury its dead!
Act,—act in the living Present,
    Heart within and God o'er head.

Lives of great men all remind us
    We can make our lives sublime
And, departing, leave behind us
    Footprints on the sands of time!

Footprints, that perhaps another
    Sailing o'er life's solemn main,
A forlorn and shipwrecked brother,
    Seeing, shall take heart again.

Let us then be up and doing,
    With a heart for any fate!
Still achieving, still pursuing,
    Learn to labour and to wait.

I sat there in silence, still savoring the sounds her melodious voice lent to the rhyme of that beautiful poem. I was oblivious to everything around when I heard Pam ask, "Irish, are you all right?"

"I'm sorry, honey, that was so beautiful coming from your sweet lips that it put me in a trance."

"Oh, Irish, it does fit the mood I'm in and it does stir all the emotions I've been feeling since it happened. But what does it really mean and what is he really trying to tell us?"

"Well, honey, I believe he wrote that poem to soothe the feeling of someone who had suffered a tragic loss, perhaps even more tragic than the loss we are suffering right now. I get the impression that person no longer cared to go on living and wanted to die himself. The poem tries to give him faith and courage. The poem explains that death is not the end, only the beginning of something warm and beautiful. When Long-fellow said, 'Trust no future howe'er pleasant,' he was telling us to live each day as if it were our last day on earth; for it may well be. When he said, 'Let the dead Past bury its dead,' he was telling us not to grieve the loss of our loved ones, for they were happy and had gone to their final reward. That is what life is all about, that dying is as much a part of life as being born."

"And when he said, 'We can make our lives sublime/And, departing, leave behind us/Footprints on the sands of time,' he was telling us to show the world we have accepted what has happened as inevitable and to set an example for others to see. Perhaps if they see us bear up under the load, then when they have a similar situation, they will be able to cope with it by remembering the example we set for them."

" 'Let us then be up and doing,/With a heart for any fate!' That's simple enough. He's telling us to get on with this business of living our lives and to accept things as they happen. He's trying to tell us that we will not get very far if we try to drag all our yesterdays along with us."

" 'Still achieving, still pursuing,/Learn to labour and to wait.' I get the feeling here that he's telling us that each day is a new beginning. A day in which we can achieve what our hearts desire and even if we don't achieve our desires that particular day, to keep on pursuing them. 'Learn to labour and to wait.' All things come to he who will work for them and has the patience to wait for them."

"Those are the impressions I get, honey, and that's what the poem means to me. Of course, it could mean something entirely different to you."

"Oh, no, Irish, I interpret it exactly the same as you do. I just didn't realize it until you analyzed it for me. You're such a deep thinker and see warmth and beauty in everything. You really have an analytic mind, Irish. I could have read it perhaps a hundred times and never fully understood what he was trying to tell me."

"Oh! I'm not that great, honey. I had another tragic event in my life and looked to that exact poem for consolation and analyzed it then. It is ironic, though, come to think about it, that you would look to the same source for consolation. I get the feeling that we were two free spirits wandering around out there in the world, knowing each other from the beginning of time and having only to meet and join forces. We think and act alike on so many different things that to me it had to be more than a coincidence. How do you feel about it, Pam?"

"Irish, I feel I've known you all my life and cannot possibly consider a future without you in it. I love you, Irish, and I'm going to keep this poem handy, and if I find myself feeling sorry for myself ever again, I'm going to read it and remember this beautiful morning and the way you interpreted it for me. You have a way of taking ordinary moments and turning them into memorable occasions, Irish, and I love you for it."

"Well then, let's get on with this business of living then. I'll buy you an ice cream cone if we can find a store open."

"You've got a deal, Irish."

We kissed and held each other tightly, secure in the knowledge that we would be able to face the future together. We finally made it back to the car and drove to town to find an ice cream parlor. We found one, got our cones, and went walking through the almost deserted Sunday morning streets making small talk and trying to out-flatter one another. We wandered back to the car and drove back to the house.

I told Pam I wanted to go back to West Virginia for Moose's funeral and hoped she would go with me. She agreed. I wasn't sure I had the plane fare for both of us, but I figured I would worry about that when the time came.

By three that afternoon the funeral arrangements had been completed for Carol. We attended the viewing that evening and after the rosary, Pam and I extended our condolences to Carol's parents.

Her father took me aside in the hallway and thanked me for what I had said to him in San Francisco. He told me my philosophy had made it a lot easier for him and his wife to accept their daughter's death.

I told him I was glad he didn't have any animosity toward me and to let me know if there was anything I could do.

He asked me if I was planning to attend Moose's funeral. I told him I was, and that I planned to take Pam back with me. He explained that he and his wife would be unable to attend and asked if Pam and I would extend their condolences for them. I said we would. He then gave me an envelope with eight hundred dollars and two credit cards in it, saying he would be grateful if I would let him pay for the trip. I told him it wasn't necessary, but he insisted, saying he would be hurt if we didn't accept. I thanked him. Pam and I then drove over to the airport and bought our tickets for the flight back east.

Although I was still grieving, I hadn't lost touch with reality, so I bought the tickets on one of his credit cards, choosing to keep the eight hundred dollars for out-of-pocket expenses, so to speak.

Along with Pam's parents, we attended the funeral the following morning. Two hours later we were in the air on our way to West Virginia to pay our final respects to Moose. We landed at an airport about forty miles from his home, rented a car, and drove the rest of the way.

It was almost 8:00 P.M. when we finally arrived. Moose's mother threw her arms around Pam and his father shook my hand and put his arm around my shoulder as they escorted us into the house. I introduced Pam to them and they introduced us to the relatives and friends gathered there.

They had Moose laid out in the living room with a military guard at one end of the casket. Pam and I walked up to the casket, knelt down, bowed our heads, and said a short prayer. This was something usually done only by Catholics and these people were awestruck that we had that much respect for one of their own.

We got up and returned to the kitchen, where his mother offered us something to eat. We were not hungry yet, so we just had coffee. His dad and mother wanted to know what happened, so we filled them in as best we could.

We told them all about Carol, and Moose's relationship with her. Pam had brought along an eight by ten inch colored photo of Carol as well as a dozen or so snapshots, including some that we had taken on the beach with Moose and Carol. Pam presented them to his mother; a pot of gold couldn't have made her any happier. Those pictures kept floating all evening from hand to hand. We told them that Moose and Carol were in love and most likely would have been married, had they lived.

His mother was so grateful that Hank (Moose's real name) had found a girl. She said she always worried about him. He was so kind and gentle, but extremely bashful when it came to girls. She explained that he had always been big for his age and awkward. He was good as gold, though. I reassured them that no man ever had a better friend than Moose.

By now everyone had congregated in the kitchen. I think the main attraction was Pam. To them she was like something out of a picture book. When she spoke, you could have heard a pin drop. They simply hung on her every word. When someone would ask if she wanted some more coffee, about six of them would almost break their necks trying to get to her cup first, so they could fill it.

She was really enjoying all the attention she was getting; it was such a contrast to all the pomp and ceremony she had been used to all her life. I had warned her before we arrived not to expect anything fancy, since they were plain and simple mountain folk. Instead, I had told her to be ready to be showered with hospitality and attention, the likes of which she had never experienced.

We were sitting there talking when Moose's little brother, who couldn't have been over eight years old, asked if his big brother was a hero.

"Indeed he was. As far as I'm concerned, he should be awarded every decoration the army has to offer."

I then started telling them stories of how Moose and I had met. I began recalling some of the incidents Moose and I had been involved in. Before long, everyone was asking for more.

I told them how I had to get Moose drunk to get him on his first plane ride. They just howled with laughter. I told them about our first night out in Japan, and the wild rickshaw ride Moose gave me, and the fight we started between the British and the Aussies (dressing up the English and leaving out as many of the four-letter words as possible, of course!).

By now they were stomping their feet and having the time of their lives. They never imagined Moose in situations like those I was describing to them. They had known him only as a gentle person who never was or gave anyone any trouble.

Pam had heard very little of our escapades before and could hardly believe all the situations we were involved in. She thought they were the funniest things she had ever heard in her life.

Word had spread all over the hills of this beautiful girl down at Hank's house. (I found this out later). As the evening rolled along, we must have had a hundred people in the house, on the front porch, and on the front yard.

They examined the car Pam and I were driving from stem to stern. I gave one old boy the keys and told him to take it for a spin. Twenty fellows must have piled into it and off they went into the night. Everyone else wanted to hear more about Moose and me.

I couldn't help thinking: This is how Moose would have wanted it—everyone happy and in a good mood. So I continued. I told them about the ill-fated flight on our way to Korea. When I told them the part about bending down to kiss our asses good-bye, the roof almost came off the house. I told them the rest of the story and how Moose had vowed to take care of me in return for my saving his life.

I told them how we wound up in Pusan, Korea; about the lieutenant crashing his jeep into the oil drums; about the crap game Moose and I broke up. They kept hollering at one another the rest of the evening, "fifteen is your point." I described the whiskey running and how we disarmed the MPs and disabled their jeeps. They could really relate to that situation because most of them had been running moonshine all their lives and fighting with the revenuers.

They kept saying, "That's our good old boy, Hank."

I told them about being shot down by the MIG fighter, our ordeal in the jungle, blowing up the weapons cache, and how the lieutenant got killed. I then told them how Moose had carried me for over fifteen miles on his back after I came down with malaria, commandeered a plane to get me to Japan, and saved my life. I told them about the riot we had started in the psycho ward and how we ran a lottery to get money to come back on leave.

It was so unbelievable to them. They couldn't imagine this gentle giant of a man who was always so peaceful and serious getting into all those situations.

Pam was laughing so hard she was crying.

Finally I told them how Moose and I met Pam and Carol.

There was such a feeling of joy and contentment in the air. Moose's dad and mother were smiling and you could tell they were proud to hear that their son was a real hero and had had so much fun and happiness while away from home. Most of all, I believe they were happy that Moose had found someone to love before he died.

We all knew what was ahead the next morning and by now it was 4:00 A.M. They made room for Pam to sleep in with the girls, and I slept in with Moose's brothers.

The next morning was there before we knew it, and we got on with the business at hand. Moose's mother asked me if I would say a few words at graveside, and I told her I would be happy to.

The little mountain chapel was about a block from the house, so everyone gathered at the house.

The army had sent a burial detail to conduct the ceremony. The flag bearers led the procession with the military pallbearers carrying the casket directly behind them. The remainder of the military contingent fell in behind them. The family and friends and relatives fell in line as the procession made its way down the road. Pam and I walked with Moose's mother and dad.

There must have been five hundred people there, and the little chapel only held thirty. Everyone who couldn't get into the chapel gathered in the churchyard. These were plain and poor folks in bib overalls, work boots, and just whatever they had to wear.

The service was plain and simple, with the old country preacher leading the singing of a couple of old standard hymns:

"On a Hill Far Away," "Bringing in the Sheath," and "Nearer My God to Thee." He then gave a short eulogy and asked everyone to gather in the churchyard for the graveside services.

The military pallbearers carried the casket over to an open grave with two planks across to support the coffin. They then folded the flag which draped the coffin and presented it to his mother.

She stood up and announced that she would like to have Hank's best friend say a few words in his behalf.

I was so choked up by this time that I could hardly speak. I had no idea what I was going to say and simply started in by thanking all in attendance for being there to pay their last respects to Moose, my dearest and most trusted friend.

"I'm sure he wouldn't want anyone grieving for him, but he would rather have people pattern their lives after his. Be gentle and kind to your fellow man; help him when you can. Do, say, and think what you think is right, regardless of what others might think, say, or do. Most of all, do not be intimidated by other people. Moose never was."

"There is an old saying: 'Only the good die young.' Moose was not only good; he was the greatest. He would want you to remember him for all the good things he represented, all the joy he got out of life. And perhaps when you remember him you will smile. Moose would like that."

I leaned over, picked up a little dirt and gently sifted it through my fingers and watched it fall on Moose's coffin while I said, "Good-bye, good buddy."

I stepped back and the officer in charge of the detail gave the order for "order arms." Then "ready, aim, fire." Then they repeated it three times.

The bugler started playing taps. Even the hounds were baying at the top of their voices. I remember thinking Moose would have gotten a kick out of that. I don't think they were baying for Moose; it was just that the sound of the bugle hurt their ears.

That concluded the services. Everyone started to fade away into the hills. We returned to the house and had dinner with the family and relatives before getting ready to leave.

His mother and dad, followed by everyone else, walked us to our car. They couldn't thank us enough for coming.

She told Pam, "You two have spread more joy and sunshine over them hills in the few hours you were there than the Good Lord himself had provided in years."

"That's pretty big company to be compared with," I said. She just smiled.

His dad told us that we had made a hero and a legend out of their son, and that all those stories would become folklore and be passed on for generations to come.

We told them we were glad to be of whatever help we could and promised to return again someday.

As we passed through that little place in the road where the general store was, I pointed out to Pam the little saloon over on the left and told her what happened to me in there when Moose and I were on our way overseas. She got to laughing hysterically at the thought of me up on that toilet hanging on for dear life.

Then she settled down and started talking about the vast differences between the two funerals. I let her do all the talking and commented only when she asked me to.

"Carol was laid out in a beautiful new funeral home with literally hundreds of floral arrangements. The funeral services were conducted in a cathedral with a huge organ and a choir of over one hundred singing in perfect harmony. There must have been fifty chauffeur-driven Cadillacs, not to mention the big Chryslers, Buicks, and Lincolns in her funeral procession. The graveyard with its perfectly manicured grass and roads lined with trees and shrubs. All those well-dressed and prominent pillars of society in attendance. The graveside services conducted by three priests under a huge canvas awning with padded chairs and a purple velvet cloth covering the grave opening."

Pam said she couldn't help wondering how many of those people at Carol's funeral were her friends or even cared or knew who she was, and how many were just attending because it was the socially accepted thing to do.

"I don't know, Pam. I'm sure you can figure that one out for yourself."

129

She went on, "At least at Moose's funeral, all the people were sincere and were there because they wanted to be and not because they had to, just to look good. Those folks back there seem to be able to cope with life better and accept death as a part of life, just like being born. It was like you pointed out to me Sunday morning, Irish, when you gave me your interpretation of that poem I read to you."

"I can't get over how they were able to accept their tragic loss and still be able to laugh like they did when you were telling them about your exploits with Moose. I'm certain Carol's parents are under a doctor's care to help them cope with their loss. I don't think they will ever really be able to accept it. Whereas Moose's parents seem to have already accepted it and although their loss is just as tragic as is Carol's parents, I have a feeling they will have their lives straightened out in no time at all."

"I'm sure you're right, honey. In two days and thousands of miles apart, we have experienced two vastly different life-styles. From the upper-upper class to the poorest of the poor. Most people never, in a lifetime, get to make that comparison."

"Oh, Irish, I love you and thank you from the bottom of my heart for inviting me to come back here with you. I got to see another side of you on this trip. Even though I loved you before we started, after seeing what you did for those people back there, taking a sad and pitiful occasion and turning it into, perhaps, one of the best days of their life. . . . Well, it only made me love you more. If I live to be one hundred years old, I'll always be grateful to you for letting me share that experience with you."

"Thank you, Pam, just for being you and coming with me." I went on to tell her she was really the main attraction and that she was the most beautiful, warm, and loving individual ever to grace those hills. "Those people not only loved you, Pam. It went much deeper than that; they worshipped you. I was so proud that you were with me. If they thought anything of me, it was because I was with you."

"Oh! Irish, you flatter me too much!"

"I'm only telling the truth, honey."

We had decided that after the funeral, we would drive up to Pennsylvania to see my mother. We were well on our way there when I got a flash.

"Pam, let's get married today."

She was a bit surprised.

"No, I'm serious, honey. We can go over to Winchester, Virginia, and be married this evening.

"Do you think we should, Irish?"

"I think it's a good idea, but it's up to you."

We stopped to get gas and were having a cup of coffee when I asked Pam if she wanted to call her parents to let them know everything was all right.

She agreed that she should.

"I'll leave it up to you to ask for their blessing on our getting married back here."

"I'll tell them our plans, Irish; but I know they're not going to like it."

She reached them and when she told them of our plans, her father must have gone through the roof. Her mother got on the phone and asked to talk to me. She was extremely sweet and pleasant as we talked. I had the feeling she was conning me. I could hear the old man in the background hollering. I guess he was making an ass out of himself.

Her mother told me she knew Pam and I were meant for each other and regardless of what her husband said, there was no way they could prevent us from getting married if that was what we wished. "If you do decide to get married there, you have my blessings."

I thanked her for her vote of confidence and told her I was only interested in doing what was best for Pam.

She told me she was sure that I was and went on to tell me that if we decided to wait and get married back in Sacramento, she would personally take charge and provide us with a church wedding and reception.

"What about Mr. Taylor?"

"Don't worry. I stood by all these years and watched him bully and badger people to get his own way. I can assure you he will do nothing to interfere with the wedding. I know in my heart that you two kids were meant for each other and as far as I'm concerned, no one is going to stand in your way. It's just that I've planned all my life to have a church wedding for Pam and would be eternally grateful if you'd consent to let my dream come true."

"Well, Mrs. Taylor, under those circumstances, how can I refuse?"

She thanked me and I turned the phone over to Pam. They talked for a while longer and then said we'd see them in a day or two.

We got back in the car. "Well, it's off to Pennsylvania, I guess. I hope you're not too disappointed, Irish."

"No, Pam. As anxious as I am to have you for my wife, I'd rather wait and do it right, especially if it means not coming between you and your parents."

"Thanks, Irish. You won't be sorry, I promise."

"The only thing, though, honey, your father will probably think we were just trying to force his hand. I'm sure that didn't endear me to him any more than if I had kicked him in the nuts. . . . I mean face."

"Irish, I'm going to get a can of red-hot pepper and pepper your tongue." She laughed and added, "Don't worry about Daddy. Mother will take care of everything. She promised you, didn't she?"

"I know now where you get all your warmth and charm from, honey. It's from your mother. I'm sure she is right. Things will work out better for all concerned this way."

"After the way Daddy has treated you, Irish, I'm surprised you can still consider his feelings."

"Pam, I know you love and respect both your parents, as well you should. I'll have to say that your father leans pretty hard on your love and especially hard on that parental respect bit. I'm sure he feels he is right and it's up to us, not necessarily to prove him wrong, but to let him down as gently as possible."

"You big, sweet, lovable person you. Mother told me she knew you were right for me. She told me anyone else would have gone through with the wedding and then called to let them know it was all over. She said to thank you and that she loves and respects you. Most of all, she wanted me to thank you for agreeing to come home for a church wedding."

"I only want to do whatever will make you happy, Pam, and I'm sure granting your mother's wish will do that. As far as your father goes, I'm sure with time we'll win him over also."

"I know you're right, Irish, and if anyone in this world can win Daddy over, you're the one who can."

After a four-hour drive, we arrived at my mother's. As I knew it would be, it was love at first sight. Pam and my mother hit it off right from the start.

We spent the next two days there. I showed Pam all the old haunts I used to frequent—the neighborhood I grew up in, the schools I attended, the old movie theater we would sneak into, the polluted river we would swim in, the old pool hall where I spent many a night just killing time. I showed her the railroad freight yards and the skid row where all the drunks and winos hung out. I pointed out the tracks where my brother got killed by a train while I stood helplessly by. I pointed out the old two-story apartment building where I grew up. It was all boarded up now and ready to be torn down.

I took her up on a hill and repeated what my mother had told my brother and me one Sunday afternoon while we were walking. I was nine years old at the time. She told us "There is a whole world out there, boys. You can own all or any part of it you want. All you have to do is be willing to work for it and pay the price." I remember that she told us our beginnings were humble and the influences around us bad, but that we could live with the worst people in the world, and not become like them. She told us exactly who we were, why we were born, and that we were going to die some day. She pointed out to us that when we did die, we would have to face our Maker alone and he would accept no excuses. We had to be totally responsible for our own actions. We couldn't tell him that someone else made us do it or told us it was all right. We had a mind and free will to do anything we wanted, good or bad, but we had to be ready to pay for the bad.

It seemed like no time at all before we were saying good-bye to my mother and winging our way back across the country to California. We were both exhausted and slept almost the whole trip. We took a cab from the airport to Pam's home. Her father wasn't home, and I was thankful for that.

Her mother came in and welcomed us with open arms. She put her arms around us and escorted us into the living room.

She told Pam, "Your father and I have been talking. I guess we never wanted to admit it, but you're all grown-up now and able to make your own decisions. I would like to apologize to both of you for the way he's been acting. We love you, Pam, and I'm sure we can get to love this young man of yours also."

"Thank you, Mrs. Taylor."

"No, let me thank you for being considerate enough to bring Pam home for a church wedding. You're the man in my little girl's life. I guess I always knew it had to happen someday, but never really wanted to face up to it. I know in my heart that you'll be good for her, and I hope she will be good for you."

"There is no doubt in my mind, Mrs. Taylor, that we'll be good for each other."

She told Pam and me of all the plans she had in store for us. I cautioned her that we had agreed to a church wedding and a reception, but plans after we were married would have to be strictly between Pam and me.

She smiled and remarked, "You'll go a long way in this world, young man."

"With Pam at my side, I'm confident there is nothing I can't do."

She told Pam that her father was still being rather difficult about things. "You know how he is when things don't go his way. But don't worry, I have everything under control."

Pam and I excused ourselves, saying we wanted to go for a walk. She said she understood. As we were leaving the room, she took my hand and kissed me on the cheek, saying, "Welcome to our family."

"Now I know where your daughter gets all her warmth and charm from."

She smiled as Pam warned her, "He'll charm your heart away, Mother, if you let him."

Pam and I went walking around the grounds, enjoying the view and joking with one another. She suddenly reached up with a devilish grin on her face and pinched my nose and started to run. I ran after her. We both ran until we were out of breath and fell into each other's arms. I spun her around and as her feet left the ground, I kissed her for all I was worth. As we sat down on the grass, she whispered in my ear that she thought she was ready for that more meaningful relationship I had spoken of.

I assured her that I felt exactly the same way and there was nothing in the world that I wanted more than to make love to her. But I cautioned her that we had managed to resist the temptation so far and that she would be a lot happier entering into marriage a virgin than if we gave in to the temptation. She kissed me and told me I was too good to be true and that if anything ever happened to me she would not want to go on living herself.

I said, "Now, it's you who flatters me too much. Once we started, Pam, we wouldn't be able to stop. If you were to become pregnant before we were married, it would break your mother's heart, not to mention your father never letting us live it down. I feel our child would only bring us closer together, if that's possible; but I wouldn't want to be responsible for putting a spot on your perfect and unblemished personality and reputation. I love you too much to harm a hair on your pretty little head."

"Now I know why I love you so much, Irish. You're always putting other people's feelings ahead of your own. Perhaps that's why you get hurt so often. You're honest almost to a fault and that makes you vulnerable—especially to people like my father. He takes your honesty and truthfulness and uses them against you."

"Perhaps you're right, Pam. I realize we're living in a world of half-truths and falsehoods. As far as I am concerned, the whole world moves forward on a curtain of bullshit . . . I mean crap."

Pam laughed and asked, "Where's my pepper can?"

"No. Seriously, I never worried much about what people thought of me—that is to say, until I met you. I never thought about truth much, one way or the other. Come to think of it, I don't know why I am or why I think the way I do about most things, except when it comes to my friends and loving you. The one thing I cherish most in this life is my love for you and your love for me. I'm sure there is no sacrifice too great to preserve our love. I love you, darling, with every fiber of my being, and I'm going to have to ask you to be the strong one and tell me "no" until after we're married. I want you so badly that I'm not sure I can restrain myself."

"I understand, Irish. I'll do my best. But what if I falter?"

"Like we always tell each other, we'll play it by ear."

We held each other tightly, not wanting to let go and wondering how long it would be before we could stop tormenting ourselves like this.

Finally we headed back to the house. It was almost supper time—pardon me—dinner time. The upper class doesn't eat supper; they have dinner.

9

Mr. Taylor and Irish Clash

Pam and I washed up and were sitting in the living room waiting for Arnold, the butler, to announce, "Dinner is served," when her father walked in and sat down.

He asked me if I would like a drink before dinner.

"No, thank you."

"Irish doesn't drink, Daddy."

"Oh? I'm rather surprised to hear that. I thought that was all you soldiers liked to do when on leave—drink and chase women."

I thought to myself, here we go. I didn't bother to answer, so he got up and fixed himself a drink.

"Tell me, Irish. That is your name, isn't it?"

"Yes, sir, my nickname."

"Oh well, that's good enough for now."

Pam reached over and took my hand and smiled her beautiful smile at me. I acknowledged with a slight grin. She knew he was getting to me, and she was so right.

"Do you play golf?"

I remember thinking to myself, this lousy bastard knows

damned well I don't play golf. So I shot back, "Oh, yes, sir; in the low seventies."

"In the low seventies? Well . . ." he said, getting ready to exploit it for all it was worth.

"Yes, sir. If it gets any colder than that, I don't bother going out."

Pam started laughing, but her father didn't seem amused by my little joke or at least he wouldn't let on.

"So you two want to get married, do you?"

"Yes, sir."

"Your mother tells me she is going to arrange a big church wedding and reception for you, is that right?"

Pam said, "Yes, Daddy."

"I wonder how much that will cost?"

At that I piped up and said, "If you're worried about the money, I'll pay for it myself."

"Don't be absurd, Irish. You only make seventy-two dollars a month in the army, and your chances for advancement are practically nil."

"You've done your homework rather well, haven't you, Mr. Taylor?"

"My, my, we're getting awfully testy now, aren't we?"

"You're damned right we are, and if this conversation doesn't take a turn for the better, I'm afraid we'll have to terminate it."

"You seem to have a pretty good command of the King's English for a high school dropout. Has Pam been brushing you up on your vocabulary? I'm an English major myself and enjoy the use of proper English."

"You're also obnoxious and overbearing, and really should refrain from employing monosyllabic words while conversing with those of lesser stature than yourself as it is not only utterly obnoxious and a rude display of your pseudo intellectualism, but also it indubitably lessens our esteem for you, thereby jeopardizing your opportunity of stimulating our lifelong friendships, which would prove to be one of your worthiest assets toward leading a highly successful life. Now, put that in your English major pipe and smoke it."

Just then I heard Pam's mother call out, "Bravo! Good for you, young man. He had that coming, and I have waited a lifetime for someone who would stand up to him and tell him exactly what a big bully he can be. I was standing in the doorway and enjoyed every moment of it. Looks like you met your match, George."

Pam squeezed my hand and leaned over and kissed me on the cheek. I was like a loaded pistol sitting there waiting for the counterattack. Surprisingly enough, it didn't come. He just asked his wife to see if dinner was ready. I was sure I hadn't heard the last of it yet. I was sure he would still be fighting while escorting Pam down the aisle of the church. I had managed to temporarily deflate his ego, and he was not accustomed to anyone talking back to him. I guess all he had working for him was a bunch of yes-men.

We went on into dinner and managed to make it all the way up to dessert before he spoke again.

"What is your present situation with the army, young man?"

"You have the dossier on me, don't you? I've lost track of things these past few days. Suppose you tell me."

"All right then, I will. You have four days before you have to report back to that hospital in Japan where you and your friend were malingering for the past several months. Then, you have the option of either going back to Korea to finish your tour there or staying in Japan and working as a clerk for some doctor over there. I believe he is a psychiatrist and you and Moose were his patients. A couple of mental patients on convalescent leave, if I'm not mistaken. I also understand you have been in scraps at every place you've ever been stationed but cleverly managed to escape punishment. Is that not correct?"

"You have the floor, Mr. Taylor. Please continue."

"By all means."

"I know your mother is a widow and you have one brother; that your mother raised you both by herself. You and your brother were little hellions when you were growing up and neither one of you finished high school, although you did manage to get to twelfth grade. I know you couldn't find gainful employment; that's why you joined the army. You were looking for a meal ticket. Now you have the audacity to want to marry my daughter and become heir apparent to everything I've worked all my life for: You have done a fine job on my daughter, smooth talking her into thinking you were somebody and something. You're trash, plain and simple. You couldn't hold a candle to my daughter's breeding and education."

"Do you think you can support her on seventy-two dollars a month or would you expect me to subsidize your marriage with a monthly check? I think you had better give up this fantasy of yours and get on the next bus back to San Francisco and forget you ever knew my daughter."

"Are you quite through, sir?"

"Yes, I guess that is all I have to say, and I consider the matter closed once and for all."

Poor Mrs. Taylor had a look of shock and disbelief on her face. I'm sure this was the last thing in the world she had expected from him. Pam held onto my arm as if to lend moral support. I felt like telling him to go to hell; but instead I started in on him by saying, "I shouldn't dignify your remarks with an answer, but I'm going to. You're right about my mother being a widow and raising my brother and me alone. I guess to people like yourself, we were considered poor white trash. My mother cleaned hotel rooms and scrubbed floors, took in washing and ironing, just to pay the rent on a run-down apartment in the wrong part of town. My brother and I carried papers, set pins in bowling alleys and did anything we could to make a few pennies."

"You're right, we were considered hell raisers. We were the only two Irishmen in an all Polish school. We had to fight our way there in the morning and back home at night. My mother bought all our clothes at a Salvation Army store—clothes that people like you would discard because they were out of fashion or you didn't like the color or something. As a result, we were the laughing stock of the school. Yes, we even did a lot of stealing. We didn't have money for such things as a Christmas tree. We would steal one. We would steal milk bottles and pop bottles and take them to the store for the deposits. We never had money to go to the movies. We would get seven or eight kids and scrape up a quarter between us and pay one guy's way in so he could open the exit door for the rest of us to sneak in."

"We never could afford to go to ball games either, but we always managed to get in. We would wait until they played the national anthem and the cops would be standing at attention. Then we would walk right on by them, sometimes thumbing our noses at them and disappearing into the crowds. We stole bread from the bread man and milk from the milk man. Real desperadoes, my brother and I. Hell, we even stole pop and pop corn from the priest out of the bingo hall at church. Of course, they put better locks on the doors after we told them what we were doing in confession. Thank God for the seal of the confessional. Otherwise, I'm sure he would have broken our necks."

I happened to look over at Mrs. Taylor and she was holding her napkin over her mouth to keep from bursting out laughing. I continued on.

"My brother is dead now. Do you want to know how that bad boy died? Well, the police didn't shoot him for stealing a loaf of bread. He was run over by a train after pushing some drunk who had been standing on the tracks to safety. That's right. That bad boy gave up his life to save someone he didn't even know and who probably hadn't drawn a sober breath in years. He didn't ask first who the guy was or what he was doing on the tracks. He instinctively saw a life in danger and gave up his life to save it."

"I was only fifty feet away, frozen in my tracks, helpless to do anything, even scream. I watched for hours while they worked to retrieve his body from under the train. Real bad fellow, my brother was, according to you. Of course, he had already dropped out of high school and was washing dishes for a living when he died, so it was no great loss to the world. Right?"

"Shortly after that I dropped out of high school myself. I was supposed to be the valedictorian of my class, but they chose to give that honor to a doctor's son whether he deserved it or not. His father was prominent. Who was I? Anyway, I told them what part of their anatomy they could stick my diploma and award up and walked out into the cruel, cruel world. . . . That wasn't the only reason though, I mean, now that we're being perfectly honest about everything. You might say that I was a coward and lost my courage. It was almost more than I could stand to see everyone else buying graduation pictures, yearbooks, rings, going to the proms and all. All I could do was stand around in my hand-me-down dungarees and tee shirt and envy them."

"I had nothing better to do when I was going to school, so I did my homework all through school and read everything I could get my hands on because I was determined to make something of myself by myself, with no help from anyone, especially those rich people who would stop by for a shoe shine and couldn't even leave a nickel tip. You thought I was putting you on when I told you I didn't drink. Well, let me tell you why. If you had lived in the slums that I did and seen all the drunks and winos lying in the gutters with their faces in their own vomit, seeing how it destroyed their lives, you wouldn't have to be too bright to vow not to start drinking, knowing it could lead to something like that."

"You're right. I did join the army. I felt that it was better than waiting around to get drafted. There was not going to be any college deferment for me or phony medical evidence to help me beat the draft. I might have been able to beat the draft with my bad eyes, but chose not to, figuring I would be on equal footing with everyone else. But I was wrong. There is just as much discrimination in the army as anywhere else on earth. I was always told one of the biggest flaws in my character was that I had no respect for authority. Well, I always felt respect was something you had to earn, not something that was automatically handed out with a birth certificate or position of authority. When I was ten years old, I would see policemen taking bribes from bookies to keep quiet about their activities. One-arm bandits in the country club were illegal; yet they were there, and the members could go there after church on Sunday and get drunk. Drinking was illegal on Sundays unless you were rich and joined the country club. How can you respect people like that?"

"From my first day in the army I knew I had made a mistake, because it was the same old story, only in uniform this time: favoritism, rooms handed out by rank, nepotism and cronyism on every level. As far as being in scraps with them, it's true that I had my share of them; but you don't have to be too bright to outwit a bunch of nitwits. Do you know what I really think about the army? It's nothing but the unwilling run by the incompetent to do the unnecessary. As far as the Pentagon goes, they are like a bunch of piss ants floating down a river on a log and every damned one of them thinks he's steering."

"You said Moose and I were ex-mental patients. Do you know why we were in the hospital in the first place? Moose and I were shot down along with a first lieutenant by a MIG over North Korea and had to walk back to our own lines. The lieutenant was killed when he stepped on a land mine. I contracted malaria, and Moose carried me on his back for over fifteen miles, and commandeered an airplane to get me to Japan. The only reason he got away with it was that he told them I was an officer. They get preferential treatment. I was unconscious for over a week and there was nothing wrong with my head—or with Moose's for that matter. If you had dug a little deeper into your investigation, you would have found out that it is standard procedure to give psychiatric examinations to all persons who have been missing in action or prisoners of war."

"Moose and I were lucky. We escaped with no stigma. But some of those poor devils will be in insane asylums for the rest of their lives, and for what? To fight a war even the South Koreans don't want. To make defense contractors like yourself rich. We were over there dispensing your goods for you. Wasting them, so that you could sell more to the services and get even richer than you are. You made a comment that I only make seventy-two dollars a month. You probably spend seventy-two thousand dollars a month wining and dining and paying lobbyists to get even more defense contracts and make more profits."

"What do you know about people? Only that they are necessary evils that you have to pay in order to advance your own cause. If you were to lose a big defense contract tomorrow, with a stroke of a pen, you might lay off as many as fifteen thousand people. Does it bother you? I think not. You won't miss a meal or do without anything if they all starve to death."

I was really up on my soapbox now and figured I'd let this bastard have it with both barrels.

He said, "Just a minute, young man; you're in my house now."

"That is absolutely right, sir, but not for long. Before I go, I'm going to have my say. You asked for it. You had the audacity to call my mother "poor white trash.' Mister, you're not fit for her to wipe her feet on. Poor she was, but you couldn't hold a candle to her when it comes to love and understanding. She could give us only the bare necessities in life as far as material things go, but she was always there when we needed her. She would always take time to listen to our problems. As far as I'm concerned, she had the wisdom of Solomon and the patience of Job. She could have sent my brother and me to an orphanage, and perhaps started a new life for herself; but she didn't. She loved us and understood we needed her and was always there. Poor white trash? I hardly think so."

"What did you give your daughter? One boarding school after another so that she would be protected from poor white trash such as me. Where were you when she wanted to be tucked in at night or needed someone to listen to her troubles? Off to some fancy ball somewhere? I'll bet you even had a nurse for her when she was a baby, so she wouldn't mess up your social life. My mother gave me far more than you ever gave your daughter. She gave me her time and her love when I needed them most. When I first met Pam, she reminded me of the little girl in an orphanage who wrote a note and threw it from the main gate into the street. The note read: 'To anyone who finds this, I love you.' Well, sir, I found that note. I wanted to give her all the love and attention I could possibly muster and only prayed that perhaps she might love me in return."

"It may interest you to know that I fell in love with Pam long before I knew you existed. In fact, Pam told me nothing of you or Mrs. Taylor until we were on our way here last Friday night. It didn't make me love her any less that she didn't tell me sooner. But I knew exactly how you would react to our being in love and wanting to get married."

"You see, Mr. Taylor, our plights were similar. Only through accidents of birth was Pam born with everything and I with nothing. Neither one of us had any choice in the matter. Here I was struggling up the ladder and Pam was on top of the ladder already trying to find a way down. You had taken your wealth and influence and hung them around her neck like a millstone. In a manner of speaking, she was drowning. We met on neutral ground, found each other, and fell in love. Is that so hard to understand?"

"Would it surprise you to know your daughter is the first girl I've ever really dated seriously and would it surprise you to know that your attempted character assassination has not diminished our love for one another one single bit?"

"Let Pam speak for herself."

"Irish is right in everything he said, Daddy. Many a night in those boarding schools I cried myself to sleep wanting you and Mother to be there, but you never were. All those boys you arranged for me to date were just as phony as Irish has painted you to be. I don't love him any less in spite of your attempt to destroy him. I only love him more. If you wanted to know about Irish, all you had to do was ask him or me. Irish has no identity problems, Daddy. He knows who he is, why he was born, and that he is not immortal. You didn't have to sneak around and come up with half truths, falsehoods, and things taken out of context. We would have told you anything you wanted to know. I never told Irish about you and Mother because I was afraid of losing him. I was afraid if he knew he wouldn't want to see me anymore. If anyone was deceived, Daddy, it was Irish, not me, and certainly not you or Mother. He told me he was in love with me on our second date, and I knew I loved him after the first night we met."

"Oh, God! I wish we had run off and gotten married and just

145

forgotten I even had parents. If I had known that you were going to do this, Daddy, I swear to God, you would never have heard from me again."

"Pam, you don't know what you're saying!"

"Yes, I do, Daddy. That you could take someone as sweet and kind as Irish and try to destroy him, just to satisfy your own ego, and then call his family 'trash' is despicable. I'm sorry you're my father, and if Irish will still have me, I'm leaving here with him tonight and don't ever want to see you again."

Pam's mother, who had been sitting silently through all this, broke her silence. "Pam, Irish. Please don't go. Not just yet, anyway. Every word Irish spoke was the truth. We were too busy making money, getting ahead and taking care of our social life to be real parents to you, honey, and I'll never forgive myself for that. Your father has been driven by a lust for power that has caused him to become cold and callous. Everything he does is based on what's in it for him. Even his charitable contributions are calculated as to where they will buy him the most prestige or favors and are only given for the tax advantages they offer. We never realized how cold and lonely our lives have become. Even with all our wealth we are not happy people. Everything we do is for appearances and not for enjoyment and pleasure. We don't even go where we want on vacation; we go to the socially accepted places that are in that year."

"It is a sad thing to realize what fools we have been all these years. And our biggest mistake—and one we'll pay for the remainder of our lives—is the way we raised you, Pam. I'm sure your father thought in his own way that what he was doing was to protect you and was in your best interests. I hope that he realizes now just how wrong he was. There are still some things in this world that his money cannot buy. There are people like Irish who cannot be bought for any price. I thank God you two kids found each other in time, before your father and I had completely destroyed your life, Pam." By now she was crying openly.

Emotions were at a fever pitch. Pam was sobbing and I could even feel a tear or two in my eyes. I got up and went to Mrs.

Taylor and asked for forgiveness. "I get started on my damned soapbox and I never know when to quit."

She was still crying, so I knelt down beside her, took her hand and said, "Mrs. Taylor, please, I have no animosity toward you or Mr. Taylor. I want to love you both as much as Pam does, and I don't want to take her away from you. I want you and Mr. Taylor to be a part of our lives, but not to dominate them. I want you to be grandparents to our children and share our joy in raising them. I want us to come here for the holidays, Thanksgiving, Christmas and the like, to truly share our lives. The only thing we have to do is to put everything in its proper perspective and we'll all get along just fine."

"I was raised to believe that nothing is worth having unless you work for it. I know I'm too damned independent, but I would have to refuse any help from you folks. I couldn't become the stupid son-in-law that your husband had to continually make excuses for, or have people be nice to me because I had married the boss' daughter. That's a phony world filled with all kinds of deceptions and before you know it, you're deceiving yourself. I love your daughter just for her sweet, wonderful self and nothing more. She has accepted me for what I am, and with that foundation to build on, I'm sure we can grow and prosper on our own. Please forgive me and say you'll still love us."

Pam came over directly and put her arm around her mother.

Her mother reached up for her, and Pam knelt down beside her. She said, "God has been better to your father and me than we deserved. I know you both should hate us, and I couldn't blame you if you did and never wanted to see us again."

"Oh, Mommy!"

"That's the first time you called me 'Mommy' since you started school. It sounds so wonderful to hear you say that. Hold on to this young man of yours, Pam, for all you're worth. He'll make you happy and love you always. I hope you can find it in your heart to forgive your father and me. We've been such fools; but fools can learn. I only hope it's not too late for your father and me."

"Oh, Mrs. Taylor. Don't pay any attention to all those things

147

I said. I didn't mean to hurt you or put you down and I'm sorry
I made you cry."

"You can find it in your heart to forgive us after what Mr.
Taylor did to you?"

"Sure. Besides that, once I let off steam, that's it. It's all over.
I couldn't carry a grudge from here to the other end of the table.
That's just the way I am."

"Don't ever change, son. You don't mind if I call you 'son,'
do you?"

"Certainly not. I'd be delighted. In fact, I'm so bright, my
mother calls me 'sun.' "

At that, she began to laugh a little.

"Oh, Mother, of course we love both you and Daddy, and we
want you to be happy—just as happy as Irish and I are."

A bright smile came over her face as she dried her tears.
"Come on, you two, let's go into the living room."

"Does this mean we can't have dessert, Mrs. Taylor?"

Pam and her mother broke up laughing, but Mr. Taylor just
sat there in a somber mood.

"I'll make you all the dessert you can possibly eat, you sweet,
lovable character, you. Now I know why my daughter loves
you. Of course, you're going to take a little getting used to. We
never laughed much around here before, but I have a feeling we
are going to love every minute of it."

As we started for the living room, she stopped by Mr. Taylor's
chair, leaned over and kissed him, and asked him if he would like
to join us in the living room.

"You go on ahead. I'll join you later. I have some thinking to
do."

"All right, dear, but don't be too long. We have a lot to talk
to these young folks about tonight."

We went into the living room. Pam and I sat down on the
couch. Mrs. Taylor pulled a chair over and sat in front of us. She
leaned forward with a tear still glimmering in her eye and said,
"I love you two with all my heart, and I thank God for letting
you and Pam find each other. They say marriages are made in
heaven. I don't know if that is true of all marriages, but I'm
certain this one was." Then her thoughts turned to her husband.

148

"Don't be too hard on Mr. Taylor, Irish. He is a proud man and has never found it necessary to apologize to anyone for anything in his life. I'm certain he's trying to find the proper words to use."

"There are no apologies necessary, Mrs. Taylor. I was just as hard on him as he was on me. In fact, I was hitting below the belt a few times and I should be apologizing for that. Perhaps in his position I would have acted the same way."

"Oh, no, son. He owes you an apology and we both owe you a debt of gratitude which we'll never be able to repay."

"Oh, Mrs. Taylor, you're embarrassing me now."

"How about that dessert now?"

"Sounds wonderful."

She got up and left the room, leaving Pam and me alone there on the couch. I took her hand and told her I believed the worst was over and things should get better from here on.

"I truly hope so, Irish. I want to thank you for being so understanding of my parents. No one else would have been able to handle the situation and come to such a happy conclusion."

"Well, honey, I'm positive your mother is our ally; but your father is still not sold on me, I'm sure."

"I think he is, Irish. I've never seen him in the mood he's in right now."

"I'm sure your mother is right and he will come around. I have a feeling that everything is going to go our way from now on."

"Did I really look like a little orphan girl crying our for love, Irish?"

"Perhaps I was the one crying out for love, honey. I only knew you were the most warm and loving individual I had ever met in my life and I wanted to love you with all my heart and soul, and like I said, I only prayed you would return my love. Now that you have, you've made me the happiest guy in the world. I believe we were like two magnets. Once we came close to each other there was no keeping us from being together."

"Thank you, Irish. I'll always be there when you need me. I love you with all my heart and soul."

Pam's mother returned with a tray of coffee and cream pie.

We were sitting there enjoying ourselves and making small talk when Pam's mother remarked, "You know, tonight is the first time I've laughed in years and it really felt good. I feel this is a new beginning for all of us and I can actually see joy and contentment in the years ahead—watching you two kids grow and love each other and being a grandmother. I was really worried about growing old, but now I'm content to let it happen."

"Well, here's to a bright future for all of us, Mrs. Taylor."

Pam's mother was a very beautiful woman, about forty-two years old, neat and petite like her daughter. In fact, they were so much alike that at a glance from a short distance you could easily mistake one for the other. I pointed this out to her.

Pam said, "I'll have to keep my eye on you, Mother, so you don't steal him away from me." Her mother smiled and said, "He's just trying to flatter me."

As we talked, the conversation came around to Carol. Pam described the vast differences between the two funerals and, of course, went on to tell her mother all that happened at the house the night before the funeral and how I eulogized Moose at graveside and made him a legend to his family and friends.

Her mother was fascinated and listened intently to every word. Then she said, "I can believe it. I was talking to Carol's mother yesterday, and she told me of the talk they had with you two in San Francisco and how much better they felt after talking to you. She told me what a warm and wonderful person she thought you were and what a wonderful husband you would make for Pam."

"Oh, Mrs. Taylor, please let me assure you that Pam is the source of my strength and courage. With Pam by my side I feel complete. She is the catalyst that attracts all the sunshine and happiness wherever we go and whatever we do."

Her father entered the room, came over and put his arm around his wife's shoulder, and asked, "How's everything going?"

"Couldn't be better, dear."

"Can I get anything for anyone?" We all said, "No thank you, we're all fine."

He then asked me if I played billiards. When I said I did, he asked me if I would like to join him for a game or two. Pam's mother gave me a pleading smile, as if to say she would be very pleased if I did. Pam sensed what was happening and urged, "Why don't you, Irish?"

"Well, all right. It sounds like fun." I got up and told the ladies not to go away, that we would return shortly. We all sensed that Mr. Taylor wanted to get me alone so that we could talk, and all seemed pleased that I accepted his offer.

He led the way. We walked for what seemed like a quarter of a mile before he opened the door to the game room. There was everything imaginable in there to do, from table tennis to a poker table. I thought to myself, all this for two people. But then, they must do a lot of entertaining here.

We walked over to the pool table and while he was uncovering it, I picked up a cue and started to chalk it up. He racked the balls and asked me what I would like to play.

"How about eight ball?"

He said, "Fine," and told me to break.

I did and didn't make anything. He made the next three shots in a row and then missed passing the first three shots off as luck.

I thought I would take the initiative and said, "Look, Mr. Taylor, I'm sorry for popping off like I did at your dinner table tonight. I wish you would accept my apology."

"No, no, Irish. I was wrong and you don't know how hard that is for me to say. I can't recall ever saying that before in my life. As it turns out, I was wrong about a lot of things that you pointed out to me. I was so sure I didn't like you and that you were not sincere about my daughter that I used every means at my disposal to try to destroy you. That dossier I had put together on you must have cost one thousand dollars in man-power, telephone calls, telegrams, and private investigators. I took things out of context and gave only half-truths. I'm sure any lesser man than yourself would not have been able to stand up under the abuse I gave you. Most would have folded their tents and stole away into the night. Not only did you stand up

151

under it, but you countered in a manner, the likes of which I've never seen. I'm impressed. You never raised your voice once to me. You patiently listened to me cut you down and then you methodically destroyed my arguments and made your points very clearly and very succinctly."

"Of course, you had a few things going for you that I didn't. You had Pam's love and devotion; you were sincere and perfectly honest, and you spoke straight from the heart. I've seen men of very high stature falter under much less pressure than you were under tonight, and I commend you for the way you stood up for your family, friends, and my daughter. It does seem awkward to be thanking someone for standing up for her when I should have been doing that myself."

"You were, Mr. Taylor. You felt at the time you were doing it for her."

"Thank you, Irish. I certainly was taken back by your candor about big business, rich snobs like myself, the military and discrimination. I know every word you spoke was the truth. But I never wanted to admit it to myself. I more or less closed my eyes to all the corruption around me and simply tolerated it as the way things were. I would tell myself all my married life that I was doing it for my daughter's future. I could justify almost any action with that rationalization to soothe my guilty conscience. I know now that I was just on an ego trip and would do all those things, not for my daughter, but to inflate my own ego. Lord, when I think of some of the things I have done in the name of profit, I could almost throw up."

He continued. "It's ironic that Pam would find someone like you. Now I don't even have her to use as an excuse, to say I'm doing it all for her. She doesn't want it and she never wanted it. All she ever wanted was to be loved and have our love. I never even let her have that. I was protecting her, all right. I didn't want her going out into the world. I thought my money and position would protect her all her life. I was so wrong. God, if I could only do it all over again."

"Well, Mr. Taylor, we can't undo the past any more than we can predict the future. The way I look at life is that it's too late to worry about yesterday and too early to worry about tomorrow. So that just leaves us today to worry about. Right now, this very minute, is the only time we can do anything—good or bad, right or wrong."

"I wish I had your outlook on life."

"It's simple enough: 'Don't worry!'"

"Simple as that?"

"Yes, it is as simple as that."

I took another shot and missed. He made two more balls and missed.

"Do you think it's too late for Pam to love me, Irish?"

"She never stopped loving you, Mr. Taylor. But I think it's time you started returning her love."

"How do I go about that?"

"Just play it by ear and I'm sure you'll have plenty of opportunities."

"You're quite a remarkable young man, do you know that?"

"Well, your daughter tells me so, but I'm sure she's prejudiced."

"Where you are concerned, I'm certain she is, as I found out when I tried to come between you two. I never looked at Pam in that light before, taking someone else's side against mine. I guess I always knew it had to happen someday, but never wanted to face up to it before."

"Well, I'm sure it will work out for the best for all concerned, Mr. Taylor. I know Pam and I are dedicated to seeing that it does."

"And I want to thank you for that. Most people I know would not make the effort but instead would have stormed out, making all kinds of threats and leaving wounds that probably couldn't be healed in a lifetime. I respect you for being man enough to make the effort, and I'll do my best not to interfere in your lives."

I took my shot and managed to clear the table making the eight ball in the corner pocket to win the game.

I said, "Losers rack!" I could have bitten off my tongue as soon as I said it. Poor choice of words, I thought to myself.

153

"Somehow I don't feel like a loser tonight, Irish. I feel like a winner for the first time in a long time."

He racked the balls and asked me, "Would you like to make it interesting?"

"Why not?"

"How about ten cents a ball, any ball, any pocket?"

"Fine."

I broke and made the next five shots in a row.

"You know, Mr. Taylor. I'm going to have to do a lot of changing myself. I think I'll be able to do it with Pam's help."

"What do you mean, Irish?"

"Well, as you already know, I'm street wise and, I guess, somewhat resourceful, you might say. I've been living on my wits for so long that it will be a little difficult to settle down to a nine-to-five job once I get this army rap off my back. I'm not a saint or a knight in shining armor. I learned about life by living it and keeping my eyes open. By the age of ten my philosophy in life was that there were three areas in which you could live—black, white, and gray. If you stayed in the white area and were perfectly honest about everything you did, you were going to starve to death. If you got into the black area you were going to jail. That left the large gray area in the middle, where you could live comfortably and stay out of jail without starving to death."

"Well, Irish. Come to think about it, there is a lot of truth in what you say. For instance, I myself have probably lived most of my life in that gray area you spoke of. But I'm sure you'll do all right in whatever you choose to do."

He then took his shot and missed.

I took my shot and cleared the table. He paid me and racked the balls. I broke and made eight more.

"You're pretty good at this game, aren't you?"

"Well, I had a lot of practice in the hospital—nothing much else to do."

He made the next four and I cleared the table.

He asked, "Do you want to go double or nothing next game?"

"Sure, why not?"

I broke and ran the table.

"I think I'm being hustled, Irish."

"You know, Mr. Taylor, I think you're right. Old habits are hard to break."

He started to laugh and said, "Your honesty amazes me. It does make you vulnerable to people like me, though."

"I know, Mr. Taylor. Pam told me the same thing."

"I didn't realize Pam was so perceptive."

"Well, when you love someone, you try to know all there is to know about them, good and bad."

"Do you really think she still loves me, Irish, after the way I raised her and after that episode at the dinner table tonight?"

"There is no doubt in my mind, Mr. Taylor. Otherwise we wouldn't be here."

He was really ecstatic at what I had just told him. You could almost see a look of contentment and relaxation come over his face—like everything was going to be all right from now on.

"Come on, Irish, I want a chance to get even," he said.

He racked them up and we got down to some serious shooting.

It went back and forth for a while. Then I got the jump on him and kept pulling away. No one had ever told me I was supposed to be gracious and let my host win. Hell, I was shooting as if my life depended on it.

It was after midnight when he finally said, "We'll have to call it a night. I must get up early in the morning. How much did you get me for?"

I pulled my money out and counted it. "Almost eighty dollars."

"Well, it was worth a hundred times that to me. I won't forget this, Irish, and I want you to know I appreciate what you've done for Mrs. Taylor and myself."

"Like I was telling Mrs. Taylor, you owe me nothing. It is Pam you owe the debt of gratitude to. If it were not for Pam, I wouldn't be here, would I?"

"Of course, you're right. Let's go see what they are up to."

We walked back into the living room. They were both looking a bit apprehensive as we entered the room.

Mr. Taylor smiled, and said to Pam, "Honey, this young man

of yours is quite a billiards player. He won eighty dollars from me this evening, but promised me a rematch. I want you to see that he does!"

Everyone was smiling now. Pam promised, "Oh, I will, Daddy, don't worry."

"Well, I'm going to turn in. I'll see you young folks in the morning."

Mrs. Taylor told him she'd be along shortly. He went on ahead.

Pam looked at her mother. "I told you so, Mother. That was the first time I ever remember Daddy calling me 'honey.'"

Mrs. Taylor turned to me. "Thank you, son. I've never seen him in a better mood."

"Don't thank me, Mrs. Taylor; thank your daughter. She made it all possible."

"Well, I thank you both. Now, I think I'll run along. See you two in the morning."

We called out "Good-night" as she left the room.

I looked over at Pam and asked, "Did you miss me, sweetie?"

She smiled, gave me a kiss and said, "I didn't think you were ever coming back."

"A team of wild horses couldn't keep me away from you. Did you and your mother have a nice talk?"

"Yes, we did, Irish, a real nice mother-daughter talk. I've never felt closer to my mother in all my life."

"I'm glad to hear that, Pam. She's a lovely lady. I wouldn't want to hurt her."

"Did Daddy make his peace with you, Irish?"

"Yes, he did, honey. I think he's at peace with the world now."

"I'm glad, Irish. Say! I just realized something, Irish! We're all alone!"

"Well, what do you know about that? You look kinda tired, honey. Why don't you lie back and let me rub your neck for you?"

She lay back on the couch, while I knelt down and took her shoes off. I put my hand under her legs, lifting them over on the couch. I then got up and turned the lights off. I sat down beside her and removed my shoes, while she turned over on her side. I knelt down again and began massaging her petite little neck. I undid the thingamajig that was keeping her hair in a perfect pony tail. I kept running my fingers through her lovely hair until I had it all undone. I continued on rubbing her shoulders and back.

She sat up and put her arms around me. I held her ever so tightly. I laid her back on the couch very gently, while joining her there. We shared a kiss that must have lasted for fifteen minutes before we came up for air.

I continued to run my fingers through her beautiful light brown hair that lay there shimmering in the moonlight coming through the window.

I whispered in her ear, "Is this the time for us?"

Her heart was pounding madly as she clung to me.

"Oh, darling, you know I want to more than anything in this world. It is going to take all the strength on earth to refuse you, but you told me I had to be the strong one and say no."

I put my finger to her lips to silence her. "I won't put you in that position, darling. We'll wait like we planned this afternoon. I'm sure we won't be disappointed. I love you, Pam, with all my heart."

"Hold me, Irish. Tell me this feeling I'm feeling now will last forever. I feel so safe, secure, and serene when I'm in your arms."

"Hush! Hush now, let's just close our eyes, lie here for a while and try to drift back to earth."

"I don't ever want to come back from where I'm at right now, Irish. I feel my feet will never touch the ground again."

I kissed her on the forehead, and as we lay there in total silence we both drifted off to sleep.

I woke up with the sun shining in my eyes. Sleeping beside me was the sweetest, most precious ninety pounds of femininity that the Good Lord ever gave the breath of life to.

Then it hit me right between the eyes. "Oh, God! I have to report back to that goddamned army by tomorrow at the latest. Why does life have to be so cruel? It just isn't fair, now that we

157

have found each other that we'll be separated again. There must be some way to beat this rap, but I'll be damned if I know how, outside of going AWOL. If I do that, well, that will destroy everything Pam and I have worked so hard to build up. Oh, God! what am I to do?"

I made up my mind I was not going to let it bother me just then anyhow. I wasn't going to let it spoil what might be our last day together for a long time. I eased myself off the couch so as not to wake my sleeping beauty. I walked across the room, sat down on the piano bench, lit a cigarette while trying to get my mind off my dilemma. I turned to the piano and started picking out little tunes with one finger.

My thoughts drifted back to when I was eight years old. I could almost see myself sitting in front of that old upright piano in the convent with Sister Margaret trying to teach me the scales. We couldn't afford formal lessons, so she would have me over after school and tutor me on her own time. That old upright was a far cry from the baby grand I was sitting at now, I thought.

Still half dreaming and half in reality, I put my cigarette in the ashtray and began playing "Moonlight Sonata." That was Sister Margaret's favorite. It had taken me over a year to get it down pat. I did it to please her. As I grew older I would think back on all she had done for me.

I must have been halfway through when I happened to look up. There was Mrs. Taylor standing there watching me. She had on the most beautiful red crushed-velvet robe, accented with white lace, that I ever laid eyes on. The sunlight was shining off her beautiful face. She looked so magnificent standing there that it almost took my breath away. I stopped playing and said in a somewhat startled voice, "I'm sorry, Mrs. Taylor. Did I wake you?"

"Please continue, Irish."

"Are you sure it's all right?"

"It's just fine."

I continued on and finished the whole score.

"That was simply beautiful. Where did you learn to play like that?"

"From a very dear friend of mine, Sister Margaret."

I looked back across the room at Pam still sleeping on the couch. "I'm glad I didn't wake our little sleeping beauty."

She smiled and said, "Pam and I are closer now than we ever have been. I owe it all to you, Irish."

"Wrong, Mrs. Taylor. We owe it all to her."

"I don't want to embarrass you, Irish; but Pam told me how you two met and how you didn't take advantage of her and promised to let her enter into marriage a virgin. I want to thank you for that. I guess all mothers have a tendency to worry about things like that where their daughters are concerned. I can only tell you, it has put my mind at ease. I know how much you two love each other and what a sacrifice it must be for both of you. But believe me, Irish, you'll both be better people for it. You won't regret it. I know, for Pam is a love child. Even though Mr. Taylor and I loved each other very much, there was always that stigma there that could never be erased."

"You don't have to tell me all this, Mrs. Taylor."

"No, I wanted to. I hope you won't betray Pam's confidence in me. I'm sure it would embarrass her if she knew I mentioned it to you."

"My lips are sealed, dear lady. I know mother-daughter relationships are sacred and not to be shared by fathers or even prospective sons-in-law."

She leaned over, kissed me on the cheek, and said "Thank you."

"Do you play the piano, Mrs. Taylor?"

"I played a little when I was in college—mostly for my own amusement."

"Did you ever play 'Boogie Woogie'?"

"Yes, I did."

"Well, come on and sit down here."

"You play the top half of the keyboard, and I'll play the bottom half. Okay?"

I started off, and she picked right up on the beat. Before long we were sailing along on the breeze.

Pam was awakened by the noise. She came over and stood there leaning on the piano, not really believing what she was seeing and hearing.

We played for five minutes or so and then quit. I reached over and shook her hand, saying "Very good, Mrs. Taylor."

I turned to Pam. "Good morning, Sunshine. Did your mother wake you with all that noise she was making on this piano? I tried to stop her, but she insisted. I just don't know what we're going to do with her, do you, Pam?"

"Well, I think I'll give her a big kiss and hug for starters."

"Hear, hear! I second the motion. Hugs and kisses all around for the pretty lady."

Her mother gave me a little punch on the arm saying, "Oh, you big nut, you."

Pam came around, put her arms around her mother, and gave her a big hug and a kiss on the cheek. "I got two surprises this morning. Why didn't you two tell me you played the piano. I never heard you or Irish play before. You're really good."

"Thank you, dear; but this young man here is the one who can play. You'll have to hear him play "Moonlight Sonata." It is simply beautiful."

"I thought I heard it playing while I was asleep on the couch."

"You did, dear. It was your young man playing it."

"I thought I was dreaming. I won't tell you what I was dreaming, only that it was beautiful." She kinda blushed and I said, "I'll bet I know." Her face really got red then. "You were dreaming that we were all in the kitchen raiding the icebox for something to eat."

She and her mother both laughed. Her mother said, "Come on, we'll see what we can find."

We went into the kitchen. She told Pam and me to have a seat while she fixed us a bite to eat.

About that time, the cook came in from another room and looked startled to see us all in her kitchen.

Mrs. Taylor greeted her. "Good morning, Maggie. We're just

raiding your icebox looking for something to eat. Anything here we can snack on?"

"How about if I fix you all some ham and eggs? I have a fresh pot of coffee on."

Mrs. Taylor turned to Pam and asked, "How about it?"

"Sounds great. Bring on the coffee."

Mrs. Taylor joined us while Maggie poured the coffee and started fixing breakfast. Mrs. Taylor asked what time it was.

I looked at my watch and said, "A quarter 'til."

" 'til what?"

"I don't know, I lost the little hand."

She smiled and said, "Come on, Irish, 'til what? 'til six? Oh, never mind what time it is. Come on and tell me about Sister Margaret, Irish."

Pam asked, "Who is Sister Margaret?"

"Well, sweetheart, I guess you had to find out sooner or later. She was the other woman in my life."

Her mother laughed, "Yes, when he was eight years old."

They both laughed. "You never know what he's going to say next, Mother. He's got such a sense of humor."

"Yes, so I found out last night when he was describing stealing the pop and popcorn off the priest and then admitting it in confession and adding, 'Thank God for the seal of the confessional'. I wanted to laugh so badly that my stomach hurt."

We sat there laughing and joking back and forth, and I began to tell them about dear sweet Sister Margaret.

"Sister Margaret and I first met when I was in third grade. I guess she kinda took pity on me and took me under her wing. Here I was, a poor little ragamuffin with blond curly hair, no bigger than a peanut. I kinda stuck out like a sore thumb; my brother and I were the only Irish kids in the school—all the rest were Polish. As a result of being different, all the other kids would pick on us. Sister Margaret became my great protector and was determined that no harm was going to come to me. I imagine that is why she would often take me to the convent with her after school—so the other kids wouldn't pick on me. I always liked to go over there, for nine times out of ten, the nuns would invite me to have dinner with them. I think they would get a kick out of watching me eat. I could almost consume my own weight in food. After dinner, I would always clean up the kitchen and help with the dishes."

"I think if they could have, they would have let me stay there permanently. My mother had always taught my brother and me to respect our elders and to be polite to people. After the way most of those kids threatened them, I guess we were like a breath of fresh air to them."

"I always loved the piano, so Sister Margaret taught me how and would let me play as long as I liked. She would only run me off so I could get home before dark. I would hate to see the summer come, because school would close and the nuns would go on retreat."

"This went on for four years. Sister Margaret got me out of the most embarrassing moment of my life. I can't tell you about that though."

"Come on, Irish, you won't embarrass us."

"No, it's me who is chicken to tell you. Okay, then, you asked for it. It was in third grade and they cut us loose for recess. We had to go to the little boys' room before we were allowed out on the playground. So naturally, we made that pit stop as quickly as possible. Well, in my haste, I got my zipper caught and was helpless to do anything about it. I stayed right in there all during recess and when I didn't return to class Sister Margaret came looking for me. She came right on in. There I was, her lost little sheep hiding over in the corner too embarrassed to tell her what my problem was. She soon discovered what it was and got me undone. I made her promise not to tell anyone about it. She promised she wouldn't."

Pam's mother was laughing so hard she was crying.

I continued. "Sister Margaret would teach me about anything I wanted to know. I had an inexhaustible curiosity about every-thing. I guess I would really put her on the spot at times with some of my questions, especially when I reached the age of puberty and found out that girls were more than just soft boys. She was real cool and suggested I ask my mother or Father Currey."

DONALD R. WAGNER

"I knew there was a better life than the one my brother and I were leading. I would ask Sister Margaret about it. Her answer would always be the same. She would tell me that the harder you have it in this life, the easier you will have it in the next. I would always believe what she told me, for as far as I was concerned she had no peers. Her word was gospel to me. She could have told me the moon was made of green cheese and I would have believed it and challenged anyone who would dare dispute it. There wasn't anything I wouldn't do for her. She would take me over to the church and we would polish the candelabrum, dress the altar, put out mass cards, and clean the whole church. I didn't care what had to be done, all she had to do was say the word and I wouldn't stop until it was complete."

"I never realized just what she meant to me until the last time she had to say good-bye to me. I was twelve years old by then, and Sister Margaret was being sent on a new assignment up in New York State. She sat me down and told me she was leaving and wouldn't be returning ever again. I sat there and cried my eyes out."

"She told me that she had chosen to do God's work and that we had to be strong and accept things as they happen. She told me to get through life I had to do, say, and think what I thought was right regardless of what others might think, say, or do. She also told me not to be intimidated by other people. That the Good Lord would look after me and provide me with everything I would need to get through life. 'I know you hurt now,' she continued. 'Perhaps I shouldn't have let you become so attached to me; for that I apologize. I'm sure the Lord has great things planned for you. You'll most likely feel as if you're walking around under clouds until one day, somewhere, someway, the sun will come shining through, you'll fall in love and tell yourself it was all worth it.' "

"I told her that I loved her. I didn't want God to take her away from me. "She got up—and I know now it must have broken her heart—and she told me to stop acting like a baby, because it was time I grew up and faced reality."

"At that she walked out the door, leaving me to my own devices. I must have sat there crying for two hours. Then, for

163

some unexplained reason (perhaps I had cried all the tears I had left in me), I began to feel better about things and finally got up the courage to leave. On the way home, I vowed never to forget her and to try to live up to all the things she had taught me. I never did get to see her again. I really don't know if she is even alive; but I hope to find her again someday and thank her, for her prediction came true. One day, just like she said, there was Pam. That's how I was so sure it was love, because the clouds parted and Pam, you were the sun shining through."

Pam and her mother were spellbound. They said they had never heard a more beautiful story in all their lives.

I turned to Pam and said, "We can't lose, can we? We wouldn't want to disappoint Sister Margaret now, would we?"

Pam smiled her loving smile. "Of course not. I love you, Irish."

Maggie, who had been hovering around waiting for me to finish my story so that she could get a word in edgeways, told us our breakfast was ready and wanted to know if we were eating in the dining room.

"Well, I'm comfortable here. How about you two?"

They both said "Fine." Maggie, still not believing what she was seeing, served us breakfast there.

I asked for the ketchup. Pam's mother looked at me a little strangely. "Ketchup? On eggs?"

"Sure, it's delicious. You really should try it."

Maggie came over with the ketchup, and I put some on my eggs and handed the bottle to Mrs. Taylor. She poured some on a little piece of egg, tasted it, and said, "That is really good," while picking up the bottle and adding more ketchup to her eggs. "Try it, Pam," she urged, "you'll really like it." Pam did, and she commented she liked it also.

Mr. Taylor came through the door. He looked a little surprised to find us eating in the kitchen. "Well, here you are! I was beginning to think you had all left home!"

His wife insisted that he sit down and she told Maggie to fix him breakfast. Still a little surprised, he agreed, "Sure, why not?"

He asked what Pam and I had planned for the evening. I told him we had no plans at the moment and added, "As much as I hate to admit it, I must report back to the army tomorrow."

"I've been awake almost all night thinking things over," Mr. Taylor began. "It almost completely slipped my mind, what with the events of the past few days, but today is our twentieth wedding anniversary. I had planned a party for Mrs. Taylor over at the country club and if it is all right with you and Pam, we would like to have you two join us and help us celebrate."

Mrs. Taylor added, "We would love to have you join us. Also, I have another wonderful idea."

"How would it be if we made it a double celebration? It would be a perfect time to announce your engagement. What do you think of that?"

Pam said, "I'll leave it up to Irish."

"If it will please you and Mr. Taylor, we'll be delighted to join you," I said.

"Fine. Then it's all settled."

Mr. Taylor looked over at his wife's plate and asked what was on her eggs.

"Ketchup, dear. You should try it; it's delicious."

Maggie brought him his breakfast. He reached for the bottle of ketchup and was converted to ketchup and eggs on the spot. We were all talking, laughing, and finishing up our second cup of coffee when Mr. Taylor excused himself saying he had some important things to take care of this morning. On his way out he commented, "Incidentally, I enjoyed the piano concert this morning."

Mrs. Taylor said, "Well, kids, let's get down to some serious planning. It's going to be a black-tie affair. Do you mind terribly, Irish?"

"Of course not. I'll just place myself in your capable hands. You must tell me what you want me to do and wear and how to act. I can assure you, your wish will be my command."

"Thanks, Irish! I just want you to be yourself. As far as the formal attire we can run into town and rent you a tuxedo. Would that be all right?"

"I'm completely at your mercy. Just don't let me make a fool out of myself, okay?"

"You're too smart to ever do that, Irish, you sweet, lovable character you."

At that, we all left for our respective rooms to get cleaned up and dressed for our trip downtown.

I was in the guest room getting cleaned up when Mr. Taylor came in and asked if he could talk to me man-to-man.

"I wouldn't have it any other way, Mr. Taylor."

"I don't want to embarrass you or put you on the spot, Irish, but what is your financial situation? I know that with the seventy-two dollars a month the army pays you, you must be broke by now."

"No, sir. On the contrary, I'm solvent at the moment." I pulled out my wad of bills and showed him I had over thirteen hundred dollars on me, plus a lot of back pay the army owed me.

He was amazed and said so. He asked me if it would be asking too much to tell him how I was able to accumulate that kind of money from a salary of seventy-two dollars a month. He said he knew it was none of his business, but that he was just curious.

"No, I don't mind, Mr. Taylor; I'll be happy to tell you. Of course, you already know that I am resourceful." I went on to tell him about the lottery Moose and I had run over in Japan, about Carol's father insisting on paying for the trip back east, and reminded him that he had contributed over eighty dollars of his own money to the pot.

"Yes, you are resourceful. I guess I'll never have to worry about my daughter going hungry, will I?"

"I should hope not, sir. As long as I still have my two good hands, I plan to provide her with everything she'll ever need."

"Of that I have no doubt. But let me ask a favor of you, Irish. I don't want you to get mad or think I'm trying to insult you, for nothing is further from the truth. As a personal favor from me, would you accept the money to buy Pam's engagement ring?"

"Well, I'd rather not be beholden to you like that, Mr. Taylor.

Although I really do appreciate the gesture, I really couldn't let you do that."

"Come on, son; I insist. It's you that I'm beholden to. No one need ever know, and God strike me dead if I ever breathe a word about it to another living soul. I want to do something for someone in my life without asking or wanting anything in return. Please let me do this, not only for you, but for Pam too."

"Well, since you put it that way, Mr. Taylor, how can I refuse?"

"Good." At that, he reached in his pocket and pulled out his wallet. He gave me five one-hundred-dollar bills and four credit cards to the fanciest department stores in town. He said, "The sky is the limit; please don't worry about it."

I was flabbergasted. He shook my hand and said "Thanks, son. Remember, this is strictly between you and me."

"Any way you want it, sir." At that, he went on out.

I finished dressing and walked out into the hall. Pam and her mother were downstairs waiting for me. I suddenly got this irresistible urge to slide down the banister. I hollered down to Mrs. Taylor and asked her if she would mind if I slid down. "Be my guest, Irish."

I mounted the railing and slid down hell-bent before election. I slid right off the end and landed pretty hard on my fanny. It gave me a good jolt and knocked the wind out of me. I lay on my back trying to catch my breath. They both ran over, knelt on either side of me, and asked if I was all right.

By now I had caught my breath, so I reached up and put my arms around both of them, pulling them down to me. "With two beautiful ladies to attend me, how could I possibly not be all right?"

We sat up and were sitting there on the floor laughing for all we were worth when this stuffy old butler named Arnold came in and asked if everything was all right. Mrs. Taylor assured him that everything was just fine. He threw his nose in the air, turned, and haughtily left the room.

Mrs. Taylor laughed and said "The old stick in the mud."

"Yea! The old fly up the creek!" I added.

We got up and went outside where the chauffeur was waiting to take us shopping. I let Pam and her mother get in first, as a gentleman should, but the seating arrangement didn't suit me. I asked Pam if she would mind terribly changing places with me.

"Of course not, Irish."

She got up and was leaning forward over the front seat. As I was scooting over, I couldn't resist giving her a little swat on the fanny. She sat down instinctively and had such a surprised look on her face. I laughed and said, "Now, that's for nothing. Now do something."

She reached up and started to squeeze my nose.

"I surrender; I surrender."

We were all in a gay festive mood, as if we didn't have a care in the world. I even commented on the new seating arrangements. "There, now isn't this much better? A thorn between two roses." They both smiled.

Mrs. Taylor hesitated and then asked, "I hate to be the one to bring it up, Irish, but did I understand you correctly when you said you had to report back tomorrow?"

"As much as I hate to admit it, Mrs. Taylor, I'm afraid that is my fate."

"Oh! I'm so sorry to hear that. How long will you be gone?"

"If I go back to Korea, it will be at least four months."

"Well, the time will pass quickly for you and Pam."

"Not quickly enough to suit me, Mrs. Taylor."

Pam, with a tear in her eye, said, "I wish with all my heart and soul that you didn't have to leave me so soon, Irish."

"Let's try not to think about it and enjoy ourselves today, okay?"

They both agreed. Before long we were in town.

First they took me to rent a tux. They insisted that I try the outfit on. I came out all dressed up and asked, "Well, how do I look?"

The tuxedo really didn't fit me right, and I could see it in Mrs. Taylor's eyes, although she was too kind to say anything. I said, "You're right. It looks awful. Wait right here; I'll be back."

I went back into the fitting room and got hold of the asshole who had been waiting on me. I told him to get me some rags that fit and to make it fast, for I didn't have all day to piss around there with him.

This snobby holier-than-thou bastard didn't know how to take that and said with disdain, "Well! I never!"

I shot back, "Well, you had better start."

Within fifteen minutes, he had me looking as if I had just stepped out of *Esquire* magazine, and I presented myself to the ladies. Mrs. Taylor looked genuinely pleased. Pam said I looked just marvelous. Mrs. Taylor offered him her credit card. I told her not to worry; I would take care of it.

I went back in, changed, and gave this squirrel-headed bastard one of Mr. Taylor's credit cards to write it up on.

"Will this be a rental?", he asked, in his superior tone of voice.

"Hell, no, my good man. I'm buying."

At that, he boxed everything up and wrote up the sales slip. I signed it, and we were on our way again.

Pam and her mother wanted to buy new gowns, so off we went to the fanciest department store in town. While they were shopping for gowns, I wandered off to the jewelry department to look for an engagement ring.

I was standing in front of the showcase when this suave sophisticated-looking salesman came over and looked me over carefully. When he was through looking up one side and down the other, I asked him if he liked what he was seeing. He snapped, "What can I do for you?"

"Well, for starters, you can show me some engagement rings."

"Oh, really?"

"Yes, really." By now I was getting so sick of these snotty bastards saying "Oh, really," I could have screamed.

He went behind the counter, reached down, and pulled out a case of the most expensive rings they had.

I guess he figured he'd insult me and put me in my place quickly rather than fool with me. I looked them over and asked, "How much for this one?" It was a beautiful solitaire diamond that almost knocked your eye out when the light hit it.

"Twenty nine hundred dollars, plus tax."

I said, "Well . . ." He broke in and asked, "Too expensive for you?"

"Hell, no! I was just wondering if you had something a little more expensive." He assured me that he did and asked how much I wanted to spend.

"Cost is no object." At that, he had to back down and confess that I had chosen the most expensive diamond they had on hand, but added, "We could order anything you wanted."

"No, that's all right. I'll take this one. Wrap it up."

"Will that be cash or charge?"

"Charge." I flipped him Mr. Taylor's credit card. He recognized it instantly and asked me where I got it. I told him it was none of his goddamned business.

"Well, you don't mind if I call him, do you?"

"Be my guest. If you want to get your ass chewed out, that's up to you."

He called the manager instead and was almost speechless when he hung up the phone. I guess Mr. Taylor had anticipated something like this and had phoned his approval ahead. This snob of a salesman looked like he had just been kicked in the balls. He wrote up the sales ticket, which I signed, and I told him not to take it so hard. "Life is full of surprises."

I wandered back through the store and found the ladies; they were still having trouble deciding on gowns. They asked my opinion. I told them that was strictly out of my league. They finally decided, and we were on our way again.

We stopped to have lunch at a real swank restaurant and were making plans for the coming events.

Mrs. Taylor said, "I would imagine you two will want to get married as soon as you come home, Irish." To which Pam said, "The sooner the better for me; I can hardly wait."

"All right then, let's plan on two weeks after Irish gets home."

"If it's all right with Pam, it's just fine with me, Mrs. Taylor. Remember, it's up to you as far as the arrangements go."

"Well, Pam and I will have four months to plan and get things ready. It will give us something to do while you're away."

"Mrs. Taylor, I'm leaving my life in your hands by leaving Pam home with you. Without Pam there is no life for me."

"Ah, how sweet, Irish. Don't worry about a thing. I'll take very good care of her for you."

I took Pam's hand and said "You had better listen to your mother or she'll turn you over her knee and paddle your behind." They both chuckled at that.

Two of Mrs. Taylor's friends, who had been watching us from a distance, came over to say hello, or so they said. They were curious about me, for as soon as they had said hello they asked "Who's the handsome young man you have with you?" Mrs. Taylor told them she was proud to introduce me as her prospective son-in-law.

You should have seen the eyebrows raise as they said, "Oh, really!" She shot back with an emphatic, "Yes, and I couldn't be happier about it. We're making the formal announcement at the country club tonight at our twentieth wedding anniversary party. I do hope you'll be able to attend."

They both said they wouldn't miss it for the world. They said their farewells and departed from the premises. Mrs. Taylor looked at Pam and me. "Those are two of the biggest gossips in town, and I'm sure we'll have a large crowd there tonight. Those two will spread the word."

"No telephone, no telegraph, tell a woman."

"That's exactly right, Irish."

"I don't mind, Mrs. Taylor, as long as those two bitches are talk. . . ." Pam and her mother both broke out laughing. "What did I say that's so funny?"

"Never mind, Irish."

"Did I make a boo-boo?"

"Yes, you did."

"Well, if I did, I apologize. What exactly did I say?"

Pam whispered in my ear that I had referred to them as "bitches."

"I'm truly sorry. It's a nasty habit I picked up in the army, and I slip once in a while."

Mrs. Taylor said, "Well, perhaps you're right, Irish. I never heard them referred to as such before, but maybe they are. Besides, it was worth it to see your face so red."

"That, too? Wow, I'm really messing up by the numbers, aren't I? Well, like I was saying, as long as they're talking about me, they are leaving someone else alone."

"Oh, Irish, people can be cruel. I just hope and pray to God that none of them insult you tonight. If they do, I swear I'll drop out of the club."

"I don't understand, Mrs. Taylor. Why would they want to insult me? I didn't do anything to them. I'm sure I don't mean anything to them one way or the other."

"They're rich snobs, Irish, who look down their noses at anyone who isn't as rich as they are or doesn't hold a position in society high enough to suit them. Funny, I never before realized just how mean and cruel people can be. I must confess that before you came along, Irish, I guess Mr. Taylor and I were the same way."

"Oh, Mrs. Taylor, I could never believe that about you. And don't you worry about me; I can take care of myself."

"I'm sure you can, Irish. I guess I'm just a natural worrier."

"Well, put your mind at ease. With you, Pam, and Mr. Taylor there to look after me, I'll feel safe as a babe in arms."

They both smiled at me. Pam added that everything was going to be fine. "Once they get to know Irish, they will love him just as much as we do."

"I'm sure they will, honey. He's the most lovable character in the whole world, but I hate to subject him to that baptism of fire."

"You promised not to worry, remember?"

"All right, I'll try not to worry."

We finished lunch and continued our shopping spree with Pam and me sneaking off to buy them an anniversary present. Now, there was a challenge. What the hell do you buy for someone who has everything? We pondered the question. Finally I said, "I think I got it. Let's tell them that you're pregnant and that is our gift to them."

Pam laughed and said, "That's not a half-bad idea."

172

"What? Your being pregnant or telling them?"

"A little of both, Irish."

"You devil, you."

We wandered around, hand in hand, both hoping tomorrow would never come. We finally wound up in a jewelry store and settled for a silver serving tray. We had it engraved "For your Twentieth Anniversary from Pam and Irish." Then we caught up with Mrs. Taylor and returned home.

Pam and I had a couple of hours to ourselves and decided to go for a walk. We walked to a beautiful little park about a mile from the house. It was a warm afternoon and there was a very gentle breeze blowing through the trees. We sat down beside a little pond and began throwing pebbles into the water, watching the ripples spread out. It was like the setting of a fairy tale.

We were both in a very somber mood by now, contemplating my impending departure. We both realized it was inevitable and found it painful to talk about.

"Oh, Irish, hold me and tell me everything is going to be all right."

I took her in my arms. She was crying openly by now. I reassured her as best I could that everything was going to be fine, and there was nothing to worry about. "The next four months will go by so fast that it will make our heads swim. We'll keep busy and the time will pass quickly."

"Will you write to me every day, Irish?"

"I promise I will, darling; and I want you to write as often as you can."

"Oh, Irish, I wish you didn't have to go away. It just doesn't seem fair."

"I know, Pam, and if there were any way in the world I could get out of it—short of destroying our lives— you know I wouldn't go."

"I know, Irish. I love you so much. I hope I can find the strength and courage to let you go tomorrow."

"It's going to be all right, honey. Absence makes the heart grow fonder, or so they say. I'll bet *they* never had to say good-bye to someone as lovely as you, though.

We lay back on the ground unashamed to openly share each other's passionate affections for one another. We lay there for the longest time, not saying a word, locked in each other's arms, sharing one tender and passionate kiss after another. If we hadn't been in a public park, I'm sure there would have been no turning back, and all our secret longings and desires would have been fulfilled. As it was, it was almost impossible to bring ourselves back to earth and to regain our composure enough to head back to the house, still longing and yearning for fulfillment of our desires.

We had promised each other; and I was determined not to betray her mother, for I had promised to let Pam enter marriage as a virgin. And no matter how badly it hurt, I was determined to keep that promise. Pam realized just how much it meant to her mother and felt that it was going to be worth it to wait until she walked down the aisle and we were finally married, at last able to make love, uninhibited, unafraid, and unashamed.

We entered the house through the side door. Her mother was sitting there. I asked to be excused for a few moments. Her mother asked where I was going.

"To take a cold shower." Pam, only half-thinking, asked, "Does that help?" Her mother laughed and said, "Yes, it does, dear."

"Come on, now, you guys are making me blush again." At that, I hit the stairs and headed for the shower.

10

The Anniversary Party

It seemed like only an instant later and there we were, all dolled up and at the country club, where we were seated at a big round table, front and center. I was very nervous and apprehensive, not knowing what to expect next. I guess it must have shown, for Mrs. Taylor told me to relax and enjoy myself.

I told her, "For you, I'd do anything."

"Okay then. Relax and enjoy yourself."

It wasn't long before that baptism of fire she had spoken of descended upon us. Mrs. Taylor's old spinster aunt came over and plunked her big fat ass down at our table and started right in on Pam and me. "So, this is the young man you intend to marry, is it?"

Pam, being as polite as she knew how, said, "Yes, Aunt Minnie, he is," and introduced me to her.

Aunt Minnie was unimpressed and said, "Well, Mrs. Bloomfield called me and told me she saw you and this young man, I guess, in the park across from her house this afternoon in a vulgar display of what, I suppose, you would call affection."

This really got my dander up. But I kept my cool and watched my language and said, "Oh, really, and where was Mrs. Bloomfield watching from—her upstairs window? You would think she would have better things to do with her time than to be gawking out the window watching people, wouldn't you?"

"Well, young man, that kind of behavior is totally unacceptable in this part of the country. I don't know what is acceptable where *you* come from; but it *certainly* is not acceptable here."

"Oh, really!" (I picked right up on that 'Oh, really!' bit that had been used against me by others today.) "If you call a couple of young lovers, walking through a park and sharing a kiss and an embrace totally unacceptable behavior, then I feel sorry for you, because you've really missed a lot in life."

"Well, I guess we all know where that kind of behavior leads to, don't we?" she said, in her nastiest, most insinuating tone of voice.

"What's that supposed to mean?"

"Well, we had one scandal in our family years ago, and I would hate to see it repeated in this generation. You know what I'm talking about, don't you, Paula?" (Paula was Mrs. Taylor's first name.)

Mrs. Taylor, very embarrassed, looked down at the table and never spoke a word.

I remember thinking to myself, "For Christ's sake, after twenty years, this old bitch can't put it to rest." I got a little hot under the collar; but I managed to keep my voice just above a whisper as I lit in to her. "If you're referring to the fact that Pam is a love child, you're perfectly right. Just look at that radiant face beaming love from every pore of that lovely white flesh. That, my dear lady, is love personified. As for Mr. and Mrs. Taylor having to get married, my dear lady, I can assure you they didn't have to get married."

"What do you know about it, sonny? You were still wet behind the ears when all this happened."

"Yes, I was; but I know people. And I'm sure they got married because they wanted to, and not just because Mrs. Taylor was carrying Pam at the time. They had other options they could have exercised. Like having an abortion. Or Mrs. Taylor could have gone away, had the baby, and put it up for adoption. That is the usual way to handle it, isn't it? No. They loved each other and their unborn child and chose to get married because they were in love. And they did so in spite of all your criticism and that of all your friends with their wagging tongues. It took strength and courage—and above all, love—to do what they did. To go through with it and subject themselves to all that cruelty and gossip, when their only sin was loving each other. I submit to you, dear lady, nothing but love and understanding went into the making of their marriage."

"As for Pam and me. You and all your gossiping friends can go ahead, mark your calendars, count the days, weeks and months. But I can assure you and your friends that you're going to be sadly disappointed."

At that, she turned to Mr. Taylor and said, "Are you just going to sit there and let him talk to me like that?"

Mr. Taylor said, "The truth really hurts, doesn't it, Minn? I find no fault in what he told you. I'm only sorry it was he, not I, that told you."

At that, she gasped. "Well, I never!"

I rebutted, "Well, perhaps if you had, you wouldn't be the way you are today."

She got up and stomped off in a huff.

As soon as she was out of earshot, Mr. and Mrs. Taylor started to laugh a polite little laugh. You could tell they were well pleased.

"Pam, this young man of yours could walk with kings."

Pam smiled, "Yes, I know, Daddy. And I'm sure he's going to make you proud of him."

"He already has."

Mrs. Taylor added, "I second the motion." Her face was beaming a glow I had never seen before, as if the stigma of living with all that gossip for all those years had suddenly been lifted off her shoulders. She said, "I propose a toast."

"I'll drink to that."

Pam asked, "What are we drinking to?"

"I don't know, your dad will think of something. How about it, Mr. Taylor, what are we drinking to?"

"Slow down, slow down; you have my head spinning with all this. Let me catch up. I'm not as quick as I used to be."

"Well, here's to twenty years of marriage for Mr. Taylor and myself, and to forty years for you kids."

"I'll drink to that." We all raised our glasses and drank a toast.

It seemed one by one and two by two, people kept coming over to our table to congratulate Mr. and Mrs. Taylor, and to get a look at this outsider, who they felt was trying to invade their ranks. Hell, nothing was further from the truth. Not that I had anything against money per se. It was all this phony holier-than-thou bullshit I had trouble contending with.

The time came to make the announcements. We assembled on a little stage about a foot above the dance floor. The MC made the announcement of Mr. and Mrs. George Taylor's twentieth wedding anniversary. Everyone clapped and cheered them.

Then Mrs. Taylor took the microphone and made the announcement of the engagement of her daughter, Pamela, to Mr. Bryan O'Malley, affectionately known to all as "Irish." They all applauded politely, but not too enthusiastically.

I walked over to the bandleader and told him I would like to sing the "Anniversary Song" and wondered if the band would accompany me. He said they would be glad to, and when I finished they would play it again so that everyone could join in the dancing. I thanked him and walked over and told Mr. and Mrs. Taylor what I had in mind.

They stepped onto the dance floor. I put my arm around Pam and took the mike from the stand and nodded to the bandleader. As he struck up the band, I began to sing the "Anniversary Song" in my best Irish tenor voice.

They had dimmed the lights with only a spot on Mr. and Mrs. Taylor. They really looked elegant out there waltzing away. The good vibrations they were giving off seemed to fill the room.

I sang on and on with Pam looking longingly up into my eyes every time I would glance down at her.

After I finished, I put the mike back on the stand. Pam and I stepped onto the floor while the band picked up the tempo just a pitch or two. I took Mrs. Taylor's hand while Pam took her dad's hand and we waltzed off in different directions. Instead of everyone else joining in like we thought, they threw another spotlight on Mrs. Taylor and me, while keeping the other trained on Pam and her father.

We waltzed the whole number through. After wild enthusiastic applause, the band started playing it for the third time, and everyone took their partners and joined in. At the conclusion, everyone cheered and applauded. They were urging me to sing another song. I respectfully declined, saying "It was the Taylors' celebration—not Pam's and mine."

Mr. and Mrs. Taylor insisted. I consented only if Pam would join me on stage.

I asked the bandleader if they knew any Irish numbers. He assured me they knew them all. I took the mike from the stand and asked if there were any Irish folks in the crowd tonight. An overwhelming response came back.

"That's good. I'm afraid all I know are Irish songs. Any special requests?"

Mrs. Taylor asked if I knew "I'll Take You Home Again, Kathleen."

I turned to the bandleader, who gave me a perfect pitch, and I began to sing. The house lights went down, and they trained a spot on Pam and me. It seemed I had hit the jackpot. Those dining at the club tonight were at least eighty percent Irish and loved their Irish music. Of course, being Irish myself, I began to feel more at ease.

I finished. The lights came up and someone hollered, "How about 'Galloway Bay'?" I said, "Maestro, if you please." The lights went down again, and I sang "Galloway Bay." After the lights came up again, I announced, "For my next number, I would like everyone to sing along. Does everyone know 'When Irish Eyes Are Smiling'?"

I got back a roar of approval. The band started playing and immediately everyone in the room was singing his heart out. People were getting up from their tables and crowding around the bandstand. I looked down and there were Mr. and Mrs.

Taylor, beaming a radiant smile at Pam and me. I put my hand over Pam's head and pointed down with one finger as if to say it was Pam making it all possible. She acknowledged, with a smile and a slight nod of her head. There was no doubt in anyone's mind by this time that Pam and I were meant for each other. Funny how beautiful music brings out the best in people. We sang one beautiful Irish lullaby after another for the next forty-five minutes, finally ending up with "Danny Boy."

"With your kind permission, I would like to profess my love for this beautiful young princess, and I would like to do it with a song. Maestro, do you know, 'All the Way'?" He nodded that he did.

I reached over and pulled up a stool and had Pam sit on it. I then said, "Maestro, if you please."

The band started playing, and I began to sing to her:

> *If somebody loves you,*
> *it's no good unless he loves*
> *you all the way;*
> *through the good and lean years,*
> *and for all the inbetween years,*
> *come what may.*

She looked remarkably like a princess sitting there with the spotlight shimmering off the tiny little tiara on top of her beautiful light brown hair that was all done up to perfection. She looked radiant in her long white sleeveless gown, accented with pearls, matching earrings, and long white lace gloves. She was truly the picture of love and purity with her radiant smile, a testimony of love and affection for everyone to behold. She had already won my heart, and now she was captivating the hearts of everyone in the room.

I took her hand and knelt down on one knee and continued singing just to her, oblivious to the rest of the world.

> *Taller than the tallest tree is,*
> *that's how it's gotta be.*
> *Deeper than the deep blue sea is,*
> *that's how deep it goes,*
> *if it's really real.*

Tears of joy were streaming down her face by now. I got caught up in the emotion of the moment and could feel the tears running down my cheeks also. I kept right on singing and at the end I sang.

"So, if you let me love you,
it's for sure I'm gonna love you
all the way; all the way."

We both stood up, with the spotlight still trained on us. I said "I love you, Pamela Taylor." She smiled and said "And I love you, Irish Bryan O'Malley."

We embraced and shared a tender kiss.

You could have heard a pin drop in there as I returned the mike to the stand and Pam and I stepped off the stage and made our way back to our table. The crowd made a path for us with Mr. and Mrs. Taylor close behind.

No one applauded, for to do so would have been almost sacrilegious. Every eye in the room was on us as we sat down. Mr. and Mrs. Taylor stood behind us, with Mr. Taylor placing his hands on Pam's shoulders, and Mrs. Taylor placing her hands on mine. Although they never spoke a word, it was as if the Taylors were saying that they were giving us to each other and the world.

The looks we were getting were those of love and admiration —not those goldfish-in-a-bowl stares we had been encountering when the evening began.

To complement the mood of this scene, the band started playing a soft dance number. Slowly everyone started dancing and returning to their tables, and things were getting back to normal.

I excused myself and headed for the men's room. I had to go so bad I thought I was going to bust. I was washing my hands when Mr. Taylor came in smiling from ear to ear. "You're really something, Irish, do you know that?"

"Well, just so your daughter thinks so, Mr. Taylor."

"Oh, you can rest assured of that, Irish."

"Say, do you know what? In all the excitement, I forgot to give Pam her ring."

"Do you have it with you, Irish?"

"Yes, would you like to see it?"

I pulled it out and opened it up.

He commented that I had very good taste.

"Well, Mr. Taylor, I'm afraid I've been casting your money around like a drunken sailor today."

He started to laugh and said he had never heard it put quite that way before, but he was sure that, no matter what I had spent, it was perfectly all right.

"Well, it was quite a nick out of your bankroll."

He laughed some more and said "Don't worry about it."

"Altogether, I must have blown four grand."

"Is that all? What the hell is money for if not to enjoy?"

That was the first time I had ever heard him use a four-letter word. I wasn't sure he knew any until then. I gave him back his credit cards and asked him if he would return Carol's father's cards to him.

He said he would, but insisted I keep his for as long as I wanted. I declined, stating, "Where I'm going, I wouldn't need them." I offered him his five hundred dollars back. He refused, saying, "Not on your life."

About that time this stuffy looking character came through the door and said, "Well, this is the lucky young man, is it?"

I said, "Luck, is that what you call it?"

"What else could it be but luck, your catching George's daughter like that?"

"Did you ever hear of love?"

He laughed and said, "Luck, pure and simple luck."

Mr. Taylor was starting to get hot under the collar, so I figured I had better bring this conversation to a close in a hurry.

I said, "Well, you're lucky, too."

"Oh, how's that?"

"You can kiss my ass, and I can't."

I thought Mr. Taylor was going to bust a gut, he was laughing so hard. He kept going, "Oh, my God, that was a good one," and laughed some more. This other character concluded his business there and left without saying another word. Mr.

Taylor was still laughing hysterically. I finally said we had better rejoin the ladies so they wouldn't think we had got lost. He no sooner had sat down at the table than it hit him again, and he started laughing all over again. His wife cautioned him that everyone was watching him. He said, "Let them. I don't give a damn."

He finally regained his composure and told Pam and his wife how I had put old Roger down in the men's room.

We all sat there giggling when I said, "Oh, by the way, Pam, I have something for you." I reached in my pocket and pulled out the box with the ring and handed it to her. Her eyes lit up in surprise. And when she opened the box, she was speechless, for she hadn't expected a ring just then. I took it from her and placed it on her finger, leaned over and kissed her, saying, "All my love goes with it, darling." "Thank you, Irish."

Mr. Taylor proposed a toast, but instead of keeping it to our table, he stood up and quieted everyone down.

After he got the crowd quieted down, he said, "I propose a toast to my daughter and future son-in-law, and may they be blessed with ten children just like their mother and father." Everyone raised their glasses, and Mr. Taylor kept going, "Hip, Hip, Hooray. Hip, Hip, Hooray."

He finally settled down. Pam and her mother were astonished; they had never seen him act that way before. He was normally a very suave and sophisticated character. A real stuffed shirt, I gathered, from what Pam had told me of him. He was certainly letting his hair down tonight, though, and having the time of his life.

"Pam, we almost forgot their present. Let's go see if it's here yet." (The store was going to finish the engraving and deliver it to the club for us.)

"What is it?" they asked. "You'll know soon enough," we replied.

We went out to the desk in the lobby to ask if our package had arrived yet. We were in luck, for there it was. We rejoined her parents, and Pam presented them with the package. They opened it and were thrilled. We wished them a happy anniversary. They both said this would be the most memorable anniversary of their marriage.

By now Mr. Taylor was becoming inebriated from the champagne. He started wandering around the room, telling anyone who would listen how I had put Roger down in the men's room. Poor Roger could have crawled out under the door without opening it after the job Mr. Taylor did on him. You always knew where Mr. Taylor was—wherever the laughter was coming from. Pam and her mother couldn't get over the good time he was having. They commented they had never seen him laugh or enjoy himself more in his life.

"By the way, Irish Bryan O'Malley, where did you learn to sing like that?"

"Would you believe Sister Margaret was Irish and taught me to sing all those Irish songs? We would sit at the piano and sing together for hours on end."

"I kinda thought so. And where did you learn to waltz like that?"

"Sister Margaret, of course. You know, I believe now she must have had ESP and knew I was going to meet Pam and her wonderful parents one day, and so she prepared me for this special occasion. Of course, there are a few words in my vocabulary that I'm sure she wouldn't approve of, but I'm trying to eliminate them."

Pam laughed and said, "I would love to meet Sister Margaret someday, Irish. Do you think that would be possible?"

"Someday after I get back, we'll make a concerted effort to track her down. For I really would love to see her again and thank her for all she's done for me."

Pam leaned over and gave me a kiss on the cheek and said, "I love you, Irish."

"No more than I love you."

The party lasted long into the night, and we all hoped it wouldn't have to end; but end it did. Following all the fanfare, handshakes, and congratulations, we arrived back at the Taylors' house and were sitting in the living room.

Mrs. Taylor was still holding on to the serving tray we had

given them, trying to decide where she was going to hang it after she had a hanger made for it. "This is a perfect piece of memorabilia to commemorate the happiest night of our lives."

We recounted all the events of the preceding evening. Pam, her mother, and dad all agreed it was a night with memories they would cherish for the rest of their lives. I shared their sentiments exactly.

Pam's mother wanted to know if Pam had planned for me to sing the "Anniversary Song" for them.

"No, Mother, I was as surprised as anyone when he did. I didn't even know he could sing. He's so full of surprises."

"Well," I said, "you have all been so nice to me that I wanted to do something nice for you in return. It was just an impulsive notion I had."

"Mr. Taylor and I both want to thank you from the bottom of our hearts."

"Pam's the catalyst, remember."

"We'll always bless the day you two kids found each other." At that, they said good-night and looked like they were floating out of the room as they left Pam and me alone to savor the events of the preceding evening.

I held her hands in mine and said, "Just let me look into those beautiful eyes for a moment, darling; I don't ever want to forget how you look tonight. You're as majestic as a snow-capped mountain and as gentle as a flower in bloom. If I had it in my power, we would have no future or no past—only this very moment together for all eternity—with you opening passages of my mind that I never knew existed and filling my heart with sweet imagination, wondering if all your magic charm will engulf me into your mystic spell. Oh, Pam, listen to me carrying on. I don't even realize what I'm saying. I want to take all the beautiful phrases I've ever heard and recite them to you in their entirety tonight. I somehow want this last night we have together to be very, very special, for it will have to last for four long months. Now I know what Cinderella must have felt like coming home from the ball."

"No, Irish, you're the Prince Charming and I'm the Cinderella; but this is all real, darling. I feel more alive now than I ever have in my life. Oh, Irish, I wish it were four months from now and this were our wedding night."

"If it were, what would you do?"

"That's not a fair question, Irish, knowing how I feel about a more meaningful relationship and all."

"I know, sweetheart. There are a million things my heart wants to say, but my heart and I both agree there is no future without you in it. Perhaps we could just go to the moon tonight, and when I return you can take me to Jupiter and Mars."

We kicked our shoes off, and I helped her off with her tiara, jewelry, and gloves. We lay back on the couch and began to passionately caress one another. I inserted my tongue in her mouth and let it dart from corner to corner in quick bird-like motions. I loosened the zipper, letting her topless gown fall down. I began fondling her lily-white breasts in my hand. My lips were on hers and my hands started to gently explore her body. We almost forgot everything except the wonderful sensations we were experiencing when we suddenly came back to earth and realized that we had vowed to wait until we were married.

"Oh, Irish, I despise doing this to you. Are you sure you're all right, darling?"

"I'll be all right, Pam. I know it's just as hard on you, honey, but we'll be just fine." As hard as it was, somehow we found the strength not to go all the way.

I helped Pam compose herself and walked her to her room, kissed her good-night, wished her pleasant dreams, and returned to the guest room. I stood under a cold shower for twenty minutes. It didn't help much, and after much tossing and turning, I did manage to fall asleep.

I woke up about nine o'clock and went on downstairs where Mr. and Mrs. Taylor were having breakfast in the dining room. She saw me at the door and invited me in. I sat down while she told Maggie to bring me some coffee and fix me some breakfast. I asked them how they were feeling this morning. They both said they hadn't felt better in years.

"I wish I felt that way. I'm afraid I'm feeling a little blue this morning."

Mrs. Taylor said, "Yes, I know, Irish, and I'm so sorry for you and Pam. I know how you must feel having to leave and all."

"Well, that's the way the cookie crumbles, I guess."

Mr. Taylor asked me what my plans were for returning. I told him I would go over to Travis AFB, get my name on a flight list, and sit around and wait until I was called. "Then, it's back to Japan and on to Korea, I'm afraid."

"Would you be allowed to fly a commercial airline to Japan, at least?"

"I think so, just as long as I report back on time. I'm sure that is all they're interested in."

"Will you let me make arrangements to get you on a commercial flight?"

"Oh! I couldn't do that, Mr. Taylor."

"Nonsense, I'd love to do it." Mrs. Taylor added, "Why not, Irish? It will be our way of thanking you for singing the "Anniversary Song" for us last night."

"Heck, that was nothing, Mrs. Taylor."

"Oh, yes, it was to us, Irish. And remember it takes as much grace to receive as it does to give. So what do you say?"

"You know, Mrs. Taylor, I think you could talk me into standing on my head over in the corner, if you had a mind to."

"Then you'll accept. Good. Now, I must run along. I'll call you later and let you know what arrangements I was able to make."

I thanked him, and at that he was on his way, leaving Mrs. Taylor and me there to talk.

Maggie brought my breakfast in, and Mrs. Taylor and I were just chitchatting away until I finished.

"Don't you think you had better go wake Pam up, Irish?"

"No, ma'am, I don't."

She was a bit surprised and said she didn't quite know what I meant.

"Well, Mrs. Taylor, if I go to Pam in her room now, we might not make it downstairs for the remainder of the day."

She reached over and patted my arm saying she understood perfectly.

"We went to the moon last night, Mrs. Taylor, and I promised her Jupiter and Mars when I return and we are finally married."

"I know how you feel, Irish. I know it sounds like a broken record, but you kids won't be sorry. You had an example of how cruel people can be last night with my aunt."

"I know, Mrs. Taylor, and I want to thank you. I love you too much to ever betray you. I did make you a promise, and I intend to keep it."

"Thank you, Irish. I love you, too. Now, if you'll excuse me, I'll go wake our sleeping beauty."

"Thanks again, Mrs. Taylor." She smiled and left the room.

Maggie came in with more coffee and said, "I don't know what you drink, young man, but I sure would like to get some of it myself."

"My friends call me 'Irish,' Maggie. I would like you to be my friend. As for what I drink, would you believe it's love, Maggie —pure and simple?"

"All I know is I haven't seen so much sunshine in this house in the last ten years, and it didn't start shining until Miss Pam brought you home."

"Well, thank you, Maggie, you big flatterer, you."

She smiled and went on into the kitchen.

Pam and her mother returned shortly thereafter. I got up and gave Pam a great big good-morning kiss. I asked her if she slept well.

"It took me quite a while to fall asleep, but with all those beautiful dreams I was having, I didn't want to wake up."

"Would you care to share your dreams with your mother and me?"

"Perhaps. But one at a time, and in separate rooms." We all laughed.

Her mother told her I had consented to fly back to Japan on a commercial airline.

"That will make it a lot easier on you, won't it, Irish?"

"Anything that takes me away from you, darling, won't be easy."

She looked up at me with a tear in her eyes and said, "I know, Irish, and I feel the same as you do."

"Enough of this now, how about some breakfast?" She smiled, "All right, honey."

We managed to make it through the day taking care of the last-minute things like calling my mother and telling her of the engagement party and all.

I gave Pam all my money except for two hundred dollars and told her to open a savings account for us. I told her I would send her my back pay as soon as it caught up with me. "That will be our little nest egg to get us started when I come home."

We kept busy, hoping somehow the day would never end. But the inevitable happened, and there we were at the airport. Mr. and Mrs. Taylor came along to see me off. We were standing at the gate with the airplane about to take off. Mr. Taylor shook my hand and told me to take care of myself. I assured him I would. I gave Mrs. Taylor a big hug and a kiss and told her to look after Pam for me. She assured me she would.

Then the hardest part of all. It was time to say good-bye to Pam. I took her in my arms and held her so tightly that we two were almost one. I gave her a kiss and another squeeze. I suddenly jumped back and exclaimed, "Oops! I've busted both of them!" It took them a second or two to catch on. Then they all burst into laughter.

At that, I turned, ran through the gate and up the steps of the plane, turned and waved good-bye before going inside. They were all waving and smiling for all they were worth. I wanted to remember them that way. I was never very good at good-byes anyway.

The door closed and we taxied to the end of the runway. As the engines roared, the plane headed down the runway and finally lifted into the air. I could contain myself no more. I sat there with big tears running down my cheeks thinking to myself, "How can life be so cruel?"

I don't think I really regained my composure until we landed in Japan. I stepped off the plane, and the smell of Japan hit me in the face. I kept telling myself, "My God, tell me it isn't true."

True it was, and before long I was back in the hospital looking for the Doc.

11

Back to Korea

I was sitting in the Doc's office waiting for him to return, when this joker came walking through the door and sat down beside me. He said hello and quickly asked for a cigarette.

I gave him one. He then asked for a match. I asked him if he would like a kick in the lungs to get it started. Without cracking a smile he said, "Say, that's pretty good. Where did you hear that one?"

"I don't know."

"You new 'round here, buddy?" he asked.

"No, I've been here longer than I care to remember, and can't wait to get the hell out of here."

"I ain't never seen you 'round here before."

"Well, it's probably because you ain't been lookin', or we were lucky enough not to run into one another before."

"Are you waiting to see the Doc?"

"Fuck no, I was just looking for a place to jack off and saw an empty chair in here. What the hell do you think I'm doing in here?"

"Well, you don't have to get sour about it, buddy."

"Look, in the first place, I'm not your buddy, and in the

second place you're bugging the hell out of me, so why don't you just shut the fuck up and leave me alone?"

"Okay; okay! you sour ass. See if I ever talk to you again."

"Thanks, and I'll try not to lose any sleep over it."

I remember thinking to myself at that moment, "Yep, I'm back in the goddamned army."

The Doc came in and spotted me sitting there. "Hey Irish! Come on in. Where's Moose?"

We went on into his office and he closed the door. I told him Moose wasn't coming back and, of course, he wanted to know why. I told him Moose was dead. He said he was sorry to hear that. Naturally, he wanted to know what had happened, so I filled him in on all the details, as best I could. I guess he was really sorry to hear about old Moose, at least in his own way.

"Well, then, I guess there is no question that you'll want to stay on here as my clerk for the remainder of your enlistment?"

"No, no, Doc. I want to go back to Korea and finish my tour over there, so I can get back to the States."

"Why would you want to do that, Irish? I thought you hated Korea and all it represented."

"I do, Doc. But it's the quickest way back to the States."

"It's also the quickest way to get yourself killed."

"You wouldn't understand, Doc."

"Try me, Irish! I've got nothing but time.

"I want to get married, Doc."

"Funny, you never mentioned anything about a girl before."

"Well, there wasn't any girl before, Doc. It's someone I met in San Francisco our first night back there."

"That's kinda sudden, Irish. Are you sure she feels the same way?"

"I'm as sure of it as I have ever been of anything in my life."

"Perhaps you'll both feel differently about it in a coupla months. You know how it goes, Irish—out of sight, out of mind."

"Yes, I'm aware of the 'Dear John Club' and that possibly as many as eighty percent of all relationships break up when people are separated, especially those who are not married. The girls are back home running around, and the guys are over here shacking up, so who do you blame? But it's different with Pam and me. In just twenty-six short days we traveled thousands of miles together, back to Moose's funeral, and to see my mother and all. We have experienced things together that most people never get to experience in a lifetime. We are totally committed to one another for life. All I know is I must get back to her as soon as possible. If that means swimming back across the Pacific, then I'll have to swim."

"Aren't you making a bit too much of it all, Irish? Just because a little filly has you pussy-whipped, wouldn't it be better to give it more time? You know what I mean. All of us have a little fur burger stacked away somewhere."

"Doc, you had better change the direction this conversation is taking right now or I'm going to forget you're an officer and see how many bruise marks per square inch I can put on your head."

"I'm sorry, Irish! I was testing you. I just wanted to make sure how you felt about her. I see so many guys go on leave, come back full of hope, only to be sadly disillusioned later on."

"Well, you needn't worry about that in this case, Doc. We're totally committed to each other for life."

"So, Irish; now that we have established the ground rules, perhaps you would like to tell me about your newfound love."

"No, I wouldn't mind, Doc. She and her family are my favorite subject." I went on to tell him the whole story of how Moose and I had got in trouble on our first day back in the States and how we had wandered around and wound up in the nightclub where we had met Pam and Carol. I filled him in on all the good times we had before Moose and Carol got killed. I told him about both funerals, the stiff opposition her father had put up, the anniversary party, and our engagement announcement. I even told him how Mr. Taylor had arranged for me to return on a commercial airliner.

The Doc was flabbergasted and said, "I guess you have your future pretty well secured then, Irish."

"As far as Pam and I getting married, that's a foregone conclusion. But I still don't know what I'm going to do for a living."

"I'm sure your new father-in-law will find you a job."

"Not on your life, Doc. I have to do it my way, without any help from anyone."

"Suit yourself, Irish. But everyone needs help sometime or another in their life, and you shouldn't be on the defensive like that. You're a bright boy, and with a little help from the old man, you could wind up on top very quickly."

"No, I wouldn't want to be beholden to the old man like that. As long as Pam and I have each other, we'll make it just fine."

"I'm sure you will, Irish. I guess you've made your mind up, so I'll get you released from the hospital and sent to your headquarters for processing back over to Korea, if that is what you want."

"Yes, sir; that's what I want."

"Okay, Irish. I'm sure gonna miss you, and I sure was sorry to hear about Moose."

"Tell me something, Doc. Do you really mean that or are you just saying it?"

"No, I really mean it. Why do you ask?"

"Well, when Moose and I left here, you were trying to split us up. You know, break up the team, so to speak. I figured you didn't like Moose and that was why you were doing it."

"No, nothing is further from the truth, Irish. You and Moose were inseparable—a real good team. Under any circumstances other than the military, I would have had no objections to your friendship. But in the army, we are all supposed to be individuals and take orders independently of others or their feelings. You and Moose were not individuals as far as the military was concerned; it was a bad situation. One that could only lead to trouble for the military and you and Moose. That's the only reason I was trying to break up the team. Not because I didn't like Moose, but to save you both a lot of trouble later."

"Well, thanks, Doc. I guess the Good Lord took care of that situation himself, didn't he?"

"Yes, he did, Irish; and I'm truly sorry it turned out the way it did."

"Oh well, Doc, when the man rings your bell, you're a goner and there isn't a hell of a lot you can do about it, is there?"

"No, I'm afraid not. I'll have your orders for you in the morning, Irish. So you might as well check in here for the night and go get some chow."

"Yea, that sounds like a good idea, Doc. See you in the morning."

The next morning I checked out of the hospital, after saying good-bye to the Doc, and caught a cab back to our headquarters in Tokyo. I checked in there, and after much explaining and red tape, I finally convinced them that everything was on the up-and-up.

I was still in civies. They wanted to know where my government issue was. I explained I didn't have time to pack when I left Korea. I finally convinced them, filled out a few forms, and got an emergency issue of clothing.

It took about three days in all before I had all my processing completed and was on board another troop carrier on my way back to Korea. I couldn't help remembering the last time Moose and I had been on one of these "flying cheese crates" and what had happened. However, this time we made it to Korea without incident.

I caught a truck on its way to Seoul, bummed a ride, and before long had made contact with our liaison officer at Eighth Army Headquarters. He loaded me in a jeep and drove me back to my old outfit. It seemed that it took forever to get there. I guess they had moved several times since I was last with them.

We finally arrived and got onto the compound. I checked in at the orderly room. The old major was still there and looked at me like he was seeing a ghost. "Good Mother of Christ! Irish!"

"Yes, sir. In the flesh."

"We all thought you and Moose were dead. We couldn't get any word on you after your 'copter went down."

"Well, it's a long story, sir. I hardly know where to begin."

"Yeah, I imagine it is, Irish. So why don't you get settled in, then come on back over. We'll talk then."

"Thanks, Major."

At that I headed for the tent area, looking for an empty bunk. Most of the old guys were gone, either killed, wounded, or had rotated back to the States by now. I found an empty bunk and put all my gear away and went to the supply tent to get all the paraphernalia like blankets, sleeping bag, rifle, mosquito netting, helmet, and everything I would need to survive over there. I took all this shit back to the tent, got it all sorted out and in its proper place.

By now, some of the good old boys had heard that I was back and came in to welcome me. Of course, they all wanted to know what had happened to Moose. It was kinda hard to tell them that Moose had gone back to the States to get killed. With all the death and destruction around them, it was almost incomprehensible to think someone could go back to the States and get killed. You figured once you made it back to the States, you were home free.

After two hours of getting reacquainted with the old guys and meeting the new ones, I went back over to the orderly room to talk to the major. I told him the whole story from start to finish. He was as broken up over Moose's death as I was. It was like telling him his own son had been killed.

"Well, Irish, I would like you to continue as my company clerk, if you will. I won't ask you to go on any more courier runs. You've done enough already, and I would hate to see anything happen to you too."

"Thanks, Major. All I want to do is get my time in, so I can get back to Sacramento and marry the prettiest girl in the world."

"I understand, Irish. I'll see you in the morning."

I headed back to the tent area to get some sleep.

Things went along smoothly for the first six weeks. We were in a quiet zone with no enemy activity reported within fifty miles of our location.

Pam's letters started arriving after the first week and I would savor and hang onto every luscious word in them. In one of her letters she had included some newspaper clippings and pictures of the anniversary party. Seems we had made the society section of the Sacramento paper, and the writeup was something out of this world. They made me sound like a visiting dignitary or something. I never did show the pictures or the story to anyone except the major. I felt I wasn't up to the ribbing and the hassle that was sure to follow.

I was super straight and never ventured off post, except to drive the major into Seoul for a staff meeting occasionally. Other than that, it was work, work, work, and then laying in my bunk, either writing letters or reading and rereading Pam's letters.

All the old boys couldn't get over the change in me. They had remembered Moose and me and all the hell we would raise—the whiskey running and the whole bit. Things were different now. I'm sure if Moose had lived and planned to marry Carol, he would have been as straight as a judge himself.

I just kept myself going with the thought that my hitch couldn't last forever, and every day was getting closer to the day I could get the hell out of there for good.

I was with the major one morning when the orders came through for us to break camp and move north. It seemed the communications we were intercepting from the gooks were of little or no value. They wanted us to get closer to the action so we could listen better.

In less than twenty-four hours we had broken camp and were on our way north. I was driving the major, with the executive officer riding with us to read the map and tell us which way to go. We were to take up a position on a ridge about forty miles above the 38th Parallel.

We made the ridge, deployed our vehicles and radio vans, and had the antenna set up, tents and all. We were in business in less than forty-eight hours.

I had just settled down for the night and was sleeping like a baby when I was rudely awakened by a mortar shell going off next to our tent. I woke up looking at the stars. The tent was gone. Then another shell went off down the line.

I got up and ran like hell for the orderly tent, where I found the major and asked him what the hell was going on.

"Looks like they have zeroed in on us, Irish. We have to get the hell out of here."

"I'll get the jeep. I went out the door and found it and was waiting for the major to clean out the company safe. By now mortars were falling all around us. The major came on a dead run and gave the order to evacuate the area. We started pulling out with every vehicle we could move when they started hitting us with everything they had. We were flying down the road with shells exploding all around us. The radio truck directly behind us took a direct hit and blocked the road, trapping the other vehicles behind it.

Everyone abandoned their vehicles and started running for their lives. I drove about a half a mile down the road when the major had me stop. We waited for the others to catch up. In no time at all about fifty guys showed up. The major was trying to calm them down while I stayed on the radio, reporting our position and trying to get someone to come to our aid.

The major decided to march the survivors another three miles down the road and out of danger. As we were trying to regroup, the Marines showed up. We explained to them what had happened, and they took over from there and prepared a counter-attack. They moved out leaving us there.

We spent the rest of the night there. At daybreak the major and I took the jeep and went back up the road to survey the damage. When we got there it was enough to make you want to throw up. Dead bodies all over the place—maimed, mutilated or burned beyond recognition. We had lost two hundred and fifty men, all our equipment—gasoline and all. There was nothing left worth salvaging.

We had surveyed the scene for thirty minutes when the infantry appeared on the horizon. They took complete charge of the cleanup operation with the medics and corpsmen gathering pieces of bodies and putting them in rubber bags until they had one complete (you know, like two arms, two legs, one torso and one head). They would then seal it up and tag it, to be thrown on a truck that was driving around to pick up bodies for shipment to the morgue at the rear of the lines.

As the major and I were standing there, a corpsman came walking by with one of my buddy's head. He was carrying it by the hair like it was a mangy old dog or something. He opened a rubber bag not ten feet in front of us and threw it in. I threw up all over the ground. He walked back up to me and asked, "What's the matter, buddy? Were you afraid it was going to bite you or something?"

I saw stars and lashed out at that son of a bitch, hitting him in the face at least six times before he hit the ground. I jumped on him and must have hit him another two dozen times at least before the major could drag me off him. I really meant to kill him.

The major had my arms locked behind my back so I couldn't move. I was crying for all I was worth. He led me back to the jeep, held me there, and let me get it all out of my system before he would cut me loose. I finally settled down, and he loaded me up and drove us back to where the other survivors were waiting for us.

We proceeded to a signal outfit nearby to get rations and await further orders. Our order came through the next day. We were to catch the next convoy heading south for Seoul for reassignment to other groups.

The Major got a new command and took me along as his orderly. The rest of the outfit was scattered over a dozen other reconnaissance groups.

The major and I headed out for his new command, and arrived there a day and a half later. This outfit was in about the same situation as the one we had just left—sitting on a ridge. The first thing the major did was to have all the vehicles moved under cover and camouflage the tents and antennae as well as could be done under the circumstances.

The old company commander had been killed a week earlier, and these guys were not quite ready to accept a new one. They were even more standoffish to me because they looked on me as the major's fair-haired boy. I was not to be trusted, for fear I would tell the major what they really thought of him. I didn't much care what they thought of me. As far as I was concerned, I only had a little over two months left before I would be on my way back to the States and chances of ever seeing any of these guys again were remote.

I let it be known just how I felt, in no uncertain terms, and after a week or so, they came around and accepted me as one of the boys. They even grew to like the major; he was one hell of a guy, and there was nothing he wouldn't do for his men. He insisted on at least two hot meals a day for his men. And that was hard to do sometimes with the conditions we were operating under.

We were right in the middle of the rainy season and everything was just a sea of mud. It rained day and night for what seemed like weeks. You couldn't even walk without your boots sinking in the mud up to your ankles. The only consolation was that it was just as bad for the other side, so the action had hit a lull which didn't make me one damned bit mad.

We would sit around at night hovering close to our little pot-bellied oil heaters trying to keep warm and bullshitting the time away. You almost hated to crawl into your sleeping bag since it was cold and damp, and it would take forever to get warm enough to go to sleep.

There was one second lieutenant that I particularly disliked. He was a real ass from the word go. He received his commission from ROTC and he was spending his two years on active duty. His efficiency ratings were the poorest the major could possibly give him and his chances for making first lieutenant were about as good as mine were of becoming general of the army.

He and I had a running battle going on all the time. He talked like a sissy and acted like a fairy. A real prissy bastard and stupid as hell. I would get a kick out of setting him up for my little jokes, and he would go for them without fail. I would throw the line out and he would grab it hook, line, and sinker.

I remember one day in particular, he came bouncing into the orderly room and asked if the major was in.

"Who wants to know?"

"I do."

"What for?"

"Personal, personal."

"Try the chaplain. The major doesn't have time for your personal problems."

"Well, if you must know, smartass, my mother is getting married."

"It's about time, isn't it?"

"What's that supposed to mean?"

"Oh, nothing, it just confirms what some of the men have been saying about you."

"Are you suggesting that my mother had sex before marriage?"

"Don't take it so hard, Lieutenant. You don't buy a new pair of shoes without trying them on first, do you?"

"Irish, you're just lucky that I'm an officer and a gentleman and so even-tempered."

"Yes, Lieutenant, you are even-tempered all right—pissed off all the time".

"Irish, you smell."

"No, Lieutenant, I stink. You smell."

"If you don't let me in to see the major, Oh! Gee! Gosh! and Golly! Who should I call first?"

"Try your English teacher, Lieutenant."

I didn't think he had it in him, but he made an obscene street gesture to me and turned around. He found himself looking the major dead in the eyes, with his finger still up in the air and right under the major's nose. The major had been in his office listening to all this and had a grin on his face, as he said to the lieutenant "I hope that gesture is not intended for me."

"Oh, no, sir, no, sir. . . ." I interrupted him saying, "The lieutenant was just giving the victory sign with one finger. Right, Lieutenant?"

"Right, right, I was. . . ."

"Never mind, Lieutenant. Don't you have something better to do than hang around in here bothering my clerk?"

"Well, I wanted to see you, sir."

"What did Irish tell you?"

"He told me so many things that he has me confused. You know, Major, he suggested that I'm a bastard just because my mother is getting married."

The major laughed and said, "Well. . . ."

"Oh, forget it, I think I'll go see the chaplain."

I said, "Here, Lieutenant, would you like a card for the chaplain to punch?" He reached out and grabbed it out of my hand.

I don't know for sure, but he probably never read it and presented it to the chaplain. It was what we called a "T S Card" (Tough Shit). It read something like this:

> *Your story has touched my heart. Never before have I met anyone with more trouble than you. Please accept this token of my sincere sympathy.*
> *1 2 3 4 5 6 7 8 9*

Each visit (theoretically) you had the chaplain punch a number.

After he cleared the door, the major and I sat there and laughed for nearly five minutes. "That guy is something else, isn't he, Irish?"

"He sure is, Major. He's about as worthless as tits on a boar hog."

"I was talking to him the other day, Irish, and told him I didn't believe he could make a decision. That dumb bastard said, 'Well, Major, yes and no.' I've about given up on him. I told him he should stop acting like a fairy and start acting like a man. All he said was, 'Different strokes for different folks.'"

"Yeah, I know, Major. He just doesn't do things like normal people. The other day we saw him in the mess tent eating a banana sideways."

"What did he want in the first place, Irish?"

"Well, his mother is getting married, and I think he wanted to see if he could get leave to attend. I believe she wanted him for ringbearer."

The Major just shook his head, muttered "Good Mother of Christ," turned, and walked into his office.

I was sitting there typing away when I heard a commotion out by the main gate. I walked to the door and looked out. There was a Red Cross Commissary truck parked there with a mob of guys hanging around it, cussing and raising hell. It was raining like hell, so I grabbed my helmet and poncho and walked over.

When I got there it didn't take long to discover what the trouble was. The bastards were selling coffee and doughnuts for a dime apiece, cigarettes for two bits a pack, and so on. It really made my blood boil that they could do that and get away with it.

I commandeered a couple of guys and told them what I had in mind. "I'll get them off the truck and you herd them over to that shack and keep them there until I tell you to cut them loose."

I made my way through the crowd and walked to the truck and told them they had an urgent phone call and to hurry. Before they knew what was happening I herded them out the door into the arms of my coconspirators, who whisked them over to the shack and closed them up inside.

I then began to dispense the coffee and doughnuts myself, along with the cigarettes, razor blades, candy, stationery, cards —every last item on the truck. I even cleaned out the cash drawer, keeping the money for myself (for services rendered). After the truck was empty and the crowd disappeared, I nonchalantly walked back to the orderly room, and told my coconspirators to cut their captives loose.

They ran back to their truck and started raising all kinds of hell when they found out they had been robbed. They kept pleading with the guard at the gate to let them on the compound so that they could use the phone to call the MPs. He told them it was restricted, and no one was allowed on.

They finally gave up, and left. Two days later a captain from the provost marshall office showed up to make an investigation. The guard called from the main gate, and the major and I walked out to meet him. He had a million and one questions, but our story was the same. "This is a restricted area and no vehicle of any outfit—not even the Red Cross—was allowed on, so he must have the wrong outfit." He finally gave up and left in disgust.

It was so ridiculous and disgusting to begin with. Here are these guys standing in the pouring rain, cold, miserable, home-sick, and lonely, not to mention being six thousand miles away from home fighting a war. Then to have some son of a bitch pull up with hot coffee and doughnuts telling them if they didn't have a dime they couldn't have any. In my book, it was grounds for justifiable homicide. Charity, my ass!

As we were walking back to the orderly room the major said, "I don't suppose you want to tell me what really happened, do you, Irish?"

"Well, sir, I have to keep our motto in mind. We only dispense information to those who have a need to know. What you don't know you can't testify to, can you?"

He laughed and said, "Okay, Irish, okay. I get the message."

We hadn't been anywhere to hear any new jokes, so the old standbys would get tossed around a lot. Everybody knew them by heart they had heard them so often.

Someone would holler, "Into the woods, little girl." Someone else would pick right up on it and say, imitating a child's voice, "My mother won't like it." Then you'd hear, "Your mother ain't getting it."

Everyone would laugh, not because it was funny anymore, but because laughing was a way to break the monotony. They would keep it up for hours on end. Even the Civil War was forgotten, things were so depressing. You knew things were bad when you couldn't even get a rise out of a Rebel after insulting the South.

We were standing around our little heater trying to keep warm one evening when this guy came bursting into our tent with a newspaper under his arm, hollering, "Hey, Irish, you got your picture in the paper." (If you got newspapers they were always at least six weeks old. They were shipped third-class on boats and you would get about thirty at a time.) I thought to myself, "Oh, shit, the cat's out of the bag now." So I said "What paper?"

"The Sacramento paper right here."

Someone grabbed it off of him and started reading the story aloud. There it was. There was no getting out of it. Pictures of me dancing with Pam and Mrs. Taylor, of me singing to Pam, and a few overall shots of the party.

They could hardly believe this guy was reading about me. "Why didn't you tell us all this, Irish?"

"Well, you know, I figured you'd think I was just bullshitting you or something."

The guy who brought the paper in was from Sacramento, and although he didn't know Pam or her parents personally, he knew of them. I guess everyone in Sacramento knew of them; for they were the upper crust of society there.

This old boy was flabbergasted that I was engaged to the Taylors' daughter.

I said, "Well, you just can't stand in the way of true love now, can you?"

"You know, Irish. I knew from looking at you that you were more than you seemed to be on the surface. Do you come from money, too?"

"Fuck, no. If it would have cost a nickel to shit when I was growing up, I would have had to throw up. I'm just a poor boy."

"Well, how the hell did you ever get to know someone like Pam Taylor?"

"You know, my boyish charm and all."

"Yeah, yeah, you big bullshitter, you."

"Well, you asked me, didn't you?"

By now everyone was full of questions. I answered the ones I wanted to, while deferring the others until later and simply forgetting about them.

They said, "Holy Hell, a celebrity right in our midst and we didn't even know it. How about singing a few songs for us, Irish?"

"Fuck you guys. I only sing to pretty girls, and I'm afraid you ugly bastards don't fit the bill."

"What are you going to do with all your money, Irish?"

"What money?"

"I hear the old man is worth millions. In fact, I hear only Howard Hughes and J. Paul Getty have more than he does."

"What's that supposed to make me, left-handed or something?"

"Shit, that automatically makes you a millionaire; that's what it makes you."

"Not on your life. I wouldn't be beholden to the old man like that. I intend to make it on my own."

"Yeah, yeah, sure you will, Irish. He'll probably make you vice president of one of his corporations at a salary of one hundred grand a year, set you up in a new house, and the whole bit."

"You can all think what you want, but I know what I want and what I'm going to do."

"Are you going to get us all good jobs when we get out of here, Irish?"

"You fuckers can fend for yourselves. I didn't take any of you to raise as my own."

Some of them actually got pissed off at that remark. It was as if the seed of greed had been planted and was already beginning to fester and grow. As if I really owed it to them or something. People are really something else when they take a mind to be— greedy, overbearing and downright parasites. It was like a bunch of vultures standing around ready to swoop down on what they thought was my good fortune and play it for all they could get out of it.

I remember thinking to myself, "If these bastards act like this over the prospect of perhaps getting something from me, it's no wonder rich people are so damned standoffish. Everyone trying to pick their pockets and play them for all they're worth. Not because they like them or give a damn about them, but because they are looking for something for nothing. Crazy damned world," I thought.

Life wasn't the same for me after that day. Every SOB and his brother would seek me out and want to be my buddy. I would ask them where they were before they heard I might be worth something. Some of the answers would amaze me. "Well, hell, Irish, you've only been here a short while. I meant to look you up." Or they would say, "What's that supposed to mean—that I want something or something?"

"I don't know. You tell me."

Some were as bold as brass. "Well, I thought, since we're in this war together, perhaps after we get back to the States, you can introduce me to your father-in-law and maybe he'll take care of me like he's gonna take care of you."

I'd tell them I'd like to see them get ahead. I thought they could use one. I'd tell them to get the fuck away from me or I'd call them parasites. I could say almost anything I wanted to them and they wouldn't get discouraged. They would just keep plugging away.

About the only person I could hold a decent conversation with was the major. He was the only one who understood that Pam and I were just two people who met and fell in love. He'd say, "Fuck them guys, Irish. You don't owe them a damned thing."

Hell, I didn't even dare run out of cigarettes and ask someone for one. I would always get a bunch of shit to go with it. "Why don't you have your father-in-law send us over a few cartons?" or some such crap as that. If someone did give me one, he thought he was my asshole buddy and had the inside track to the old man and his money.

They say money talks. Well, I not only believed that, but also that it jumps right up and shouts. Even my mail wasn't sacred any longer. I would get a letter from Pam or her mother, and everyone would have a wisecrack to make. "Did they send you a check for a coupla grand, Irish? How about sharing your letter with us? we ain't never read a letter from a millionaire before. Do they talk like other people?"

I would always try to laugh it off, but it was really beginning to hurt. I was beginning to wonder, "If these bastards are like this over here, what's it going to be like when I get home and Pam and I are married? Will everyone be trying to get to the old man through me?" I really had some soul-searching to do.

As far as all these bastards were concerned, I figured in a few weeks I'd be gone and they would be out of my life forever, so I could put up with their bullshit for that long. As for when I got home, Pam and I would have to start our lives off someplace where we could be out from under the influence of the Taylor family. I never wrote and told Pam any of this, for I didn't want to worry her. I always tried to keep my letters to her as cheerful and happy as I possibly could. I would always include the number of days I had left.

Like I said, the major was the only one who understood that it was plain and simple love. You could have preached that until you were blue in the face and no one else would have ever believed it. This common bunch of bastards couldn't comprehend anything so pure and untainted.

We struggled on day after day until finally the rain let up and things started to dry out.

It wasn't long until the North Koreans, along with the Red Chinese, started a new offensive. We stayed right there in the thick of things with our radios intercepting everything they were broadcasting while the Marines, Aussies, British and others were going up and down the road like a bunch of yo-yos.

The roads were constantly filled with refugees carrying all their worldly possessions. It was really pitiful to witness, especially the children. Poor little bastards didn't even know what was going on, and they damned sure didn't start the war, but were suffering the most. You didn't dare invite them onto the compound for something to eat. If you did, you would have started a riot. People, when they're hungry, have no sense of logic, and it is impossible to reason with them. It was like they were out of their minds from hunger. All you could do was watch them go by and hope they made it to a refugee camp.

Even if they made it, conditions there were so subhuman that they would die by the hundreds. Life was so cheap; if they sensed someone was dying, they would stop feeding him, figuring it was a waste of food. Even the garbage we would throw out would cause bloody battles. They would go after it like a pack of wild dogs, clawing and scratching, and practically tearing each other apart just for a few scraps of food. It was so disgusting and bestial it is impossible to describe.

Things were not going too well for our side. We received orders to stand by and be ready to pull back. The major had all the rigs broken down and ready to travel on a moment's notice. We could tell it would not be long before we would have to hit the road from the waves of troops that were heading south. We finally got our orders to retreat. The major and I were standing on the ridge watching the hills beyond us with field glasses. The major got the convoy started and we were waiting for the last of it to get under way when we witnessed one of the most grotesque examples of disregard for human life that you could ever imagine.

What seemed like a half million Red Chinese soldiers came running over a hill about a mile and a half from our vantage point. The infantry had built miles and miles of barbed wire fences to try to stop them or at least slow their advance. But it didn't seem to bother them. The first ones to hit it would simply throw their bodies over the fences, and those who followed would run right over their backs.

Our artillery was throwing everything we had at them. Old boots, dirty socks, and what have you—but they still kept coming. The amazing thing to me was that only every other wave had rifles. The second wave would look for someone who had been killed or wounded, snatch his rifle, and keep on coming.

We had air support. They kept buzzing and strafing and dropping napalm on them, but still they came. It was so frightening to witness that when the major finally said, "Let's get the hell out of here." I looked down, and I noticed I had pissed all over myself.

We jumped in the jeep and headed south just as fast as that thing would go. There were our troops and allies lining both sides of the road in full retreat. It took no time at all to catch up with the convoys.

We were about five miles down the road when suddenly everything came to an abrupt halt. The major had me go around the columns to see what was holding things up. When we got there, we saw a truckload of ammunition on fire. The driver had already abandoned it for fear it would blow up. Couldn't blame him much for that, although it had to be removed or hundreds of lives and millions of dollars' worth of equipment were going to be lost.

I don't know where my mind was or why I did it, but I

jumped in the damned thing and got it started down the road as fast as I could. I came to a bridge. I figured if I could get the truck in the water the fire would go out. So I cut the wheel hard to the right and ran off what must have been a forty-foot cliff along the river.

I jumped, but not in time. I remember flying through the air right out over the cliff and hearing the truck blow up. Then everything went blank. The next thing I remembered was being in a field hospital somewhere in the southern part of Korea. I had jammed my spine and had a multitude of cuts and bruises. I lay there, not even able to move a muscle for a couple of weeks, I guess, and then I was evacuated to the big hospital in Japan.

All my cuts and bruises were healing nicely, but the fall had left me paralyzed from the waist down. They tried to tell me it was only temporary and that I would be able to walk again in time, but I was having none of it. I figured they were just telling me that to keep me from trying to commit suicide. I knew that I would never walk again, and what hurt even more was the fact that I no longer felt I was a man. I had become impotent, and in spite of all their reassurances that my potency would return and that I would be able to function normally, all went for naught. I knew in my heart and soul that paralysis and impotency were to be my fate for the rest of my life.

12

Recuperating at the Taylors'

I had already tried unsuccessfully to commit suicide on two occasions. My attempts had been foiled on both occasions by the doctors and nurses.

I hadn't written to Pam since I got hurt and I refused to read any of my mail, although there was at least one letter from her every day, sometimes two. There were also letters from her mother, and her father had even written six or more letters to me.

I never opened any of them, for I was trying to forget. I had illusions of being the strong one and breaking off with Pam. There was no way I could condemn her to a life of taking care of an invalid. I reasoned in my mind that everything was different now. Hell, I couldn't even take care of my own basic needs, like taking a bath. I knew Pam would never walk away from me regardless of what sacrifices had to be made or how difficult it might be to stay with me. I figured if I made them hate me, they would go away and leave me alone. That would give Pam another chance at happiness. Perhaps to find someone who could take her to Jupiter and Mars. I couldn't satisfy her most basic needs any longer.

It tore my heart out to see those letters sitting there, to remember all the wonderful times we had had together, and to think of all the beautiful plans we had made for the future. It felt as if someone had reached in and tore my heart out by the roots, leaving only a big empty cavity there. "Oh, God! Why didn't you let me die over there? I must have really done something bad in my life to be punished like this."

I reasoned, "Even though I'm being punished, there is no reason why I have to condemn Pam to a life of pain and misery also. The only answer is to break it off. And the first chance I get, I'll simply end my own life, for there is no earthly reason why I should go on living in my vegetated state."

"Oh, God! Why in all your mercy can't you let me die and spare all concerned this pain and agony?" I would pray. They say God always answers your prayers. But I'm afraid he was tuned out on me or at least was saying no every time I would ask him to let me die.

I was laying there under my blanket of self-pity, crying to myself and praying out loud for God to spare me the agony of living when I heard a familiar voice say, "Hi, Irish."

I pulled the blankets over my head. It was Mrs. Taylor, and I was too ashamed to let her see me like this. I desperately hoped she would go away and leave me to my own miserable self. But she didn't. She came over to the side of the bed, took my hand, and stood there in silence for what seemed like forever. Then she said, "You're going to have to come out from under there sooner or later, and I'm not leaving until you do."

"Oh, please, Mrs. Taylor. Go away and forget you ever heard of me."

"Oh, no, Irish! We'll never forget you. It's not fair that you should ask us to. You came into our lives and filled them with joy and happiness. We're not about to turn our backs on you now."

"It's me asking, Mrs. Taylor. I'm the one who is breaking it off. You good people have nothing to do with it. How the hell can I ask you to tolerate a hopeless cripple like me in your family? Most of all I have to give up on Pam. I'll never be able to face her again. Remember, I'm the guy who took her to the moon. Now, what am I supposed to tell her? 'Sorry, sweetheart, the moon is as far as we go. The trip to Jupiter and Mars has been called off.' What kind of a cruel hoax is that to play on someone as sweet and lovely as she? I'm sorry, Mrs. Taylor. All bets are off, and you all can pull your money out of the pot, as far as I'm concerned."

"Are you quite through, Irish?"

"There is nothing more to say, Mrs. Taylor."

"Well, you listen to me, young man. You're making me mad. We've got you covered for life. And just because you crapped out this time, you'll get another roll of the dice, as soon as they come around again. Sure, it's a bum rap you got, but it's not the end of the world. I'm not going to let you get away with it. If you can tell me you no longer love Pam and that you never want to see her again, then I'll let you alone and go away. Then and only then will I let you wallow and drown in this pool of self-pity you have created for yourself. Do you still love Pam?"

"What the hell kind of a damned fool question is that to ask?"

"It's the kind of a question this damned fool deserves an answer to. One that you're going to answer, Irish O'Malley. Now you're making me mad."

I was shocked. I had never heard Mrs. Taylor talk like that. I had never even heard her raise her voice before, and I told her so. "Oh, Mrs. Taylor, please don't talk like that. It's not becoming you. I never heard you talk like that before."

"Well, then, answer my question, Irish, or you're going to hear a lot more."

"Okay, okay, Mrs. Taylor. Of course, I still love Pam. I could never stop loving her. Why do you think I have to break it off? I love her too much to ask her to spend her life taking care of a helpless cripple."

"Goddamn it, Irish; you're not a helpless cripple. The doctor said your condition is fifty percent physical and fifty percent mental. With the proper care in the right atmosphere, you can walk again."

"That's just fine, Mrs. Taylor. But did he also tell you I'm no longer a man? I'm just an it now."

"Damn you, Irish, you stop that. Time will take care of that situation also. Now you just have to give it time. As you regain the use of your lower limbs and the circulation gets back to normal, then your treasured manhood will come back. If you think that getting your rocks off is all there is to marriage or that is as far as love goes, then you're not the man I thought you were. Where is the guy who sang that pretty love song to my daughter and made her cry?"

"How did it go, Irish? *'All the way.'*

Deeper than the deep blue sea is;
that's how deep it goes,
if it's really real.

Are you trying to tell me you didn't mean it?"

"Of course I meant it, Mrs. Taylor, every damned word of it. Without Pam there is no life for me. That still is no reason why I should ruin her life. I love her too much to even consider asking her to go on with me."

"All right, Irish, I'm going to see just what the hell you're made of. I have Pam here with me and I'm going to bring her in here. If you can tell her to her face that you no longer love her; that you want her to go away and leave you alone; then, and only then, will I take her back home and try to mend her broken heart for her. For that is exactly what you're doing, tearing it up in little pieces and throwing it back in her face."

"Oh, please, Mrs. Taylor, don't bring Pam in here. I can't face her."

"What are you, a coward?" At that, she went to the door and asked Pam to come in.

I was still hiding under the covers when I felt Pam's warm hands come under the sheets and caress my face. She said, "I love you, Irish, and we've come to take you home."

I could contain myself no more and was sobbing my heart out. All the defense barriers I had built up had suddenly fallen and all my defense mechanisms failed to work. There I lay, completely at their mercy.

Mrs. Taylor was on the other side of the bed. They both took hold of the covers and gently pulled them out of my hands, exposing my face.

I looked up and saw Pam's radiant face with those big tears streaming down. I could contain myself no more. I reached for her and hugged her for all I was worth. We kept that posture for five minutes or better just sobbing our hearts out. There was no more question as to whether or not we were going to spend the rest of our lives together; it was a foregone conclusion.

We finally regained our composure after that tearful reunion. I reached over and took Mrs. Taylor's hand and pulled both Pam and her mother to me. I gave them both a big hug and asked, "Do you know what this reminds me of?"

"What?"

"Remember the day I slid down your banister and landed on my fanny? You both came running over to see if I was all right." We all started laughing.

"I have a feeling everything is going to be all right from now on, don't you?"

"Are you really sure that I have a chance to walk again, Mrs. Taylor?"

"Yes, Irish. And even if there were no chance, we would still be here. But we have every reason in the world to believe you will walk. I couldn't be so cruel as to build up false hope in you, Irish! I love you enough to tell you the truth."

"Look, I'm sorry I made such an ass out of myself . . . I mean hinny."

Pam laughed and said, "Irish, I still have my pepper can, and I'm going to pepper your tongue."

"My tongue! Wow! You should hear your mother cuss!" and I laughed.

Mrs. Taylor said, "You're just lucky I didn't lose my temper, or you would have really heard some cussing."

Pam was a bit surprised herself. "Mother cussed at you?"

"She sure did, but I've never been cussed at by anyone so lovely in all my life. I don't think we'll have to pepper her tongue, do you?"

"No, Irish, I don't. She's a pretty nice mommy."

We had talked and reminisced for a long time, and then Mr. Taylor walked into the room. I guess I had a quizzical look on my face, for he was really the last person on earth I expected to see there. I guess it showed, for my voice must have raised five octaves as I exclaimed, "Mr. Taylor! What in the world are you doing here?"

"The ladies want to bring you home, and I came along to help them."

"Home! You must be kidding!"

Pam said, "You weren't listening, Irish. I told you we have come to take you home. I have your orders right here in my hand. We're taking you back to Sacramento to recuperate in our home."

"I can't believe it. Pinch me to prove I'm not dreaming."

Pam and her mother pinched me on either arm.

"Ouch!"

"It's true, Irish. The army is through fooling around with you and they have given us a shot at you."

"Do you really mean it? I mean, really? I can't believe it. How? Why would you want to?"

"We all love you, Irish, and want to help you get better."

"Oh, Pam, with you by my side, how can I miss?"

Mrs. Taylor said, "We intend to see that you don't, Irish. Now, enough of this. George, see if the nurse is in the hall. We want to get started for home as soon as possible."

I lay there with all the fight gone out of me. It would have done no good to protest anyway. I wanted to be with Pam so badly that I would have consented to cut my right arm off.

"Well, Mrs. Taylor, you taught me that I have to be as gracious in receiving as giving, so how can I refuse?"

"You can't, Irish. You just relax and we'll have you back home in no time."

"How will I ever be able to repay you for all your kindness?"

"When we see you take your first step, that will be payment enough for all of us. Right, Pam?" "Right, mother."

"Pam, this is some lady you have for a mother. But there is just one thing I want to know."

"What could that be, Irish?"

"Where did you learn all that crap game jargon and all those streetwise phrases you were throwing at me a while ago?"

"Well, Irish, it was you who pointed out to Mr. Taylor, when you two were talking about how perceptive Pam was, that when you love someone, you get to know all there is to know about him. So I anticipated you. I read a few books and picked up a few phrases and the latest sayings, so that I could come back at you in your own lingo and make you understand that we love you and want to take you home with us."

"Well, I'll be darned."

"You mean, damned, don't you, Irish?"

"Ssh, Mrs. Taylor, Pam still has her pepper can, and we wouldn't want her to use it, would we?"

The nurses and the doctor came in. While the nurses got me out of bed and onto a stretcher, the doctor filled Mrs. Taylor in on my medication, the type of therapy I would need, and gave her my medical records. Pam packed all my personal gear, and the next thing you knew there we were at the airport with me being loaded aboard a plane.

I don't remember much of the trip home. They had me pretty well sedated. That was a good thing, because I was feeling so good that I probably would have wanted to fly the plane myself. I was full of joy and eager anticipation at how things were going to turn out.

The next thing I knew I was in the Taylor's house, all propped up in a hospital bed with all the latest trappings and gadgets. They had even hired a special nurse to live in and care for me. I remember everyone gathered around the bed. I felt like it was all a dream and told them so.

Mr. Taylor, who hadn't been saying much up to this point,

assured me that it was all real and that if I would be gracious enough to let them handle things and do what the doctor ordered, they would see to it that I walked again.

I gave him my solemn vow that I would do nothing to hamper or delay the day when I could walk down the aisle and make Pam my wife. "I'm completely at your mercy; but I don't know how I'll ever be able to repay you."

"Well, like the ladies told you, Irish, your walking again will be payment enough for us all."

"You know, you're all too good to be true. I intend to prove your faith in me has not been misplaced."

Mrs. Taylor said, "We're sure it hasn't been, Irish. Now, enough of this. It's time to get down to this business of making you better."

Mr. Taylor went to the door and showed two doctors in. They came over to the bed and introduced themselves.

I was surprised. They knew more about me and my condition than I did myself. They reassured me that the paralysis was temporary and could be cured with therapy. What they prescribed was massages every two hours and daily whirlpool baths. They instructed Pam and her mother in massage techniques that they felt would be most beneficial. They told me they would be dropping in daily to see me and, most important, they reminded me not to worry.

Mr. and Mrs. Taylor saw them to the door, leaving only Pam, the nurse, and me in there. Pam leaned over the bed and asked me if I was happy to be home.

I assured her that I was ecstatic. I apologized for making her life so miserable and promised to make it up to her as soon as I could. I told her I was sure nothing would stand in our way now and that all I had to do was get over this paralysis and then we could get our lives moving again.

Pam's mother came back into the room smiling from ear to ear. "You certainly look happy tonight, Mrs. Taylor." She assured me that she was and told me I had restored the sunshine in her life.

"Oh, come on, Mrs. Taylor. You're embarrassing me again."

"Why, Irish, I didn't think anyone could do that. But enough of this now. We have work to do so we can get Irish out of this bed. Who knows, he may get to like it if we pamper him too much, and then he won't want to get up."

"Oh, don't worry about that, you two. I'm committed to getting up and walking. I promise I'll do whatever you want me to do in order to speed the day I can walk again."

"Good! Pam, get the covers on the other side of the bed and let's get on with Irish's therapy."

Before I knew what was happening, they had the covers off me and began massaging my legs and hips. My face must have turned beet red. Pam looked up at me and said, "Why, Irish, you're blushing." I covered my face with my hands to hide my embarrassment.

Mrs. Taylor said, "Now, Irish, you promised." I was speechless.

"Well, we finally found a way to shut him up," laughed Mrs. Taylor as she put a towel over my face and said, "Go ahead and be as embarrassed as you like, Irish. We won't pay any attention to you. Besides that, I think your embarrassment is very becoming. Don't you agree, Pam?"

"Yes, I do, mother." They both laughed at me.

They kept up the massage for about a half hour and then covered my legs up again. Mrs. Taylor took the towel from my face. She and Pam were grinning from ear to ear.

"You're still blushing, Irish."

"Yeah, now I know what an ostrich feels like with his head buried in the sand. Anyone could come up behind him and kick him in the rear and he would never know what hit him."

"Well, you had better get used to it, Irish. We're going to keep up these massages for as long as it takes to get you better." Mrs. Taylor added, "If you think this is bad, wait 'til we get you in the whirlpool in the morning."

I reached out for their hands and told them, "God has been too good to me, giving me you two to look after me. I have never felt so safe and secure in my life, and I promise you this: I'll beat this rap and make you all proud of me."

Mrs. Taylor leaned over and kissed me on the cheek and said, "Of that, there was never any doubt. Now, I'll leave you two alone; I'm sure you have a lot of things to catch up on."

"Thanks, Mrs. Taylor. You're really too good to be true."

She smiled and said, "Don't forget the whirlpool in the morning."

"I'll try to remember, Mrs. Taylor."

Pam leaned over the bed and I held her for all I was worth. I could feel the tears of joy in my eyes as she lay down beside me and began feverishly kissing me, saying, "Oh, Irish, you'll never know how happy you've made me by coming home with us. I'm just sorry we didn't come for you sooner, but we had no word for such a long time and all."

"Shh! I know now just how wrong I really was, honey. I'll never forgive myself for any heartache I caused you or your parents. I accused your dad of being proud and vain, but I'm the one who almost let my pride and vanity destroy myself and those who love me. I know now how hard it was for your father to say he was wrong that night in the game room. Now I find myself in the same position. I was just as wrong as two left shoes, Pam, and I'm truly sorry."

"Now, you hush up, Irish. Mother and I understand pride is a fierce thing in a man, and we don't think any less of you for it. In fact, this little setback you're experiencing now will only serve to bring us all closer. Perhaps God planned it this way to make us realize just how much we have to depend on each other."

"I know, Pam. 'I cried because I had no shoes, until I met a man who had no feet.'"

I kissed her again and told her I only prayed I could walk again and be the man to take her to Jupiter and Mars.

She smiled and comforted me, "The trip to the moon was quite sufficient for now, and I am sure the trip to Jupiter and Mars is in the stars for us."

We lay there for the longest time enjoying the pleasure of each other's company. Suddenly Pam had a really somber expression on her face.

I asked her what was troubling her. She told me she had some bad news for me but didn't know how to go about telling me. I reassured her nothing could be that bad, but I was wrong again.

She told me my mother had died eight weeks ago. She started to cry, "Oh, Irish, I didn't know how to tell you! Please forgive me for not telling you sooner."

I was stunned by the news, but I quickly came back to reality and said "Pam, please don't cry. I'm sure Mother wouldn't have wanted you to. True, hearing of Mother's death is the saddest news I have ever received, but we can't let it stop us cold like this, Pam. My mother wanted nothing more in this world than to see us together and happy. She wouldn't want us saddened by her departure. I'm truly sorry I wasn't with her when she died and didn't get to attend her funeral, but we both know the Lord works in strange ways. Although I have no reason why he planned it this way, I'm sure it was his will, and we'll have to be brave and accept it."

"Thank you, Irish."

Although I was grieving and wanted to cry, I managed to contain myself, if only for Pam's benefit.

There was a knock on the door. Pam got up and went over and opened it.

It was Maggie with a tray of coffee and cakes. She set them down on a table next to the bed and greeted me, "Welcome home, Mr. Irish."

"Where did you get that 'Mr.' stuff from, Maggie? I'm just Irish."

She smiled and said, "You a lot more than Irish. This sure was a sad old house after you left. Now that you're back, it's a happy house again."

"Why, Maggie, I didn't think you cared."

We all laughed. Maggie let me know that if there was anything I needed I should just ring the bell.

"As long as I have Miss Pam here, Maggie, I won't need another thing in this whole wide world."

Maggie laughed and said, "I'll see you two later."

"Where did you get this 'Miss Pam' business from?"

"I think it's cute. Yeah, I like it. I think I'll call you that from now on."

"Don't you dare, Irish, or I'll call you 'Mister Irish.' "

"Okay, okay, you win, Pam, love of my life, my precious little baby doll."

She smiled her loving smile at me. I knew all was right with the world.

"Tell me, Pam, how did Mother die?"

She went on to tell me that my aunt had called her one evening and told her that my mother was gravely ill. "She wanted to know if we knew how to get in touch with you. We called the Red Cross. That's when we found out you had been wounded and were in a hospital in Korea. We managed to get through with the help of the Red Cross. But your condition was so grave that they felt the news of your mother's condition would be more than you could handle. Therefore, they advised against letting you know at that time."

"Mother and I flew to Pennsylvania and were with her before she died. She spoke of you and wanted to know if you were coming. We were at a loss for words to tell her. She seemed to sense the situation and told us it was perfectly all right. She was glad we were there and said to tell you that she apologized for not being able to give you a better start in life."

"I assured her, and so did Mother, that she gave you a better start in life than most children and should be very proud of you. She told us she was very proud of you. She wished us all the happiness in the world, and said she would be waiting for us in heaven. Mother and I were both with her when she passed on, Irish. She suffered very little and was very much at peace with the world."

"Yes, that sounds like Mother. Did she have a nice funeral, Pam?"

"Yes, she did, Irish. She really had a lot of friends."

"I'm glad. I'm truly sorry that I couldn't be there but will be eternally grateful to you and your mother for going back there and being with her when she died."

"It was the least we could do, Irish. Although I had only met her once, I loved her so very much. Mother said she never met a more gracious lady in all her life."

"Thanks, Pam. I'll always be grateful to you and your mother."

"Say, by the way, there was someone at your mother's funeral who was very interested in you and how you're doing."

"Who was that?"

"Remember Sister Margaret?"

"Do I ever! Was she there?" I was so excited to hear her name.

"Yes, she was. Mother and I spent one whole afternoon with her. She is every bit as lovely and loving as your description of her to us. Wait a minute, Irish. Mother has something I want to show you." She left the room and returned shortly with her mother.

Mrs. Taylor had a sad look on her face. "Look, Irish. I'm awfully sorry about your mother and that we didn't tell you sooner."

"Please, Mrs. Taylor, don't be sorry. I understand. Like I was telling Pam, I will always be grateful to you for doing what you did for her."

"Thank you, Irish. We were only too glad to do it."

"Say, Pam tells me you met Sister Margaret there."

She was smiling now. "Yes, we did, Irish. And look what she gave to Pam." She opened an envelope and pulled out a picture of a little choirboy dressed up in a cassock and surplice with a big red bow tie. He was standing on a pulpit in a church. It looked as if he was singing, for his mouth was wide open.

"Who in the world could this be?"

"Why Irish, that's you!"

"Me? I never laid eyes on this kid before in my life."

"Yes, you have, every time you look in a mirror. When you were in third grade at midnight mass you sang, 'Oh, Little Town of Bethlehem.' Do you remember now?"

"Well, I'll be darned. I had forgotten all about that."

"She told us all about it—and a lot more about you."

"Oh boy! Here we go. All good, I'm sure."

"Remember this?"

She opened the envelope again exposing the prettiest golden locks of hair you ever laid your eyes on.

"Who do they belong to?"

"Those are your golden locks, Irish. Remember the haircut Sister Margaret gave you that Christmas Eve?"

"Yes, I remember."

"Well, she said she didn't have the heart to throw those precious golden locks of yours away."

"Dear sweet Sister Margaret. I was really unkind to her putting up such a fuss when she had to leave. I'm sure she didn't want to go anymore than I wanted her to."

"She told us about that day, Irish. She told us it was the saddest day of her life and the hardest thing she ever had to do. Leaving you alone like that to your own devices almost broke her heart."

"Oh, how I wish I could see her again and tell her how sorry I am for doing that to her."

"You will, Irish. We have her address. You can write to her if you like and after you're all better, we'll go see her."

"I'd like that. I really would."

"She really did love you, Irish. She told us all about that Christmas Eve and she had tears in her eyes as she was recalling it. She had your mother drop you off at the convent about ten o'clock that evening. She and several of the other nuns got you ready for your solo number at midnight mass. She said you were so little it was almost unbelievable. They bought you a new pair of shoes and gave you a haircut. They got you all dressed up in your cassock and Surplice that one of the ladies in the parish had made specially for you. One of the nuns had made a little halo out of foil and when they topped it all off with that big red bow tie, you really resembled a little angel."

"You went stomping around the halls of the convent showing all the nuns your new shoes and telling them you were going to sing at midnight mass for Sister Margaret. All the nuns simply loved you. When the time came, they took you behind the altar and told you to watch for their signal from the first pew. When you got it, you were supposed to go up on the pulpit, wait for the organist to start, and then sing your song just like you had rehearsed it. Everything went just perfectly. You went up on the pulpit, climbed up on your stool, and started to sing right on cue."

"The lights of the church were all down. With the light from the candles on the altar as a backdrop, you looked exactly like a little angel up there singing 'Oh, Little Town of Bethlehem' in your beautiful Irish tenor voice. Sister Margaret told us that you had a little ham in you anyway, and by the time you were finished, there wasn't a dry eye in the church."

"You were so anxious to win her approval that instead of going back behind the altar when you finished, you came running across the sanctuary, opened the altar railing gate, scampered over to the pew where she was sitting, and crawled past four other nuns on the kneelers just to get to her. She moved down to make room for you. You were not to be denied. You crawled up on the seat, sat down beside her and looked her straight in the eyes, and asked, right out loud, 'Did I do good, Sister Margaret?' Everyone in the church simply went, 'Ahh!' Even Father Currey stopped saying mass; he turned and smiled his approval from the altar. She put her finger to her lips to caution you to be quiet and whispered, 'You did just fine.' At that, you stood straight up on the seat, threw your arms around her, and gave her a big hug and a kiss. You had won the hearts of the whole congregation by now and everyone thought you were the most adorable little boy."

"You settled down and snuggled into her side and fell fast asleep. After mass you were still sleeping. She didn't have the heart to wake you, so she picked you up in her arms and carried you out of church. When she got outside, everyone was crowding around to get a look at you. You were so precious sleeping there in her arms. It almost broke her heart to hand you back to your mother. If she could have, she would have taken you back to the convent and kept you."

"Well, subconsciously, I was probably afraid she wouldn't invite me back to the convent for supper anymore if I didn't do a good job for her."

"Sure you were, Irish."

Pam went on to tell me about the gifts I would bring to her daily. Some were rather unusual, like half a baked-bean sandwich, a can of sardines, or perhaps half a cookie. "She said you had something for her every day without fail. It got to be a ritual, and the other nuns would always ask her, 'Well, what did Irish have for you today?' They would really get a kick out of it."

"I'll bet they wouldn't have thought it was so cute if they had known I was swiping most of the goodies I would bring to her. I would always stop in the little corner grocery store on the way to school and pick up something for her. Of course, I didn't have any money to pay for it and could justify it in my own mind by saying as long as it was for Sister Margaret it was perfectly all right. Except for the cookies; I had another way of getting them without stealing them. I would stand outside the bakery with my hands and nose pressed against the glass until this lady that worked there would spot me. She would always put a big sugar cookie in a little brown bag and hand it to me out the door. That posed a new problem to me, though. I sure loved Sister Margaret; but I loved those cookies also. I would always compromise, break the cookie in half, eat half and give the other half to Sister Margaret. That way I could satisfy both loves."

"Irish, you really must have been a character when you were growing up."

"Well, it was just that my sense of values was a little out of kilter. Father Currey got me straightened out in sixth grade, though. I remember that my brother and I had been swiping a few boards from the railroad for this old man who ran the apartment building we were living in. He would use them for kindling wood to start his fires in the old coal boiler that heated the place. Anyway, I told Father Currey about it in the confessional, and when it came time to hand out the penance he asked me if I knew how to make a novena. I didn't know it was a series of prayers and visits to the church made over several days. I told him no, but if he could get the plans, my brother and I could get him the lumber. He refused to grant my absolution that day and told me to go sit in the church because he wanted to talk to me after he was through hearing confessions. Needless to say, he pointed out the errors of my ways and got me started on the path of righteousness."

"Irish, you're too much. You really didn't tell him that, did you?"

"Yes, I'm afraid I did. I was just being honest with him."

After they stopped laughing at me they went on with Sister Margaret's dramatic recollection of my youth.

"She told us how the other kids would always pick on you and how quick you were to retaliate. She would always hate to punish you, for nine times out of ten, it wasn't you who started the trouble. She would smack your hands with a ruler, and it truly hurt her more than it did you. You would stick your little hand out there and before she could even hit you, you would get big tears in your eyes and say to her, 'I know it's not your fault, Sister Margaret; I know I was a bad boy and you have to punish me.' Instead of hitting you, she would want to take you in her arms and squeeze you."

"Well, Sister Margaret could do no wrong in my book. Besides that, I was just trying to con her so she wouldn't hit me so hard."

"Sure you were, Irish."

"She told Pam and me that she prays for you every day, and she knew in her heart and soul that you would turn out to be a fine man someday. She said it would have been easy for you to turn astray with all the corruption and bad influences you had around you, but you were so eager to learn and always sensed that there was a better life, a life that held far more than you were ever accustomed to."

"It was just like you told us, Irish. She told us she always tried to prepare you for the finer things in life. That's why she taught you to play the piano and sing. She and the other nuns would teach you your table manners and not permit you to eat with the wrong spoon or fork."

"Ah, they were just trying to make a big sissy out of me. That's all they were doing."

"Well, if that's what they were doing, I'm glad I found that sissy and fell in love with him."

"Well, if that's what it took, then I'm happy about it too."

My thoughts began drifting back to my mother and her funeral and of Pam and her mother being there.

"Tell me, honey, how did my aunt know to call you?"

"Well, I had been writing to your mother before she died. I suppose your mother told her about me."

"You sweet, adorable, precious baby doll, you. That was the kindest thing you could have done, writing to her like that. I'll always be grateful and bless the day I found you. I'm sure your letters meant more to her than anything else on this earth. I guess that's why I love you so much. You always know the right thing to do."

Then I panicked. "You didn't tell Sister Margaret that I got myself all messed up like this, did you? I mean, I wouldn't want her worrying about me and all, you know. She always worried about me anyway."

"We simply told her you were in the hospital and would fully recover in time."

"Oh, that's good. I wouldn't want her to worry."

Mrs. Taylor said, "Well, Irish, that is something we have no control over. People will worry in spite of everything."

"I know, Mrs. Taylor. And say, I really do want to apologize for the bad time I gave you in the hospital. That's not the first time you had to step in and keep me from making a serious mistake. When I think of how depressed I was less than forty-eight hours ago; well, I can hardly believe it. I sincerely hope I didn't hurt your feelings, Mrs. Taylor."

"Oh, come on now, Irish, that's ancient history. But if you want to know the truth, you were no match for me."

"Oh! You think not?"

"That's right! I couldn't lose. I had the ultimate weapon with me."

"I know." I reached for Pam's hand. "I guess I'm just a big pussycat at heart anyway."

Pam and her mother both agreed. Pam looked at her watch and saw what time it was. "It's time to embarrass Irish again."

"Oh, no!"

Pam, raising her voice a little, "Irish, you promised."

"Yes, I know. I know. Can I have my towel back again?"

"Sure, you can, Irish," said Mrs. Taylor, as she playfully threw it over my face.

The nurse who had been hovering around the room all evening joined them by the bed. They rolled me over on my stomach and while the nurse rubbed lotion on my back, Pam and her mother massaged my legs.

I peeked out from under my towel and spotted a picture of the Mona Lisa hanging across the room. For want of something better to say, I asked, "That's the Mona Lisa hanging over there, isn't it?"

"Yes, it is."

"You know, they finally discovered why she was smiling like that."

"Why was that?"

"She found out she wasn't pregnant."

They all broke up laughing. Pam said, "I had to ask, didn't I?"

The nurse said, "Now I know why you folks went so far to bring this character home. He's really something, isn't he?"

Pam and her mother both agreed.

"Well, they're just prejudiced, Helen," I told the nurse.

"Now, Irish, you behave yourself, or I'll get a ruler and smack your hands like Sister Margaret would do."

I held my hand out and said, "Go ahead, Mrs. Taylor. It's not your fault; I know I was a bad boy."

They all laughed.

I asked them if they knew how long it would be before I regained the use of my legs and hips. They assured me it would take no time at all.

"Good, then I can get out of bed tomorrow, right?"

"Don't rush things, Irish. If you'll behave yourself, we are going to try to get you into the wheelchair in the morning and down to the whirlpool for a couple of hours there. It's going to take time, so you just be patient, okay?"

"I'm completely at your mercy and, I must confess, it's a good feeling."

"We're glad you feel that way, Irish. With a little patience and a little time, you'll be as good as new."

After they finished my massage they rolled me back over and

tucked me in. It was truly a joyous occasion. We sat there until the wee small hours of the morning reminiscing the past and planning the future. It must have been two o'clock in the morning when Mrs. Taylor finally said good-night. Pam stayed with me all night, choosing to sleep in a big recliner next to the bed.

She was so precious sleeping there. I could hardly believe someone so adorable was in love with me and would one day be my wife. I remember thinking to myself, "This is the stuff that memories are made of."

I finally drifted off to sleep and slept until ten o'clock the next morning. When I opened my eyes, there were Pam and her mother hovering over me like a couple of mother hens.

I greeted them. "Good-morning, everyone! Isn't it a beautiful morning to be alive?"

They agreed that it was, and it was about time I woke up. "How about some breakfast, you old sleepyhead, you?"

"You talked me into it."

Mrs. Taylor went to the door and called Maggie while Pam leaned over the bed and gave me a good-morning kiss.

"I love you, sweetheart." She smiled. "I love you too, honey."

Presently Maggie made the scene with a tray of food fit for a king. Pam and her mother got me all propped up; then Maggie set the tray in front of me. Everything was so delicious. I simply devoured everything on the tray.

"How do you feel now, Irish?"

"Like I could whip the world, Mrs. Taylor."

"Good! We'll give you a few minutes to settle your breakfast. Then we'll get you out of that bed."

"You're the boss; anything you say goes."

"Look what I have for you, Irish," said Pam, holding up a pair of kelly green swim trunks.

"Are we going back to the beach today?"

"Well, not just yet; but it won't be long before we go back again."

"I want to go back to the exact same spot where I first kissed you and then walk to the place where I first told you I was in love with you."

"I would like that, Irish."

Mrs. Taylor said to Helen, "Well, will you listen to these romantics? Someone who didn't know you two would swear you've been married for fifty years."

"We will be married for fifty years someday. We'll have dual rocking chairs and fifty grandchildren running all around."

"Well, first things first, Irish. What do you say we get you into these swim trunks and down to the whirlpool first?"

"Okay; I'm sure I don't have any options anyway."

"You're right, Irish; you're completely at our mercy. And if you give us any trouble, it's "duke city" for you."

"There she goes again with that street jargon," I observed. Then Pam chimed in with, "Do you want a fat lip, Irish?"

"You too?"

"That's right; now let's get these trunks on." So, on went the trunks.

Helen brought the wheelchair over. Pam held the chair while Helen and Mrs. Taylor slid me around and got me under either arm and stood me up. Pam pushed the wheelchair up behind me and they sat me in it.

I didn't realize until then how weak I really was or how much weight I had lost. Christ, I was like a toothpick. I could hardly hold myself up in the wheelchair. Everytime I would ease my grip I would start to fall forward and have to catch myself. Mrs. Taylor asked me if I was all right. I explained my dilemma to her, so the nurse got a sheet and put it around my chest and tied it to the chair. That sure made it a lot easier, but just that little bit of effort had me exhausted.

We made it to the indoor pool. Mr. Taylor had one end of it converted into a whirlpool. I must say it certainly looked inviting. They managed to get me out of the wheelchair and into the water. I was clinging to the side of the pool and it really felt great.

We were joking and laughing. I didn't realize it, but I couldn't hold on any longer and slipped under the water. I was immediately joined in the pool by the nurse, Pam, and her mother. They got me up and were asking me if I was all right.

231

"Sure, I slipped so you all would jump in and get all wet."

We stood there laughing so hard like a bunch of nuts that they forgot themselves and let go of me. I immediately sank to the bottom again. They got hold of me and stood me up again. After we stopped laughing, they decided they had better come up with a better plan so that I didn't drown. Pam jumped out and got a straight-back chair and put it in the water. They sat me on it and stood there holding me up.

Mrs. Taylor sent Pam for some towels and robes. I asked Mrs. Taylor if she was enjoying her whirlpool bath. "Never had more fun in my life, Irish."

I apologized to her and the nurse, saying I was sorry they had to get all wet. At that, Mrs. Taylor reached down, took off one of her shoes, and emptied the water out of it over my head, saying, "Irish, we only planned on baptizing you today; but it looks like you baptized us also."

The nurse added, "This is the most unusual assignment I've been on in a long time."

I assured her, "Things will get better."

"Well, I'm sure you'll get better, Irish," Mrs. Taylor said, "but as for me, I'm having the time of my life. I can't tell anyone about it. Who would believe me? I hardly believe it myself. I think I'll bring my swimsuit tomorrow."

Pam returned with the towels and robes. She had changed into her swimsuit. She came over and jumped right in the water and began splashing water in our faces, daring us to try to catch her.

I told the ladies that I would hold on to the pool and they should try to catch her and dunk her head under the water. I grabbed the side of the pool and they went after her. By the time they turned around, I had lost my grip and was back under the water.

They got me up again and decided, "We had better stop fooling around before we drown poor Irish."

"If I do drown, I can't think of a better way to go, surrounded by all this warmth and beauty."

We carried on like that for the better part of two hours before they finally dragged me out of the pool, placed me back in the wheelchair, and returned me to my room.

They dried me off and got me back into bed. I was really exhausted by now and hungry as a horse.

Mrs. Taylor and Helen went to change clothes while Pam and I talked. I drifted off to sleep as I was gazing into her beautiful eyes.

When I woke there was Pam, her mother, and Maggie with lunch.

"Hi! Ready for lunch, sleepyhead?"

"You talked me into it."

"She didn't have to twist your arm too hard, though, did she?"

"Not at all. As a matter of fact, I'm starved." I reached for the bar hanging down from the ceiling and tried to pull myself up, but I was still too weak.

"I'm glad you found that bar, Irish. By the end of the week we'll expect you to be doing at least ten pull-ups before each meal."

"Oh, yeah? And if I won't?"

"You will," said Mrs. Taylor, "or we'll get Maggie here to cut out the chow."

"I'll do twenty, if that's what it takes."

"Good! Now, Pam, let's get this goldbrick propped up so we can fatten him up."

"I swear you two must have gone through basic training the way you are throwing all those military terms around."

"Never mind, Irish. You just clean up your plate or we'll put you on KP for a month."

"You don't have to tell me twice." I dug in and ate everything in sight.

After lunch the doctor showed up again and gave me a thorough examination and supervised Pam and her mother while they gave me a massage, pointing out the most effective methods to maximize the results. After they were through, I asked him point-blank if there really was a chance for complete recovery.

He told me to put my mind at ease, there was nothing to worry about. He went on to say that we should be getting some positive results in a week or so. He also pointed out that the more I cooperated, the quicker I would recover.

He suggested I receive thirty-minute massages every two hours, around the clock, to stimulate the circulation and build up muscle tone. I objected, saying, "That's asking a lot of these lovely ladies now, isn't it?"

Pam and her mother both jumped on me, saying that they would be the judge of what was too much for them, and they ordered me to be quiet and pay attention.

"Okay, okay; I'm sorry. It's just that I feel I should be able to do more for myself."

"As you get better, you'll be expected to do more. In fact, I am eventually going to insist on it. You have some painful days ahead. As the feeling starts coming back and you start using your legs, the pain is going to be excruciating. I just hope you'll be up to it, Irish."

"I'll have to be, Doc. Otherwise, I'm afraid they'll beat the daylights out of me."

"That's right, Irish; I'll get Mother and Helen to hold you, and I'll beat you up."

"See there, Doc. What choice do I have?"

"None that I can see. You know, there is one thing here in your file that doesn't make much sense to me."

"What could that be, Doc?"

"It says here that you are supposed to be severely depressed. But from my observations, you are anything but depressed. Quite frankly, from the picture they have painted of you here in this report, I thought we really had a challenge on our hands. With your attitude now, I can only be optimistic for a speedy recovery."

"Well, you know how those service people exaggerate, Doc," I thought about it for a second and then said "No, I'm afraid it's all true. As for my attitude now, all you have to do is look around the room to see what brought about the change of attitude. This lovely little lady and her beautiful parents came all the way to Japan to bring me home because they love me. Well, I'm on top of the world now, Doc. I'll have to admit I was very depressed because I thought I had walked my last steps and had become impotent. I simply lost my will to live. They came to my rescue and brought me back to my senses. They made me realize that life was really worth living after all. I'll never be able to repay them for all they are doing for me; but I'll always love them and be grateful to them. I'm totally committed to doing whatever they say so that I can get out of this bed and make them proud of me."

"Well, Irish, you're a lucky man. I can tell you that love and understanding will do more to get you up than all the medicine in the world."

"I know, Doc. And don't you agree with me, they are the most beautiful ladies you ever laid eyes on?"

"I agree, Irish. In a way, I envy you. You wouldn't consider changing places with me, would you?"

"Not on your life, Doc. I may have been depressed; but I don't think anyone has ever accused me of being out of my mind."

"You'll do just fine, Irish. Now, I must be running along. I'll look in on you tomorrow."

Mrs. Taylor saw him to the door and returned directly.

"Do you know what, Mrs. Taylor? I feel like crying, I'm so happy."

"You go right ahead, Irish, and we'll cry with you, if you like."

Just then I could feel a big tear running down my cheek. Mrs. Taylor took my hand and assured me, "All is right with the world today, so why don't you get some rest? Pam and I will be back before you have a chance to wake up."

"Well, if you promise."

Pam gave me another kiss and said, "We promise."

They left the room. I closed my eyes and was fast asleep before I knew it. When I woke up, there they were, just like they had promised.

"Ready for dinner, Irish?"

"You bet, I am, Mrs. Taylor. My cup runneth over."

"Well, don't fill it so full next time, Irish," Pam retorted.

I laughed, "That's pretty good, Pam. Where did you hear that?"

"It just seemed to fit so I threw it in. I guess I've been around you too long."

"Not long enough, sweetheart. If I have anything to say about it, you'll never get away. I'm hooked on you for life."

"I feel the same way, Irish. Now get hold of that bar so we can get you propped up."

I reached for the bar and struggled and did manage to pull myself up about halfway. They came to my aid. "Very good, Irish; but you'll have to do better tomorrow morning."

"You slave drivers, you. It looks like my get-up-and-go-got-up-and-went."

"Oh, yeah! Well, we know where it went and how to get it back. So eat up, Irish, or I'll hold your nose and have mother shovel it in."

"Hold it! Hold it! I'll behave myself. Just give me a little slack."

"What will you give us if we do?"

"I'll do two chin-ups in the morning. How will that be?"

"It's a deal, Irish."

I again ate everything in sight and was having a second cup of coffee when Mr. Taylor came into the room.

"Good evening, Irish. How are you doing?"

"Couldn't be better, Mr. Taylor. I hope to be up and around in no time at all."

"Are the ladies taking good care of you?"

"No man has ever had more love and attention than I'm getting, Mr. Taylor. They're spoiling me rotten."

"Okay, Irish; I guess we'll have to start getting rough on you."

"I was just kidding. I didn't mean it. Really, I didn't."

"Just for that we want four chin-ups in the morning instead of two."

"Okay, okay, I'll behave."

Pam and her mother excused themselves to take the tray back to the kitchen, leaving Mr. Taylor and me there to talk.

13

Irish and Mr. Taylor Reach a Meeting of Minds

Mr. Taylor pulled up a chair and sat down.

"I'm glad we have this chance to talk, Mr. Taylor. I have a much better understanding of things now that I've had a lot of time to think things out."

"You know, even before we met for the first time, I knew we were on a collision course; but I really didn't understand why. All I knew was that there was a gap between us wider than the Grand Canyon."

I related to him the treatment given me by my so-called buddies after the guy from Sacramento showed up with the newspaper account of the anniversary party. I told him it was like someone had planted the seed of greed in them and they acted like a bunch of parasites. I told him that I now understood the position he took a lot better and could understand why there had been the gap between us.

"I know now just how bad it really must have looked on the surface. Here was your beautiful young daughter coming home with some guy she met in a nightclub, a soldier to boot. Everyone knows what a reputation they have, deserved or not. Then to find out he was a high school dropout with a questionable

237

background and without even a prospect of a job when he did get out of the service. All that stacked up against Pam's background, her family, education, the whole bit. There was really no other conclusion you could have come to. I was just a gold digger trying to worm my way into your daughter's heart to get at your fortunes. I could almost see myself sitting in your chair at the dinner table saying everything you said to me."

"There was no way you could have known how unhappy Pam was in the world you had created for her. She realized that you had knocked yourself out trying to make her happy, and we both know she is much too kind to ever throw it back in your face. There was no way you could have known that Pam had kept her family and background from me until after we had fallen deeply in love. She was so afraid of being rejected as a poor little rich girl just out looking for kicks that she kept it from me as long as she could. That showed a lot of character on her part, I believe. She wanted so desperately to find someone who loved her just for being herself and not for all the frills that go with being rich that she took the chance of jeopardizing our relationship by keeping it a secret. It was just like I told you, Mr. Taylor; I fell in love with your daughter the first night we were out together. She is the most warm, affectionate, loving human being on this earth, as far as I'm concerned."

"As for me, I told her everything there was to know—all the good and the bad. I wanted her to hear it all from me, and hope against hope she would return my love, in spite of it all. She did, Mr. Taylor, and we couldn't love each other more if we tried. As for our wanting to get married back east, Mr. Taylor; well, I want you to understand that it was not a power play. I know it's a hell of a thing to talk to a girl's father about, but I'm sure you'll understand. Pam and I were both going through a tragic time in our lives with Moose and Carol being killed. We were so in love and both felt at that time we needed all the love and affection we could muster for one another. I had vowed to let Pam enter marriage as a virgin, and we both felt the only way we could fulfill our need for each other was to be married back east and spend the last few days of my leave as a honeymoon.

We both wanted it more than anything on this earth. But by the same token, neither one of us wanted to hurt you or Mrs. Taylor."

"Believe it or not, Mr. Taylor, parents are very high up on the priority list with both Pam and me. Of course, my parents are both gone now, but I love them just the same. That's why we called you before going through with it. In retrospect I guess we both wanted you to say no and used you for a way out of our predicament. I must say, Mrs. Taylor came through with flying colors. She really is something special, isn't she, Mr. Taylor?"

"Yes, she is, Irish."

"I could no more have denied her her dream of Pam's wedding than I could fly to the moon. I just wanted you to know our motives, that's all."

"I understand, Irish; and I'm sincere when I say that I have never been so wrong about anyone in my life as I was about you and your intentions. I especially want to apologize again for the bad time I gave you at the dinner table that night."

"Oh, no, Mr. Taylor; there is no apology warranted. That was the best thing that could have ever happened. It gave us both a chance to get things out in the open where we could look at them and put them in their proper perspective. Who knows, if we hadn't had our little chat that night and you had kept quiet about all your doubts and suspicions, hell, we might have gone through life hating each other. I think it gave us all a firm foundation to build on. We got down to bedrock, so to speak."

"You know, Irish, you're something else yourself. You have an exceptionally analytic mind and you're definitely a deep thinker. Any guy so considerate as to take the time and put forth the effort to understand someone else's position, as you have, has to be all right in my book; and I'm sure you're just what the Good Lord ordered for my daughter's happiness. I agree with my wife, that you two were born to be with each other."

"Thank you, Mr. Taylor. As your lovely daughter put it, it was not our intention to prove you wrong. It was our intention to let you down as gently as possible while trying to let you know just how much we loved and needed each other. Pam really loves you, Mr. Taylor, as much as any daughter ever loved her father."

"Well, now, that really makes my life worthwhile, Irish."

"There is just one thing though, Mr. Taylor. If my so-called buddies treated me the way they did merely because of the prospects of my marrying your daughter, it must really be rough on you. Quite frankly, I don't know how you can possibly cope with it. You never know who your friends are and always have to wonder what ulterior motive they have for being nice to you. I've about come to the conclusion that Pam and I are going to have to start our lives off somewhere by ourselves so that we don't have to put up with such nonsense as that."

"It's going to be kind of hard on you kids to get a start, Irish. People will seek you out no matter where you go. There is one fact in life, Irish, that you might as well know right now. If you have a dollar, there are eight people lying awake at night dreaming up ways to get it away from you. As for friends, Irish, I'm sure you'll have no trouble there. I'm sure you can spot a phony a mile away. And even if you can't, it doesn't take people long to let their true intentions be known."

"There is nothing wrong with being wealthy, having and enjoying the finer things in life. It's when you become obsessed with them, like I was, that you get into trouble with those you love. Wealth begins to destroy you and all you hold near and dear to you. And you were kind enough to point this out to me. I guess the secret lies somewhere between both worlds. It is elusive, and unfortunately, hardly anyone ever finds it. I'm sure you could find it, Irish, with your intelligence and grasp of human nature. There is no doubt in my mind you could be both the wealthiest and the happiest man on earth if you wanted to."

"Well, I thank you for saying that, Mr. Taylor; but I firmly believe that happiness is not a place or material possessions; happiness is a state of mind. I believe that people get into trouble when they try to equate happiness with possessions. I guess if you were to pursue that line of thought to an ultimate conclusion, you would find that the only way to be perfectly happy is to own absolutely nothing. What Pam and I are looking for is going to be difficult to find—a place where we can be both comfortable and happy, without going to either extreme. Anyway, that's what we're going to pursue. I'm going to do my damnedest to be a good husband to Pam and a son-in-law you and Mrs. Taylor can be proud of."

"I'm sure you will, Irish. Do you have any plans as to what you'll be doing after you get out of the service?"

"Not really, Mr. Taylor. I'll have the GI Bill and a chance to go to college if I want; but nothing is settled yet."

"You'll do all right, no matter what you choose to do. I'm sure of that."

"Look, Irish, I hate to leave such good company, but I have to attend a meeting this evening. I'll be looking in on you from time to time."

"Thanks, Mr. Taylor. I'll be looking forward to it. Now, if you'll allow me this one observation before you leave."

"Go ahead, Irish."

"Well, when I first laid eyes on this beautiful house and your lovely flower gardens, the manicured green, green grass, and the trees lining the driveway at perfect intervals, I was really impressed. In fact, I said to myself, "Just think what God could have done with the world if he would have had this guy's money."

He laughed and said, "You're all right, Irish. Now, I must go. I'll be talking to you later."

"Just one more thing before you go, Mr. Taylor. I really want to thank you for all you've done for me. I really do appreciate it."

"Oh, Irish; there is no credit due me. My wife and daughter are the ones responsible for bringing you home. They were on that phone day and night, cutting through miles and miles of red tape, and making all the arrangements. So if there is any credit due, it goes to them and not to me."

"I know better, Mr. Taylor. They would not have been able to pull it off without your help, and I'm grateful."

"Well, thanks, Irish," he said while reaching for my hand. We shook hands and at that he departed.

Shortly after that Helen came in and asked me if I needed anything. "Yes, I do. I need to get out of this bed and start walking again."

"Patience, Irish; you have to be patient."

"I know, Helen. It's rather difficult. I have so much to do, and I can't get anything done lying here like this."

"With all the help you're getting, Irish, you'll be up in no time at all. So just settle down, will you? You know, Irish, I've worked around a lot of people in my time. But I don't believe I've ever worked around two people as much in love as you and Pam. You two just seem to radiate love and affection whenever you're in the same room. It's really a pleasure to work around you two. I'm sure you'll be happy together for the rest of your lives."

"Thanks, Helen. Pam's the girl I've waited for all my life, and I couldn't love her more if I tried."

"She feels the same about you, Irish. They hired me a week before you came home and have had me living in ever since. They had me teach them all there was to know about taking care of a bed patient. All the dos and don'ts, right down to giving a back rub. You were all they talked about. Quite frankly, from their description of you, I felt I already knew you when you arrived. In fact, the whole household was so anxious to get you back here—even the maids and Maggie—that I got caught up in the emotions of the situation. I could hardly wait to greet you myself."

"They really are special people, aren't they, Helen?"

"Yes, they are. They certainly love and think the world of you."

"It's a mutual admiration society, because I certainly love them with all my heart. Say, I do want to apologize for getting you all wet this morning, Helen."

"Forget it, Irish. It was fun. Like I told you this morning, I really enjoyed myself. I'm sure on any other job, if that would have happened, I would have been fired on the spot."

"For what? It certainly wasn't your fault."

"Yes, it was. I should have realized you were too weak to hold on like I expected you to do."

242

"Shoot, I really enjoyed myself. That was the most fun I've had since before I went back overseas. I'm glad I slipped. I wouldn't have had it any other way."

"Thanks, Irish."

"I'm sure you'll never forget me. After all, it's not many of your patients who try to drown you, is it?"

She laughed and said, "No, Irish, you're the first one. But you did give us a fright for a moment."

"Well, it was worth it just to see you all standing there in the pool with me, laughing your heads off."

"Yes, I guess it was."

Pam and her mother walked through the door with Mrs. Taylor saying, "Guess what time it is, Irish?"

"Is it Howdy Doody time?"

"It's time for your massage; so let's get on with it."

"Can I have a kiss first?"

"Well, I don't know. What do you think, Helen?"

"I think he deserves one."

"Okay then." Pam leaned over the bed and put her arms around me and kissed me passionately.

"Do you suppose we could get rid of these other two, and just you and I will sit here and talk?"

"Not on your life, Irish. You're just trying to con me, aren't you?"

"Well, it was just a shot in the dark."

Off came the covers and they proceeded with the massage.

"Mrs. Taylor?"

"Yes, Irish."

"You forgot my towel."

She laughed and gave me my towel saying, "I thought you'd be over that by now, Irish."

"What can I say, Mrs. Taylor?"

"You can say anything you like, Irish."

"How about if I say, thanks for bringing me home and being so good to me."

"You're welcome, Irish. Now we want to try something new. We are going to start working your legs, so you let us know if you feel anything."

"I sure will, Mrs. Taylor."

They got my feet and started pushing on them, forcing my knees and hips to bend.

"I can feel it pulling in the upper part of my back, but not in my hips or legs."

"Okay, we'll keep working them for a while. I would imagine they would be stiff by now from not being used and when you start walking, we don't want you to have to build them up, so we'll try to keep them limbered up for you."

"You're the boss, Mrs. Taylor. And Helen and Pam are the enforcers so whatever you say goes. Seriously though, you're not going to take that doctor at his word and keep this up around the clock, are you?"

"Yes, we are. Why do you ask?"

"Well, I'd hate to see you interrupt your sleep just for this."

"Don't worry about it. Between Helen, Pam, and myself, we'll take turns at night, and it won't be that hard on anyone. Right, girls?"

"Right, Mrs. Taylor."

"Right, Mother."

"Why are you worrying about things like that, Irish? You should be worrying about how you're going to be able to do those four pull-ups in the morning."

"Oh! You remembered, did you?"

"Yes, we did, and we're going to hold you to them."

"In that case, I'll have to do them, won't I?"

"You sure will, Irish."

14

Pam and Irish Bare Their Souls

After they finished my massage, Mrs. Taylor and Helen left the room, leaving Pam and me alone at least.

She lay down beside me. I caressed her beautiful face in my hands and began kissing her. I told her I was on cloud nine and still climbing, and that I loved her more than life itself. I asked her to hold me and never let me go. "I truly feel like a stranger in paradise, no more hunger or thirst—you are my angel and lover, my heaven and my earth."

She held me ever so tightly and there was no reason to question the love in her heart. "I'm the stranger in paradise, Irish; I never knew love could be this wonderful. I'm way past cloud nine and still climbing."

"Oh, Pam, how could I have been so foolish and hurt you the way I did? I must have taken leave of my senses."

"Hush, Irish, I don't want to talk about it. Remember, let the dead past bury its dead. I know you never stopped loving me, and I know what your reasons were. I only love you more for being so thoughtful. Remember, I once told you that one of the reasons I loved you so much was because you are always putting other people's feelings ahead of your own. We're in this together now, and we'll work it out; just you wait and see."

"I'm sure we will, darling. Kiss me and tell me you love me, for I still have trouble believing someone as wonderful as you could be in love with me."

"Believe it, Irish. As far as I'm concerned, you are my origin, my nature, and most definitely my destiny. I love you with every fiber of my being. If it were possible to love you more, I would; but I don't know how."

"You know, Pam, I'm not ashamed to tell you that when I got back to Korea I would cry myself to sleep at night because I wanted to be with you so badly. I never felt so lost or lonely in my life. All that kept me going was the thought of coming home to you. If it hadn't been for your letters, I'm sure I would have gone out of my mind. Then when I was dumb enough to get myself messed up like this, I just knew it was the end of the world for me. I loved you so much. And I was so ashamed of becoming impotent that I didn't know what to do. I knew I couldn't disappoint you, honey. I felt so badly at how things turned out that I simply wanted to die."

"Oh, Irish, you don't have to tell me all this. I understand, and I can tell you now that I also cried myself to sleep at night, praying to God to find a solution to our problems. I feel God has answered our prayers, and we have the solution in hand."

"I'm sure you're right, darling, and I'll always bless the day I found you. Hold me and take me to the moon."

I began to feverishly kiss her, and run my fingers through her beautiful hair. I could feel a churning in my stomach, the likes of which I had never experienced before. It was a tingling churning sensation, and the closer I held her, the greater the sensations would become.

"I told Pam about it and she began to massage my abdomen.

"Do you think it's coming back?"

"I know it is, Irish. You'll be as good as new in no time at all."

"Kiss me, darling. I'm so overjoyed; I want to squeeze you to pieces."

As our lips met, I whispered in her ear that I felt like I was a man again.

"You were always all the man I ever wanted, Irish."

"Thank you, darling; I'll love you always."

We held each other tightly until it was time for another massage.

Helen and Mrs. Taylor showed up right on time. They rolled me over on my back and started right in.

Should I tell them, Irish, or do you want me to?"

"Tell us what?" inquired Mrs. Taylor.

"Give me my towel back and you can tell them, honey."

Pam draped the towel over my head and told them my manhood was coming back.

They greeted the news with a loud cheer. "Good for you, Irish."

"Shh! Someone will hear you. Besides that, you're embarrassing me again."

"Poor Irish, you're right. We'll keep it to ourselves, if you promise to give us a kiss when we're through here."

"It's a deal."

After they were through, I paid them all with a big kiss. Mrs. Taylor pinched my cheek and said, "I told you, didn't I?"

"Yes, you did, you dear, sweet precious lady, you."

"Well, Helen, should we take our leave and let these young folks get back to themselves again?"

"I don't know if we should, Mrs. Taylor. Why don't we stay in here and torment them?"

I stuck my lower lip out and pouted. "I'll give you both another kiss if you promise to leave."

"How can we refuse?"

So I kissed them and they departed, promising to return again in two hours.

"Well, we may not be here. As much progress as I'm making, we might jump out the window and elope tonight."

"If you do, be sure to call us, so we won't worry."

"Oh, we might."

"Now then, what were we doing before we were interrupted?"

"Come over here; I can show you much better than I can tell you."

She lay down and snuggled close to me. We began to reminisce.

"You know, honey, I'll never know where I got the courage to ask you to dance that first night we met. In the first place, I had never rock and rolled before; and in the second place, I was so afraid of being turned down that I almost chickened out. Old Moose and I were so lonely and wanted to meet some nice girls so badly that I guess we would have moved heaven and earth if we thought it would help. I'll have to remember to thank that waitress for tipping us off as to your presence there."

"How did she do that, Irish?"

"We explained our dilemma to her. She told us there were two very lovely young ladies at the table over by the door who were unattached and suggested we ask you to dance. Poor Moose couldn't dance a step, and I only knew how to waltz; but something told me to give it a go and see what happened. I was so scared when approaching your table that my stomach was full of butterflies. It was all I could do to ask you, and when you said, 'Sure, why not?' I just knew I was going to faint."

"Oh, Irish, how sweet."

"The plan was that I would ask you to dance and then invite you both back to our table. Moose had so much faith in me and just knew there wasn't anything I couldn't do if I put my mind to it. But even he had his doubts as to whether or not I could pull this off. Needless to say, when you and Carol agreed to join us, you really made me a hero in Moose's eyes. I really appreciated that, for I did owe Moose my life."

"Well, Irish, I'll tell you something. Carol and I spotted you and Moose when you first walked in. It was like magic or something. Carol said she sure would like to get to know the big guy, and I said I thought the little one was simply dreamy. We both hoped you two would ask us to dance but figured we didn't have a chance of meeting you two. We had also talked to the waitress and asked her if she could steer you two over to our table. She said to leave it to her. I guess she felt like a real cupid."

"I think it was fate, our meeting like that, don't you, Pam?"

"I guess so, Irish. I still think about Carol and Moose an awful lot. You know what I mean? Do you suppose we could have had a double wedding if they had lived?"

"Perhaps, honey; I would have like that." "I would have, too, Irish."

"Well, I'm sure they're together in heaven now, and wouldn't want us worrying about them. They'll always be part of our lives, though, honey; I'm sure of that."

"Say! You made a statement before I went away, and I never had a chance to ask you about it. I was just wondering if you would care to expand on it now."

"Whatever in the world are you talking about, Irish?"

"When your father and I were having our spirited discussion at the dinner table the night before the anniversary party, you told him you knew you loved me the first night. Would you like to elaborate on that statement for me now?"

"Well! I don't know if I should."

"Please, pretty please, with sugar on it?"

"Okay. Do you remember when Carol and I asked you and Moose what you did?"

"Oh, Boy! Right; and I tried to lie to you."

"Yeah! Your face got as red as a beet. I knew right then and there that I loved you."

"You fell in love with me for trying to tell you a lie?"

"No, I fell in love with you because you had such a basic honesty about you that you couldn't even tell a little fib like that. I don't know; something just clicked and told me you were the one for me."

"Well, why didn't you tell me so the first time I told you I was in love with you?"

"You have to let us girls keep something in reserve, don't you?"

"Why?"

"Oh, I just wanted to make you suffer a little, that's all."

"You devil, you. Just for that I'm going to squeeze you 'til you holler."

"No, seriously, Irish, I wanted to make sure it wasn't just an infatuation on either of our parts."

"Well, I was sure it wasn't. Remember the clouds, the sun shining through and all?"

"I know, Irish. I'm sure it was love at first sight on my part also."

"What about the happily-ever-after part, Pam?"

"Oh! We'll have our smiles and a few little tears along the way; but together, we'll make out just fine."

"Kiss me, sweetheart. I want you to promise to kick my fanny if I ever as much as say a cross word to you."

"I'll hold you to that, Irish."

"I want you to, sweetheart, and I'm going to reserve the same right."

"Oh, that's not fair, Irish."

"Okay, I'll give up my right to kick your fanny, only if you'll give me the right to kiss you whenever I please."

"Okay, it's a deal, Irish."

"We'll start paying off then."

She began smothering me with kisses, and when we finally came up for air, she said, "You said something that night, also, that has me kind of curious, Irish."

"Whatever it is, I confess; I know nothing about it."

"Oh, yes, you do. But you don't have to tell me if you don't want to."

"Oh, love, I have no secrets from you. It is already an established fact that I'm a terrible liar, so feel free to ask me anything you like and you can be reasonably sure you'll get a straight answer."

"Well, okay then. You said I was the first girl you ever really dated."

"I see. Ah ha! And, you're jealous that there might have been another girl, aren't you?"

"No, Irish, I'm not jealous of anything you might have done before we met. It just struck me as kind of odd that someone as handsome as you never had a steady girl and sat at home all the time. I'm sure if you had wanted you could have had all the dates you ever wanted. Either that or there are a lot of dumb girls back there."

"You think so?"

"You bet I do. As far as I'm concerned, any girl with any sense would be proud to date you."

"Well, I'll tell you, honey, I guess I could have had lots of dates; but I never had a car, good clothes, or any money to speak of. Actually, I guess those were just excuses I would use. The truth is I was always bashful when it came to girls. I guess I had an inferiority complex. I was so afraid of being rejected that it was less painful not to ask rather than take a chance of being turned down."

"Oh, Irish, I find that hard to believe about you. You have such a wit and sense of humor; you could cope with any situation."

"It's true, Pam. I developed a sense of humor and a wit and used them as defense barriers to keep from getting hurt. Kinda like the song 'Laughing on the Outside; Crying on the Inside.' I thought if I could make people laugh and was able to outwit them, no matter what they said to me, that somehow they would like me and could not possibly hurt me, no matter what they said."

"Oh, Irish, I'm so sorry. I shouldn't have pried like that. I should have known, or at least guessed, after you made that boo-boo on the beach that first day. I don't believe I've ever seen anyone so sorry for saying anything in my life. I was at a loss for words myself; but I could see the deep hurt in your eyes. Like you had just lost the love of a lifetime, or something just as tragic. When you got up and started slowly walking down the beach, I felt so sorry for you that I wanted to cry. I had to come after you and let you know everything was all right."

"Oh, Pam, darling, you'll never know just how low I was feeling. I was convinced I had blown the whole thing. I sat there on that rock and admonished myself. I asked God what I had become with my foul mouth. I felt like I wasn't even a human being any longer. The very thing I had been trying so hard to avoid had happened. I had vowed and, so had Moose, that we were going to watch our language. And you'll never know just how hard that was to do."

251

"In the service every other word is a cuss word, and before you know it, you're saying them without even realizing it. It's all men and no one has any peers. For someone who has never been through it, it's almost impossible to comprehend just how low a level your vocabulary can fall to. I remember once a second lieutenant was giving a lecture on morality of all subjects. I counted the number of times he used the most popular four-letter word. In twenty minutes he used it one hundred thirty-seven times. He used it in every way possible. As a noun, pronoun, adjective, descriptive adjective, transitive verb, and intransitive verb. He used that word to express anger, love, hate, joy—even happiness. When you stop to think about the way he was using that word, it has to be the most versatile word in the English language."

"What really hurt was the fact that I knew I was in love with you, and I had done something as stupid as that just when I was finally coming out of my shell. Well, I just wanted to find a rock, crawl under it, and die. When you walked up behind me and put your hand on my shoulder, it was almost as if I was touched by the Good Lord himself, and that I was forgiven. An unbelievable surge of joy and love went flowing through my veins. That was the moment when love first touched me. You were so sweet and kind to me. You knew it was just a slip of the tongue and the fact that you were so willing to forgive me, well, it is almost impossible to explain my feelings at that moment."

"I knew somehow, someway, I had to tell you that I loved you and wanted to spend the rest of my life with you. I suddenly had all the strength and courage I needed. When I took you in my arms and kissed you for the first time, my feet left the ground. To this very day I still feel as if they haven't come down."

"Thank you, Irish. I really did understand, and I can assure you that when you kissed me that day, I knew somehow there would never be anyone else for me. It was so beautiful, Irish. I never knew a kiss could be so tender and generate so much love and affection."

"Well, thank you, darling. If we live to be one hundred, I'll never forget our first day together. I never really understood what Sister Margaret meant when she told me I would feel like I was walking around under the clouds, and that one day I would fall in love and tell myself it was all worthwhile. I understand now. She knew me like a book. She never told me; but she knew I was bashful and shy and had an inferiority complex. She also knew that I was going to spend years being unhappy and lonely because I was afraid to take the first steps with girls. She hit it right on the button. You were exactly what she was talking about. You were so sweet and loving and made everything so easy for me. You never asked direct questions and made me feel completely at ease. It was simply beautiful. Like I was half a person; then you came along. We joined forces, with you providing everything I was lacking—like the strength and courage to face life and giving me something to believe in and to look forward to. You gave me love and taught me how to be loved. Without you, I'm sure I would go right back into my shell and the clouds would descend upon me again. You've made me both happy and comfortable."

"Comfortable, that's the word I've been looking for, Pam. That's the feeling I get when I'm with you—comfortable, at ease with myself and the world. I don't have to put on an act or set up the defense barriers. Everything is so natural when I'm with you. Like at the country club that night. I would never have been able to get up and sing if you hadn't been by my side. It seemed so natural, the two of us together like that. Also, I would never have been able to stand up to your father without you by my side. If it had just been me, well, I probably would have left without saying a word in my own defense. You made me feel that I was important and that I had a right and a duty to stand up for both of us, regardless of the outcome."

"Since we fell in love, darling, I feel like a whole person, probably for the first time in my life. I'll always love you and as long as we live, you will be my source of strength and courage."

"Thank you, Irish, and I'm sorry I pried."

"I'm glad you did, honey. I wanted to tell you all this before but could never find the words to explain it. See what I mean?

You made it so easy for me to do so now. It's incredible. Oh, Pam, hold me, touch me, tell me you'll never let me go."

"Irish, you couldn't drive me off with a stick even if you wanted to."

"I can never imagine wanting to. I just want to smother you with love and affection. You have to be the most affectionate, loving human being God ever gave the breath of life to, and to think you are going to be my wife is almost more than I can comprehend. Me, Irish O'Malley, married to the most beautiful girl in the world. It's fantabulous, that's what it is."

"What's 'fantabulous' mean, Irish?"

"It's fantastic and fabulous all rolled up in one."

"I love you, Irish. It's just a matter of time until our union will be official. Mr. and Mrs.—doesn't it sound wonderful?"

"It's the most wonderful sound in the world."

She snuggled closer to me and lay her head on my chest. I ran my fingers through her beautiful hair and continued to bare my soul to her.

"I guess you thought it kinda strange that I never made love to you on the beach, didn't you?"

"Well, no, Irish, you explained your reasons then for not going all the way, and I'm glad now that you didn't. Like you said, no one would ever believe that it is pure and simple love if I were pregnant."

"That's true enough, sweetheart. I just don't want you to think it was because I was bashful and shy. Perhaps with any other girl on this earth, that may have been true; but not with you. I had other reasons and believe me, darling, I wanted to, more than I ever wanted anything in my life. It was just that I was so afraid of losing you; I thought that if we did make love, you would get the idea that that was all I was after and would be upset with me. You hadn't told me you loved me yet and I was so in love with you and wanted so badly for you to love me that I put forth that superhuman effort. If you had decided you were not in love with me, I just know I would have died."

"Oh, Irish, I'm sure it would not have made me think any less of you. The thought of making love to a boy hardly ever entered my mind before you came along. I'm sure if any of them would have tried, I would have fought them with my life. That was just the way I felt about it, until you. You were different; I was in love with you, and if you had wanted to, well, it would have been the most natural thing in the world to do."

"Well, you know that reputation GIs have—drinking, raising hell, and trying to screw every woman they come in contact with. I didn't want you to think that of me. I wanted you to be my wife and spend the rest of your life with me. Even though I wanted to make love to you more than anything I ever wanted in my life, I simply couldn't take the chance of losing you. The stakes were simply too high."

"Oh, Irish, I wish now that I had told you sooner that I loved you. I promise to make it all up to you. I never realized you were suffering like that, or I would have."

"Oh, no, honey. I'm sure now it only made our love stronger. And just think how much more rewarding it will be when we are finally able to make love, uninhibited, unashamed, and unafraid."

"I'm sure you're right, Irish. I promise I'll make it all up to you. I'll be there whenever you want me. I'll make you a night like no night has been or will be again. Jupiter and Mars will be way behind us. We'll fly to the top of the universe."

"You know, love, I just know I've died and gone to heaven and you're a beautiful angel that God has appointed to look after me and see that no harm comes to me. I'll never stop loving you, darling. I can assure you, even though you're too kind to ask, that you will be the first girl I will have ever made love to."

"Do you mean that, Irish?"

"It's true, honey. No hits, no runs, no errors."

"I'm glad, Irish. You won't be sorry."

As we lay there, savoring still another new dimension of our love for each other, we drifted off to sleep.

It was about seven the following morning when I woke up, with the sun shining through the window. There were Mrs. Taylor and Helen, both standing at the foot of the bed. I asked what time it was and they told me.

"Oh, we're in trouble for goofing off all night, aren't we?"

"Certainly not, Irish. We didn't have the heart to wake you two last night. You both looked so peaceful and radiant sleeping there together that to disturb such peace and tranquillity would have been the unforgivable sin."

"Thank you, Mrs. Taylor; I promise to work that much harder today to make up for lost time."

Pam woke up and was a little surprised that the sun was shining. I gave her a kiss. She smiled her loving smile at me and said, "Good-morning, precious; are we in trouble?"

"You bet, we are. Just look there at the foot of the bed; we're both in for it now."

Pam got up and excused herself saying she wanted to powder her nose.

"Well, as they say in West Virginia, be sure to stay away from the door."

She broke into laughter as she was leaving.

"What's so funny, Irish?"

"I'll let Pam tell you when she returns."

"It must be a good one."

"I didn't think so, but Pam sure got a kick out of it."

"Okay, Irish, we can wait; but right now how about getting hold of that bar and showing us how many pull-ups you can do?"

I got hold of the bar and with much groaning and struggling I managed to do four.

"That's just great, Irish; we really didn't expect you to do four this morning."

"With all the TLC and Maggie's good cooking, I'll be as strong as Superman by the end of the week."

"What's TLC, Irish?"

"Tender loving care."

"How sweet! Now, let's get you all prettied up so you can dig into another one of Maggie's delicious breakfasts."

"It's a deal, Mrs. Taylor, and thanks again for last night."

"You'll never know what last night meant to all of us, Irish; we should be thanking you and Pam."

"I'll have to get you to explain that to me later, Mrs. Taylor; I don't quite follow you."

"I will, Irish; you bet I will."

Pam returned, all bright-eyed and bushy-tailed. Immediately Mrs. Taylor and Helen wanted to know what was so funny when she left the room. Pam told them the whole story of the hillbilly shooting through the door of the men's room, and of me jumping up on the toilet and hanging onto the pipes for dear life. I thought they were all going to die from laughter.

Helen said, "I don't think I'll ever be able to go in a bathroom again without thinking of you standing up on that toilet."

"Thanks. It's nice to be remembered."

Mrs. Taylor said, "Irish, you're too much."

They finished getting me prettied up, and Maggie came in with breakfast. "Thanks, Maggie. By the end of the week, I'll be up, or at least in my wheelchair, and I'm coming down and raid your icebox."

"You're welcome there any time, Irish. Just tell me what you like, and I'll have plenty of it on hand."

"Anything that's edible will be just fine, Maggie."

I finished breakfast, and they wasted no time getting me out of bed and down to the whirlpool. I was strong enough by now to hold on, but as a precaution Pam had her bathing suit on and joined me in the pool.

We began to heckle Mrs. Taylor and Helen, telling them they were chicken to jump in. Before long they left and returned with their bathing suits on and jumped in with us.

They would get me over on my back and float me around the pool. Every time I would make a wisecrack, they would let me sink and told me to behave or they would drown me. It was really a beautiful time. I know they were enjoying it as much as I was.

We spent most of the morning there in the pool; but they finally talked me into going back to my room. They placed me in bed and told me to try to take a short nap before lunch.

15

The Taylors and Irish have a
Heart-to-Heart Talk

I was getting tired of that bed and decided to do some exercise on my own. I started pulling myself up on the bar. I finally got my arms over it and was kinda hanging there by my armpits ordering my legs to start moving. I was saying, "Come on, Goddamn it, start moving," when Mrs. Taylor came into the room.

I guess I was quite a sight hanging there like that. She said, "That's the spirit, Irish," and started laughing at me. "Please forgive me, Irish; but if you could just see yourself," and she started laughing again.

I started laughing with her and said, "I don't think I can get back down, Mrs. Taylor."

"Here, let me help you." She put her arms around me and helped me lay back down.

"Mrs. Taylor, whatever in the world would I do without you?"

"Oh, you'd make out just fine, Irish; I'm sure of that."

I was in kind of a melancholy mood. "No, Mrs. Taylor, you've saved my bacon too many times for me to believe that. I guess I'll always count on you to keep me straight. I have more respect for your opinion than that of any other person on this earth."

"Irish, you don't have to call me 'Mrs. Taylor,' if you don't want to. You can call me 'Paula' if you like."

"Oh, no, Mrs. Taylor. I love you and have too much respect for you to ever call you anything but Mrs. Taylor. You'll always be dear, sweet, precious Mrs. Taylor to me. I like the sound of it, Mrs. Taylor. It's like the sound of sweet music to my ears. I get a warm feeling every time I hear it. Mrs. Taylor."

"Oh, Irish, you big flirt, you. You're just saying that, aren't you?"

"Oh, no, Mrs. Taylor, I'm sincere. The first time I ever laid eyes on you, I thought the world of you. You were so gentle and kind to me. You knew I was ill at ease and not feeling very welcome here. You were kind enough not to ask direct questions of me or try to embarrass me. I really do want you to know that I appreciated that. I made up my mind right then and there that I'd never do anything that might cause me to lose favor with you. Now that my own mother is gone, I'm going to need someone to come to for advice when I have a problem. I would like that someone to be you, Mrs. Taylor. For I know you are sincere and will give both Pam and me your wise counsel."

"Thank you, Irish. I'll always be here whenever either you or Pam need me."

"Thanks, Mrs. Taylor. I think I'm finally starting to grow up. I realize now that no one can make it alone. Everyone needs someone they can count on, someone to turn to. Please tell me you'll always be there when we need you."

"I will, Irish. Don't fret about such things now. We still have a lot of work to do in order to get you walking again. Remember we have a wedding to plan for. If you're as anxious as Pam, and I'm sure you are, why the sooner the better."

"Okay, Mrs. Taylor; you're the boss."

"Now, how about trying to take a little nap before lunch?"

"Anything you say, Mrs. Taylor."

She had big tears in her eyes as she leaned over and kissed me on the cheek and said, "I won't be far away; if you need me just let out a holler."

"Thanks again, Mrs. Taylor."

She smiled and left the room.

I closed my eyes and was fast asleep in no time at all.

The pattern was pretty well established by now and things went sailing along smoothly for the next three weeks. Day by day I was getting stronger and spending more time in the wheelchair and less time in bed.

The ladies relentlessly kept up the massages and the whirlpool baths. By the end of the third week the feeling had started to return to my legs. As they would work my legs, the pain would increase day by day. But I welcomed the pain as a sign I was getting better. The more it hurt, the harder I tried.

Pam would have some of her girl friends over from time to time, and they would bring their boy friends with them. We would sit around and talk for hours on end. The girls were making wedding plans, choosing gowns and all. They were planning the biggest wedding ever held this side of the Mississippi, or so it seemed to me. When consulted about this or that, I would simply say that whatever they wanted was just fine with me.

While the girls would be chewing the fat, I would lure the guys down to the game room where we could bullshit or they could play pool. Occasionally, I would teach them the finer arts of playing poker. I figured they could afford the lessons I was teaching them, and I managed to see that they left with a lot less than they came with. They thought they were real pros, for after all they played poker with their fraternity brothers at the frat house all the time. I felt kind of guilty at first, taking their money like that; but then I figured it was good experience for them.

They were very standoffish and cool to me at first. After all, they were all draft age but had managed to beat the draft with their college deferments. Then after college it would be marriage or some phony medical report to keep them out. I let them know right from the beginning that I knew what the score was and that I didn't hold it against them if they were smart enough or rich enough to beat the system. I told them it had been going on since the beginning of time. Hell, in the Civil War you could pay someone three hundred dollars to take your place. I'm sure it didn't make them feel any less guilty. But it at least let us all know where we stood and that I had no animosity toward them for being draft dodgers.

If I had learned anything up to this point in my life, it was that very little is fair about life. All the puritan principles that had been drummed into my head all my life seemed only to apply to me and no one else. The higher up the ladder you would climb, the less these principles would apply, until you got to a point, as in a large corporation, where you became a law unto yourself. From where I was looking, it appeared anything or anybody had a price tag on it or him. I didn't invent the system, and I sure as hell wasn't going to change it. I could bitch about it all I wanted, but things, I was sure, were still going to be the same tomorrow.

I figured when you have a society where ninety-five percent of the wealth is controlled by less than five percent of the population, then you were going to have lopsided rules and regulations to go with it. It appeared to me that the laws were being written by people with money for people with money. To justify that theory in my mind, I took a look at the tax laws. Lo and behold, all the advantages went to the rich. I took a look at just what it cost to become a United States Senator versus the salary the position paid; lo and behold, the difference was staggering. Someone had to be making up the difference, and I don't believe it was coming from one- and two-dollar political donations. Hell, even back in my hometown the mayor's job paid only five thousand dollars a year and the office seeker would spend as much as one hundred twenty-five thousand for the privilege of getting a twenty-thousand dollar return for four years in office. Who was kidding whom?

But then, I figured if they were to suddenly gather all the wealth in the world and redistribute it equally, within six months those who had it initially would acquire it again anyhow, so what was the difference? There have always been rich people and poor people from the beginning of time and this was going to continue for the foreseeable future at least.

I had come to the conclusion that the democratic system at

best was no damned good; but it was so much better than anything else on earth that we should be thankful for it, rather than bitch about it. Like I say, I wasn't about to change the world single-handed and there was no use in my being mad at anyone or holding anything against anyone. I adopted a live-and-let-live attitude toward life; for no matter how hard you fought life, you were never going to get out of it alive.

Anyway, this wasn't a bad bunch of guys. Terrible poker players but, what the hell, no one is perfect. Besides that, this was a new audience for me to tell all my old jokes to; and we really did have some good times there at the Taylors'.

Mr. Taylor and I became good friends and would bullshit for hours on end. I think he would enjoy talking to me for he was sure that I would give him a straight answer and tell him what I really thought and not just what I thought he wanted to hear, like all his other associates and friends would do.

He was just as fascinated with my world and exploits as I was with his. Our worlds were oceans apart and so foreign to one another that it was almost unbelievable. It was so seldom, I would imagine, that he had a chance to brag about his accomplishments; consequently, he really enjoyed my interest in them. I was a good listener and was genuinely fascinated by big business and its internal workings. He would get to talking about fifty- to one-hundred-million-dollar deals and what it took to put them together and see them through to a conclusion. It was as fascinating to me as my exploits were to him.

We had bridged the gap and had become the best of friends. He would ask my opinion on different subjects and problems. I would always try to keep from expressing an opinion. But he would insist, saying it would give him a different point of view in making his decision. I would always tell him exactly what I thought. I'm sure he didn't always agree with my opinions. He would, however, always say that he appreciated them; for the more input he could get, the sounder his decision would be, and then the more chance there was that it would be the right decision.

He told me that was one of his biggest problems—getting

people to make decisions. He wasn't sure whether they couldn't or were afraid to. These were top executives he was talking about. I was very surprised and told him so.

"Well, Irish, perhaps it is because the stakes are so high that they are reluctant. But personally speaking, I find my first instincts in a given situation are usually my best, and I base my decisions on them. I would rather make a wrong decision and do something about it than make no decision at all. Even if I goof and make a wrong decision, I can usually spot it before it does too much harm and from that experience, I can make the right one. If I make no decision at all, I get nowhere. I also find that by putting off decisions that have to be made, it's not long until all my indecisions overwhelm me, and everything comes apart at the seams."

"I really believe the problem is people won't think for themselves. I guess we've spent hundreds of thousands of dollars sending people to seminars, special college courses, and training programs all designed to get them to think for themselves. If I could just find the magic formula and give it to them so they would simply think it would be worth millions to me."

"Well, now, Mr. Taylor, that fascinates me. The answer to that one is so simple it's no wonder everyone, including yourself, has overlooked it."

"Explain that to me, Irish; I don't follow you."

"Well, ever since I can remember, people have always been telling me to think, use your head or what have you, all leading back to the same thing—thinking. So I got to thinking about thinking one day. It always struck me as rather peculiar that people would always tell me to think; but never once did anyone ever tell me how to think. I would always wonder why, and then one day it hit me; that was the answer. Ask why, and that will start the thinking process. This will force you to think."

"Wow! Give me a minute or two to digest that one, Irish. That's kind of a hard pill to swallow."

"Take as much time as you like, but you'll find that it's true."

He sat there in silence for a few moments. I'm sure he was trying out his new discovery. Then he said, "By God, Irish, I believe you have the answer." He hurriedly wrote it down so as not to lose it, for fear it might somehow escape him. He then leaned back in his chair, with a real contented look on his face, and asked, "Well, how much do I owe you, counselor?"

I laughed and said, "No charge."

"Irish, I've wrestled for years with these problems and consulted some of the greatest minds in the country, not to mention the huge sums of money spent on trying to solve them. You sit there nonchalantly and solve them right off the top of your head. How do you do that?"

"Not so fast, Mr. Taylor. I can't take credit for the answers. They're just the sum and substance of years of reading, listening, picking up a little goodie here and a pearl of wisdom there."

"Horseshit, Irish; I can't buy that. It took that analytical mind of yours to put it all together and come up with the answers you did. How do you do it?"

"Well, if pressed for an answer, all I can say is that I get all the input I can possibly get on a given subject and simply forget about it. It all seems to register in my subconscious along with everything else I know or have forgotten, and it all mixes together in my mind. Then all of a sudden—maybe days later—I'll be walking down the street, or wake up in the middle of the night, and the answer is there."

"I guess this business of decision making and thinking came to the foreground after I joined the army. I was simply amazed at how little incentive there really was. All you had to do was keep your nose clean and do exactly what you were told. I couldn't get over how few people were making the decisions. Everyone was simply following orders. Absolutely no challenge at all. They told us when to get up in the morning, when we could eat, what we would wear, what we would be doing for the day, and even what time to go to bed at night. After a few weeks of that routine, I was bored to death and could actually find my mind slipping. That's why I would pull a lot of the shit I did, just to break the monotony and for the challenge of trying to beat the system. It's the only place on earth that I know of where they encourage a guy to bitch; they figure as long as you're bitching, you're at least getting the boredom out of your system. Could you just imagine twenty years of that shit?"

"Anyway, I would be lying in my bunk at night and for want of something better to do, I thought about all these people, robots, taking orders, if you will. It really bugged the hell out of me. That's when I started to ask why, and one thing led to another. Before long I had come to the conclusion that decision making and thinking were synonymous. It was hard to separate them. Then one day, just like I was telling you, they had us out there doing drills and the answer about thinking hit me right between the eyes. I simply had to carry it a step or two further to come to conclusions about decision making. What really hurt the most was, it opened my eyes to a lot more things that were wrong with the world. It was like opening up a Pandora's box or something."

"What do you mean, Irish?"

"Well, in pursuing that line of thought back to my school days, I came to the realization it was no better there. Hell, all they were doing was preparing you to go to work for someone else. Same thing: If you kept your nose clean and did just what you were told, nothing more, you would be promoted from grade to grade. They sure as hell didn't teach you how to think or make decisions. There is a hell of a lot more they could teach you to prepare you for life than what they do."

"Is it any wonder there are so many passive people in the world, just satisfied to get by, not wanting to make waves or change their sorry lot in life? It's sickening when you come to think about it, isn't it? I hope I'm not boring you, Mr. Taylor, going on like a preacher giving a sermon."

"Boring me? Hell no, Irish; I'm fascinated. Boring me, Christ! Irish, I learn something new every time I talk to you. Irish, let me ask you something point-blank. How about going to work for me?"

"What, so you can exploit my mind?"

"Irish, I want to tell you something; I think I know you well enough by now to talk to you man-to-man."

"Well, I certainly hope so, Mr. Taylor."

"You're an intelligent young man, and I don't feel a college degree will do you one damned bit of good. With your grasp of human nature and all you have going for you, you are already had and shoulders above ninety percent of those college graduates out there working. All a college degree does for you is open doors. It's just the fact that you go and finish, never mind learning anything."

"There is still a hell of a lot you don't know yet, Irish, and there is no sense in your having to find it out the hard way, like you've had to find out everything else. Permit me to point out a couple of things to you before you make any hasty decisions. Your question about me exploiting you is a fair one. That is exactly what I'd be doing, and you know it. Did you ever stop to think that no matter who you go to work for, they'll be doing exactly the same thing? Let's face facts. The employer only pays a worker enough money so he won't quit and get another job. The employee only does enough work to keep from getting fired. I wouldn't think of fraternizing you, Irish. Fraternization breeds contempt. It would be strictly an employer-employee relationship—while at work, at least."

"Well, Mr. Taylor, faith, hope, and charity also breed contempt."

"I don't follow you, Irish."

"Right now, you have faith in me. Should you find your faith misplaced, it would turn to hope. You would hope I wouldn't let you down. Then if I did, it could turn to charity on your part, and charity certainly does breed contempt."

"Irish, I should know better than to lock horns with you, but I'm going to. I have thousands of employees—passive employees, as you pointed out—content to draw a paycheck every week, and that's all. No drive, no ambition, really unhappy people. I need people like you who can think and who are not afraid to take chances and make decisions. I think I know people pretty well myself, Irish, and my faith would not be misplaced."

"Well, Mr. Taylor, I'm sure what you're saying about your passive employees is true enough. I'm sure ninety percent of those people would rather be doing something else besides what they're doing for a living. Few people, as far as I can see, ever choose a career. They just seem to take what is available at the time. Let's face it, they're already passive. They get into a rut and find it less painful to stay put and put up with an unpleasant situation than to put the effort into trying to change it. It's hard to explain. I think Shakespeare said it best:

> *To be, or not to be,*
> *That is the question:*
> *Whether 'tis nobler in the mind to suffer*
> *The slings and arrows of outrageous fortune;*
> *Or, to take arms against a sea of troubles,*
> *And, by opposing, end them?*
> *Ah! but then the fear of what may happen,*
> *Makes us rather bare those ills we have*
> *Than to fly to others we know not of.*

"You know, Irish, you never cease to amaze me. Come to think of it, I would imagine that quotation could apply to any unpleasant situation we become involved in, couldn't it?"

"Yes, that's true, Mr. Taylor. Remember the first time we locked horns? We were both in an unpleasant situation, and we sure as hell took arms against our troubles and by opposing we ended them. Fortunately we were able to reach a happy ending."

"What are you trying to tell me, Irish? That you wouldn't be happy working for me?"

"No, Mr. Taylor. It has nothing to do with you personally. I simply feel it would be an awkward situation for both of us. You know what people would think and say as well as I do. Not that I give a damn what people think of me, for I just put myself out to the world. Here I am—no more, no less. If you like me, wonderful; if not, leave me alone. It just wouldn't be fair to place you in that position, Mr. Taylor."

"What position, Irish? I wouldn't give a damn what people thought, and I wouldn't be doing you any favors either. You would earn every penny I paid you."

"Well, there is one other problem, Mr. Taylor. I just don't think I could pay the price or measure up to the standards you would set for me. Let's be truthful. I'm somewhat of a novelty to you now—a different point of view, and so on. What would we do when the novelty wore off and I ceased to amaze you? Would you feel obligated to keep me on for your daughter's sake? I'm sure you can see the possible complications down the road, Mr. Taylor."

"I think I have some idea of just what it took for you to get where you are today and, perfectly candidly, what it almost cost you. I just don't feel I could pay the price of success that you had to. Pam and I want to take time to watch the trees bud in the spring, to enjoy the warm summer sunshine, and to feel the warmth of a sweater against the fall breezes. I want to take time to love Pam and help her raise our children. I feel a lifetime is too precious to waste building a fortune, only to look around and find out life has whizzed right on by you. I don't want you to think for one minute that I don't appreciate your concern for me, Mr. Taylor. I really do. Perhaps I have a warped sense of values when it comes to worldly things. I guess my outlook, and Pam's also, has been altered by the fact that I almost lost my life on several occasions. Also, we buried our two best friends at the tender age of twenty."

"Irish, I really do appreciate your candor. Believe me, I've learned my lessons and learned them well. I'd never expect anyone to go through what I did. All the hell and lonely nights at the office, away from home for weeks on end, all those lousy cocktail parties, bridge with people you hated, and one social function right after another. I'm living proof that it's not worth it."

"You have had so many lousy breaks in your life, Irish, that I feel it's time you get a good break for a change. Not because of my daughter or because I feel sorry for you either. I like you, and you have talent. As far as being exploited, you're smart enough to know that every living human being on this earth is exploited to some degree or another. All I'm asking is that you give yourself a chance for once instead of beating your head against a brick wall. What the hell, Irish. You have balls enough to quit if things don't suit you. I give you my word I'll respect and understand your decision, if it should ever come to that. So, what do you say?"

"Well, Mr. Taylor, by the same token, I'm sure you have balls enough to fire me if things didn't go right, and I'm smart enough not to throw it back in your face. I will, however, have to consider all the pros and cons, and talk it over with Mrs. Taylor."

"With Mrs. Taylor? How about Pam?"

"Well, Pam and I already have an understanding. She wants to be a housewife and mother. What I do for a living is strictly up to me, just as long as I take time to be a husband to her and a father to our children."

"As for Mrs. Taylor, as you pointed out, I do have a lot to learn. It really is amazing how much you have to know in this old world before you realize you don't know anything. I have asked Mrs. Taylor to be my confidante, for I realize I do need someone older and wiser than myself to help me with such important decisions."

"I'm sure she'll be fair and give me her honest opinion. She did intervene and talk Pam and me out of getting married back east, and she did bring me back to my senses when I was wasting away in that hospital over in Japan. I hope you're not offended that I have chosen Mrs. Taylor as my sounding board."

"Not at all, Irish. I'm a bit surprised, but I shouldn't be. I should have known you were too smart not to figure that one out for yourself. I'm glad you chose Mrs. Taylor for your confidante, and I can assure you she has the patience of Job and the wisdom of Solomon, as you said your own mother had. After all, Irish, she has put up with me all these years, hasn't she?"

"Remember, you said that. I didn't. Thanks, Mr. Taylor; I knew you'd understand."

Almost as if it were timed, Mrs. Taylor came through the door. "I hate to break up this conference, but it's time for your massage, Irish."

"Speak of an angel, and one is sure to appear."

"That's not the way I heard it, Irish."

"Oh!"

269

"Yes, but I like your version better."

"Well, thank you, Mrs. Taylor; and I will definitely give some serious thought to your proposal, Mr. Taylor."

We were joined in my room by Helen and Pam. "You're really getting along famously with Daddy these days, Irish. Do you suppose he's mellowing with age?"

"He's quite a guy once you get to know him, honey, and opposites always attract. . . . I'm sure you'll agree we are as opposite as two people can be."

Mrs. Taylor said, "Oh, I don't really believe that, Irish. You both have a lot in common. You both love Pam; you both play billiards; you both like to tell stories."

"Yes, and we both love you, Mrs. Taylor."

"Irish, you're going to make Pam jealous."

"No, Mother, I couldn't be happier that Irish loves you. I want him to, just as much as I do."

"You two are going to make me cry if you don't stop all this."

"Should we make her cry, Irish?"

"Well, she's even more beautiful with a tear glimmering in those beautiful eyes; so why don't we see if we can get those beautiful eyes to glimmer a little. Then we'll let her off the hook."

"Say, not to change the subject, for I really love all this flattery, but I have a letter for you, Irish."

"A letter for me? I didn't think anyone knew I was here. Would you read it to me, please?"

She opened it and read it out loud. It was from the major, my old company commander. He was coming back to the States and wanted to drop in and see me when he arrived. He gave me the name of the hotel where he would be staying in San Francisco and the date he expected to arrive.

"Gee, I thought he would have forgotten all about me by now. It sure will be good to see him again. He looked after Moose and me and really got us out of some tough scraps. When will he be in San Francisco?"

"On the 14th."

"Say, that's the day after tomorrow, isn't it?"

"Yes, it is, Irish."

"Will you call him and invite him over?"

"Sure, Irish. If you like, he can stay right here while he's visiting you."

"Are you sure it will be all right with you, Mrs. Taylor?"

"Certainly, Irish. You must know by now that our home is your home and you can invite whomever you like."

"Isn't she the sweetest, Pam?"

"Sweetest what, Irish?"

"Sweetest mother a girl ever had."

"Yes, she is, Irish. I keep trying to back you into a corner, but you're too smart for me, and keep sidestepping me."

"Well, there is one time when I won't sidestep you, you can believe that."

"When will that be, Irish?"

"When the good padre asks, 'Do you take this woman to be your lawful wedded wife?' I'll stand there straight as a judge and say, 'You bet I do.'"

"Irish, I don't think that's the proper response."

"Well, I want him to know that I really mean it."

"I'm sure he'll get the message if you simply say, 'I do.'"

"Do you think he will, Mrs. Taylor?"

"Yes, Irish, I believe he will."

They started to exercise my legs. I began to grit my teeth; the pain was excruciating.

"Does it hurt that much, Irish?"

"Yes, it does, but don't stop on account of that. The Doc said the more it hurt the better. I've been goofing off so long that I've lost all my muscle tone and now payday is here. I have to pay the price for all that goofing off."

"Come on, Irish; no one can ever accuse you of goofing off, as you put it. No one in the world has tried harder than you. I just hate to see you in pain like this. I'm going to ask the doctor if he can't give you something for it."

"Oh, no, Mrs. Taylor, I don't want anything. The pain is like

271

a barometer as to how I'm doing. Besides, I don't feel it's going to increase any and should start to subside soon. Then as the pain decreases, my chances for walking will be better."

Pam leaned over and kissed me. "I wish there were some way I could help you bear the pain, Irish."

"I feel you all are, darling. I would never be able to see it through alone. It's like I told you, you're my source of strength and courage. So you just push as hard as you can on my feet and make those knees and hips do their work. I'll hold on to my monkey bar here and not pay any attention to you."

"Okay, Irish, we'll do as you say, and I hope your ordeal is over soon."

"I'm sure it will be over soon. And when it is, I'm going to run you around the block a hundred times."

"Gee, I hope I can keep up."

"Well, if you can't, I'll carry you."

We started making wisecracks back and forth. Mrs. Taylor started off, "Yes, yes; but other than that, Mrs. Lincoln, how did you enjoy the play?"

"Funny as a rubber crutch, Mrs. Taylor."

"Did you hear about the guy so dumb he studied two weeks for a urine test?"

"Irish, I'd like to see you get ahead; I think you need one."

"Oh, Yea! When they passed out the brains you thought they said 'canes' and you said you didn't need any."

"Okay, Irish, when they passed out the noses you thought they said 'roses' and you said, 'Give me a big one.'"

"Har! har! har! What if I told you I was pregnant?"

"Go ahead, Irish; I think I heard it."

"Oh, well, I just thought I'd run it up a flagpole and see if anyone saluted."

"How about throwing it out on the stoop and see if the cat licks it up."

"Gee, I hope this rain keeps up."

"Why?"

"Well, if it keeps up, it won't come down."

"Now, enough of this, you guys. How do you feel, Irish?"

"Well, as compared to what, Mrs. Taylor?"

"A knuckle sandwich, Irish."

"Oh, fine, Mrs. Taylor, just fine."

"No, seriously, Irish, is the pain still so bad?"

"Not as bad tonight as it was this morning, Mrs. Taylor."

"Should I try to skin the cat on my monkey bar now?"

"No, no, Irish; you settle down now. We still have fifteen more minutes to go before you can start goofing off again."

"You slave driver, you."

"Do you really think so, Irish?"

"Well, if you are, you have to be the prettiest slave driver ever born and I have to be the luckiest slave ever born to have you for a master."

"Okay, slave, give me a kiss."

"Your wish is my command."

"Tell me some more stories, Mrs. Taylor."

"What do you want to hear about, Irish?"

"Oh, it doesn't matter. I just like to hear the sound of your melodious voice."

"Would you listen to that? Pam, I don't know what you're going to do with this character."

"I do, Mother. I'm going to love him for as long as I live and see that he never gets too far away from me."

"Well, honey, I promise you there will be no lonely nights or empty days. But you'll probably get tired of me and won't be able to wait to kick me out of the house to go to work."

"Do you really think so, Irish?"

"I hope you never tire of me. I plan to shower you with so much love and devotion that you won't have time to even think about getting tired of me."

"I feel the same way, Irish; it sounds like heaven to me."

"Yes, I know. I feel like I've already died and gone to heaven. But if I'm dead, how come I have to go to the bathroom?"

"Do you, Irish?"

"No. It just seemed to fit, so I threw it in."

They all laughed and Pam said, "You got even with me, didn't you, Irish?"

"Hey, that reminds me of a story."

"Everything reminds you of a story, Irish, doesn't it?"

"Now, Helen, you be good."

"Well, if I can't be good, will it be all right with you if I'm just careful?"

"Okay, and if you can't be careful, how about naming it after Pam and me and calling it even."

After the laughter died down, Mrs. Taylor said, "Someday, Irish, we're going to get ahead of you."

"Say, did you hear about the little kid who wanted a watch for Christmas?"

"Hum! No!"

"They let him."

"Irish, I'm going to bop you on the nose."

"Okay, okay, I'll behave myself. I was going to say I'll be good but . . . . ." "Yes, we know if you couldn't be good, you'd be careful. . . . . right . ."

"See there, that's the only exercise you get—jumping to conclusions."

"That's one for you, Irish; we'll get even, though.

"Look, you're all such good sports and I just like to kid you a lot. I want you to understand, I wouldn't knowingly hurt anyone's feelings."

"We know that, Irish. If it takes your mind off the pain, wonderful. We like to kid with you, too, and we really enjoy your sense of humor."

"Okay, then, how about the moron who thought a mushroom was a place to neck."

"Or thought 'no kidding' meant birth control."

"Or took a roll of toilet paper to a crap game."

After regaining their composure, Mrs. Taylor said, "I've got one you won't be able to top, Irish—thought a sanitary belt was a drink from a clean shot glass."

When the laughter died down, I exclaimed, "Mrs. Taylor! I concede; I wouldn't touch that line with a ten-foot pole. You win, Mrs. Taylor."

"Oh, come on, Irish. I didn't embarrass you, did I?"

"No, Mrs. Taylor; but I'll have to remember that one. It's better than the one where he spent two days in Sears looking for wheels for a miscarriage."

"We give up, Irish; you're just too much for us."

Helen said, "Well, that should about do it for now, Irish. Do you want to get back in your wheelchair?"

"Yes, I'd like that." So they got me out of bed and into my wheelchair.

Pam asked me if I'd like to go out on the patio for a while.

"Yes, I'd like that, honey; lead the way."

I turned to Helen and Mrs. Taylor standing there smiling. I told them to sharpen up their wits because I wanted a chance to get even with them.

"Irish, you're so far ahead of us, we'll never get even with you."

I blew them both a kiss and said, "Drive on, lover, and let's see what the great outdoors looks like."

It was truly a magnificent night. The rain had stopped and the moon and stars filled the skies. There was a cool breeze rustling the leaves on the trees. Pam's beautiful eyes sparkled in the moonlight as if every star in the universe were reflecting in them. We sat there in the still of the night, with the crickets providing their calming effect to the serenity of the moment. I asked Pam to sit on my lap and as we melted into each other's arms, we got lost in a world all our own. I prayed to God at that moment that we would never be apart again for the remainder of our lives. I never knew such happiness and true bliss ever existed, and really had trouble coming to the realization that it was actually me experiencing all these wonderful feelings.

I related my feelings to Pam who said, "Oh, darling, it's all real and we'll make it last forever. Just hold me tight."

I leaned forward and began feverishly kissing her when it happened. I had forgot to lock the wheels on the wheelchair. We were too far forward and fell out of the chair. The wheelchair went crashing against the patio door while we went sprawling to the ground.

Pam wound up about five feet from me. I was so shocked and

surprised at what happened that without even realizing what I was doing, I crawled over to her, took her in my arms and asked her if she was all right. She assured me that she was fine, and was more concerned about me. After we assured each other we were all right, we began to laugh in nervous relief, like a couple of nuts. All the noise had attracted everyone in the household, and they all came running.

When they arrived on the scene, there we were sitting on the ground, holding each other. They were all inquiring as to what had happened and if we were all right, but all we could do was laugh. We finally settled down and Pam told them what had happened. I added that a wheelchair is no place to do any necking.

Suddenly Pam cried out in amazement, "Irish! do you realize what you did?"

"Yeah, made fools out of both of us."

"No, no! You crawled over to me on your hands and knees. That means your paralysis is going away, and you're regaining the use of your legs."

"You're right; let me try it again." I sat there and for the first time in months began moving my legs and knees under my own power.

I exclaimed, "They work, they work! Help me up and let's see if I can walk." The pain was really bad, but I had no trouble contending with that. I wanted to stand up and walk. They tried to talk me out of it, saying I was rushing things; but I insisted.

They helped me to my feet and were holding me up when I asked them to let me go. They did. I stood there for an instant and immediately began to fall. They grabbed me and made me sit back down in the wheelchair, saying that enough is enough for tonight.

"We won; we won, didn't we? My legs are working!"

Pam was so overjoyed she was crying like a baby. In fact, everyone was so happy that the tears of joy were flowing like water. All those weeks of work, worry, and waiting were finally coming to an end.

Mr. Taylor told Arnold to bring a bottle of champagne to toast the occasion.

I said, through my blurry tear-filled eyes, that I was grateful and owed them a debt of gratitude that I would never be able to repay. "You all had more faith in me than I had in myself. You never gave up hope. When I think of lying in that hospital over in Japan feeling sorry for myself, well, I'm ashamed for ever having lost faith and hope. They say love conquers all. I'll never doubt that statement again."

Mrs. Taylor said, "Don't be so hard on yourself, Irish. You were as responsible as anyone. A great deal of the credit has to go to your efforts. All we could do was love you and help you. But in the end, you were the one who had to want to walk again."

"Oh, thank you, one and all. You'll never know how wonderful it felt to at least stand up under my own power. I hope to start walking by tomorrow, at the latest."

"Well, Irish, let's just celebrate your accomplishments of this evening. We'll consult the doctor in the morning and see where we go from here."

"From here to the altar. Do you have those wedding invitations ready to be typed, Mrs. Taylor?"

"We're way ahead of you, Irish. All I have to do is call the printer and give him a date to put on them and we're all set."

"Oh, love, are you sure you didn't get hurt when we fell?"

"No, Irish, not even a scratch."

"That's good, for I would never forgive myself if I ever hurt you."

"How about you, Irish, are you sure you didn't get hurt?"

"No. I got better."

Arnold returned with the champagne and glasses and poured everyone a glass, including himself, the maids and Maggie.

Mrs. Taylor proposed a toast. "Here's to Pam and Irish and to their wedding day."

We all drank to that and I said, "Here's to the most wonderful people in the world—the Taylors—and everyone associated

277

with them, for the superhuman effort put forth on my behalf.
I wish to thank you one and all from the bottom of my heart."

They all cheered and drank up.

"Say, aren't we supposed to break a bottle of champagne over
my head or something, to launch me?"

"No, I don't think so, Irish. But I'll tell you what we can do."

"I have a feeling I shouldn't ask."

Mrs. Taylor walked over to me and poured her glass of champagne over my head, and was quickly followed by Pam and
Helen, who followed suit.

"There, Irish; you're officially launched."

I laughed, "Do you believe this, Mr. Taylor?"

"I have to, Irish; I'm standing right here watching it."

At that, I raised my glass over my head and emptied it.

Everyone laughed and clapped. Mrs. Taylor said, "We're just
getting even with you for all those wisecracks, Irish, but we still
love you."

"I'll never stop loving all of you. Say, Pam, do you want to
sit on my lap again?"

"Sure, Irish; if you'll remember to put the brake on this time."

Helen said, "Come on, Irish, I think you've had enough excitement for one night. Let's get you cleaned up and back in bed.
Then we can talk some more."

"What are my options?"

"None."

"Mr. Taylor, these ladies sure are tough taskmasters. Don't
ever get sick and plan to do any goofing off around them, because they won't let you."

"I'll try to remember, Irish."

"Come on, tough guy. It's off to the showers for you."

"See you later, Mr. Taylor, Arnold, Maggie, everybody," I
was shouting as she wheeled me through the door and back to
my room. She got me all cleaned up and in clean PJs and
wheeled me back over to the bed where Pam and Mrs. Taylor
were waiting to help me into bed.

They got me all settled down, and I told them I felt like I was
floating on air.

"Oh, Irish! We're all so happy for you. Isn't it just great?"

"Yes, it is, and I'm ecstatic. Say, I really do want to thank you three for all those sleepless nights you spent making me better. How can I ever thank you enough?"

"Well, how about a kiss for starters?"

"You got it."

I kissed and hugged each one of them and was so happy that the tears would not stay put in my eyes; they started escaping down my cheeks. Pam leaned over and dried my tears and kissed me.

"Whatever in the world would I have done without you, sweetheart?"

"That goes both ways, Irish. I would be just as lost without your love. I was born to be with you. I love you, Irish."

I started moving my legs and wiggling my toes. Mrs. Taylor asked if it was painful.

"I'm oblivious to pain, Mrs. Taylor; it's just beautiful."

"I'm happy, Irish. Would you and Pam like a sandwich or something?"

"Sounds great to me; how about you, honey?"

"Great!"

"Okay, I'll send Maggie up with something. Anything special?"

"Oh, surprise us."

"Okay. We'll see you two later."

Pam lay down beside me and snuggled close to me. "Oh, Irish, I'm so happy I don't know what to say. It's a dream come true. I'll never forget this night, Irish."

"How far in advance do we have to plan our wedding, honey?"

"The wedding is all planned. All that remains to be done is to send out the invitations."

"Well, what do you think would be a reasonable time?"

"Perhaps two weeks would be a respectable time, Irish."

"I think that's great, honey. This wedding is long overdue."

"I have something else to tell you, honey."

"What's that, Irish?"

I whispered in her ear that I was one hundred percent better in all categories now, and ready for that trip to the top of the universe.

"Oh, Irish, I'm so happy for you. My prayers have been answered. I just hated seeing you lying there full of doubt and worry. It's such a relief to know it's finally coming to an end. Tell you what, Irish. I feel you've suffered long enough. I want to put you on notice that all bets and promises are off. I love you, Irish, and want to make love to you so badly that I don't want to wait for a piece of paper. That piece of paper couldn't possibly make me love you any more than I do now."

"Oh, Pam, let me hold your hands, touch your face, and gaze into your beautiful eyes. You'll never know how I worshiped you when we were apart; how I longed for and adored you. I dreamed of the day we would make love. I feel exactly as you do, darling, and I don't want to wait a moment longer. Hold me in your arms and take me to wherever it is that lovers go."

We were locked in a passionate embrace with our hearts beating madly. We were in complete accord and on perfect wavelengths. Our passions were at a fever pitch. I never experienced such wonderful feelings in all my life.

Pam whispered in my ear she wanted to go to her room and change into something more fitting the occasion. "This will be a solemn moment for me, Irish, and I want everything to be just perfect."

"Hurry back, honey, I don't want to wait a moment longer."

"I'll be back before you realize I'm gone, sweetheart." She got up and started out the door.

I lay there like a child in wild anticipation. All my wildest dreams were about to come true.

As I lay there, slowly drifting back to earth, all the promises and vows of letting Pam enter marriage as a virgin started to come to the forefront of my mind. I was beginning to have second thoughts. After all Mrs. Taylor had done for me, I thought, how could I betray her like this? We had managed to fight off temptation up to this point, and although I was impotent for so long, the basic promises and vows still held true.

I knew I had to keep those promises, but I felt I was in an impossible situation. I wanted to make love to Pam more than anything else. I also knew I wouldn't have the strength and courage to refuse her this time, and I knew she felt the same way. I made up my mind not to think about the whys and wherefores. I would wait for Pam to return and would simply let whatever happens happen.

While I lay there suspended somewhere between heaven and earth, Pam returned. She was still in her skirt and blouse. She came over to the bed and lay down beside me and began to cry. "Oh, Irish, I'm so sorry. I got my negligee out, the one I was going to wear on our wedding night. I started to think of how much we both have longed for that night, and all we've been through anticipating it. I remembered promising Mother I would be a virgin when we were married. If we made love tonight, Irish, I'm afraid it would make our wedding night anticlimatic. Irish, I'm so sorry I did this to you. If you want me to, I'll still make love to you tonight, darling."

"Oh, Pam, darling, don't do this to yourself. I'm the one who should be sorry, honey. Please don't cry. If you hadn't backed down, I would have. After you were gone, I started having second thoughts, also. I guess we simply got carried away, sweetheart, and with you, that is so very, very easy to do. I guess that is why we're so good for each other. We both think alike."

"Oh, Irish, I love you. You're so understanding. You really are a superhuman person. I don't believe anyone else on earth would have let me get away with what I have done to you."

"Nonsense, sweetheart. Think how proud and happy we'll both be on our wedding night. How much more rewarding our love will be. Last, but by no means least, how proud it will make your mother of you."

"I know, Irish, and you know what a natural worrier she is anyway. I put her mind at ease by telling her I would be married a virgin. It means so much to her. You know all the abuse my great aunt gave her all those years until you put her in her place that night at the anniversary party."

"You made my mother so proud of you that night, Irish, that

I would hate to be the one to ever say a cross word about you in front of her. I'm afraid she'd kill me if I ever did."

"I know, she worries a lot about me, and I certainly do appreciate her concern. I somehow feel she is my mother too, especially since my own mother is gone now. I look to her for the help and guidance I would look to my own mother for. I think we both owe her that much, to make the sacrifice, don't you, honey? It won't kill us and will only make our love stronger."

"Yes, I do, Irish. I apologize for getting you all shook up tonight."

"Please, honey, I enjoy your shaking me up, and I don't ever want you to stop. All you have to do is look at me with those beautiful eyes and I'm all shook up. Can't you just picture us, after we've been married for fifty years, still shaking each other up?"

"I hope I can still shake you up, honey."

"You will; you will."

There was a knock on the door. Pam went to answer it. It was Maggie with a tray of sandwiches and coffee.

"Come on in, Maggie."

"How are you feeling tonight, Mr. Irish?"

"Great, Maggie; simply great."

"Here's your snack; I'll set in here on the table and I'll see you two later."

"Thanks, Maggie."

After she was gone, Pam and I looked at each other and started to laugh. "Are you thinking what I'm thinking?" "Yes. Wouldn't it have been something? We would have been somewhere between Jupiter and Mars by now and would never have heard Maggie at the door."

"Oh, well, at least we managed to work up an appetite. Our other hungers will be satisfied in time."

"It won't be that long now. I'm planning on walking tomorrow, and as soon as I do, you can shoot those wedding invitations out in the mail."

"You bet I will, Irish."

We were going over our wedding plans and planning a honeymoon when Mrs. Taylor came into the room. Pam and I both laughed and, of course, she wanted to know what was so funny. "We'll tell you later—much later," we promised.

"Well, Irish, are you ready for a massage?"

"I thought we could give them up now that my legs are working again."

"Not so fast, Irish. It will still be required for a week or so until you have your muscles built back up to a point where you can walk with a cane. I was lucky enough to get hold of the doctor at home tonight and gave him the good news. He told me to keep up the massages and the whirlpool bath and to get the whip out and start you with the walker in the morning. He said we don't want any relapses at this point. You can exercise as long and as hard as you can."

"Oh, I will, Mrs. Taylor. Believe me, I'll go until I drop."

"I believe you, Irish."

Mrs. Taylor asked Pam if she would like to be excused from night duty. Pam's face got a little red. I smiled and took her hand. "It's all right, Pam; your mother knows exactly what the score is and what we're going through right now. She truly has the wisdom of Solomon and the patience of Job."

Pam smiled, "I guess Mother knows best."

"Yes, she does, honey, and she'll keep us straight."

"Thanks, kids; I know how impossible it would be for you, especially now that Irish is fully recovered. I don't want you to torment yourselves like that. Pam, you will be the proudest girl in the world walking down the aisle, and Irish, all your patience and understanding will be rewarded a thousand times over."

"I know you're right, Mrs. Taylor. Pam and I are both grateful to you for seeing us through this most difficult period."

"Mother, you have to be the most precious mother a girl ever had. You're so understanding and know exactly the right thing to do. How will Irish and I ever be able to repay you?"

"You already have, both you and Irish. When I see you walking down the aisle, honey, I'll be crying. But they will be tears of joy, believe me. I'll be so proud of both you and Irish. I couldn't love Irish more if he were my own son."

"I couldn't love you more, Mrs. Taylor, if you were my own mother."

"I'm glad, Irish."

Pam asked her mother how she knew that I was one hundred percent again.

She smiled and told Pam, "We'll embarrass Irish if I tell you."

"Oh no, Mrs. Taylor. It's true when I first came home I was so bashful that I just knew I was going to die the first time you two gave me a massage. But your love and understanding got me over that."

"I know, Irish, we discussed that at length. We all knew you were so bashful, but also what had to be done to get you up again. We decided the best way to handle it was to make light of it and hope you would understand."

"I did, Mrs. Taylor, and the towel over my head sure helped."

They both laughed. Pam said, "You're still blushing a little, Irish. It's becoming to you, though; I don't ever want you to get over it."

"Thanks, sweet pea."

"No, I'll tell you, Pam. When I came in last night to give Irish a massage, he never woke up; but he must have been having some beautiful dreams."

My face must have gotten red again; for Pam and her mother both agreed, "He's as bashful as ever," and started to laugh again.

"Well, last night was the first time I knew for sure." I reached for both their hands and said, "God has been good to me. I'm not only getting a beautiful wife, but also a beautiful family I can call my own. I'll never let any of you down and will love you all as long as I live."

"We know that, Irish, and we'll always love you. It's past midnight now, honey, so if you want to turn in, I'll look after Irish for you tonight."

"Well, you had better take good care of him now."

"Just how do you mean that, Pam?"

"Now, she has you backed into a corner, doesn't she? It should be interesting to hear you talk yourself out of this one."

"Well, you two know what I mean."

"No, honey, explain it to us." We all started laughing.

Pam leaned over and gave me a good-night kiss, saying she'd see me in the morning.

"Good-night, Mother." "Good-night, honey."

"She really is special, isn't she, Mrs. Taylor?"

"Yes, she is, Irish. It seems like only yesterday she was just a baby. Now, she's all grown up and ready to start a family of her own. It doesn't seem possible."

I took Mrs. Taylor's hand. "I'll take good care of her, Mrs. Taylor. It's not like you were losing her; I want you to understand she'll still be as much a part of your life as ever. Perhaps more so, when we have children. If our first child is a girl, we're going to name her after you."

"Oh, Irish, you wouldn't want to do that."

"Oh, yes, we would. We both agree. We would love to name our baby after you."

"You kids are too much."

"It's because we love you, Mrs. Taylor."

She pinched my cheek. "Why don't you try to get some sleep, Irish. You have a busy day tomorrow."

"Oh, I couldn't sleep if I wanted to, Mrs. Taylor. I feel better now than I have in years. If you're not sleepy, I would like to talk to you for a while."

"I'm not a bit sleepy, Irish. We can talk as long as you like."

"I have a problem I would like to discuss with you, if you will."

"That's what I'm here for, Irish."

"Mr. Taylor has asked me to go to work for him."

"What did you tell him, Irish?"

"Well, I pointed out all the pitfalls I could think of and told him I was not willing to pay the price for success that he had paid. I pointed out to him that I was somewhat of a novelty to him now and asked him what he'd do when the novelty wore off."

"What did he say, Irish?"

"Nothing, really; he's thoroughly convinced everything will work out fine."

"Don't you plan to go to college when you get away from the service?"

"I had thought about it, Mrs. Taylor, but I'm not too keen on the idea. I told Mr. Taylor that I would be strictly a nine-to-five man. I made it clear that I wanted to take time to watch the flowers in spring, enjoy the summer sunshine, love Pam, and help her raise our children."

"What did he say, Irish?"

"That he had learned his lessons and would not expect anyone to go through what he had gone through. He also told me, quite frankly, that he doesn't know how you put up with it all those years."

"I know, Irish. Since you came into our lives, Mr. Taylor and I are closer than we have ever been. All that love and affection you seem to generate rubs off on people. Remember the night you and Pam fell asleep here together? Well, I promised you I'd tell you about that night, and I will now. Mr. Taylor came up with me to say good-night to you. When we looked at you and Pam sleeping there together and all the love and devotion you two were generating, well, Irish, it brought tears to our eyes and got all the good juices flowing again. Mr. Taylor and I had reached a point in our marriage where we more or less took each other for granted. We seldom, if ever, had sexual relations. We were really at a low point in our marriage, but after seeing you two kids together like that, it brought back all the good memories of just how it used to be for us when we were young and in love."

"Oh, Mrs. Taylor, you're still very young and very beautiful. I can hardly imagine Mr. Taylor ever losing his desire for you."

"No, Irish. I don't believe he did. It's just that we were always so busy, on the go all the time. There never seemed to be any time for each other. That's all changed now, Irish. We're more in love, and make love more now, than we ever have before in our marriage. The only thing we can attribute it to is the love you and Pam show for each other."

"I'm glad for you, Mrs. Taylor. You deserve a meaningful and rewarding relationship, and so does Mr. Taylor. God only knows the sacrifices you two have made over the years. I'm happy for both of you that you found out before it was too late that you have to take time for each other. As I see it, without each other nothing else matters."

"You're right, Irish. The only reason I'm telling you this is because I don't want you to forget it, Irish. I don't want you and Pam to make the same mistakes we did. Life is too precious to waste even a day of it."

"As for Mr. Taylor, I can assure you he is a changed man. He's not the same man you had the run-in with at the dinner table that evening, Irish. It's phenomenal, the change that's come over him. Like you said, Irish, if you get everything in its proper perspective, and you both know what's expected of you as employer to employee before you start, I see no reason why it shouldn't work out just fine."

"Well, he hasn't told me what I'd be doing for him, and we haven't discussed salary or anything. As a matter of fact, Mrs. Taylor, I'm not even sure what Mr. Taylor's business is, or if I would fit in."

"He's a defense contractor, Irish, and has holdings in at least eight major corporations and dozens of subsidiaries. I'm sure in all that there has to be a place for a very special guy named Irish."

"Do you think I'm special, Mrs. Taylor?"

She laughed, "You're fishing for a compliment, Irish; but yes, I do. You're very, very special to Mr. Taylor and to myself. I think you would be well-advised to accept his offer, and I'm sure everything will work out just fine."

"Well, I do want to talk it over with Pam, but I'm certain she'll agree with you. I'd be willing to give it a try. If it doesn't work out, I can always go someplace else, right?"

"Right, Irish. But always be mindful of your marriage to Pam and your relationship with her. That's the important thing."

"We're in complete accord, Mrs. Taylor. I love talking to you. You're so honest and I can count on your advice as being sincere. I want to thank you again for all you've done for me. I never would have made it without you, Mrs. Taylor."

"Oh, come on now, Irish; you're making me blush. Irish, I want to tell you something. After Pam was born, I found out I would never be able to have another child. Perhaps that is why we were so protective of her. I always wanted a son and was brokenhearted when I found out that could never be. That might account for why Mr. Taylor and I were the way we were, and perhaps that is the reason we grew apart the way we did."

"Do you think it would be presumptuous of me to assume God has sent you to us as our son? Mr. Taylor shares my feelings. If we had a son of our own, we couldn't ask for one to fit the bill any better than you do, Irish. I know you never knew your father, and your mother is gone now. We would both like to think of you as our own, Irish. I don't mean I'll ever replace your memories of your own mother; but I would like to carry on and love you just as she would have, had she lived."

"Oh, Mrs. Taylor, you're so perceptive. You know I'm grieving for her, don't you?"

"Yes, I do, Irish. You've been keeping it all bottled up inside of you, along with all your other little doubts, fears, worries and anxieties. I think you'll feel better if you let them all out and get them out of your system."

I reached for her. She lay down beside me and put her arm around me. She opened the top of her robe exposing her lily-white breasts and gently maneuvered my head into them. I began to weep.

"Look at me—big tough guy—as helpless as a babe in arms."

She assured me everything was going to be all right now. "It's perfectly natural to grieve the loss of a loved one, and I only wish there were more I could do to help you, Irish."

"Oh, you dear, sweet, precious lady, you. You're the only woman on this earth who could ever replace my mother. I'll always love her and cherish her memory, Mrs. Taylor; but I'll always need you. I would be proud to have you consider me your son. Just as proud as I'm going to be to be Pam's husband."

"Thank you, Irish. Do you feel better now?"

"Hold me a moment longer, Mrs. Taylor. I'll be all right."

"I'll hold you as long as you like, son."

"That sounds so good to hear, Mrs. Taylor. It's kind of tough being grownup, isn't it? After my brother was killed, I felt nothing could ever possibly hurt me ever again, as long as I lived. I was wrong. I try to remember what Sister Margaret told me about being strong and accepting things as they happen and all. She taught me that it's God's will, but it still hurts so badly. When you see hundreds of people stacked up like cord wood waiting for a bulldozer to dig a common grave for them, you'd think you would become immune to death. It's not so. When the lieutenant got killed, I cried like a baby. When most of our outfit got wiped out, seeing your buddies and guys you had been talking with just hours before, laying on the ground, arms and legs missing, decapitated or burned beyond recognition—it's enough to shake your faith in God."

"Some things you count on more than others in this life and feel they will be constant in your life. When you lose them, it's a deep hurt that takes a long, long time to heal. I've learned to accept Moose and Carol's deaths and all the others. But my own mother, somehow I felt that would never happen, that I would have her forever, to go to when I needed her, or just to talk things over. Now that she is gone, Mrs. Taylor, I'm having trouble coping with it."

She kissed me on top of the head and began rubbing my neck and the back of my head, saying, "Oh, Irish, I wish there were more I could do for you. If only there were some way I could help you. I have a pretty good idea of what you're going through. My parents were both killed in an automobile accident shortly after we were married, and it took me a terribly long time to accept it. All I can do is be here when you need me, Irish, or when you feel you need someone to talk to, to get over the rough spots."

"Oh, Mrs. Taylor, you already have. You all have. Your love and understanding has kept me going and enabled me to face it. I really do appreciate your giving me this opportunity to talk about it. It really helps to get it out in the open where I can look at it and face up to it. I feel you and Pam are helping me bear the load, and I'll always cherish the knowledge that my mother died in the presence of my new family. You'll never know what that meant to me, Mrs. Taylor."

"You know, when Pam first brought me home, I was a pretty cocky guy. I had found the love of my life and thought I had all the answers. No one or thing was ever going to hurt me again. Looking back, I'll have to admit that I was proud, and perhaps a little vain. I felt I needed no help from anyone and that I could face any situation, climb any mountain, or solve any problem by myself. It was you, Mrs. Taylor, who came to my rescue and brought me back to earth. You taught me a virtue I was lacking —humility. In your own sweet, lovable way, without ever saying so or saying, 'I told you so,' you made me realize just how much I needed people and all the help I could possibly get. Perhaps that is why God permitted me to get hurt in the first place—so that you could come along and point out the errors of my ways."

"Do you know, Mrs. Taylor, if I live to be one hundred, I'll always be indebted to you for teaching me how important other people are, and how beautiful and moving an experience it can be to be totally and completely dependent on others. I'll never be proud or vain again in my life. I'll always be aware that I can never make it alone and that I'll always need people."

"I always thought to be humble was to be weak, but you taught me that to be humble was to be strong. That it takes more courage to be humble and accept help than it does to be proud and refuse help. I'll always love you for that, Mrs. Taylor, and I'll always be humble in your presence."

"Oh, Irish, you poor baby, you. You're much too hard on yourself. We never thought of you as proud or vain. We realized you were young and vulnerable and could be hurt very easily. You never came across as a wise guy or a know-it-all. You spoke with a wisdom far beyond your years and you did seem to have all the answers, or at least were highly opinionated on what you felt about certain things. Mr. Taylor and I both agreed that all you needed was to be mellowed with age and experience. Basically, Irish, you had it all together. I can truthfully say that the first time I ever laid eyes on you I prayed to God no harm would come to you. I hoped one day you and Pam would be married."

"Everyone needs people, Irish. We need you, probably more than you need us."

"Thank you for saying that, Mrs. Taylor. I really do feel I'll be able to accept my mother's death now, especially since I'll always have you to turn to. I couldn't love you more if you were my natural mother."

"I'll be here, Irish," she said as she gently pulled me closer to her.

She reached up and turned out the lights, and as we lay there, a peaceful calm seemed to descend over us. We lay there in silence for the longest time, still holding onto each other. Mrs. Taylor broke the silence by asking me very softly if I was still a virgin. I confessed that I was and went on to explain that it wasn't that I didn't have wants and desires like everyone else, but rather that I had never had any opportunities when I was growing up and was afraid of catching venereal disease in the service.

"Oh, Irish. I don't mean to embarrass you or to pry. It's only that I want to help you. I know how bashful and shy you really are, and I don't want you to have any problems on your wedding night. God only knows how you two kids have suffered and denied yourselves. I feel responsible for that, Irish. I didn't realize you had to go back to the service so soon when you and Pam wanted to get married back east. I feel I denied you two that little bit of time to make love before you had to go away."

"Oh no, Mrs. Taylor. Please don't feel guilty."

"Irish, what I'm about to tell you and ask of you will have to be a sacred trust just between us two—a secret bond, if you will. I want your wedding night to be absolutely perfect for both you and Pam, and I want to teach you the art of making love. I want you to accept what is going to happen in the spirit that it is offered as an ultimate expression of my love for you."

"Oh, Mrs. Taylor! I couldn't. Please, I'm not that strong. You're a very desirable woman, and I'm afraid you tempt me beyond my will to resist. I couldn't accept your love out of pity, charity, or because you feel guilty about Pam and me."

"It goes much deeper than that, Irish. I have a deep need to give of myself. I have been taking all my life and never really had an opportunity or was in a position to ever give much in return. Please, Irish, let me do this for you. If you have never gone through with the physical act, how do you know you can or that you won't freeze up at the last minute? Once you've done it, Irish, you'll never have to worry about it again. It's a once-in-a-lifetime opportunity for me to do something for somebody without asking or expecting anything in return. Please accept it out of love, Irish—nothing else."

I had tears in my eyes as I said, "Mrs. Taylor, just the fact that you're willing to help me is the ultimate expression of love, as far as I'm concerned, and we wouldn't have to go through with the physical act. To be perfectly honest, Mrs. Taylor, I wouldn't even know how to begin."

"That's why I want to help you, Irish. I not only *want* to help you; I *need* to help you. It's for me, Irish, please. Let me fulfill this need to give of myself, for I'll never have another chance as long as I live. Please."

I lay over on my back while she got up and went over and locked the door. She returned to the side of the bed and disrobed. She leaned over and helped me out of my pajamas and lay down beside me again. As our lips met, I could feel the warmth of her tender flesh pressing against mine.

She was so gentle and kind with me as she maneuvered into position and told me exactly what to do. My penis rose quickly to erection, and she directed me to enter her. As I made the slightest penetration, my arms gave way and I collapsed on her. I buried my head in the pillow next to hers and began to cry.

She ever so gently moved her hips until she had me completely engulfed. The warm and sensuous sensations were flashing from the tip of my toes to the top of my head. Even the slightest movement brought more of the wonderful sensations.

As I lay there crying my eyes out, all my worries, doubts, fears and frustrations seemed to be melting away like April snow.

We lay in that position for several minutes, until I had cried out all my frustrations, with Mrs. Taylor encouraging me to get it all out of my system. She held me ever so tightly and kept running her fingers through my hair.

She asked me to kiss her. As our mouths met she inserted her tongue into my mouth and again began to gently rotate her hips. I began to withdraw my penis ever so slowly and just as gently let it glide back in. I was truly in heaven and didn't ever want it to end. When I finally reached a climax, I never knew anything could feel so wonderful. My heart must have tripled its beat, and when I finally got up the courage to withdraw completely, I rolled over on my back, completely exhausted.

She then maneuvered herself into a position with her breasts next to my face, and guided one of them to my mouth. As I lay there nursing it like a babe-in-arms, she explained to me all the different ways to make a woman happy and to see that she reached a climax before the man did. She explained all the different positions and instructed me, "Your bodies are for each other's pleasure."

"At last, I know I can do it, Mrs. Taylor. I never knew it would be this wonderful. This is beyond my wildest dreams, and I want to thank you."

We talked for better than an hour when she asked me if I would like to try some other positions. I had already had a taste of paradise, and was more than willing for her to take me back there again. She told me it was important to not reach a climax until we had experienced all the different positions. I agreed to let her know when we should change positions. She took me to the top of the universe in sensual excitement, until we finally were back in the position we first started with, and I climaxed again.

She helped me back into my pajamas and got dressed herself. She lay back down, and I took her in my arms and told her she truly took the boy and gave me back the man. She cautioned me that this was a sacred trust and bond between us, and that I must never, under any circumstances, tell anyone of it. I gave her my word, and sealed it with a passionate kiss.

"Thank you, Irish, for letting me give myself to you. I feel as close to you now as if I had conceived you, bore you for nine months, and gave birth to you."

"Thank you, Mrs. Taylor. Although my lips are sealed, I'll always remember this night as the most perfect night of my life. This was the night when I finally grew up and became a man. Most of all I'll remember how sweet, gentle, kind, and patient you were with me; how giving you were; how tonight was the ultimate expression of your love for me and mine for you."

"Thank you, Irish. I'll cherish this night forever, Irish. Now, why don't you close your eyes and go to sleep."

"You're still the boss, Mrs. Taylor."

"Goodnight, Irish. I'll see you in the morning." She got up, turned and walked slowly out the door, while I closed my eyes and drifted off into a beautiful dream world.

I woke up about seven o'clock in the morning. Mrs. Taylor was standing there, holding my hand, and smiling a brilliant smile at me. "Good morning, Irish! How are you feeling this morning?"

"Need you ask, you precious, adorable lady, you?"

"No remorse, no regrets, Irish?"

"None whatsoever, Mrs. Taylor. I feel more alive this morning than I ever have in my life. You took away all my worries, fears, and doubts. Words are woefully inadequate to express how I feel for you and what a wonderful new outlook on life you've given me. I'll never stop loving you, Mrs. Taylor, and I'll conduct my life in such a manner as to make you proud of me and to show you your faith in me has not been misplaced. I'll always cherish the knowledge that you loved me when I needed love more than anything else on earth. Last night was both humbling and rewarding, and it seems so inadequate to simply say, 'thank you,' but I do, and I love you, Mrs. Taylor."

"Thank you, Irish, but it was not all that one-sided, you know. You fulfilled a deep, deep need in me. Last night was one of the most rewarding experiences of my life, Irish, knowing I was able to help and to love someone who really needed me. And what was even more rewarding was the fact that that someone was you, Irish, whom I love very dearly. It is I who should be thanking you, and I do, Irish. Last night gave me a new outlook on life also. I'm happier now than I've been in a long time."

Pam and Helen came in. Pam ran over to the bed, smiling from ear to ear. I sat up and threw my arms around her as she bounced up on the bed. We hugged each other and kissed like there was no tomorrow.

"You're in a beautiful mood this morning, Irish. I haven't seen you this happy before in my life."

"Today is the first day of a brand new wonderful and glorious life for us both, darling. Your dear, sweet, precious mother let me cry on her shoulder last night. She took all my little worries, doubts, fears, and hang-ups over there to the window and threw them into a stiff breeze. They will never return to haunt me ever again."

"I'm glad, Irish. It's so good to see you so happy. When you're happy, I'm happy."

"Can I kiss your mother and thank her, Pam?"

"Irish, you don't have to ask such a silly question. You can kiss Mother any time you like, and don't ever worry about me getting jealous, either. I simply love your love for each other. It makes me feel more secure."

"I'm glad, honey." I reached for Mrs. Taylor, kissed her, and said, "Everything is going to be simply beautiful for the rest of our lives."

Mrs. Taylor took the initiative and said, "Okay, what do you say we get Irish all prettied up and make him walk down to breakfast in his walker this morning?"

All three of them were scurrying around like busy little bees and finally got the job done. They had me standing next to the bed when Pam brought the walker over. I took hold of it and tried to manipulate myself around the room. My coorindation was all gone. My legs were working like wet noodles, and I was really having a bad time of it. Although the pain wasn't that bad, I felt like I was really walking on my hands and dragging my feet along for the ride.

I made it to the door with them right behind me, smiling, and giving me all the slack I wanted. I finally made it to the top of the stairs.

"Let's take the elevator, Irish."

"I think I can make the stairs."

"We don't want you to fall, Irish."

"Okay." Then I sat down and started letting myself down the stairs on my rump, one at a time. When I got to the bottom, they helped me back up and I got hold of my walker again and proceeded to the dining room. Pam and her mother helped me sit down while Helen took the walker and set it aside.

"How was that?"

"Not bad, Irish, but you can do better. No. We're just kidding you. It was great, Irish."

After breakfast and much joking and carrying on, I continued to work out in my walker. After an hour or so and falling several times from sheer exhaustion, they directed me to the whirlpool, which really felt great and seemed to relieve all the little aches and pains I was experiencing. After three hours in the whirlpool, during which time I showed off my swimming abilities, they insisted I go back to my room for a nap before lunch.

I was much too tired to argue, so I put up very little resistance. It didn't take long after I hit the bed before I was fast asleep.

16

Irish has a Visitor that could Change His Life

When I awoke, there was Pam, right beside me.

"Hi, Irish," she said in her cheery, little-girl voice. "Have a nice nap?"

"I slept like a baby, honey. What have you been up to?"

"Well, Mother and I went shopping in town and happened to find some nice slacks and shirts that perhaps might fit someone your size. Would you like to try them on and see?"

I reached for her hand and kissed it. "I'd love to, darling. It's been so long since I've had street clothes on, it's going to seem strange."

"Well, let's see, shall we?"

"You bet, honey."

"You have a visitor coming this afternoon, Irish."

"Oh, yeah, the major."

"Right. I called this morning, and he's on his way now."

"I thought he wasn't due until tomorrow. It sure will be good to see him. I know you'll like him. I don't know how a nice guy like that ever got to be an officer in the army in the first place."

"You still hold a grudge against the army, don't you, Irish?"

"No, not really. I'm just kidding."

Pam helped me into my new duds.

"Why, Irish, you don't look like the same person."

"Better or worse than the old one?"

"Better—much better."

"When will the major be here?"

"In an hour or so. Why don't we go down to the living room and wait for him there?"

"You're the boss, sweetheart; whatever you say goes."

The trip downstairs wasn't as bad as the one in the morning, but I still had to negotiate the steps on my bottom. When we made the living room, Mr. Taylor was sitting there.

"It's good to see you out of that wheelchair, Irish."

"It feels great to be out of it, Mr. Taylor. Did Pam tell you we have a visitor coming this afternoon?"

"So I heard, Irish. I guess you'll be glad to see him, won't you?"

"Yes, I will, Mr. Taylor. I'm sure you'll like him. He's quite a guy."

"I know I will, Irish."

We were soon joined by Mrs. Taylor and Helen. We were passing the time of day with idle chatter when the doorbell rang.

Arnold answered the door showing the major, a three-star general, and a captain (the general's aide) into the living room where we were sitting. We all stood up, with me hanging onto my walker, flanked by Mrs. Taylor and Helen, in case I decided to fall.

The major came over and put his arms around me and said, "It sure is good to see you on your feet again, Irish."

"Thank you, Major. Let me introduce you to my family. This is Mr. and Mrs. Taylor, and their lovely daughter, Pam, the love of my life, I might add. This is Mrs. Jenkins, the most beautiful nurse in the world. This is Major Lewis."

They all exchanged niceties and he introduced us to General Lloyd and his aide, Captain Gunther. We again exchanged niceties with them and we all sat down.

Mr. Taylor had Arnold fix everyone a drink. The major asked

me what I was drinking. I told him my usual, 7-up on the rocks.

"Do you know out of an outfit of 350 men, Irish was the only one who didn't drink? But when he and Moose were in the outfit they saw to it that everybody had their fill, including myself."

The general looked a little surprised.

The major explained to him that Moose and I had been running whiskey up from Seoul. "At a profit, too, I might add. They were the greatest morale boosters north of the 38th Parallel."

The General laughed, "That's what it takes to win wars—ingenuity."

"Speaking of ingenuity and resourcefulness, with Moose's brawn and Irish's brains, there was absolutely nothing we ever needed that they couldn't come up with. I never knew how, why, or where they would get it—and I wouldn't dare ask, for Irish was very honest and would tell me exactly right down to the last detail. Believe me, after the first time, I was better off not asking, figuring what I didn't know I couldn't testify to. All I had to do, though, was let it be known what was needed and it would appear like magic—like a fifth in my desk drawer or fresh meat in the mess hall. I guess it's safe to ask you now, Irish. Where in the world did you and Moose come up with those twelve cases of frozen steaks?"

"From the navy in Inchon."

"How in the world did you guys get to Inchon?"

"That chopper would take us any place we wanted to go as long as we supplied the booze."

"Well, how did you get the steaks away from the navy?"

"We traded them six cases of booze for them."

"That really cut into your profits, didn't it?"

"No, not really. We showed them what we had by opening a case of Seagrams and they went for it without opening the six cases we gave them. They only had bricks in them."

Everyone, including the general, was laughing. The major added, "That's Irish. I'll tell you, though, Irish was the best company clerk I ever had. He would anticipate my every need and was a wealth of information. He knew what was happening before I did. It wasn't long before he was signing my name to orders and taking care of the whole operation himself. I would simply look things over. He would have things so well organized they could have sent me back to the States and I would never have been missed."

"Well, you know my motto, Major. 'Work smart; not hard.' There are no rewards for effort; it's results that count."

"Yes, that was Irish. He would get the maximum with the least amount of effort of anyone I've ever run across. He would play a game when I would give him a project. He called it 'what if?' What if I made it bigger, what if I made it smaller, and so on, right down the line until he would come up with a way to make it easier and do it faster."

"I would get a kick out of the way he would screen everyone who wanted to get in to see me. No one, but no one, got in to see me without first going through Irish. It would make a lot of them mad, especially my officers. But Irish was one of the few in the military that didn't draw a line between enlisted personnel and officers. He would simply treat everyone alike. It made no difference to him if you were a full bird colonel or a private. He'd treat you just the same."

"I could go on for days with stories about Irish, but let me get back to his screening of my visitors. If he thought their reasons for wanting to see me weren't good enough, he simply would not let them in or he would solve their problems himself. I can never remember a time when his decisions were not in complete accord with what I would have done myself."

"Well, I liked you, Major. And besides that, you helped Moose and me out of some tough scrapes, like that day we disarmed the MPs."

The general said, "I'd like to hear this one; it has to be good."

So the major told him how we had disarmed the three MPs. He described how we disabled their jeeps, outran them back to the company area, and came into his office and dropped their .45 pistols on his desk. He said he could hardly believe it when we told him we had a case of whiskey in the jeep. Since we were being that truthful, what else could he do but concoct a story to get us off the hook.

Mr. Taylor and the general, along with everyone else, were simply roaring with laughter.

"Oh, and his sense of humor; he has to know more stories than anyone on earth. I've known him for over a year and have never heard the same one twice. I think he makes them up as he goes along. Even though he was as homesick and lonely as anyone over there, he always kept everyone's spirits up with his story-telling. I never heard tell of anyone topping him. He always had the last word."

"Well, Major, happiness is not a place; it's a state of mind."

"Irish, you might tell that to anyone else on earth except me. I have something here you left behind. He reached in his brief-case and placed a forty-five recording of 'I Left My Heart in San Francisco' on the coffee table. Remember this, Irish?"

"I sure do, Major. But how did you know it was mine?"

"I shouldn't tell this story on you, Irish, but I'm going to."

"Irish was not a happy man, although no one would ever have guessed. I found out quite by accident. He would sneak back into my office late at night and play this record over and over again. I happened to go over there one night for something, I walked in, and there was Irish sitting behind my desk, with his feet propped up on it. He was playing this record. I said, 'Hello, Irish,' but he was in a trance and never even knew I was in the room. He had big tears running down his face, and the only movement he would make was to move the needle back to play it over again. He might have been over there in body, but his spirit was truly right here with you folks. So if you ever doubt that Irish loves you, young lady, just remember him sitting over there, dreaming of the day when he could come home to you."

Pam took my arm and said, "I never doubted Irish for a moment, and I thank you for telling me, Major. It only makes me love him more, if that's possible."

"Well, you got me, Major; you spoiled my act as a clown. I really was hurting."

Mr. Taylor had Arnold fix everyone another drink. The major said, "Irish, when I saw you going over that cliff with that ammo truck blowing up, I just knew you were a goner."

"Ah! You can't kill a good man, Major. Besides that, I had too much to live for." I smiled and took Pam's hand. "You wouldn't have wanted me to disappoint this pretty young lady, now, would you?"

"Well, Irish, I never witnessed such an act of heroism in all my time on active duty."

"It was nothing, Major. If I hadn't done it, someone else would have."

"Irish, I have a feeling you're being modest and haven't told these good folks just how you got wounded in the first place, have you?"

"They were too kind to ask, and I didn't want to bore them with war stories."

Mrs. Taylor came up behind me and put her hands on my shoulders and said, "No, Major, he didn't tell us. Believe me, anything pertaining to Irish doesn't bore us. I think we would all be interested in knowing what a hero Irish is." She squeezed on my shoulder blades as if to tell me I was getting out of line. I turned to her and smiled my knowing smile and said, "Okay, Mrs. Taylor; I'll be quiet." She reached over and pinched my cheek.

"You know, Major, she's tougher on me than you ever were."

"Well, Irish, the treatment you're getting certainly seems to be effecting the cure. Let me show you folks something," he said, reaching in his briefcase and pulling out a map of South Korea. He explained our position along with those of the North Koreans and the Red Chinese.

He explained how we stood there, watching through field glasses the onslaught of over one hundred thousand Red Chinese who bridged the barbed wire with their own bodies. He detailed how we were in full retreat across the river when everything suddenly came to a stop and we drove around the column and came upon the burning ammunition truck. He explained the chaos and how, without a second's hesitation, I jumped in the truck, drove it over a quarter of a mile and finally went over a cliff into the river.

He continued, "I followed Irish in my jeep, praying that he

would jump. When he finally did jump, I felt it was too late. I saw him in midair, and then he disappeared right out over the cliff. I stopped my jeep and hit the ground just as the truck blew up while hitting the water. I got up and hurried over to the edge of the cliff and saw Irish lying down there."

"By now the column was moving again, and I commandered the first ambulance to come along. I helped them get him in a stokes basket and pull him back up from there. They all thought he was dead and didn't want to bother; but I made them go down and get him out of there. I ordered them to take him to the nearest evacuation pickup point across the river and told them if he didn't make it, I was holding them personally responsible. That was the last time I laid eyes on Irish until today."

"Now, let me show you the significance of what he did. If that truck had blown up where it was, blocking the road, we would have lost millions and millions of dollars' worth of equipment and hundreds, perhaps thousands, of lives would have been lost. All our forces from the south were converging on the river. We had planned to make our stand there and keep the enemy from crossing the river. We still had five thousand troops to get across that bridge and very little time to do it."

"If our men had been forced to take a stand on that side of the river, the odds are twenty to one they would all have been killed. If Irish hadn't driven that truck off the cliff, it would have blown up on the bridge, and our men would have been trapped anyway."

"But, because of his presence of mind and an act of heroism far above and beyond the call of duty, every single man and piece of equipment made it across that bridge before we blew the bridge up ourselves. There at the river we were able to stop their advance with our reinforcements from the south. Within a week we were able to drive the enemy back across the 38th Parallel again."

Mrs. Taylor said, "Well, Irish, what do you have to say for yourself now?"

"It was nothing, Mrs. Taylor."

The general piped up with, "It was to the five thousand men

who owe their lives to you, not to mention the millions of dollars' worth of equipment that were saved. I often wondered what goes through a man's mind at a time like that, Irish. Would you be kind enough to tell me what was going through your mind and what made you do it?"

"Well, sir, I don't feel like much of a hero. For that matter I don't know what a hero is supposed to feel like. As to why I did it, someone had to. I seemed to be the closest one; that's all. I had no particular thoughts going through my mind—only to ditch that thing somewhere where it would do the least amount of harm."

"Well, weren't you afraid for your own life, knowing it could blow up at any moment?"

"I never gave it a thought. Perhaps if I had stood there, even for an instant, and thought of the consequences, I would have run for the woods like everyone else was doing. I just wasn't thinking at all. When I saw the bridge, I figured if I could get the truck in the water, perhaps the fire would go out. That's probably why I didn't try to cross the bridge. I didn't figure on that cliff, though. When I saw it, I jumped. But it was too late, and I went sailing right out over it. I heard the truck blow up, and that's the last thing I remember until I woke up in a field hospital."

"So if you say I'm a hero, it would simply be defined as opportunity and reflexes. It certainly wasn't planned or calculated."

Pam asked, "Weren't you scared, Irish?"

"I'll tell you the truth. When the major and I were watching the onslaught of those Red Chinese, I was so frightened, I wet myself."

"Well, Irish", said the general, "your country is grateful and wants to show its appreciation for what you've done by awarding you the Congressional Medal of Honor."

"You've got to be kidding! I'll have to think about that for a moment. I find it almost impossible to believe."

Mrs. Taylor, in her cool, efficient manner, seized the initiative. "Gentlemen, it's time for Irish to take his medicine; so if you'll excuse us, we'll rejoin you shortly. I want to hear what else Irish has been keeping from us."

"Certainly. You run along now, Irish."

Pam helped me up, and she and her mother helped me into the library across the hall. As she closed the door, I turned to her, puzzled and said, "Mrs. Taylor, I don't take any medicine."

"I know, Irish, I wanted to get you away for a few moments so you could think things out."

Pam looking a little bewildered, asked, "What's wrong, Mother?"

"I'll let Irish tell us."

"You're afraid I'm going to turn that medal down, aren't you?"

"I'm scared to death that you're going to. That's why I wanted to give you some time to think about it."

"Will it make you proud of me, if I accept it?"

"Yes, it will, Irish; very, very proud."

"How about you, Pam?"

"Yes, sweetheart. Regardless of what you think about the army, it's a personal achievement equaled by very few people. It may not seem like a big deal to you now; but in years to come just think how proud your sons and daughters will be to brag that their daddy won the Congressional Medal of Honor."

"Do you both think Mr. Taylor shares your feelings?"

"We're sure he does, Irish. Please, not just for our sake, but for your own. And Moose would have wanted you to, I'm sure. Think of how proud your mother would have been."

"Oh, Mrs. Taylor, you have come to my rescue once again. Of course, I'll accept it, and as graciously as I possibly can."

Pam gave me a big kiss and a hug and was followed by Mrs. Taylor, who did likewise. They both thanked me and told me I wouldn't be sorry.

"I know I won't. It has to be right, if you both say it is."

"We do, Irish; we do."

"Okay, let's go back in then."

They helped me back into the living room, and we sat back down on the couch.

Mr. Taylor was grinning like a Cheshire cat. He was delighted with what was taking place. I had the distinct impression that he could hardly wait to get on the telephone and tell the world about his prospective son-in-law, or at least run over to the country club and tell all the boys over there. They say that after you have all the money you want, there is nothing left but prestige. I'd say he had the ultimate in prestige now, and there was no way any of those other bragging bastards were going to top this.

The major asked, "Are you feeling better now, Irish?"

"Yes, sir. Much, much better."

"Well, Irish, the general would like to present you with your Purple Heart today, and we have a set of orders here for your Congressional Medal of Honor. The commander in chief wants to present that to you himself at a White House ceremony. What do you think of that?"

"I'm honored, truly honored."

The general read the orders and presented me with my Purple Heart. He shook my hand, and I thanked him. I handed it to Pam, who admired it and passed it around for all to see.

"I have another set of orders here for you, Irish." He then proceeded to read them. They were for a battlefield commission. I was suddenly an officer and a gentleman. He presented me with a set of gold second lieutenant bars. I was absolutely speechless.

The Major broke the silence and asked, "Irish, now that you're an officer and a gentleman, would you consider making the army a career?"

"Well, Major, Mr. Taylor has other plans for me, but nothing is settled yet. I need time to digest all this. Everything is happening so fast. I'm not even sure if it's happening to me. It's all so unbelievable."

Pam reached over and gently pinched my cheek to convince me. "It's all real, Irish."

"This is my source of strength and courage, Major; isn't she wonderful?"

"There's no denying that, Irish. And you're a very lucky man to have someone so lovely in love with you."

"Yes, and I thank God for her every day of my life."

Mrs. Taylor invited them to stay for dinner, and they accepted. While we were having dinner the major said, "By the way, Irish, I sent in the last flypaper report before I left Korea. I also recommended they be terminated."

"Fly paper report?" the general asked, quizzically.

"Yes, General; I imagine Irish was trying to make a point about all the useless reports we had to fill out monthly that no one ever read and that went absolutely no where."

"Unbeknown to me, Irish made one up on flypaper, using as his authority for the report article numbers and regulations he pulled out of thin air, I guess, for I was never able to verify any of them. He hung flypaper up in the mess tent at six strategic locations, and drew a schematic showing the location of each, and made up a report on the number of flies each one caught."

"He simply signed my name to the reports and sent them along with the appropriate number of copies through the appropriate channels, right on up the chain of command to the Pentagon. He had been doing it for the last three months he was there, and, of course, when he got wounded, the reports stopped. Well, the last week I was there, I got an urgent message from some major in the Pentagon wanting to know where my flypaper reports for the last two months were. It took me a long time to find the ones Irish had made up. And when I did, I said to myself, 'Irish had the last laugh after all.' You know, I really felt stupid trying to make out a flypaper report."

After everyone was through laughing, the general agreed. "I know it's true. I've been fighting the system for years myself, but things are slow to change. It takes someone like Irish to come along and show us how really ridiculous and out of hand things can really get. I venture to say there are over half a million different regulations and special orders on the books right now that don't belong there, and no one knows how to get rid of them."

"Don't feel bad, General. They have written over thirty million laws trying to enforce the Ten Commandments out here in civilian life, so you have a long way to go yet."

He laughed, "I guess that should make me feel better, but it doesn't; I have to obey all those laws also."

Mr. Taylor said, "Listen, I have a great idea. Why don't we take Irish over to the club for a couple of hours to celebrate. After all, it's not every day you find out you've won the Congressional Medal of Honor. What do you say?" The general said it sounded like a great idea to him. After that the major and the general's aide could do little else but agree. "How about you, Irish? Do you feel up to it?"

"Sounds fine to me, but I'd better check it out with the boss before I commit myself. What do you think, Mrs. Taylor?"

"Well, if you feel up to it, Irish, and you're sure you're not overdoing it. Do you think it's okay, Helen?"

"Okay, but take your wheelchair along, just in case."

"Pam, will it be all right with you?"

"Just fine, Irish. I think you need to get out a little after being cooped up with females all this time."

"Thank you, honey. But I must confess I loved every minute of it."

After dinner, Pam went upstairs and brought my wheelchair down. As we were getting ready to leave, I could see Mrs. Taylor was looking a little apprehensive, so I assured her I'd take good care of them, see that they didn't have too much to drink, and get them home at a respectable hour.

Everyone laughed. She smiled her loving smile and said, "I don't know why I worry about you, Irish; I'm sure you can take care of yourself."

"Well, with your help and guidance, of course."

She leaned over and kissed me and told me to behave myself. Pam told me to enjoy myself, and Helen came running over with a sweater for me.

The major said, "Irish, I don't believe any man ever had better care than you're getting. They sure think the world of you, and I hope you never let them down."

"Rest assured, Major, that that will never happen."

Shortly after loading into Mr. Taylor's big Cadillac, we were at the front door of the country club waiting for a table. Some sharp-looking dude in a tuxedo came over to our group and said something about not allowing me in because I wasn't wearing a tie. Mr. Taylor took him aside. I couldn't hear what he told him, but whatever it was, it only took about ten seconds before Mr. Taylor rejoined us, and they were showing us to the finest table in the room. I would imagine he told that guy that if he opened his mouth once more, he would buy the goddamned place, and he would be the first one he'd let go.

Things were pretty quiet for the first half hour with Mr. Taylor ordering the finest champagne in the house and hors d'oeuvres, and everyone making small talk.

After the first few glasses of champagne, the major started quizzing me.

"Irish, what's your secret for getting along with people?"

"No secret, Major. I simply say, 'Here I am. If you like me, fine; if not, leave me alone. I'm no more or no less than what I am.'"

"No, no, forget the double-talk, Irish. There has to be more to it than that." He kept insisting, so I finally said, "If you must know, Major, I figure everyone's got to take down his pants to shit the same as I do, so what's the difference?"

Mr. Taylor burst out laughing, and the general got caught with a mouthful of champagne that he couldn't spit out or swallow. His lips were sealed and his cheeks were puffed out about five times their normal size. He finally gagged it down and started to laugh like I never heard anyone laugh before in my life. By now, everyone in the room was noticing us and looking our way. The major said, "That's Irish, completely uninhibited. Ask a simple question and you'll sure as hell get a simple answer." That broke the ice, if there was any to break, and it was all downhill from there on.

As people would wander by the table, Mr. Taylor would stop them, tell them the news about me, introduce them to the general, the major, and the captain, and invite them to join our group. As the champagne flowed and the evening wore on, we must have had about thirty people sitting, standing, or otherwise milling around our table, listening to the major and me bullshitting one another and telling stories. Mr. Taylor kept ordering one bottle of champagne after another and finally had the waiter stay right there and keep pouring it for everyone gathered around. I had suddenly become his son. No more son-in-law, or daughter's fiance, or any of that other bullshit. I was his son in no uncertain terms.

Mr. Taylor urged me to tell them about the lottery Moose and I ran over there. I did, and everyone burst into fits of laughter. I went on to tell them about being hassled by the MPs on our first day back in the States and how we handled it. The general really enjoyed that anecdote and every once in a while, during the rest of the evening, he would shout, "Can I shoot your gun?" and then cackle uproariously. They were really getting drunk by now and were to the point where they were letting their hair down and not much giving a damn as to what they said. I just sat there nursing my 7-up on the rocks and watched them become more and more drunk.

It was almost midnight when I finally convinced them to head back to the house. It's a good thing the chauffeur was sober. Otherwise, we would never have made it. We pulled up in the driveway and the chauffeur got my wheelchair out of the trunk and helped me into it. Everyone wanted to push it for me, and while they all stood there arguing over it, Helen came out of the house and pushed me inside. They turned around and suddenly realized I was gone. They were so drunk they couldn't remember if I had come home with them or not, and they were actually debating whether or not to go back to the club to look for me. Mrs. Taylor went to the door and assured them that I was already inside.

They all came staggering in, holding onto one another. As soon as they were all inside, the major asked the general if he could see his pass. The general said, "Can I shoot your gun?" And they all started laughing like a bunch of idiots.

I turned to Pam and to Mrs. Taylor and said, "And a good time was had by all."

"How about you, Irish? Did you have a good time?"

"Wonderful, simply wonderful."

"How did you manage to stay sober with all that going on around you?"

"Well, someone had to drive home,"

"You drove home?"

"No, I'm just kidding you."

"Let me see if I can get them settled down for the night. It's quite evident they are in no condition to go anywhere." Mrs. Taylor went over to Mr. Taylor and suggested he show them to the spare rooms so they could spend the night there.

"Good idea, my dear. "General, since you're the highest ranking man here, you lead the parade up the stairs." So off they went, singing.

Pam, her mother and Helen were simply breaking up with laughter. "You guys must have had some evening."

"Yes, we did. You had better have plenty of ice on hand, for I'm sure there are going to be some big heads in the morning."

"Well, how about you, Irish, are you ready for bed? I'll bet you're really tired."

"Yes, I am exhausted. It's been a busy day—one that I really enjoyed, though." Off we went to my room. I reached for Pam and hugged and kissed her as if I had been away from her for months. "Did you miss me, honey?"

"Yes, I did, Irish, but I'm so glad you had a good time. I'm going to run along now, so you can get some sleep. I'll see you in the morning." We kissed again and said good-night.

After Pam left, Helen came over and turned off the lights. "I'll let you sleep now, Irish, and I'll try not to wake you when I come back for your massage later."

"Oh, Helen, why don't you forget it tonight? I'm doing just great."

"I know, Irish, but we can't let down now. We have to get you all better so I can get on to my next job."

"You know, that makes me very sad that you'll be leaving. I've grown very fond of you, Helen."

"Well, I've grown very fond of you, too, Irish. But that's life, and life must go on. We'll keep in touch, though, don't worry."

"I'd like that, Helen. I really would."

I closed my eyes and started drifting off to sleep as I heard her leave the room.

It was seven o'clock the following morning. I was laying there thinking how wonderful it was to be alive when Pam came in and ran over to the bed with open arms. I sat up and swung my legs over the edge of the bed and caught her up in my arms.

"Hi, beautiful. How's the most beautiful girl in the world this morning?"

"She's happy just to be alive and in the arms of the handsomest guy in the world."

"I'm so happy to be in love with you; to be walking again; to be going to the White House; but most of all, I'm happy about going to the altar to make you my beautiful bride. We have all this joy and happiness to share together, darling. It makes me feel the suffering, waiting, longing, hoping—all the frustrations, little setbacks and all—were worth it, and we're going to be paid off in bonuses we never dreamed of."

"You're so right, Irish. I love you, I love you, I love you."

"Say, I've got a good idea. Why don't you help me get dressed and cleaned up, and we'll sneak downstairs. Won't your mother and Helen be surprised when they come in and find us gone?"

"Okay, let's do it." While she helped me get dressed and watched me shave, we couldn't help wondering how the houseguests were feeling this morning. "Big heads, I'll bet. They must have each consumed three bottles of champagne." I laughed and said, "That's one of the pluses of not drinking. I probably had more fun than they did, and I feel great this morning."

"I'm glad you don't drink, Irish. I think it makes you more of a man to be able to exercise all that willpower. It would be easier just to go along with the crowd, I'm sure."

"I suppose you're right, honey. Once they find out you don't drink and you mean it, they quit trying to twist your arm and in the end have more respect for you."

Just as we were heading for the door, in walked Mrs. Taylor and Helen.

"They caught us, Pam! Now what are we going to do?"

"Where were you two heading so early in the morning?"

Pam said, "We were going to play a trick on you and hide downstairs, but you're too smart for us, I guess."

"Well, come on then; we'll all go down together."

We decided to go ahead and have breakfast, for it was hard to tell how long it was going to take the other party-goers to sober up enough to negotiate the stairs.

We were talking about the trip to the White House and I asked Mrs. Taylor if there was anyone she would like to invite.

"Irish, we would like to invite the world, but it's up to you to choose the guests."

"Decisions, decisions. Well, the general told me last night they prefer a party of seven, in addition to the recipient; so there's you and Mr. Taylor, Pam and Helen."

Helen shook her head. "Oh, I couldn't, Irish."

"Why not? I may have a relapse. It's not every day you get to meet the President, and besides that, I'd love to have you along as a very dear friend."

"It really sounds thrilling in more ways than one. I've never been up in an airplane and I've never been east of Arizona in my life. Then to see the White House and meet the President! It's mind-boggling! But most of all, the biggest thrill will be seeing the most wonderful patient I've ever had the privilege of taking care of, receiving the highest honor his country can bestow upon him. It certainly will be an exciting experience. I thank you all for thinking enough of me to invite me along."

"It's our way of thanking you for all your kindness and patience, Helen. Right, Mrs. Taylor?"

"You hit the nail right on the head, Irish. We never would have made it without her help and understanding."

She excused herself, got up, and walked out of the room. As she was leaving I thought I heard her crying.

"Did I say something wrong, Mrs. Taylor?"

"No, Irish. She is overwhelmed; she'll be all right in a moment or two."

"Do you suppose Sister Margaret would like to attend?"

"Why, Irish, I'm sure she'd love to. How sweet of you to think of her."

"How could I ever forget her? It will be a joyous occasion just seeing her again."

"It certainly will be a dream come true for her, Irish. All her hopes and aspirations and all her prayers for you will be paying off in a grand and glorious way."

"You know, when I look back over my life, I have to realize how fortunate I've been to have all the wonderful people I've had helping me. I've been a most fortunate man. Look at me right now, sitting here with all this warmth and beauty. It's enough to make a fellow want to cry."

"Oh, Irish, you're flirting again, aren't you?"

"Yes, I guess I am. But flattery is the highest form of praise, and nothing's too great for you two."

"Thank you, Irish. We are flattered that you think so highly of us."

Helen rejoined us in the dining room and apologized for letting herself get carried away. "I don't know what came over me; I was simply overwhelmed that you all thought that much of me." I reached for her hand and assured her that we all loved her, and the honor of her presence there would indeed be our honor. She thanked us all again, and suddenly Mrs. Taylor, in her usual fashion, began to worry about protocol and the like.

I laughed and said to Pam, "Here comes the natural worrywart in your mother again. Let me put your mind at ease, Mrs. Taylor. The captain is an expert on protocol. As soon as he wakes up, he can give you every last detail on everything we have to know, from what to wear to the proper method of shaking hands."

She gave a sigh of relief and said, "Oh, that's good."

"See there, I keep telling you not to worry."

"I know, Irish, and you sure have my number on that point, don't you? I guess I'll have to take your advice and stop worrying. You know, Irish, you don't seem to be as thrilled or impressed as we all are. Don't you realize it is the highest honor that can be bestowed upon you?"

"I'm highly impressed, Mrs. Taylor, and this honor ranks right up around the top somewhere. But the greatest honor ever bestowed upon me was your daughter's love for me. Everything else in the world has to come after that—even the Congressional Medal of Honor."

Pam took my arm and looked me in my eyes and started to cry. "Oh, Irish, what did I ever do to deserve you? Those have to be the most eloquent compliments a girl ever had bestowed upon her."

The captain was the first one to get up and face the world. We couldn't entice him to the dining room with food; just the mention of the word seemed to make him sick, so we sat in the living room while he nursed a big glass of tomato juice. Meanwhile Mrs. Taylor picked his brains about protocol at the White House. He went out to their car and brought her back a book on protocol and pointed out the chapters and pages that would pertain to our visit.

It wasn't long before we were joined by Mr. Taylor and the major, with the captain saying he had better go wake the general up. Soon we were all assembled in the living room with the other party-goers trying to get me to fill them in on their activities. Their memories were very fuzzy or they had no recollection whatsoever of what happened after nine o'clock.

I summarized our activities of the preceding night for them. I described the sing-along they had with me at the keyboard. Everyone was simply in stitches. And when I told them they came home and were singing some of the songs before they went to bed, they all seemed a little embarrassed until Pam and Mrs. Taylor assured them they really got a big kick out of it. I added, "And, Captain, I heard of taking a sobriety test by trying to walk a straight line—but on your hands?"

"Oh, Lord, did I do that? I haven't tried that since college."

"Well, you didn't do too badly. You only knocked over two tables and several chairs before everyone agreed you were stone-sober."

After everything settled down, we started having a serious discussion about the trip to the White House.

The major asked if we had decided on a guest list yet, and we told him of our plans so far. "With you and the general, that will make six." The general backed off, saying he was due in the Far East in a few days and would be unable to attend, but the major would represent him there.

I said, "Then there are two other people who I think deserve to go—Moose's parents. If it weren't for their son saving my life on more than one occasion, I wouldn't be going there myself."

The major added, "That would be a great idea. I was planning on visiting them myself. I had put Moose's name in for the Silver Star after verifying the weapons cache we blew up behind enemy lines, and was going to deliver it to them when it came through. Incidentally, Irish, you and the lieutenant are up for that one, also."

"Say, do you think it would be asking too much to have the President present it to them at the same ceremony? That would really make them proud of him."

The general said he would personally write a letter to a good friend of his on the White House staff and see if it could be arranged. We chatted on for another thirty minutes and then they took their leave. The general told me if I decided to make the army a career to get in touch with him. "Maybe together, we can bring some badly-needed changes to the army's way of doing things."

"I definitely will give it some thought, General."

We all shook hands and stood in the driveway as they departed.

We made our way back into the house, and Mr. Taylor came over and shook my hand vigorously as he remarked, "I'm certainly proud of you, Irish."

Pam added, "I told you he'd make you proud of him, Daddy."

Pam threw her arms around me, "Oh, Irish, I love you so much that words won't describe how I feel for you."

"Thanks, Sweet Pea." I made my way over to the piano, and asked Pam to sit beside me. With Mr. and Mrs. Taylor and Helen standing there, I began to play "All the Way." I was singing from the bottom of my heart. It brought back all the good memories of the anniversary party and was a reaffirmation of our love for one another. By now everyone was singing along, and when we finished, I spun around with my back to the piano, and Pam and I melted into each other's arms; we kissed like it had to last a lifetime. We knew it was only a matter of days now until we would finally be married. At last we would be able to start our lives off together with all the love and understanding any newlywed couple could ever hope for.

17

Helen's Husband Makes a
Surprise Appearance

Things started rolling along at a whirlwind pace what with wedding invitations and preparations. Mrs. Taylor was reading her book on protocol for our pending trip to the White House. At the same time she was worrying herself to death over the wedding preparations. I, along with Pam, would keep reassuring her that everything would be just perfect and that there was no need to worry so much. It didn't help her much though, for she worried just the same.

Pam and I made good use of the swimming pool. It was excellent therapy for my legs and just what the doctor ordered to regain the strength in my legs. By the end of the first week I had progressed to such an extent that I had discarded my walker and was using two canes to get around.

Pam would pack picnic lunches, and we would drive to a different spot every other day or so and have our picnic and enjoy the scenery. She was so sweet and loving and was absolutely thrilled at each new little success I would achieve. It only made me try that much harder, for I loved her so much that if standing on my head would have made her smile, I would have tried it.

She would bring along a book of poetry and read to me for

hours. I simply loved it. It didn't matter what she was reading; I simply loved the sound of her beautiful voice. She, in turn, would always try to get me to analyze the poems for her. I would where I could and if I couldn't, I would use that as an excuse to take her in my arms and kiss her, telling her that I interpreted the poem as an inspiration to shower her with love and affection. She knew it wasn't true, yet she never objected.

As we pulled into the driveway after one of our outings, we were greeted by Mrs. Taylor, who was carrying a large bundle of mail.

"Irish! Pam! They're here; they're here."

"What's here, Mrs. Taylor?"

"The invitations to the White House," she said excitedly. "Isn't it wonderful?"

She handed them to Pam, and while I looked over her shoulder, she read them out loud.

"Gee, the twenty-fifth! That's only five days away. They don't give you much notice, do they? Do you think we can be ready by then, Mrs. Taylor?"

"Oh, Irish, I think you're the one who's starting to worry now, aren't you? Of course, we can make it. You just leave everything to me." She threw her arms around me and reiterated how proud she was of me.

"Ah, Shucks! Mrs. Taylor, you're making me blush again. Say, there is one problem though, that I never thought of before."

"No matter what it is, Irish, we can solve it. What is it?"

"Am I supposed to be in uniform to receive the award?"

"Yes, according to protocol you are to be in your dress uniform."

"Got you there, Mrs. Taylor. I'm an officer and a gentleman now, and I don't have an officer's uniform—or even an enlisted man's uniform, for that matter."

"Oh, yes, you do, Irish. They arrived today too and are hanging in your closet."

"I should have known better than to ask. What are we going to do with someone so thoughtful, Pam? Have any ideas on the subject?"

"Well, Irish, we'll just respond in kind and be as loving and thoughtful as she is. Just to prove it, Irish and I are taking you and Daddy out tonight to celebrate. What do you think of that?"

"Oh, you kids! You don't have to do that."

"Nonsense. All the plans are made. We'll leave about seven for a night of dining and dancing; how does that sound to you?"

"It sounds wonderful."

"Thanks for accepting, Mrs. Taylor. It should be a lot more fun than staying home looking after me."

"Oh, Irish, don't talk like that. We all loved taking care of you. It made us happy to do what little we could for you."

"Listen to that; what little you did for me? You simply gave me back my life and made me the happiest man on earth. I don't know how you measure it, but to me those are not little things. They are everything, and I love you all for your undying faith in me."

"Well, come on, let's go on in the house and tell Mr. Taylor of your plans."

"Helen too. Will it be all right with you and Mr. Taylor if she joins us for the celebration?"

"Of course, Irish, don't be silly."

"Where have I heard that before? I know. The first time I asked you to dance, Pam. That's exactly what you said. 'Of course, don't be silly.' "

"No, I didn't, Irish. I said, 'Sure, why not?' "

"That's right. And when I asked you to join Moose and me at our table, that's when you said, 'Don't be silly; we'd love to join you!' "

"Right, Irish! I remember everything about that night. Do you know how he asked me to dance, Mother? He was so polite it almost threw me for a loop. No boy was ever that polite to me in my life. He came walking over to our table, looking mighty apprehensive and nervous, and said, and I quote 'Pardon me, ma'am, may I please have the pleasure of this dance with you?' I couldn't believe it, and at the same time, there was no way in the world I could have turned down such a polite request. What was even more amazing, which I found out later, Irish couldn't rock and roll at all. He and Moose were very homesick and wanted to meet a couple of nice girls. Irish came over to our table like the sacrificial lamb being led away to the slaughter. He told me later that he just knew I would refuse him."

"Are you sorry now that you didn't?"

"Best move I ever made in my life, Irish, accepting your invitation to dance."

"I'm sure glad to hear that. Your acceptance has certainly made my life worthwhile."

We went into the house, and I started hollering for Helen. She came in from another room and wanted to know what all the commotion was about.

"Get your dancing shoes out, Helen. We're all going dancing tonight."

"Dancing? Whatever in the world are you talking about, Irish?"

"Well, since you've been so sweet and uncomplaining about being cooped up here all this time with me, Pam and I decided to have a coming-out party for you and the Taylors tonight."

"Are you kidding me, Irish?"

"No, ma'am, we're leaving at seven. Can you be ready to travel by then?"

"Mrs. Taylor, help me. I never know when he's kidding or being serious."

"He's being serious, Helen, and we would love to have you join us."

"Well, all right, sounds like fun. I accept your gracious invitation."

"Thank you, Helen, but the pleasure and honor will be all ours. Feel like a swim, Pam? We have a few hours to get my dancing legs back in shape. What do you say?"

"Love to, Irish. See you poolside in five minutes."

"You've got it, sunshine."

So off we went, and by the time I got to the pool she was already there.

I walked over to her and took her in my arms, letting my canes fall where they may. I held her like she was ninety pounds of precious gems entrusted into my care. I whispered into her ear how I adored her and how my love had escalated into worship. I simply worshiped the ground she walked on. "Ten more days until you'll be Mrs. Irish O'Malley. Is it possible to be in heaven and on earth at the same time, darling?"

"I'm sure it is, Irish, for I'm in the arms of my angel and lover, so it must be heaven and earth."

Our lips met and sweet, warm sensuous feelings began racing through my body. Pam was breathing heavily, and I could feel her heart pounding against my chest. We knelt down, still locked in each other's arms, and slowly lay down beside the pool. I gently untied the tiny little bows holding up the top of her bikini and gradually slipped it from between us, so her warm soft breasts were pressed against me.

Our mouths were pressed together and I inserted my tongue in her mouth and ran it gently over the roof of her mouth. It aroused her to a fever pitch, and she writhed in ecstasy. Her hand began to move down my body and into my trunks. She began rubbing my penis. I, in turn, loosened the bow on one side of her bikini bottom and she turned so I could loosen the other side also. After I had it untied, I began to gently pull it away. She raised her hips allowing me to do so and giving me access to all of her. I moaned in eager anticipation.

I managed to get my trunks off and began gently kissing her stomach, slowly working my mouth up to her lily-white breasts, while gently running my fingers between her legs and tenderly caressing her vagina.

We continued to enjoy the sensations of fondling and arousing each other and Pam assured me that she was more than willing. I kissed her and told her we had three choices: Go all the way, which I wanted more than anything in the world; masturbate each other and get some relief that way; or jump in the pool and try to cool off.

"Whatever you want, lover, will be what I'll do, Irish."

I kissed her and told her she was too good to be true, and I didn't want to spoil our wedding night for her but felt if we both didn't get some relief we would both be very depressed. She agreed, so we decided on our second option.

I lay her back down and while she ran her tongue around my mouth I inserted my fingers in her vagina. My fingers were inside her, opening her up gently and lovingly. Her vagina felt warm and moist. She was so worked up that she put everything she had into it, churning her hips and encouraging me to keep it up. After she climaxed, she thanked me for stimulating her to heights she had never risen to before.

She had me lay back and reciprocated by gently rubbing my penis until it became stiff and hard and erect. When she asked me if she was satisfying me, I couldn't speak a word. It felt so wonderful. I tried to restrain myself to prolong the incredible ecstasy and, when I could wait no longer, I climaxed. She then looked lovingly into my eyes and asked me if I felt better. I never answered, but took her in my arms and kissed her breasts and sucked at the nipples while she kept running her hands all over my body.

"We're going to have such a wonderful life together, Irish," she said. "You have such a healthy outlook on sex and really know how to make a girl happy, respected, and loved. Most of all, you were able to help me reach fulfillment while keeping my virtue intact. I love you with all my heart, Irish, and if you could do this for me now, I know our wedding night will simply be heaven."

"Thank you, darling, but you have done as much for me, and I love you for it."

"Say, I have an idea, Pam. Let's go skinny-dipping. I always wanted to. What do you say?"

"You got it, Irish."

She helped me to my feet and held my arm until we got to the edge of the pool and then pushed me in. She stood there laughing at me. She looked so pure and innocent standing there in the nude, completely uninhibited. Truly magnificant. And I could feel myself getting sexually stimulated again. I invited her to jump on in, "The water is fine."

She dove in and came up beside me. We embraced there in the water, and after I kissed her she said, "You're aroused again, aren't you?"

"How did you guess?"

She reached down under the water and got hold of my erect penis and said, while giggling her girlish little laugh. "That's how I know."

"And how about you?"

"Irish, I'm always shook up when I'm near you. Do you want to do it again?"

"You know I do. But what if someone comes in here?"

"That only makes it more exciting for me, Irish! Like an element of suspense about it. What do you say?"

"I say let's do it again!"

So we crawled out of the pool and didn't even bother to dry off, and went through the whole wonderful process once more. We came back to earth long enough to get our swimsuits on again and continued our swimming and frolicking for the next two hours before giving it up to get ready for our night out on the town.

As we assembled in the living room, one by one, all dressed up to the hilt, Nurse Helen made her appearance. She had on a beautiful black dress, pearls, and white gloves. She was only twenty-six years old and had a body that would put a sex goddess to shame. We were only used to seeing her in her nurse's uniform, and even though she was stunning enough in that, she was magnificent in dress clothes. Mr. Taylor's eyebrows seemed to disappear into his hairline as he searched for words to express how lovely she looked. I simply said, "I believe I'm having a relapse," and asked her if she would hold my hand, and perhaps take my temperature.

Pam and her mother both got Mr. Taylor and myself under control by reminding us we were both spoken for.

"Yes, and we're very, very pleased about it also; right, Mr. Taylor?"

"Right, Irish."

"We can still admire a beautiful lady, though, can't we?"

"Sure, you can, Irish: that's what beautiful women are for—for you men to admire."

"I'm glad you two are not the jealous types because I'm sure going to ask her to dance with me when we get to the nightclub. How about you, Mr. Taylor?"

"You bet I am, Irish."

Helen was just standing there taking it all in, when Mrs. Taylor assured her that Mr. Taylor and myself were just two big pussycats and that she and Pam would settle our hash if we got out of line.

"Well, if they get out of line, Mrs. Taylor, I'll box their ears for them, okay?"

"Gee, we don't have a chance, do we, Mr. Taylor?"

"Looks that way, Irish."

"Well, shall we get under way, ladies?"

Off we went into the night and arrived at the nightclub a short time later. Pam had already made reservations, so we had no wait at all. We were ushered right to the head of the line and to our table. It was a really classy place and the only problem I had was with the menu. It was written in French, but it was Greek to me. Pam, on the other hand, was quite good with French. I had her order for me and told her as long as it wasn't fried grasshoppers or chocolate-covered ants, it would be fine. After the waiter took our order, Pam informed me she had ordered frog legs for me. I told her that would be all right, as long as they were in the kneeling position.

As the waiter poured the dinner wine, I noticed a good-looking dude making his way toward our table. He walked up behind Helen, put his hands over her eyes, and asked, "Guess who?"

She seemed a bit startled and asked, "Is that you, John?"

He uncovered her eyes and said, "In the flesh, darling." She jumped up and threw her arms around him. It was the mysterious Mr. Jenkins whom I have always wondered about but was afraid to ask for fear he may have been dead, or some other unpleasant memory that would be better left alone.

After their tearful reunion and the introductions all around, he took his place at our table.

"You arranged this, didn't you, Mrs. Taylor?"

"Well. Mr. Jenkins called about five, and I thought it would be a nice surprise for Helen, doing it this way."

"You're really precious, Mrs. Taylor. But you know, this creates another problem."

"What is that, Irish?"

"Well, Mr. Jenkins, we've all grown very fond of your wife. In fact, we love her. Now that you're back, I just don't know if we can let her go or not."

Mr. and Mrs. Jenkins smiled at one another and I said, "Well, seeing how happy you two make each other, we'll just play it by ear for the evening, and see how we feel about things then."

"Thank you, Irish. You don't mind me calling you Irish, do you? Helen has written so much about you that I felt I already knew you before I ever laid eyes on you."

"If you called me anything but Irish, Mr. Jenkins, I probably wouldn't answer. I wouldn't know who you were talking to, I'm so used to everyone calling me Irish."

"I didn't have a chance to tell you of his latest accomplishments though, John. Irish won a battlefield commission and is going to be awarded the Congressional Medal of Honor this week at the White House."

"Congratulations, Irish. Those are some impressive credentials you have there."

"Well, thank you, Mr. Jenkins. Look, we were planning on taking your wife to Washington with us. Would you consider joining us for the trip?"

"Oh, Irish, I couldn't. But it's perfectly all right for Helen to go with you. I'm sure she's looking forward to it, and it will be the thrill of a lifetime for her. And please call me John, not Mr. Jenkins."

"John, there is still one open place on the invitations, and we'd hate to see it go unfilled. Right, Mrs. Taylor?"

"Right, Irish; I do wish you would reconsider, John. We'd love to have you, and I know it will make Helen very happy."

"I really would like to go. Are you sure I'm not crowding my way in or that it won't be putting you all to too much trouble?"

"None whatsoever. Consider the issue closed and consider yourself a member of the party."

"Well, thank you very, very much. I'm sure it will be the thrill of a lifetime for me, also." He took Helen's hand and kissed her on the cheek saying, "They're every bit as wonderful as you described them to me in your letters."

"Helen, you wrote to him about us? I hope you didn't tell him I was in love with you. He may poke me in the nose."

"No, Irish, he's not the jealous type, and he knows I belong to him only."

"Oh, that's good. You know, I feel like a little kid with a whole bagful of sugar cookies. I know damned well I can't eat them all myself. But then, I'm too greedy to want to give any of them away. But it looks like I'm going to have to. These three beautiful ladies have become so much a part of my life that it's gonna take a lot of adjusting to be able to get along without all three of them. I'm gonna have to give Mrs. Jenkins back to Mr. Jenkins. There goes some of the sugar cookies. And then I'm gonna have to give Mrs. Taylor back to Mr. Taylor. There goes more of my cookies. Ah! But look what I have left for myself! All the sugar cookies in the world wrapped up in one precious bundle of love and affection."

The waiter showed up with our dinners and began serving. Poor Mrs. Taylor said, "I'm sorry, John. In all the excitement we never gave you a chance to order your dinner. Waiter, Mr. Jenkins needs a menu, and hold our dinners until his is ready."

"No, no, you go on ahead. I'm really too excited to eat just now anyway."

"Are you sure?"

"Yes, yes. It's perfectly all right."

"Tell you what, John. Pam ordered frog legs in a kneeling position for me, and I'll be glad to share them with you."

Everyone laughed. He declined my gracious offer.

"It certainly was a surprise your showing up here tonight, honey. I didn't expect you back for two weeks."

"Well, we finished our assignment early. Besides that, three months away from you is too long, anyway."

"I hope that's the last time you'll have to go away like that."

"Believe me, it will be. I've been promoted to bureau chief, and from now on someone else will be doing all the traveling while I come home to you every night."

Mr. Taylor asked what line of work he was in. John explained that he was with one of the large news magazines, and he was on special assignment in the Far East for the last three months, covering the war in Korea.

Mr. Taylor told him that was where I was last stationed and that is where I won the Congressional Medal of Honor.

"Wait a minute. How long ago was that, Irish?"

I told him as close as I could remember.

"Let's see, now, that was during their spring offensive. You wouldn't happen to be the guy who drove an ammo truck over a forty-foot cliff into the river, are you?"

"I'm afraid I'm the big dummy."

"Dummy, hell," he said. "I was one of the last guys to get across that bridge you saved before our troops blew it up. I, along with a hell of a lot of other guys, owe my life to you. That's all we talked about for weeks. In fact, I remember seeing them pulling you up in a stokes basket at the direction of a major. I thought for sure you were dead, but that major wasn't having any of that talk."

He stood up and reached for my hand to shake it. I stood up and shook his hand and said, "Small world, isn't it?"

He shook his head and turned to his wife and said, "Honey, if it weren't for Irish, chances are very, very great I wouldn't be here with you tonight."

Helen, with a tear in her eyes, looked at me and said, "Thank you, Irish."

"Ah, come on now, Helen. If it weren't for your efforts, I probably wouldn't be walking tonight, so we're even. Okay?"

"Well, Irish, if anyone in the world ever deserved that award, it's you."

"Oh, there are probably a lot of guys who deserve it more than I do. Like all the ones who will never be back—I think they all deserve it more than I."

"Perhaps you're right, Irish. I'm in no position to judge. But look at all the guys who did make it back due to your efforts. That's what counts as far as I'm concerned."

"Brian O'Malley, I don't know why I never made the connection before. I'm doing a feature article on you and traced you as far as that hospital in Japan. They informed me you were sent

328

home for rehabilitation. I just assumed you were in Pennsylvania. I had planned to go there to interview you. I never dreamed you were the guy named Irish my wife was taking care of. It's incredible!"

"Why do you want to do an article on me? Who'd be interested? I fail to see the appeal."

"It's a terrific human interest story, Irish. And even more so, now that you've won a battlefield commission and the Congressional Medal of Honor."

"Well, I wouldn't want to exploit it or flaunt it."

"Oh, we'll talk about that later, Irish. Enjoy your dinner now."

"Say, Pam, I wonder what kind of a frog they got these legs off of."

"Why do you ask?"

"Fileted frog legs?"

She laughed and said, "It's filet mignon, Irish."

"That's good. I don't think I could handle frog legs."

We finished our dinner and I sat there, listening attentively to all the small talk, not saying much. I was really enjoying being out and in the company of such wonderful people. To me, it was all like a fairy tale come true. Beautiful women, fine wines, lovely atmosphere, soft dance music, money in my pocket, the trip to Washington to be followed by my wedding to the most wonderful girl in the world, my choice of two careers—one in the army and one with Mr. Taylor in the business world. My cup truly runneth over.

I finally got up the courage to ask Pam to dance. "We came to dance, so may I have the pleasure of this dance with you, ma'am?"

"Sure, why not?"

I stood up and held Pam's chair until she stood up. We walked arm in arm the short distance to the dance floor. My legs still felt like rubber and as I embraced Pam for the dance, I warned her to watch out for her toes because I wasn't sure of myself yet. She looked longingly into my eyes and said, "You can stand on my feet if you like, and I'll guide us around the floor."

"No, that won't be necessary, sweetheart. Just hold me and we'll make out all right." We danced the whole number through and made it back to our table.

Everyone was smiling at us. Mrs. Taylor said, "That was wonderful, Irish. I knew you could do it."

"Yes, Mrs. Taylor, your faith in me has helped me do a lot of things I thought I'd never do again. Just as soon as I catch my breath, I would love to dance with you and Helen too."

"Relax, Irish. We have the whole evening ahead of us."

As the evening wore on I kept steering the conversation to Mr. Jenkins by asking him about his career as a correspondent and his overseas adventures. I was a little weary of being in the spotlight and welcomed a new face in the crowd to take some of the heat off me. He obliged and talked freely and willingly. In fact, he did most of the talking for the rest of the evening.

Every once in a while I would take Mrs. Taylor or Helen to the dance floor and stumble through a number with them. I told Helen that things were not going to be the same around the Taylor house with her gone, although I was very, very happy that her husband was home. "I know how hard it is to be separated from someone you love, and I wish you every happiness in the world, Helen."

"Thank you, Irish. I promise I'll never forget you. I'll always have a place in my heart for you, for more reasons than one. Taking care of you made the time pass very quickly for me, and now to find out, you saved my husband's life is simply overwhelming, Irish."

"Oh, Helen, I didn't save your husband's life. I'm sure he would have somehow made it across that river knowing he had you to come home to. And I was the benefactor of all your hard work and long hours. Just a week ago I was paralyzed, and now here I am dancing with one who helped make it all possible. I'll never forget you. For what it's worth, you can tell your husband if it will help him doing that article, I'll cooperate in any way possible. I'm not as bullheaded and stubborn as I was when you first met me. You three have taken that hard, old crab apple I was and turned me into a soft marshmallow."

"I believe you always were a marshmallow, Irish. You just tried to make people think you were an old crab apple."

"Thank you, Helen. I guess that's why I like you so much."

She helped me back to the table. As we sat down, I asked Mrs. Taylor to remind me in the morning to try to get in touch with Sister Margaret. She smiled her loving smile.

"You already have, haven't you?"

"This afternoon, Irish, and she already has permission to attend. We're going to meet her at the train station in Washington. It's all arranged."

"Pam, you're the luckiest girl in the world to have such a wonderful and thoughtful mother. I just pray we never let her down."

"We won't, Irish. We won't."

We finally decided to call it a night about one in the morning. We parted company with Helen and John Jenkins there at the nightclub. They decided to take a taxi to their apartment. Helen was very gracious in saying good-night. She told me she would be over in the morning and that if I gave Mrs. Taylor or Pam any trouble tonight I would have to answer to her in the morning. I kissed her on the cheek and told her I would do my best to behave myself. I believe I detected a tear in her eye as she said good-night. I had the feeling she was going to miss us just as much as we were going to miss her.

We arrived back home a short time later. Mr. and Mrs. Taylor thanked us for a wonderful evening and went on up to bed. Pam and I were tired by now and decided to retire ourselves. As tired as she was, she helped me get ready for bed. I still had trouble bending over, so she took my shoes and socks off for me and helped me out of my trousers and into my PJs. After she had me all tucked in, she leaned over and gave me a passionate good-night kiss as she recited,

"Parting is such sweet sorrow, That I shall say—good-night, till it be tomorrow."

"Say, honey, before I forget, how do you feel about John Jenkins doing that article on me?"

"Irish, that's up to you. Whatever you decide will be perfectly all right with me."

"You know, honey, we two are one now, and I want you to be part of everything I do. I kind of feel I owe it to him, and if you think it's all right, then I'll do it."

"I was hoping you would feel that way about it, Irish."

"How about if we get your mother's opinion in the morning? I'm sure she'll agree, but she really appreciates our consulting her. It makes her feel needed and wanted, so why don't we both approach her about it in the morning?"

"Good idea, Irish. You're so thoughtful."

"Thanks, sweet pea. Much as I hate to part company with you, you had better get your rest. These next few days are going to be a little hectic, I'm afraid."

"Whatever you say, lover. I'll see you in the morning." She kissed me again and left the room. I let my mind wander and fell off to sleep.

18

Preparing for the Trip to the White House

When I awoke, things seemed a little different to me. No Helen, Mrs. Taylor, nor Pam standing there to help me greet the new day. I thought this would be a good time to show everyone how far I had progressed, so I got out of bed and, with the help of my trusty cane, made it to the bathroom, where I showered and shaved.

I got myself completely dressed and even tied my own shoes for the first time in months. I was exceedingly proud of myself and decided to go on downstairs and wait for everyone else to get up. I thought to myself, "How pleased they're all going to be to see me downstairs on my own hook."

I wasn't alone very long when Mrs. Taylor came in. She smiled and sat down beside me. I reached for her hand and said, "Well, I guess I'm all better now."

I could detect a tear in her beautiful eyes as she said, "It isn't going to be the same around here, Irish. I've grown so accustomed to taking care of you that I'm really going to miss it. Then you and Pam will be getting married and probably want to get a place of your own. It's going to be hard to let go, Irish."

"Please don't think of it as letting go, Mrs. Taylor. We'll never be more than a phone call away, and we plan to spend as much time with you and Mr. Taylor as possible. This is only the beginning, Mrs. Taylor. We're going to need you more so now than ever. I just hope you won't get tired of us pestering you all the time. If you do, I want you to let us know. We'll have a million and one projects and problems that we'll need your advice and opinions on, and we are planning to start a family right away. I don't want you to ever get the notion in your head that you are not needed and wanted. How does the old cliche go, 'You're not losing a daughter; you're gaining a son.' "

"Oh, Irish, you'll never know how badly I want to believe that. It sounds so good to hear you say it."

"Believe it, Mrs. Taylor. I am your son, and I'll need you until the day I die, just as much as your daughter will, Mrs. Taylor. We love you and want you to be very much a part of our lives. I know you're going to spoil our kids rotten. But I'll love it because I know you'll love them just as you love Pam and me, and we love you. As long as we have love, our love will bond us together. Please don't forget the very, very special bond you and I have, Mrs. Taylor. That night is one of the most precious memories I have to cherish all my life. You taught me how to make love, and by doing so, I will be able to show Pam my love even more than I would have ever dreamed I could."

"Thank you, Irish! I'll never forget and will cherish that night forever in my memories. If you ever get depressed or feel you need love, I want you to know I'll always be here for you."

"Thank you, Mrs. Taylor. I want you to know that the feeling is mutual; should you ever need someone to help you over a low period, I'll be there for you."

I took her in my arms and passionately kissed her. She responded in kind and held me ever so tightly in her arms and whispered in my ear that she would always love me. "You have a way of putting my mind at ease like no one has ever been able to do in my life."

"I'm glad, Mrs. Taylor. I want us all to be very, very happy for the rest of our lives."

"How about some breakfast, Irish?"

"Love it, Mrs. Taylor." I stood up and took her arm and led her to the dining room, held her chair until she was seated, and called for Maggie.

Mrs. Taylor and I had a delightful breakfast, joking and laughing. It was so good to hear her laugh. She was a lady in the truest sense of the word—schooled in all the social graces, dignified and perfectly proper in her every mannerism. Still I felt I knew her like no one else knew her. I knew how warm and loving she was, and I knew of her great need to be giving of herself. I felt warm and secure with the knowledge that she loved me and that I was able to return her love without the slightest feeling of guilt or remorse. Mrs. Taylor and I were of one accord, and I told her exactly how I felt about her and our relationship.

"Oh, Irish, you'll never know how happy you make me."

"Believe it, Mrs. Taylor. I'm not one to take such things lightly. I believe you know me well enough—perhaps better than anyone else on this earth—to know that I could never lie to you about anything, especially my feelings about you."

"God, forgive me, Irish, but there was a time or two when I had a selfish feeling and hoped you wouldn't get better so that I could spend my life taking care of you. Please forgive me."

"Oh, Mrs. Taylor, don't feel guilty about it. I think those are the most precious sentiments you could bestow on me, and I love you for thinking that much of me to be so willing to give of yourself to me. Some way, some how, some day, I hope I'll be able to reciprocate in kind."

"Thank you, Irish, I had to get that off my chest. I know how wrong those feelings were, and I apologize again for having them."

"What time is it getting to be?" "It's only six-thirty, Irish."

"Feel like taking a swim before everyone gets up?"

"Sounds great, Irish. Let me go change, and I'll get your trunks for you and meet you at the pool."

I walked down to the pool and was sitting there on a chair waiting for Mrs. Taylor. She walked in about five minutes later, and I noticed she locked the door behind her. I knew what was coming next, and my heart started pounding with excitement just thinking about it.

She walked over and handed me my trunks and smiled. "Come on, Irish. Let me help you get into your trunks. She knelt down and took off my shoes and socks while I took off my shirt and T-shirt. I loosened my belt and unzipped my trousers and she gently slid them off me. We both stood up, and I pulled the belt around her robe off and slid it off her shoulders, letting it fall to the ground. She hadn't put her bathing suit on either, and there we stood nude, looking longingly into each other's eyes. I took her in my arms and told her I wanted to make love to her more than anything on this earth.

"I feel the same, Irish. Don't make me wait a moment longer."

We lay down beside the pool, and I immediately began making love to her. She was as gentle as ever. We aroused each other through extensive foreplay, and then I gently penetrated her heavenly vagina as far as my penis possibly could.

She responded with sensuous sighs of relief and kissed me like there was no tomorrow. She ran her tongue around the roof of my mouth and as quickly as she withdrew it, I would insert my tongue and respond in kind. I could feel myself plunging deep inside her moist vagina. We both were moving in a frenzied rhythm that culminated in simultaneous orgasms.

I told her she had to be the greatest lover in the world. She told me it only feels this way when you make love to someone you love.

"Thank you, Mrs. Taylor, and I only want you to think of our affair as something warm and beautiful, which it is, and never, never, under any circumstances think of it in any other way. I love you, Mrs. Taylor. If I didn't I could never make love to you."

"Thank you, Irish. I promise never to think of it any other way, and I will keep it a warm and beautiful secret between us two."

We sealed our promises with a kiss. I then slid down and took one of her lovely breasts in my mouth and started nursing it. She seemed to love it and encouraged me to keep it up. I did, alternating from one breast to the other, while running my hands all over her body as far as I could reach and finally inserting a finger in her warm, moist vagina. By now I had another erection. I ever so gently encouraged her to get on top this time, which she did. It felt even better this way, and in no time at all, we had climaxed again.

She began wondering if we would be able to carry on our affair after Pam and I were married. "It would be devastating if Pam and Mr. Taylor ever found out about it, Irish."

"I think Pam would understand, Mrs. Taylor, but I'm sure Mr. Taylor could never understand. We'll be very discreet and only meet when the need is the greatest. I think I can live with that, Mrs. Taylor. How about you?"

She kissed me and told me I was the only person in the world she had ever even considered having an affair with and she agreed we would have to be very discreet. "I love you, Irish, and you fulfill this great need in me to be giving of myself. If there were no chance for us to continue making love, Irish, I would go right back to my secret longings for fulfillment. You satisfy the need in me, Irish. I don't want you to think that I don't love Mr. Taylor. I do. His needs and wants are so much different than mine. He enjoys making love to me. But with him, it's over in about two minutes, and he just wants to roll over and go to sleep. I do love him, Irish; but sexually, he has never fulfilled my needs. The only person on this earth who can do that is you, Irish. You're so understanding, gentle, and kind. Even after you climax, after you are satisfied, you still take the time to cuddle up to me and prolong the warm, sensuous feeling that makes me feel appreciated and wanted. You are a truly great lover, Irish."

"Mrs. Taylor, I had a loving, kind, warm, and gentle teacher who was willing to share her beautiful, warm, and loving body to teach a scared and very insecure little boy how to be a man and to satisfy a woman's needs."

"I'm glad I was able to help you, Irish. It has been the most rewarding experience of my life."

"I'll always love you, Mrs. Taylor, and always love your loving me. Do you want to go skinny-dipping?"

"What in the world is skinny-dipping, Irish?"

"It's swimming with no suits on. It's really exhilarating and gives you a free feeling like you've never experienced before. Do you want to try it?"

She stood up and helped me to my feet and said, "Why not?" We jumped in the pool together and began swimming and frolicking around. I would swim under water and come up between her legs and stand up with her on my shoulders, then dump her back in the water. We carried on completely uninhibited and unashamed. We finally settled into an embrace at the shallow end of the pool. We got out of the pool and lay there with stars in our eyes. "Wasn't that exhilarating, Mrs. Taylor?"

"One of the most exhilarating experiences of my life, Irish, I love you for suggesting it."

I continued to worship her beautiful body by kissing all parts of her from her thighs right up to her beautiful and soft lips. She continued to arouse me by taking my penis in her hand and working it ever so gently until she had it erect again. She was truly mine and made love to me like we had been doing it all our lives. She kept running her fingers through my hair and rubbing my neck, and would then hug tightly as if to make this moment last forever. She had me sit up and turned herself with her legs ending up behind my back. She then cradled me in her arms while I nursed on her lily-white breasts. I felt like I was in heaven and related that feeling to her.

"This is as close to heaven as we'll ever get here on earth, Irish. I feel so warm and beautiful, holding you like this. I wish I could hold you like this forever."

"You truly are an angel God has sent to show me heaven on earth, Mrs. Taylor, and I only wish I could stay in your loving arms forever."

It took us a long time to come back to earth and get our swimsuits on and take another dip in the pool. She went over and unlocked the door so that if anyone came looking for us, we would be innocently swimming in the pool.

Our first visitor was Pam. I invited her in the pool and told her she was chicken if she didn't jump in. Much to my amazement and Mrs. Taylor's, she quickly shed her shoes, skirt, blouse and slip, leaving only her panties and bra on. She dove in and came up between Mrs. Taylor and myself. I was embarrassed, and so was Mrs. Taylor.

Pam laughed at us and said, "Don't be so Victorian, Mother. Hard as I try to seduce Irish, he has managed to keep my virtues intact, and I love him for it."

Mrs. Taylor smiled and said, "You two are going to have a happy, healthy relationship. I'm so happy for both of you."

Pam threw her arms around me and said, "Do you want to go skinny-dipping, Irish?"

"Okay, wise guy; only if your mother goes skinny-dipping with us. Now what do you have to say about that?"

"Why don't you, Mother? You'll find it exciting and ex-hilarating. And don't worry about embarrassing Irish. After all we've put him through in the past couple of months with all those massages and baths we gave him, it's not going to bother him."

"Don't tempt me, young lady, or I just might do it. What would you think of me if I did?"

"I'd think you'd be the coolest mother a girl ever had, and I'd love you for being so broad-minded. I think bodies are a thing of beauty and should be exposed for enjoyment."

"What would you think of me, Irish?"

"I'm with Pam and believe in freedom of expression, and as long as we all agree, and no one is going to get bent out of shape about it, it sounds like fun."

Pam hollered, "Last one out of their clothes is a chicken."

I got my trunks off in no time flat, and Mrs. Taylor got her suit off without too much trouble, but Pam was having trouble with her bra.

"Would you like some help with that, honey?"

"Yeah, I guess I'm the chicken."

I helped her out of her bra. I must admit it was a bit awkward for Mrs. Taylor and me for a while. But with Pam's encourage-ment and reassurances, we all three let ourselves go and had the time of our lives frolicking around there in the water. After an hour or so of heavenly bliss, we climbed out of the pool and lay down on a blanket, all of us still in the nude.

I was laying between them trying to catch my breath and think of something to say when Pam asked, "What's the matter, Irish? Are we too much for you?"

"I have a feeling my cast-iron constitution is about to get a break in it." I slid my arms under both of them and drew them as close to me as I possibly could. "I love you two more than life itself, but you two tempt me beyond my will to resist." Pam smiled, "You're all shook up, Irish, and I love it. Just think, Irish, only two weeks ago, that couldn't have happened! I'm so happy for you now."

"Oh, Pam, we're embarrassing your poor mother here. I'm sorry, Mrs. Taylor."

"It's all right, Irish. I never subscribed to those old Victorian customs of sex and prudence beyond reason. This is truly an exhilarating experience for me."

"Well, if you're enjoying it as much as I am, then you're really in heaven." Pam included herself in the heavenly atmosphere.

We decided we'd better get dressed and see what was happening. Pam put her skirt and blouse on, and we made our way back upstairs. I went into the kitchen to bum a cup of coffee from Maggie while Pam and Mrs. Taylor went on up to get dressed.

Maggie brought me a cup of coffee and set it down smiling her knowing smile.

"What's the matter, Maggie? Do the walls have ears?"

She grinned and said, "Mr. Irish, we were all so worried about you and your condition, but it looks like you have it all together again. And I for one, couldn't be happier for you."

"Why Maggie, you're going to make me blush. Whatever in the world are you talking about?"

"When I saw Mrs. Taylor hurrying down to the pool this morning, Irish, she had love in her eyes, and I haven't lived in this house for ten years without knowing my way around a little. I just want to tell you, it's the best medicine in the world for her. She really had led a very lonely life in this big house with Mr. Taylor off on trips every other week or so for all them years. I couldn't be happier for her and especially that she chose you for her lover."

"Wow! Maggie, that's pretty hot gossip! How far has it gotten?"

"I'm the only one who knows, Irish, and your secret is safe with me. When I saw you two making love there by the pool, it was so beautiful I wanted to cry."

"Thank you, Maggie. But, please, let it be our secret; don't even tell Mrs. Taylor that you know. Promise?"

"I promise, Irish. Now if you'll excuse me, I have to go grocery shopping."

"Okay, Maggie. See you when you get back."

I took my coffee and wandered into the living room, and sat down at the piano to await the return of the beautiful women in my life. I didn't have to wait long; first came Pam bouncing into the room full of vim and vigor. She sat beside me and insisted I play a pretty love song just for her.

"For you, dear heart, I would do anything in the world." I began to play "I Left My Heart in San Francisco," and before long we were both singing the words.

In the meantime, Mrs. Taylor came into the room and stood by the piano with a handful of mail. After we finished singing, I asked her what she had there.

"Here's one for you, Irish."

"Oh! Would you give it to my wife-to-be, so she can censor it for bad words and grammatical errors? Some day I'm going to have to learn to read and write."

Pam took the letter, hit me on the arm, and said, "Wise guy."

The letter was from the major. The sum and substance of it was the award for the Silver Star had come through and the White House had agreed to present it posthumously to Moose's parents at the ceremony being held in my honor. The Major had made all the arrangements for transportation and accommodations for them all.

"That's simply great, honey. It won't bring Moose back to them, but it sure will make them proud of him, don't you think so?"

"I do, Irish. I really do."

We sat there talking when the doorbell rang. It was Helen and John Jenkins. I stood up and shook John's hand and kissed Helen on the cheek. "We missed you terribly, Helen."

"I've only been gone a few hours, Irish. Now you couldn't have missed me that much."

"Oh, I did! You wouldn't believe the bad time I gave Pam and her mother last night. I refused to go to bed unless you were here to tuck me in. And even when I did, I threw my teddy bear across the room, and knocked all the junk off the dresser. I finally settled down when they promised that once they got you back here this morning, they would never let you get away again."

"Come on, Irish; that's a lot of malarkey. You were probably glad not having me around to boss you, weren't you?"

"Don't you ever believe that, Helen."

"Say, where are your canes, Irish?"

"I must have left them down by the pool. Good place for them. They can just stay there. I never missed them until you mentioned them."

She turned to her husband. "Would you believe less than two weeks ago he was paralyzed from the waist down? That's the kind of guy he is—full of love and determination. He has more heart than anyone I've ever met before in my life."

"Don't you believe a word of it, John. I had no choice with the three of them standing behind me threatening to beat the hell out of me if I didn't get off my backside and start walking. Even in my weakened condition, I really had no choice but to do what they told me, and that's the truth."

"Irish, I agree with my wife. You're full of malarkey."

Mrs. Taylor asked them if they would like some breakfast. They declined, saying they had already eaten, but joined us in the dining room for coffee. As we sat there chatting, John brought up the subject of the article and wanted to know if I had thought any more about it.

"Well, Pam and I discussed it last night but decided to wait for you this morning. We wanted to see what you had in mind and discuss it with our chief counsel, Mrs. Taylor, and get her opinion on the subject."

"Sounds fair enough to me." He proceeded to lay it out for us up to and including the award ceremony at the White House.

"What is your opinion, Mrs. Taylor?" I asked.

"Sounds fine to me, Irish.

"Well, John, I would like you to include the superhuman efforts of your wife and the Taylors. Without them, there would be no award ceremony."

"Oh, Irish," said Mrs. Taylor, "you can't let him put that in the article. It's about you, not us."

"Mrs. Taylor, without you, there would be no Irish O'Malley today. I feel you all deserve all the credit in the world. There I was, completely out of touch with reality and contemplating taking my own life, when you all came to my rescue. I want to tell the world how grateful I am. That's human interest, isn't it, John?"

"It certainly is, Irish, and personally, I think it is a marvelous story. I would like to do it just the way it happened. Why don't you let me write it and submit it to you all for your approval before it is published? Is that fair enough?"

"Sounds fine to me. What do you think, Pam, Mrs. Taylor?"

"If you promise not to publish it until we have had a chance to read it, I'd say go ahead and write it and we'll decide then."

"Say, I have my recorder out in the car and if you're free, we could get started this morning."

"I have no plans. How about you, Pam, Mrs. Taylor?"

"Looks like a clear day, Irish, so why don't you get started?"

"Okay, let me get the recorder. Where do you want me to set up, Mrs. Taylor?"

"How about the library? It will be nice and quiet in there."

"Okay, I'll be right back."

"Well, ladies, shall we retire to the library?"

"No. You go on, Irish. He wants to interview you, not us. Besides we promised to take Helen shopping one day, and today would be a perfect day for it."

"It's gonna be tough getting along without you all, but I'll give it the old college try. Would you leave a number for me to call in case I get lonesome and need someone to hold my hand?"

"Irish, you'll be so busy bending John's ear that you won't even miss us."

"Oh, yes, I will. But you all have a good time now, and if I give you the money, would you please bring me back an ice cream cone? Please?"

Pam stood up and leaned over and kissed me. "Sure, we will, you precious little sweetheart, you."

I walked them to the front door and bid them good-bye. John got his recorder and I showed him into the library where I waited until he had everything set up. We sat there and bullshitted for the next five hours with only a short break for lunch and coffee later on. He said he'd take everything to the office in the morning and have it transcribed and ready for our approval before we went to Washington.

I invited him on down to the game room to shoot a little eight ball. It had been so long since I had held a cue stick in my hand that I had forgotten how it felt. My game had really suffered from the long layoff. I couldn't make a run for anything. It was great fun, though, and we played until the ladies returned from their shopping spree. They invaded the game room with cries of, "Hurry, the ice cream is melting."

We took the cones from them and licked the soft part off until all the remaining ice cream was in the cone, not around the cone.

"Ah, that's delicious, absolutely delicious. I must be pregnant. I have this terrific craving for ice cream cones."

"Say, we left you two to do an interview, and we come home and find you goofing off here playing billiards. What happened to the interview?"

"We finished. We talked for better than five hours. Believe me, Irish gave me enough material to write a novel. Terrific material. He had me laughing so hard I was crying. And at other times I felt like crying because it was so sad. I believe we have the makings of a beautiful article, and I should have it all transcribed by the time we leave for Washington. How does that sound?"

"It sounds wonderful, and I can hardly wait to read it."

"Say, it's about dinner time. Why don't we get ready and wait for Mr. Taylor in the living room?" We all agreed and met back in the living room in ten minutes.

Mr. Taylor had arrived and was sitting in the living room with John when I walked in. "Would you like something to drink, Irish?" "No, thank you, I'm fine."

"Irish doesn't drink, John."

"Yes, so I've heard. I would love to see him drunk one time, though. With his sense of humor, I'll bet he'd be a riot with a few drinks in him."

"Believe me, Irish doesn't need any alcohol to have a good time. When the spirit hits him, he's completely uninhibited. He just lets loose on his own, without any help from the booze."

We were soon joined for dinner by the ladies. After dinner we wound up back in the living room. I asked if Pam and I could be excused to go for a walk in the park. Of course, it was perfectly all right with all concerned, so Pam and I started out the door, promising to be back before the Jenkins had to leave.

We walked with our arms around each other, not saying much of anything, finally arriving at the little park with the duck pond. We sat down on the grass facing each other. I took Pam in my arms and kissed her passionately. I whispered in her ear that I had a confession to make to her, and I only prayed to God that she would understand. I could feel the tears in my eyes as I searched for the words to tell her.

She withdrew a little and looked me in the eyes and said, "Irish, I think I know what you're going to tell me, and I do understand. I still think you're a superhuman person, and I only love you more for confiding in me after you were sworn to secrecy. Mother was feeling guilty about it too. I only want you both to understand how much I love you and that it only makes me love you both even more."

"How did you know, darling?"

"Oh, Irish, I practically forced Mother into your arms that night. I encouraged her and told her to go to you for both your sakes. You both had such a deep need for love and affection, and I wasn't in a position to help either one of you just then. Mother and I talked for hours on end about you—about how you were grieving for your mother; about your being a virgin; and about how bashful and shy you really were, in spite of the academy award performance you would put on for our benefit. She really wasn't aware of her own needs of fulfillment until I pointed them out to her and made her realize that she had never achieved sexual fulfillment in twenty years of marriage. I encouraged her, by telling her she would be doing both you and me a great service by teaching you how to make love and by getting rid of all your little hang-ups, inhibitions, and anxieties. She was afraid that if you had never gone through with the actual sex act, you might freeze up on our wedding night, making it a disaster for both of us."

"I don't believe that would have happened with you being so loving and understanding as you are, honey, but she was right. I didn't know from straight up how to make love to a woman and see that she was completely satisfied."

"She was so afraid you would get the wrong impression, Irish, and she didn't want you to know that she and I were discussing you like that, so she had me agree that if she found the courage to go through with it, she would swear you to secrecy."

"Oh, lover, you'll never know how it has been tearing at my heart, not telling you before this. I really do love your mother and I'll always be grateful to her for teaching me how to make love. It can only help me love you more, honey. I'm sorry I betrayed your mother's trust in me; but I could never live a lie with you. I love you too much to deceive you. I had all that grief bottled up, along with all those fears and doubts. And I wasn't sure, after being impotent for so long, how I would function, and I was really worried that I wouldn't be able to satisfy you. Thanks to her, all my insecurity is gone. She truly took the boy and gave us back the man."

"Oh, Irish, I do understand, and I'll always be grateful to you both. She came to me that night after she left your room and cried tears of joy in my pillow for over an hour. It was one of the most rewarding experiences for her, Irish, and she reached sexual fulfillment for the first time in her life. It was beautiful and rewarding for me, also, Irish, knowing I played what little part in the affair that I did. Like you say, she gave us back the man, and we'll have the rest of our lives to enjoy a good healthy, uninhibited relationship."

"Thank you, sweetheart. I guess it was all those puritan principles and beliefs that were really bothering me. I still have a little trouble understanding just why you encouraged your mother, though, Pam."

"It's not so hard to understand, Irish. You taught me, to thine own self be true. To do, say, and think what I know in my heart to be right, regardless of what others might think, say, or do. I knew in my heart and soul that it was the right thing to do. The fact that she was my mother and you were my fiance was unimportant. The important thing was how you two felt about each other and the great need you both had to be free of your doubts, fears, and worries. She needed you every bit as much as you needed her, Irish; you can believe that. My reward was seeing how happy it made her. I never saw her so happy. My greatest reward came the following morning when I saw you in such a happy, gay mood. All your anxieties had vanished overnight, and you were your old self again for the first time since you went away. What more could I have asked for? No one in the world could ever convince me it wasn't meant to happen just that way."

"Oh, you dear, sweet, precious baby doll, you. You have a heart as big as all outdoors. You're the most compassionate little lady God ever gave the breath of life to. To think you loved your mother and me enough to be that thoughtful of both of us. It's truly magnificent, darling. If there were just some way I could express how I love you and feel for you. I just can't put it into words, darling."

"Why don't you try kissing me and showing me then, you dummy you." She laughed as I grabbed for her and squeezed her as hard as I could. I kissed her like there was no tomorrow, and kept reiterating the fact that I loved her, until it sounded like a broken record. We got up and went walking around the pond, hand in hand, stopping every once in a while for a tender, little embrace and a kiss.

I decided to show off a little as to the progress I was making and did a handstand. I promptly fell on my butt, and just that quickly had my precious little angel sitting on the ground beside me caressing my face, and asking me if I was all right. "Never felt more alive in my life. I'm glad I told you about your mother. It really has taken the burden of guilt off my mind. I don't ever want us to have any secrets from each other. Regardless of how painful it might be, I want us to be perfectly honest with each other. Promise?"

"I promise, Irish, and since we're not keeping any secrets from one another, I feel there is something I have to tell you."

"What could that be?"

"I snore a lot and my feet get terribly cold at night."

I laughed and said, "So those are the chinks in your perfect coat of armor, are they? Well, we'll keep your feet warm for you, and once I'm asleep, your snoring won't bother me a bit."

She stuck out her lower lip and raised her eyebrows as if to pout, while teasing, "Shucks, Irish, are you planning on sleeping after we're married? I thought that was why you were resting up now, so we could dispense with sleeping, giving us more time to make love."

I laughed and said, "Well, maybe after the first year or so, we'll consider a few hours' sleep now and then."

"You know, Irish, when Mother came to my room that night, I cried with her. She told me what a gentleman and how really kind and thoughtful you were. Even after she had committed herself to making love to you, you respectfully told her that she wouldn't have to go through with the physical act, just the fact that she was willing to help you was the ultimate expression of love, as far as you were concerned. That was so sweet and kind of you, Irish. Knowing how you felt and how badly you needed and wanted to make love, to think you were thoughtful enough and respected her enough at that point to even think of her feelings was superhuman."

"I'm glad it worked out the way it did, honey. I really feel like a complete man now, and I am confident that I'll be able to take care of your every want and need for as long as we live. I love you, Pam Taylor, with all my heart and soul."

"Say, do you suppose Mrs. Bloomfield is watching us from her window? You know, kissing and hugging are totally unacceptable behavior in these parts, honey child."

"Oh, pray tell, handsome prince, what's a girl to do then?"

"Well, should she call up and tell on us, I'll just say, 'Alas, I never touched my love, for she is swift and outrunneth me.' Do you think they'll go for that?"

"Well, if she calls, I'll tell her to go sit on a tack."

"That wouldn't be very ladylike."

"Perhaps not, but it sure would give me a great deal of satisfaction."

"Temper; temper."

She laughed and said, "Should we wander back home and see what everyone else is up to?"

"Why not? I'm so happy I feel like singing. Does my lady care to join me in a song of good cheer?"

"What would you like to sing, my love? I'll have the maestro strike up the orchestra."

"How about, 'The Cow Kicked Nellie in the Belly in the Barn'?"

"I don't know that one, Irish." "Neither do I. You pick one."

"How about 'Til the End of Time'?"

"That's a beautiful song, honey, and it expresses my sentiments exactly."

As we started walking slowly back to the house, I started to sing to her, "Til the end of time, long as stars are in the blue, I'll be there for you, to care for you, through laughter and through tears." She joined in and our voices blended together beautifully. We sang it again and again, all the way up to the front door. We kissed and exchanged our vows of love for one another before going in.

We walked in the living room and sat down on the piano bench, listening to Helen and John and Mr. and Mrs. Taylor talking. When their conversation reached a lull, Mrs. Taylor asked me if I would play "Moonlight Sonata" for them.

"It's been so long, Mrs. Taylor. I'm not sure I remember."

"Sure, you do, Irish. We won't take any points off if you make a mistake or two."

Pam got up and stood by the side of the piano, and I started in playing. I must have played it a thousand times for Sister Margaret and perhaps a thousand times since then. I played the whole score through and then picked right up on "Til the End of Time" and asked Pam to sing with me. We sang our hearts out. When we were through, every one in the room gave us a warm round of applause.

John said, "Irish, do you know, you're great."

"No, John, but if you hum a few bars, I'll try to play it."

They must have laughed for a good five minutes before things settled down. Mr. Taylor said, "I told you, John. Irish doesn't need any booze to have a good time."

"Why don't you all gather around the piano and we will have a sing-along?" They did. Mrs. Taylor dug out all the sheet music she could find. We had a gay ole time for the next two hours, singing one song after another.

Finally deciding we had had enough singing, we retired to the comfort of the couch and the easy chairs. We laughed and joked around until past midnight when Helen and John decided they had better be going. He wanted to get up early and get to his office to have the tapes for the article transcribed and all. We saw them to the door and while we were saying good-night, John commented he had never had a more memorable day in his life and would never forget it.

Pam told him that I had a way of taking ordinary days and turning them into memorable occasions.

"He certainly does, young lady, and I'm sure he'll make you very, very happy."

"Thank you, John. I know he will."

350

I kissed Helen and promised to behave myself until she returned.

They no sooner cleared the driveway than we all decided to call it a day, also. Pam walked me to my room. She helped me get ready for bed. I had outdone myself and was so tired I could hardly stand up any longer. She lay down beside me for a few minutes, urging me to close my eyes and go to sleep and then she would go on to bed as soon as I fell asleep. I closed my eyes and a few seconds later was dead to the world.

19

The Trip to the White House

Time moved quickly during the next two days. Before we knew it, we were on the plane winging our way east toward Washington. John had the transcripts of the article with him and had made enough copies so that we could all read one on the plane. Everyone agreed it was a beautiful piece of work. I still felt a little sheepish about having my exploits exposed for all the world to see, and I confided these feelings to Mrs. Taylor and Pam.

With the help of Mr. Taylor and the Jenkinses, they convinced me to let it be published as it was written. As I knew I would, I agreed with their decision, and we all signed the customary release forms allowing our names to be used. John then handed me a plain white envelope. I asked what it was and he told me to open it and see. I handed it to Pam and asked her if she would do the honors. She opened it and withdrew a check for one thousand dollars with my name on it.

"Wow! I didn't think there was that much money in the whole world. What's it for?"

"That's the standard fee for the article, Irish. It's all yours."

"I can't believe it." I took the check and admired it and then passed it around for all to see. "Do you mean it's mine to keep?"

"Yes, it's all yours. And I'm sure you'll find a good use for it."

After they handed the check back to me, I gave it to Pam and said, "Quick, honey, get the parachutes. Let's get out of here before he changes his mind."

We all laughed. I told him I really hadn't been expecting anything, but that I certainly wanted to thank him, not only for myself, but also on behalf of all these wonderful people who made it possible, and especially him for being thoughtful enough to want to do the article in the first place.

"It was my pleasure, Irish. Believe me, I enjoyed doing this article more than any I have ever written."

"Well, I don't know how we'll ever be able to repay you, but thanks again."

We landed at National Airport outside of Washington and took a cab directly to our hotel. The award ceremony was to be held at three o'clock in the afternoon and it was already nine in the morning. Sister Margaret was due at the train station at ten, and Pam and I had volunteered to go down and meet her train.

We took another cab and went to Union Station to await her arrival. We had a little time to kill, so we did so by sharing a Coke at the lunch counter. I told Pam I was starting to get very nervous about the whole affair and hoped I could see it through. "I'll sure feel funny in an officer's uniform—somewhat like a traitor to all my buddies whose side I was on for all that time." I explained to her how it worked with those in authority in the service being the enemy of the enlisted men and all. "Now, I'm the enemy."

"Irish, you'll do just fine, and I'm proud that you're an officer and a gentleman. There are leaders and there are followers. You have always been a leader and are finally getting the recognition you so richly deserve. I'm sure your old buddies are just as proud of you as I am, so don't think another thought about it. You just stand tall and proud this afternoon, Irish, and we'll all stand tall and proud beside you."

"Thanks, sweet pea, you're great for my ego and self-confidence. I would never have made it without you."

"Nor I without you, Irish. That's the beauty of love, being able to give strength and reassurance to one another. I love you, Irish, with all my heart and soul."

It wasn't long before they announced the arrival of Sister Margaret's train. We walked over to the gate to wait for her. We didn't have to wait very long before I spied her coming through the gate with her suitcase. "There she is," I cried out.

We walked up to meet her. As soon as our eyes met, she dropped her suitcase. She rushed into my open arms, and I lifted her right off the ground and swung her around. I was so happy to see her after all those years that the tears were flowing like water. We never spoke a word for the first few minutes. We didn't have to. Our emotions were telling us both how glad we were that we had finally found each other again.

After we regained our composure, she gave Pam a big hug and a kiss and told her how happy she was to see her again. Pam was overwhelmed at the reunion and told her she would never know how happy she made us all by coming.

I held her at arm's length and told her she was even more beautiful than I remembered her to be.

"I see you're still full of blarney, Irish."

"Where the women in my life are concerned, I carry the blarney stone around in my pocket. Say, have you had breakfast, Sister Margaret?"

"Yes, I have, Irish."

"Well, I guess we had better get on back to the hotel then, before Mrs. Taylor sends a search party out for us."

We arrived at the hotel a short time later. Pam showed Sister Margaret to her room and said she would join us in a few minutes. I went to the Taylors' room. The major had arrived with Moose's parents, and they greeted me with open arms. I let them know how happy I was that they could make it. They told me they would have made it if they had to walk and thanked me for making it possible for them to be there.

I assured them, "I had little or nothing to do with it. If it hadn't been for your son's saving my life, I wouldn't be here today to help honor his memory. He'll be getting the recognition he so richly deserves. He was the real hero, not me."

"Well, we can't say, Irish. But we'll always remember how you and Pam eased our burden and made us feel his life here on earth was not in vain. You lightened our load considerably. We'll always be grateful and always have warm and loving memories of him and his best friend. There is no way to measure those things, Irish; they are priceless."

I thanked them and told them we were all only too glad to do what we could.

Pam and Sister Margaret showed up a few minutes later. I introduced her to everyone as my first love. I told them, "I would have married her, but I was upstaged by the Good Lord himself. He had already won her heart before I ever had a chance. He told me personally, though, that I could love her just as much and as long as I wanted to, and I took him at his word and I'll love her until the day I die."

She laughed and said, "Mrs. Taylor, will you see if you can get that blarney stone away from him? He's been carrying on like this since the train station."

"I'm afraid I can't help you there, Sister Margaret. Besides that, I believe every word he said."

The major suggested we have an early lunch since we were to be at the White House at two o'clock for our briefing on the award ceremonies.

We went to the dining room there in the hotel and were seated at a table large enough to accommodate our group. Moose's parents were ill at ease and everyone sensed it, so we all directed the conversation to them and encouraged them to do most of the talking. It seemed to work; for before we were through with lunch they were acting like their old selves and having the time of their lives.

After lunch, we retreated to our rooms to get dressed for the upcoming event. I put on my monkey suit with the gold bars on the epaulets. When I topped it all off with my new hat with the big gold eagle on the front, I must admit that the vain streak in me surfaced for a moment or two, and I stood there admiring myself in a full-length mirror. I felt a foot taller.

While I was admiring myself, the major walked into my room. He saluted and told me I made a fine looking officer. I thanked him and returned his salute.

"Christ, Major, I'm nervous as hell. Is there any chance of calling the whole thing off? It's more like an act of God than an act of Congress."

"Not a chance in the world, Irish. Relax. You'll do all right, I'm sure. Say, there is one slight problem, Irish."

"What's that, Major?"

"Well, I've made reservations for our party at the Officers' Club over at Fort Myer for dinner and dancing. Do you think the good sister will be offended being asked to go there?"

"I'll talk to her, Major, but I'm sure it will be just fine. She is really quite broad-minded, and I don't think she'll be offended in the least."

"Okay, Irish. I'll leave it up to you. I sure wouldn't want to hurt her feelings."

"Don't you worry, Major. Leave it to me. Well, shall we join the others?"

We walked into the Taylors' suite, and everyone had already assembled there. Everyone couldn't get over how handsome I looked in my officer's uniform. I was having a little trouble coping with the situation and returned their compliment by telling them they all looked super themselves. I took Pam aside and told her of the Major's plans and asked her if she would speak to Sister Margaret in case I didn't get an opportunity to do so. She said she would be glad to.

Soon it was time to leave. Before I even had time to catch my breath, we were pulling up to the White House in the two chauffeur-driven limousines. We were met there and escorted into a reception room where the gentleman in charge began briefing us on the upcoming ceremonies and asking us if we had any questions. We had plenty of questions and he fielded them all and concluded by telling us not to worry. He assured us that even if we happened to make a mistake, we shouldn't feel badly about it, because everyone would understand. "Just relax and be yourselves and everything will be just fine." The time flew by quickly and the next thing we knew, we were standing in the Oval Office, waiting for Mr. Big himself.

I held onto Pam's hand so tightly and kept biting my lower lip to hide my nervousness. In fact, I wished I could be most anywhere else in the world at that moment instead of being there. Pam sensed it, leaned over, and whispered in my ear that it was going to be just fine. "We're here to honor you, Irish—not to execute you." I smiled at her and gave her a little peck on the cheek. "Thanks, sweetheart, I really needed that."

Our wait was soon ended with the announcement of the arrival of the President.

He immediately put us all at ease by coming over and being introduced to all in attendance and welcoming us there. Then he instructed our escort to give us a special guided tour of the complete White House after the ceremony. We all thanked him. He nodded to the gentleman in charge of the proceedings and things got under way.

He started off by reading the orders for the Silver Star awards and went on to give a description of the events that made the awards possible. Another aide handed the President the medal for Moose, and he, in turn, handed it to Moose's mother, all with the thanks of a grateful country. Moose's mother and dad thanked him, and he shook their hands.

He was then handed the Silver Star to be awarded to me, which he pinned on my chest, and then shook my hand. I, in turn, thanked him.

They then read the orders for the Congressional Medal of Honor and gave all the details leading up to, and the consequences of, my actions. They handed the President the medal. As he placed it around my neck, he said he was truly honored to make this presentation. I thanked him and shook his hand, and that concluded the ceremony.

Everyone in the room hovered around me and all were congratulating, hugging, and kissing me. It was definitely my moment of glory. I actually felt ten feet tall.

The President stayed with us for another few minutes, sharing in the joyous occasion and posing for pictures with us. He really seemed to be enjoying himself, also. And let's face it, pictures like this didn't hurt his political image one single bit. One of his aides finally reminded him that he had another meeting to attend in ten minutes and they had better get started to it. He shook all our hands once more and then gracefully made his exit.

We talked for another five minutes when our escort graciously prompted us to start our tour of the White House.

While on our tour, Pam and I were able to get Sister Margaret aside and ask her if she objected to the arrangements for the celebration party afterwards. She assured us it wouldn't bother her in the least, especially since she was able to talk Mother Superior out of sending an escort with her. I kissed her on the cheek and told her I'd dance the first waltz with her. "Oh, you remember how, Irish?"

Pam said, "Does he ever. He waltzed all our hearts out at our engagement party."

"I'm glad you remembered, Irish. I thought it would be useful to you someday."

After our tour was concluded, we were ushered out the door and to our limousines. Pam had assured the major that his plans would not be an embarrassment to Sister Margaret, so we were off to Fort Myer for a joyous evening of dinner, dance, and song.

True to my word, I bribed the bandleader into playing a waltz just for us and took Sister Margaret to the dance floor. We waltzed our hearts out while everyone in the room looked rather stunned to see such an unlikely sight as a nun waltzing in a place where they served liquor. After we were through dancing and I was escorting her back to our table, I asked her if she was sure that J. C. wouldn't get mad at me for having brought her here. She laughed like I never heard her laugh before.

Helen told Sister Margaret that a little over two weeks ago I couldn't even walk, and to see me waltzing with her was the most glorious sight in the world to them all.

"Irish, I didn't know, or I'd never have put you through that."

"Nonsense, Sister, I loved it. It was a childhood dream come true. I always dreamed of dating you and taking you dancing in some fancy ballroom when I grew up, and here we are. I guess I can take that page out of my dream book and put it in my memory book now."

Everyone was smiling at us. Mrs. Taylor asked her what I said that was so funny when we were leaving the dance floor. She laughed again and said, "Irish wanted some reassurance that J. C. wasn't going to get mad at him for taking me dancing." Everyone started in laughing.

I proposed a toast to some very special people in my life that couldn't be here to share our happiness. "To Moose, my most trusted and cherished friend; his lovely fiancee Carol; and my loving mother and brother. May God rest their souls." Sister Margaret suggested we all bow our heads in a moment of silent prayer for them. It took a little while to get things back to their joyous level after I had injected that bit of sadness into the proceedings, but it wasn't long until dear, sweet Mrs. Taylor took the initiative and told me I also had promised to dance with her. "Your wish is my command, dear lady."

Mrs. Taylor asked me how I was doing and if I was feeling all right.

"Terrific, Mrs. Taylor. It will take weeks, perhaps even months, for the full impact of this day to hit me. You'll never know how happy I am that you're all here to share this memorable occasion with me."

"You'll never know how happy I am to be sharing it with you, Irish."

"Do you think Sister Margaret is having a good time?"

"The time of her life, Irish, from where I stand. She is truly magnificent, Irish. She is so sweet and kind. I can readily see why you are so taken by her warmth and charm."

"I only wish there were more I could do for her, Mrs. Taylor —something to make her truly happy and to make life easier for her."

"Oh, Irish. I'm sure she is perfectly content in the sisterhood, and you have made her the happiest person on earth today. I'm sure she feels her life as a nun has really been worthwhile upon seeing her favorite pupil receive the highest award his country could bestow upon him. I'm sure she feels it's all been worthwhile, knowing she had so much to do with getting you started on the right path so many years ago. The fact that you remembered her and thought enough of her to invite her must have been overwhelming for her."

"I'm sure you're so right, Mrs. Taylor. I've never known you to be wrong when it came to affairs of the heart. I remember Sister Margaret telling me once, a long time ago, when I asked her why she chose to be a nun, telling me:

> *I slept and dreamed that life is joy;*
> *I awoke and saw that life is duty;*
> *I acted accordingly and discovered joy and*
> *happiness.*

I understand now that she is perfectly happy and doing exactly what she wants to be doing. If in some small way, I've added to her joy and happiness, I'm only too proud to have been able to do so."

"How sweet, Irish. You're so warm and giving of yourself. You always take the time to try and understand others' needs and wants; and as Pam has told me many, many times, you are always putting other peoples' feelings ahead of your own."

"No, Mrs. Taylor. It's that being surrounded by so many beautiful and lovely people like yourself makes me want to make you all proud of me."

Without realizing it, the evening slipped away. Midnight was fast approaching when I suggested we go back to the hotel before our carriages out front turned into pumpkins and I reverted back to being a hapless chore boy again.

Everyone laughed and drank their final drink. We piled into the limousines and headed back for the hotel. On the way back to the hotel, I asked Sister Margaret if there was anything I could do for her.

"There is only one thing in the world that I can think of at the moment."

"Your wish is my command."

"I want to hear you play "Moonlight Sonata" on the piano before I go back."

"Well, even if I have to go out and buy a piano tonight, I'm sure going to fill that request."

Upon arriving back at the hotel we went into the lounge, which was practically deserted. Sure enough, they had a piano over in the corner. I asked Mr. Taylor if he would find everyone a table while I got hold of the manager and asked if he'd mind my playing the piano. He was more than happy to grant my request. Mr. Taylor had everyone seated over by the piano, and I started playing just for Sister Margaret. I'm sure it brought back a lot of pleasant memories for her. I could see tears in her eyes and I played my heart out for her. I played the whole score, and when I was through, everyone applauded. I asked if there were any special requests, and, of course, Mrs. Taylor wanted me to sing her favorite, "I'll Take You Home Again, Kathleen." I asked Sister Margaret if she would join me at the piano so we could sing together. She got up and came over and sat beside me.

"Just like old times, Sister Margaret, sitting behind the old upright, with you praying your rosary, praying for patience and guidance while I banged away on the wrong keys." She laughed, reached up and mussed my hair all up, and said, "Hit all the right notes, Irish, or I'll get my ruler out and smack your hands."

"I'll be good, Sister Margaret. Don't you worry." I began playing, and as we were singing, a peaceful calm seemed to descend over the room. It was almost as if the Good Lord himself had put his stamp of approval on the proceedings. After we finished, we played a couple of duets, and then asked everyone to join in the singing. We had a good ole time for the next two hours. It was really hard to bring such a good time to an end; but we were all so exhausted we could hardly keep our eyes open any longer. After saying good-night, we all made it to our respective rooms. I escorted Pam to her room and went in with her. It was the first time we were alone since before the trip began. We clung to each other like there was no tomorrow. I told her I was sorry for not being able to devote more time to her during the day, but I would make up for it right now.

"Oh, Irish, I don't feel slighted in the least. I was so proud of you today and I have you in my arms right now. What more could a girl ask for?"

"I don't know, honey, but if you think of something, just let me know."

She laughed and held me closer. "Oh, Irish, I love you so much. Just when I think I could not love you any more than I do, you do something nice—like making Sister Margaret so happy today—and it only makes me love you more. I don't believe I've ever seen anyone happier than her in my whole life. She was fighting back the tears of joy all day long, Irish. I'll bet she's in her room right now crying because she's so happy."

"Do you think she is? I would like to go to her now, but I couldn't do that." "I know, Irish, and besides that, women enjoy a good cry once in a while. Especially a good cry over a very meaningful occasion. In fact, if I ever get up the courage to run you out of here tonight, I'll have me a real good cry."

"Say, honey, I was just thinking, do you suppose we could rent a car and drive Sister Margaret home tomorrow? She's at a school only fifty miles away from my hometown and we could visit my mother's grave after we leave her. Do you think your folks would mind terribly if we did that?"

"I'm sure they won't mind one bit, Irish, and they will have John & Helen Jenkins to keep them company on their trip home. I think it's a wonderful idea."

"If Sister Margaret agrees, then we'll do it. Now, as much as I hate to, I'd best say good-night to you, sweetheart, so you can get some rest."

"I hate to let you go, Irish; but I know I must. Get a good night's sleep, darling, and I'll see you bright and early in the morning." We kissed good-night, and I very reluctantly backed out the door, throwing her kisses as I departed.

20

Taking sister Margaret Home

The morning came quickly and we were all gathered in the Taylors' suite, packed and ready to travel by eight-thirty. Pam and I had discussed our plans with all concerned and had everyone's blessing and consent.

Pam, Sister Margaret, and I were the first to leave after saying good-bye to Moose's parents and the major, and telling the Jenkinses and the Taylors we would see them in Sacramento.

We took a cab to the rental agency and rented the biggest, finest car they had available. Sister Margaret wanted to ride in the back seat, but I insisted she ride up front with us. I told her I needed her to pray on her beads so I could get a little divine help keeping this big monster of a car between the guardrails. We were soon out of Washington and on the open road, heading through Maryland toward the Pennsylvania line. The miles just seemed to fly by as we talked and reminisced, joked and laughed, stopping only for a short lunch break and to get gas.

It was about two o'clock in the afternoon when we arrived at the convent. School was still in session and Sister Margaret asked Pam and me if we would mind terribly if she introduced us to her students. "Of course not," we said, "we would love it."

363

We followed her over to the school. She asked us to wait in the hall to give her a chance to introduce us properly. Then she went into her classroom.

As soon as the kids laid eyes on her, school was over for the day. They greeted her with loud cheers. They were shouting about how she had her picture in the paper and how proud they were of her and all. She finally got them settled down, restored some semblance of order, and then told them she had a special treat for them. She told them that she had brought the real hero back to meet them personally. She then came to the door and asked Pam and me to come in.

We walked in and were immediately surrounded by all these well-wishing little third graders. They had a million and one questions which we tried to answer for them. They were more interested in how Sister Margaret and I became such good friends and why I invited her to the White House than they were in my receiving the Medal of Honor.

I told them Sister Margaret and I first met when I was in the third grade, same as they were now, and that I fell deeply in love with her then, and our love and friendship had lasted all these years. "In fact," I told them, "it was because of her love, patience, understanding, and above all the principles of life that she taught me, that I was able to get through life and find this beautiful girl here who will be my wife next week. Most of all, Sister Margaret taught me to face up to any situation by having faith in myself and in God."

One little girl said, "I didn't think sisters were allowed to fall in love with their students."

"Don't you believe it, honey. Sister Margaret always falls in love with her students. I'm sure she loves you all every bit as much as she ever loved me. You just pay attention to what she has to teach you, and someday, perhaps, as I am doing today, you'll thank her from the bottom of your heart for being so loving and giving of herself to make you all better people."

By now word had spread all over the school of the triumphant return of their beloved Sister Margaret. Mother Superior came in and asked if she called a school assembly, would we be kind enough to appear before the student body to be introduced. "I wouldn't expect you to give a speech or anything like that," she assured us.

"We'd love to, Mother Teresa, and we'll let Sister Margaret do all the talking."

"Thanks, Irish. You know, I'm stealing your thunder, and you've made a hero out of me, don't you?"

"I'm glad, Sister Margaret. You're only getting the recognition you so richly deserve."

Within ten minutes, all the students in the school were assembled in the small auditorium and Mother Superior stepped up to the podium, said a few kind words about their returning hero, Sister Margaret, and then turned the microphone over to her. The entire student body gave her a standing ovation and almost took the roof off the place with their shouting and hollering. She was smiling with delight. After getting them all settled down, she proceeded to tell them all about her trip to Washington and her introduction to the President and the award ceremony. She then introduced Pam and me and told them we would answer any questions they might have. They gave us a standing ovation as we stood up and walked over to the podium to join Sister Margaret.

I started in by saying, "Good afternoon, Mother Superior, sisters, boys and girls. We never expected to be afforded the pleasure of appearing before you this afternoon. Our mission was simply to return your hero, Sister Margaret, safely back to those she loves so dearly. But in her own sweet, lovable way she maneuvered us right up on stage. So, if you have any questions or if there is anything you don't know about Sister Margaret that you would like to ask me, I'll be glad to answer, for Sister Margaret has been my favorite subject ever since third grade."

One little boy raised his hand, and I acknowledged it. He wanted to know if Sister Margaret ever gave me a whipping.

"Well, she never paddled my britches, but I had my share of smacks with the ruler. One thing, though, I never blamed her. She never smacked me without a reason, and it was always when I was in the wrong."

Another little guy in the first grade raised his hand. His question was for Pam. He wanted to know if she was a movie star, being so pretty and all.

Pam told him she was flattered; but, no, she was not a movie star, just some girl lucky enough to be marrying the handsomest guy on earth.

We fielded their questions for twenty minutes or so. Before leaving, I told them I would like to teach them what Sister Margaret had taught me and what had carried me through some of the toughest times of my life, both in the military and in civilian life.

"To thine own self be true. Don't place too much importance on unimportant things. Do, say, and think what you know in your own hearts to be right, regardless of what others might think, say, or do. I know it doesn't make much sense to you now, but as you grow older and get out in the world, you'll know that Sister Margaret is right. And if you ever doubt it, just think of me, standing up here with the most beautiful girl in the world. That's how I won her heart, by listening to Sister Margaret and applying the rules she taught me."

One little guy in Sister Margaret's class had one final question. "Did you get to be a hero by doing what Sister Margaret taught you?"

"In a very real sense, yes. I learned my lessons of doing what was right from her so well that when the opportunity presented itself, I didn't have to stop and think about what to do. I instinctively knew what had to be done, and I simply did it, without thinking or worrying about the consequences. They all told me I was a hero and gave me a medal to prove it. I really don't feel like a hero. Or for that matter, I don't know what a hero is supposed to feel like. To me, it was simply a matter of opportunity and reflexes; it certainly wasn't planned or calculated. In a very real sense, the medal belongs to Sister Margaret, and all the other wonderful people who taught me right from wrong all my life.

When the President honored me with this medal, what he was really doing was honoring Sister Margaret, all the other nuns, my mother, my dear fiancee here, and all the other wonderful people in my life. They all have a share in it, and I thank them from the bottom of my heart."

"So, I'd like to sum it all up by advising you all to listen to these dear, sweet, precious nuns who have devoted their lives to seeing that you get a good start in life. If you ever get to feeling sorry for yourself or get the notion in your head that they are picking on you, just remember it's for your own good. And, just as I am doing today, someday you will be thanking them from the bottom of your hearts. I want to thank you for being kind enough to hear me out this afternoon. It beats sitting in class, anyway, doesn't it?"

They all clapped and cheered.

Mother Superior took to the podium and dismissed them for the day. She invited Pam and me to have supper with them at the convent. We told her we would love to. We retreated to the quiet of the convent and were quickly joined by several other nuns.

Sister Margaret began telling them all about when she had me for a student all those years ago. She really laid it on thick; but I managed to tell them of how she was really responsible for my growing up and how I would put her on the spot with my inexhaustible curiosity. I really broke them up when I told them the story about stealing the lumber and telling Father Currey about it in confession, and my answer when he asked me if I knew how to make a novena.

It wasn't long before dinner was served. The conversation continued right on through dinner with me telling them of how Sister Margaret was my great protectorate who would take me to the convent after school, teach me to play the piano, and invite me to stay for dinner. She countered with her favorite story of my singing at midnight mass, and then with all the gifts I could bring her. She told them she especially enjoyed the half sugar cookie I would bring in every other day or so.

Mother Superior asked, "Why only half a sugar cookie, Irish?"

I explained to her what a dilemma it was for me—loving Sister Margaret as I did, and also loving sugar cookies. "It was

367

the only way I could satisfy both loves." They all laughed and thought that was precious. I told Sister Margaret that after she left, I quit eating sugar cookies. "It wasn't fun anymore, not having you to share them with, and they would always remind me that you weren't coming back anymore. It sure took me a long time to get used to the idea of not having you to rely on, and I don't believe I ever really got over you. I love you as much now as I did when I was in third grade."

Sister Margaret went on to tell them of our sad farewell and of just how painful it was for her also.

After we finished dinner, they invited us back into the living room.

I said, "No, I'll stay out here and help with the dishes."

They all laughed and said, "That won't be necessary."

I said, "Well, well, Sister Margaret, you mean you had me do all those dishes way back then, and I didn't have to?"

She laughed and said, "You would always insist on helping."

"Yes, and I enjoyed every minute of it, also."

We talked on and on until the gong sounded for evening prayers. They invited us to join them in the chapel, which we did. The air was filled with peace and tranquillity; at that moment it wasn't hard to understand how they could devote their lives to the sisterhood. They were truly at peace with themselves and the world.

After evening prayers, Pam and I decided we had better make our way the last fifty miles and bid our fond adieu to the peace and serenity of the convent. We invited Sister Margaret to our wedding, but she had to decline, even though we offered to pay her plane fare and all. She said she would remember us in her prayers, though, and wished us every happiness in the world.

We promised to write to her and not to stay away so long next time. We were under way once more and decided to spend the night in a hotel just outside of town and finish our pilgrimage in the morning. We checked in as Mr. and Mrs. figuring we would only be using one room anyway. It was really the first chance we had to be alone in quite some time, with no one to bother us, or having to hurry here or there, and so forth.

We were both really bushed, and after taking a nice, hot

shower, we settled down in this nice soft bed to savor the events of the last two days at our leisure. We didn't have a care in the world. It just seemed so right, our being together like this. I reached over and turned off the lamp and took Pam in my arms and kissed her tenderly yet passionately. She whispered in my ear, "Irish, please make love to me tonight. I can't wait another moment, and it will not detract from our wedding night in the least. Our wedding is only four days away, and I figure I can't conceive for at least two weeks yet."

"Oh, darling, I'm so happy you feel as you do. Shall we shed our clothes and fly to the top of the universe?"

"I'm with you, lover."

All the forces of heaven and earth combined could not have denied us our love for one another at this point. As we lay back and melted into a warm and tender embrace, our lips met. Our passions reached a fever pitch from the sensation of our warm naked bodies next to each other and the anticipation of what was to happen. Almost as if it were rehearsed, we were in a position for the moment when our love would be consummated in the ultimate expression of love forever. My hands were gently exploring her body, beginning with her soft breasts and working their way down to the soft hair surrounding her vagina. Meanwhile her hands were tenderly touching my penis, playing softly with it as it rose to erection. After extensive and heavenly foreplay, I finally made the first penetration. I ever so slowly, and ever so gently, withdrew, and penetrated again and again until I was completely engulfed in her sweet and precious body. She whispered in my ear that she loved me and would be mine and only mine forever and ever. I whispered back to her that I loved her and would not want to go on living if anything ever happened to her. "You're all I hunger and thirst for; you're every breath I breathe. As I've quoted to you many, many times before, darling, 'Nothing in the world is single;/All things by a law divine, In one another's being mingle:/Why not I with thine?' Why not, indeed? I was only half; now I'm whole, at last. I feel complete. Like life's sweet promise of love has finally been fulfilled."

We continued our lovemaking, being careful that we didn't

climax so we could make this wonder last as long as possible; for we both knew that no matter how many times we made love in our lives, the first time we would cherish and hold dear to our hearts like no other for the remainder of our lives. Finally we began moving in a rhythm that became faster and faster as we rocked and moved together, up and down, in delirious ecstasy.

I lay over on my back, while Pam snuggled her pretty little head under my chin and began rubbing my chest and stomach. I ran my fingers through her beautiful, long, brown hair, as I told her, "This night will be indelibly impressed in my memory forever, darling. I only wish there were some way we could capture this moment and hold it forever and ever. I have never been happier or more at peace with myself and the world. And to think the night is only beginning."

"I know, Irish; I never in my wildest dreams dreamed it would be this wonderful. And to think we have all our lives to enjoy this sheer ecstasy is in itself enough to make me want to cry tears of joy. I love you, darling, and will through eternity." Quite by accident Pam discovered that I was ticklish and quickly took advantage of her newfound weapon by sitting on my stomach and tickling the hell out of me every time I would let one of her arms free.

Our mood had changed from one of solemn lovemaking to a jovial fun-filled session with plenty of laughter. She teased me about a name for my penis, and I told her we would just call it "Mr." and her vagina "Mrs." She laughed and said, "That sounds so funny to me. I can just see us at the table with Mother and Daddy and me asking you, 'How's the Mister?' And you'd say, 'Just fine, and raring to go. How's the Mrs.?' And I'd say, 'Likewise, lover.'"

We lay there savoring every luscious moment of our perfect love affair until I was rested enough to get another erection. She worked her way down off my stomach and into position. She gave a great sigh of delight when she had all of "Mr." that I had to give. I asked her how she felt and she responded by vigorously rotating her hips while maintaining a perfect up and down rhythm. I could speak not another word; it was so wonderful.

I could see her beautiful smile with the help of the glimmer of light that shone through the window from the lights of the street below. After five minutes or so, she collapsed on me while I threw my arms around her and held her ever so tightly. "Oh, lover, don't move. I want this to last forever and ever."

She began feverishly kissing my face and reiterating that she loved me.

"Oh, Pam, darling, it's beautiful, two hearts in perfect harmony, beating in perfect unison. If we were not meant for each other, no couple on this earth ever was." We changed positions again, and it was only a matter of moments until all the sweet juices of love began flowing again. I lay over and began nursing her lily-white breasts, first one and then the other. She was so aroused by the good feeling it gave her that she was sighing like a beautiful little kitten who had just finished a bowl of cream and was curling up in a nice warm place to take a well-deserved nap. We didn't have a care in the world at that moment; just our love and affection for one another, as we basked in the warmth of each other's affection.

She was running her fingers through my hair and rubbing my neck while I continued to softly touch every part of her beautiful body I could reach from my position.

She told me the top of the universe was way behind us now, and that she wanted to experience every warm and loving sensation her body had to offer. I extended to her the exact same wishes.

There wasn't anything we didn't do that night or any experience we didn't experience. We were so wrapped up in our love for each other that time seemed to stand still for us. We both felt that this was the most beautiful, the most rewarding, and the most magnificent night of our entire lives.

It was four in the morning when we finally drifted back to earth long enough to realize that we should try to sleep for a couple of hours anyway. So we got up and stripped the linen off the bed and decided to take a shower together.

Even our shower was an exhilarating experience for both of us. We could hardly let go of each other or stop kissing long enough to get lathered up with soap. We finally managed to dry off and went over to the bed and lay down again. I pulled a light blanket over us, as we cuddled into each other's arms. Without saying a word, we kissed each other good-night and drifted off to the most relaxed and peaceful sleep I ever experienced in my life. All the waiting, anticipating, fears, doubts, worries, and little "ifs and maybes" were completely gone, leaving contentment and tranquillity for both of us.

We woke up about eight o'clock in the morning. Pam smiled her most radiant smile at me and then kissed me, "Hi, lover! How are you feeling this morning?"

"Precious, I've not the words to describe how madly in love I am with you, and I want you to know you fulfilled my heart's desire, and oh, so much more, last night. I never dreamed I could love anyone as I love you, Pam, darling."

She smiled and said, "I'm so glad, Irish. I only want to spend my life making you happy." "And, I, you, Pam, darling."

"Do you think the 'Mrs' feels up to one little tiny lovemaking session before we have to get up and face the world?"

"Certainly! If the 'Mr' is in need, the 'Mrs' will satisfy his every need."

It was every bit as sweet and tender this morning as it was last night. The morning lovemaking seemed to top off the most perfect night of our lives beautifully. We showered together and even dried each other's backs. We wasted no time getting dressed and hurried on downstairs, checked out, and were on our way to find a good restaurant. By now we were both famished.

As we were eating breakfast, I asked Pam if she had any regrets for not waiting until we were married. "Oh, Irish, all the powers on heaven and earth couldn't have kept us apart last night, and I don't regret it in the least."

"That's truly phenomenal, sweetheart. I was thinking the exact same thing last night. All the powers on heaven and earth couldn't keep us apart. I felt it was so right and that no one had waited longer or been through more than you and me—especially you, Pam, darling. It was the most natural and the most heart-rendering experience of my life, and I hope it was as much for you."

"Oh, it was, Irish, it truly was."

We finished breakfast and drove directly to the graveyard where my mother and brother were buried, stopping only to buy four dozen American Beauty roses for her grave.

We knelt down and placed the roses in front of her headstone. I took Pam's hand as we knelt there and I said a prayer for my mother. We stood up, and I held Pam ever so close to me. I was finding it difficult to hold back the tears. Sweet, adorable Pam sensed this and told me, "Let it all go, Irish. You'll feel better if you do."

"Oh, darling, I didn't realize it was going to be so hard. There was so many things I wanted to tell her and so many things I wanted to do for her when I grew up to make her life easier for her. I'm so sorry for all the cross words I ever spoke to her, and all the disappointments I caused her. Now, it's too late to do anything, or to repay her for all she did for me, or to even say, 'Thanks, Mom.' " I could feel the tears running down my cheeks as Pam tried her best to console me.

"Irish, you were anything but a disappointment to your mother. She knew before she died that you were well on your way to being everything she ever hoped you would be. It is God's will that she is in heaven now, Irish. If you want to thank her, all you have to do is say, 'Thanks, Mom, for everything.' I'm as sure she'll hear you as I am that I love you, Irish."

I looked up to the sky and said, "Thanks, Mom, for everything." I held on to Pam a little while longer until I regained my composure. We took one final look at the graves and ever so slowly retreated to the car.

As we were driving out, I looked at Pam and said, "Thanks, honey, I could never have faced that alone. I really appreciate your words of comfort. You made it a whole lot easier for me, darling."

"Irish, I always want to be there when you need me."

"I'll always be there for you, also, honey."

We stopped by and paid our respects to my aunt, but we

stayed a little too long and had to drive like hell to catch our plane. We made it with not a moment to spare, and used our time on the plane to catch our breath and discuss plans for our upcoming wedding.

When we arrived back at the Taylors we were greeted at the door by Mrs. Taylor. She threw her arms around us, kissed us, and welcomed us home. We told her it was good to be home, and added, "We should go away more often. Just to receive your warm welcome home is enough not to make us stay away for too long."

She had Maggie serve us dinner that she had been keeping warm for us, and she started chattering away. She had saved yesterday's newspaper for us, with the picture that the wire service had sent the local paper, and she read us the nice story they had written about us. She was so happy and thrilled, so proud that she was almost bubbling over with enthusiasm. Pam and I couldn't get over how she was acting.

She asked us about our little side trip. Pam told her what a warm and rewarding experience it was taking Sister Margaret home, getting the opportunity to speak to the children, and visiting with the nuns.

"Oh, Irish, there has been a young lady calling here for you the last two days."

"Oh, yeah? I hope it's not my wife. I forgot to tell you all that I'm married."

They both laughed. "No, seriously, she is a reporter for the local paper and wanted to interview you for a feature article in the Sunday paper. I told her that was up to you."

"What do you think, Pam? Mrs. Taylor?"

"It's up to you, Irish."

"Well, it will give me an opportunity to tell all your friends and neighbors just how wonderful you all really are, and I feel the world should know and feel about you as I do. So, if you both give me your stamp of approval I'll be happy to see her. Let's face it, I may never get another chance to tell the world in print how I really feel about you and how wonderful you've been to me. Fame is fleeting, and by next week no one will even remember my name. Just as well, though, for I really feel uncomfortable in the limelight and will welcome the peace and solitude of a quiet little love nest with the most beautiful girl in the world. Outside of you and Mr. Taylor and a close circle of friends, I'd be content to let the rest of the world roll right by us."

"Irish, I'm sure no one who has ever met you will ever forget you. But I couldn't agree more with your plans for peace and solitude, and I wish with all my heart and soul that you kids have the happiest marriage on earth and find the peace and tranquillity you both so richly deserve. I want that for both of you and pray every day that your wishes will be granted."

Pam said, "We have all the ingredients for a happy marriage and it will be up to us to make it happen."

I took her hand, smiled, and said, "Can there be any doubt, sweetheart?"

She returned my smile and said, "None whatsoever."

We were soon joined by Mr. Taylor who was in an exceptionally jovial mood. He sat down and laid his paper on the table. I asked if that were today's paper, to which he replied, "No, it's yesterday's paper." We all laughed.

He asked if I would be kind enough to let him examine the Medal of Honor, saying he never really had a chance to take a good look at it.

"Why, certainly, Mr. Taylor. Pam, it's in your purse, isn't it?"

"Yes, Irish, I'll get it."

"No, no, sit still. Just tell me where you put it and I'll get it for you."

"It's on the table in the hallway, honey."

I excused myself and quickly retrieved her purse. As I was coming back in the room with it, I put it on my shoulder, saying, "I believe she has half the world in her purse."

I handed her the purse, which she quickly opened. She handed me the medal, packed neatly in its carrying case. I, in turn, handed it to Mr. Taylor. He opened the case and examined it very carefully. He seemed to be in deep thought and acted like he wanted to ask us something but didn't quite know how.

I broke his trend of thought by telling him I knew what he was thinking.

"You do, Irish?"

"Yes, you'd like to borrow that for a few days to show it off to that bragging bunch over at the country club and at your club downtown."

"How did you know that, Irish?"

"Simple. I'll bet they're always bragging about the accomplishments of their sons and daughters until you're sick of hearing about it, and they will really have to go some to top this one, won't they?"

"They sure as hell will, Irish, and I promise to take good care of it and return it to you shortly."

"It's all right, Mr. Taylor. Keep it as long as you like."

"Thanks, Irish. Look, if you'll all excuse me I have to run over to the club for a few minutes and check on the arrangements for the stag party for tomorrow night and the reception for Saturday."

"Fine, Mr. Taylor. We'll be here when you get back."

He closed the box and slipped it in his inside coat pocket, picked up his newspaper, leaned over and kissed his wife and was gone as quickly as he appeared.

"That was awfully nice of you, Irish. You've made him a very happy man."

"I'm glad, Mrs. Taylor. He's made a whole new world possible for me, and I couldn't be happier in it."

"Well, what are we going to do this evening, ladies?"

"Oh, my goodness. In all the excitement, I almost forgot, that the girls are due here any minute to go over that final preparation for the wedding. Do you kids feel up to it?"

"Certainly, Mrs. Taylor. Pam and I can do anything if we put our minds to it, can't we, sweet pea?"

"Sure, mother, there shouldn't be too much left to do, should there?"

"No, not really. We just want to make sure we haven't overlooked anything."

I laughed and said, "You're still the worrier, aren't you, Mrs. Taylor? I really do think it's precious how you look after Pam and me."

"Well, let's face it, Irish. You kids are my life and nothing is too good for both of you."

"Thank you, Mrs. Taylor, and we're proud to be in such an enviable position. Right, Pam?"

"You bet, Irish. A day without Mother in it is like a day without sunshine."

It wasn't long before the girls started arriving. The next thing I knew, with the members of the wedding party and their friends, we must have had thirty young girls there in the living room. It was a little awkward being the only guy there, but it didn't take long to start enjoying all the girl talk and the pleasant compliments they were throwing my way. I would occasionally try to return their compliments by saying something like. "This is going to be more like a Miss America contest than a wedding," or "Look at the thorn (meaning myself) among all these beautiful roses."

Our little get-together lasted for over two hours. Slowly but surely, everyone started leaving, and before long we were alone again.

21

The Wedding

Mrs. Taylor asked Pam and me if we had decided where we wanted to go on our honeymoon.

Pam told her that we didn't plan to go far or stay too long. We thought perhaps we would spend a few days in San Francisco and then return home and start looking for a house of our own.

"What did you have in mind? perhaps I could help you kids find a place."

"Well, what we would really like to have is a little Cape Cod house with a nice yard around it, so Irish can have his vegetable garden and I can have my roses."

"You wouldn't mind if I made a few inquiries for you, would you?"

"No, not in the least. In fact, we were planning on asking for your help, and here you are volunteering. Isn't she the most, Irish?"

"She certainly is, honey."

"Have you decided what you want to do yet, Irish?"

"Yes, Mrs. Taylor. Pam and I decided, with the assistance of your wise counsel, that going to work for Mr. Taylor would be the best move to make at this time. As far as the army, I'll just

378

quietly finish my enlistment and go into the inactive reserves. The only way they could touch me then is if there is an all-out war. And if that happens, we're all going back in anyway. I think that will be the best way to handle that. I don't want to hurt the major's feelings, though, so I would appreciate it if the subject comes up when he gets here tomorrow, just say I haven't decided yet. I'm sure he'll understand when the time comes."

"Of course, you're right, Irish. That's Irish for you."

Pam asked what time it was getting to be.

I looked at my watch and said, "Well, Mickey has both hands pointing straight up in the air."

"Midnight already?"

"I guess we had better think about retiring for the night. We have a busy day ahead of us tomorrow, and I'll bet you kids are tired from your trip."

"You're so right, Mrs. Taylor. If you'll excuse us, we'll crawl up the steps and call it a day."

"Good-night, kids."

"Good-night, Mrs. Taylor—Mother."

I walked Pam to her door, kissed her good-night and told her that tonight and tomorrow night would be the last times I would ever have to say good-night at her door.

"I know, Irish, and I'm so happy. Kiss me once more and I'll try to let you go."

We kissed and embraced, not wanting to let go and not wanting to give in to the temptation. Finally we managed to wind up in our respective rooms for the night. It was hard to sleep with the memories of last night still fresh in my mind. I managed to drift off to sleep with the comforting thoughts of the beautiful lifetime we had ahead of us.

The following day went by at a whirlwind pace, with all the last minute preparations: picking up our morning suits, the major's arrival, and filling him in on the duties of being best man right up to the rehearsal at the church.

Dear Mrs. Taylor, in her usual, cool and efficient manner, kept everything moving smoothly and was really carrying more than her share of the load.

As soon as rehearsal was over, Mr. Taylor, the major and ushers dragged me away from the church, hardly giving me time to kiss the ladies good-bye. Within an instant we were at the country club for my final night as a bachelor. I really wasn't too impressed with the thought of spending all evening with a bunch of guys. After all, I had become so used to female companionship that having two or three beauties at my side all the time was almost a way of life with me.

However, I decided to make the best of the stag party given in my honor. And after everyone had a few drinks under their belts things started to liven up. They were all telling me how sorry I would be to see the end of my freedom. They even went so far as to tell me marriage was a three-ring circus: an engagement ring, a wedding ring, and suffering.

I thought to myself, "If only these guys knew just how lonely and depressed I was before Pam came into my life, they wouldn't be talking like that." I figured if I ever got tired of being married, all I had to do would be to think of how miserable I had been when I was single and how Pam had given me all her love and affection. I figured we would have our ups and downs, but with love, openness, and a mutual respect for each other's feelings, I felt there would be no obstacle in our marriage we couldn't overcome. The thought of surrendering my freedom never entered my mind. I thought of our marriage as the joining of forces, with each of us bringing into our alliance all the peace, joys, hopes, aspirations and fulfillment of desires that only two people in love, as Pam and I were, could ever hope to achieve. Anyway, all their little jokes satirizing the institution of marriage were in the spirit of good fun, so I didn't get bent out of shape and managed to laugh along with them.

As I figured it would, the conversation eventually got around to the army. All the young guys were asking the major and me about Korea and wanted to hear war stories. One guy asked us if it got cold over there in the winter. The major told him that it got so cold we had to bring the brass monkeys in at night. Most everyone got it and laughed. But for those who didn't I explained it was cold enough to freeze the balls off a brass monkey.

All the guys were determined to get me drunk. They would keep slipping drinks in front of me in place of my usual 7-up on the rocks. I would politely take a sip and then leave it alone if it had alcohol in it. I figured I didn't need a hangover on my wedding day. I took a sip of one especially potent drink they slipped me and commented that it tasted like a drink we had back home called "Old Factory Whistle." One blast and you're through for the whole day.

We bullshitted and told war stories for the next hour or so, when one old boy who couldn't hold his liquor too well started making snide remarks about me. "Irish, I hear you come from a real poor family back east. I hear tell you were so poor that you didn't have enough to eat at times."

I don't know if he was jealous of me or just a natural asshole. But either way, I figured I was more than a match for him.

Mr. Taylor hastened to defend me, but I told him it was all right. I proceeded to elaborate on just how poor we really were when I was growing up. I told them, "If it had cost a nickle to shit, I would have had to throw up. We used to rob Peter to pay Paul, and that would make Peter sore, and you just can't get along with a sore peter." Everyone was roaring with laughter by now. If this asshole had any intention of embarrassing me, he was badly mistaken; for I seized the initiative and was really taking advantage of it.

I went on to tell them about our notorious landlord and how I would put him off for weeks at a time. "I remember he came to the door and told me he was raising the rent. I told him I wished he would for we were having a little trouble coming up with it that week."

"No, no, I mean it," he insisted. "It's going to cost you more to live here, and I'm only going to give you three days to come up with it."

"Okay, okay. We'll take Christmas, Easter, and the Fourth of July."

Everyone was in stitches by now, and hanging onto my every word as I continued. "I told the old bastard that we put all the names in a hat and drew them out until we ran out of money, and that if he didn't stop bothering us about it, we wouldn't put his name in the hat next month. He threatened to get the sheriff and have us thrown out. But I knew he was bluffing for that would have cost him more money. So I just told him he would have to swing by his nuts until we were able to pay him. He finally threw up his arms in disgust and left."

The major asked if I was just putting them on or if things were really that bad.

"I'll tell you how bad it was, Major. One kid on the block wanted a watch for Christmas, so his parents let him. Another neighbor was always complaining about what a dirty housekeeper his wife was. Every time he went to piss in the kitchen sink, she had it full of dirty dishes."

By now everyone in the place was cracking up and looking with a jaundiced eye at the joker who had started it all. He appeared to be suffering from a case of terminal stutter and couldn't speak a word if his life depended on it.

Mr. Taylor was really determined to put this guy in his place. "Let me tell you something about this poor boy, buddy. I'd take one of him to a hundred of you who have had everything handed to you on a silver platter. Irish is a real man, and he has the credentials to prove it." He whipped out the Congressional Medal of Honor from his inside pocket. He made the statement that no one in the room, including himself, could lay claim to an award any higher.

I was kind of embarrassed that he pulled it on them, but it sure put them in their place. It didn't dampen the spirits of the party though, for everyone wanted to look at the medal. Mr. Taylor was very protective and would let them look, but not touch. When someone would reach out for it, he'd simply push their hand away and say, "Look; don't touch." The major and I really got a big kick out of that.

John Jenkins made the scene and apologized for being late. He had just returned from New York. He told us the article would appear in next week's issue and the group pictures would be on the cover. He showed us the proof they were using for the cover and several of the other pictures to be including in the story. That certainly raised some eyebrows in the room.

Champagne, whiskey, and beer kept flowing like water and the bullshit and storytelling kept pace with the drinking. For one reason or another, they all liked my stories and kept encouraging me to tell more. The major, who had heard most of them, would say through a somewhat slurred voice, "Tell them about this one or that one," and of course, I would accommodate him.

"Do 'Twinkle, Twinkle, Little Star,' Irish," he said. Everyone laughed and told him the booze was getting to him. "Do it, Irish." So I did.

> Starkle, starkle, little twink
> Just who the fuck you are I think
> I'm not as drunk as some stinkle pep I am
> Some stinkle pep I'm under the alcofluence
> of incohol
> I only had tea Martunies
> But the drunker I sit here the longer I get.

Mr. Taylor had me repeat it for him two more times. He wanted to commit it to memory to tell all the guys at work. As soon as there was a lull in the story-telling I headed for the men's room to get rid of some of that 7-up I had been consuming.

I was washing my hands when in came the asshole who had been trying to belittle me. It was obvious he was looking for me, for he started right in on me.

"You think you're hot shit, don't you, Irish?"

"Well, at least you know my name."

"If you hadn't talked Pam Taylor into marrying you and won that medal, you wouldn't be shit."

"There you go with ifs. If the dog hadn't stopped to shit, he would have caught the rabbit, and if you hadn't been born with a silver spoon in your mouth, you wouldn't even make a good bum. So don't come around here with your holier-than-thou attitudes."

"Well, I asked Pam to marry me over a year ago."

"I know, and she told you to get lost. Let me see now. Your dad and Mr. Taylor arranged all your dates with Pam. Isn't that correct? You didn't even have balls enough to ask her out yourself. She has about as much respect for you as she does for the dirt on this floor."

"You can't talk to me that way."

"Well, I just did, Mr. son of a bitch. Now get out of my way; the air is getting bad in here."

"Wait just a minute. I have a proposition for you from my old man."

"Oh, shit. This should be interesting, but spare me the details and get to the point."

"Well, my old man figures you're just after money. Why else would you want to marry out of your class?"

"Please continue, you aristocratic bastard."

"Well, he figures if he pays you off, then I'll have another chance to marry Pam."

"Look, fucker," (I was starting to get really angry now) "you never had a chance to begin with. And if you think I'm marrying Pam for her money, you're sadly mistaken. But I'm sure I'll never be able to convince any of you pricks of that, so you can think what you will. By the way, just what kind of a payoff did your old man have in mind?"

"He gave me a check for twenty-five thousand dollars to give to you, if you'll leave town tonight and disappear."

"Sounds perfect, doesn't it? Do you have the check with you?"

"I have it right here," he said, pulling it out of his pocket and handing it to me.

I examined it. It was beautiful, made out in my name and all. I said, "You can thank your old man for the donation, but I'm not going any place, motherfucker, except to the altar with Pam in the morning."

He became infuriated and took a swing at me. I ducked, and he smashed the mirror with his fist. Blood was flying everywhere. This prissified bastard started crying at the sight of blood and then started hollering for his daddy. In an instant, we had six or eight guys in there. They wrapped his hand in a towel and a couple of them took him to the hospital to have it tended to.

His old man was going to go with him, but I advised against it, telling him he would be very sorry if he left just then. I told him I wanted a few words with him and Mr. Taylor alone. We all three went into a private room. Mr. Taylor was really bewildered, not to mention half-drunk.

"What's wrong, Irish? What happened in there?"

"Well, suppose we let Mr. Roth tell us."

"Me! I have no idea what you're talking about."

"I suppose you don't know anything about this twenty-five thousand dollar cashier's check made out to me, either, do you?"

"Give that back to me, you," he said, reaching for it.

"Fuck you, Mr. Roth. I'll just consider it a wedding present, and also an expensive lesson to you that your goddamned money can't buy everyone, and particularly not me."

"What's this all about, Roth?" demanded Mr. Taylor.

"I can explain, George, if you'll give me a chance."

I said, "Please do. It should be interesting to hear you lie your way out of this one."

"It's all a mistake. And if you'll please give me back my check, I'm willing to forget the whole unfortunate incident."

"Unfortunate for you, maybe, but I'm twenty-five thousand dollars richer. He sent his punk son in the men's room after me to try to bribe me into leaving town tonight, so his son would have another chance at trying to marry Pam and give this motherfucker the inside track to your pocketbook. Nice friend you have here, Mr. Taylor."

Mr. Taylor sobered up in a hurry, calling him one son of a bitch after another, and promising to destroy him both physically and financially.

Old Mr. Roth kept pleading for a chance to explain and to get his check back, repeating again and again that it was all a mistake and he was very sorry that it happened.

I said, "It certainly was a mistake when you let your greed for money carry you away like that. And to think it cost you twenty-five thousand big ones, to boot."

Mr. Taylor told him to get out of his sight before he personally threw him out. He warned him that if he dared set foot inside the church tomorrow, or ventured into the reception afterward, he would personally throw him out.

"But, George, what will people say if I'm not there? And what about my wife and son? What will people say? Please, George, we'll be the laughing stock of the whole community. Give us a break."

"What! Like you tried to give Irish here? Pretending to be my friend all those years, and it turns out you're nothing more than a parasite and a leech. I don't give a damn what you do; but don't ever darken my doorsill again, as long as you live."

"Should I give him his check back, Mr. Taylor?"

"Fuck him. You're right, Irish, it's an expensive lesson for this crooked bastard."

"Well, you heard the man, Mr. Roth. Now why don't you stop by the hospital and pick up your punkyass kid. And tell him the next time he takes a swing at me, I won't let him off so easily. I'll beat him to a pulp."

He was as white as a ghost and was nervously fumbling for the doorknob to let himself out. After he was gone, Mr. Taylor told me he was sorry as hell it happened, but not to let it bother me.

"No, it doesn't bother me, Mr. Taylor. People are people on both sides of the track. The only difference is that on this side, the stakes are higher and the methods of operation are a little more devious. As far as I'm concerned, the matter is closed and will go no further. I just wanted to expose him for the phony bastard that he is. As far as his check goes, he can have it back."

"To hell with him, Irish. You go ahead and cash it and use it as you see fit. He has taken me for a hundred times that amount over the years in various little deals that I always let him have the better part of because of our friendship. I guess it wasn't enough for him. He wanted to get control of it all."

"Greed and lust will make a man do crazy things, Mr. Taylor. Look, I'll just give you the check for now, and we can decide later what to do with it. I think it would be better not to say anything about this incident to anyone. We don't want to spoil what promises to be the happiest day of Pam's and my life."

"Okay, Irish. Shall we join the others and get on with the celebration as if nothing ever happened?"

"I'm with you, Mr. Taylor."

Everyone was so drunk by now that we were hardly missed. Some asked what happened in the men's room and I told them, "The guy slipped and cut his hand on the mirror." Everyone seemed satisfied with that explanation, so we let it go at that.

The party continued until one in the morning, and a good time was had by all. Mr. Taylor didn't do much drinking after that unfortunate incident. I'm sure he felt betrayed by a guy who he thought was his friend. And to be betrayed in such a devious way must have made him sick to his stomach.

After the party broke up and Mr. Taylor and I were heading home, he told me something I would never forget. "Don't worry about your enemies, Irish. Only your friends can get close enough to fuck you." He was so right, and it was so true.

We were greeted by Mrs. Taylor as we entered the house. We talked for a few minutes; then Mr. Taylor showed the major to his room after bidding Mrs. Taylor and me good-night. He told me he would see me in church in the morning. "I'll be there, Mr. Taylor. And don't you forget to bring Pam with you." He laughed and said, "Don't worry about that, Irish."

As soon as they were out of sight, Mrs. Taylor asked me what was wrong and what had happened at the club. "Oh, it was nothing to write home about, Mrs. Taylor."

"Come on, Irish. I haven't been married to Mr. Taylor for twenty years and not know when something is bothering him. And you, I can read like a book. Do you feel like talking about it?"

"Well, all right, Mrs. Taylor. Are you sure Pam is sleeping?"

"Yes, Irish, I made her go to bed about midnight, so she would be well rested for the big day tomorrow. Now, what happened?"

"Well, it was Mr. Roth and his son. Seems Mr. Roth had planned for his son to marry Pam. He wanted me out of the way so badly that he sent his son into the men's room to offer me a twenty-five thousand dollar bribe to leave town."

"Irish, I'm shocked! He actually did that?"

"Yes, ma'am. Mr. Taylor has the cashier's check, made out to me, in his pocket right now. The only reason I'm telling you is because I don't want you worrying about what is bothering Mr. Taylor and me. Now I wish you would keep it between us for now. Mr. Taylor was planning to tell you after the wedding."

"Well, tell me how it came about, Irish."

I explained to her how Junior had been trying to badger and belittle me all evening, and how I kept getting the better of him. I explained in detail the episode in the men's room, including his taking a swing at me and tearing his hand open on the broken mirror. I told her how Mr. Taylor and Mr. Roth and I had a private conference and just what transpired in there. "So, that's the whole story, Mrs. Taylor."

"Oh, Irish, I'm so sorry that this had to happen."

"Oh, it's all right, Mrs. Taylor. I'm sure Mr. Taylor feels badly being betrayed by someone who he thought was his friend. But it's better that he found out now, before Mr. Roth had a chance to do him any real harm. As for me, I know what people are like, and how they feel about Pam and me getting married. But as long as Pam and I love each other, and we have your and Mr. Taylor's blessings, I really don't give a damn what anyone else thinks, do you?"

"No, Irish, I certainly don't. People will talk and be just as mean and nasty as they can be. You have the right attitude, and as far as I'm concerned, they can all go to hell."

"Mrs. Taylor!"

"I'm sorry, Irish, but it makes my blood boil at how petty and jealous people can be. For him to think you'd take money to leave town is despicable. I never did trust that man to begin with, and for him to have the gall to think he could marry off his son to Pam is beyond belief!"

"Well, as long as we love and understand one another, we'll make out just fine."

"You bet we will, Irish."

"Promise you won't let it upset you, Mrs. Taylor."

She smiled at me and said, "I won't, Irish, and I'm glad you told me. I really appreciate your confiding in me, Irish, and I always want you to."

"I will, Mrs. Taylor, always and always. Do you suppose you

and I could sneak a peek at our sleeping beauty before we retire for the night, Mrs. Taylor?"

"Sure, Irish, why not?"

I got up and took her hand, helping her to her feet. Together we walked up the stairs to Pam's room, opened the door and softly walked over to her bedside. She had such a beautiful smile on her face that it almost brought tears to our eyes. I knelt down beside her bed and kissed her hands while whispering, "Dear God, please look favorably on our marriage, and let us always share the peace and tranquillity of this moment for the rest of our lives." I stood up Mrs. Taylor and I walked softly to the door, closing it with care so as not to wake her. We walked together as far as my room. Before saying good-night I made her promise once more that she would dismiss what I had told her from her mind and just concentrate on having the time of her life at the wedding tomorrow.

"Oh, I will, Irish. I'll not let anything or anybody spoil that for me. You can rest assured of that."

"Thanks, Mrs. Taylor. And would you do me one more little favor?"

"Anything, Irish."

"Be sure I'm up and out of here on time tomorrow. I wouldn't want to be late for my own wedding."

"I'll personally wake you, you sweet, lovable character, you. I couldn't be happier for both you and Pam, and I truly feel I'm gaining a son. I love you, Irish O'Malley."

"And I truly love you, Mrs. Taylor."

I gave her a tender embrace and a loving kiss and said good-night. In nothing flat, I was undressed, showered, and in bed, trying to go to sleep. But with all the heavenly bliss all around me, I wasn't a bit sleepy. I finally managed to drift off, though.

True to her word, I was awakened by a tender kiss from Mrs. Taylor, who scolded me, "Get up, sleepy head. It's your wedding day and you don't want to be late."

I sat up and threw my legs over the side of the bed. "Oh, Mrs. Taylor, do you really mean that all the hoping, longing, waiting of all those lonely days and lonely nights are finally over? Is this the day we've all prayed and worked so hard for? Is it really here? Pinch me to prove it is not just another beautiful dream."

She pinched me tenderly on the cheek and said, "This is the day, Irish. Now you run on in and take your shower and shave, while I lay your clothes out for you."

I stood up and kissed her on the cheek and said, "Thanks, Mother, you've made me a very happy man." She smiled her precious smile at me while I retreated to the shower. After I finished in the bathroom, Mrs. Taylor helped me get all decked out in my morning suit, tied my tie for me, and made sure everything was just perfect. I asked her how I looked and confessed I was very nervous and hoped I wouldn't make any mistakes.

"Irish, you look simply wonderful. Just carry yourself like you always do—straight and noble, not afraid of anything or anybody. When you do that, Irish, you give off good vibrations that tell the world that you're gentle and compassionate, yet not afraid to be strong nor ashamed to be kind. You're a man's man, Irish, and a gentleman in the truest sense of the word."

"Thank you, Mrs. Taylor. What would I ever do without you? Even my own mother couldn't boost my ego any higher than you have. I really love you and will be proud today to become not only Pam's husband, but also your son in the truest sense of the word."

I took her in my arms and kissed her. "I'll never let you down, Mother. Promise me you'll be there when Pam and I need a hand. We're both very young and are going to need all the help we can get."

"I know, Irish. I promise I'll be there to do what I can when you need me. Now, I have to get you out of here and over to the church, so let's go downstairs and I'll have Henry drive you over there."

After instructing Henry to drop me off, she gave me a kiss and told me to do exactly as she told me and everything would be just fine. "Now, I have a beautiful, young bride waiting upstairs that I have to get ready for you, so I'll see you in church."

390

"Thank you, Mother," I said, and Henry and I departed. She smiled and waved as I gently closed the door behind us. Henry and I arrived at the church a short time later. I thanked him and walked on in, making my way to the sacristy to pass the time before I would take my place at the front of the sanctuary to receive the bride and her father.

It wasn't long before I was joined by Mr. Roth. I was a little surprised, to say the least, that he had balls enough to show up there. But there he was, big as life, and just as brazen. I knew no good could come of this situation. Therefore, I decided to get rid of him as quickly as possible.

"What can I do for you this morning, Mr. Roth? Did you come here to make me another offer? Just what's on your crooked mind?"

"I want you to intervene for me with Mr. Taylor and tell him it's all a mistake."

"Why the hell should I?"

"I'll let you keep the twenty-five grand if you do."

"Go to hell, Mr. Roth. And get your ass the hell out of here before I throw you out."

"Wait a minute, Irish. I can have you arrested for assault and battery on my son last night. Don't forget that."

"Go ahead and try it, you silly bastard. And as far as your check goes, Mr. Taylor has it. So if you want it back, go see him."

"Look, Irish, I'm sorry for what happened last night. I couldn't tell my wife, and she's waiting at home for me to bring her to the wedding. Have a heart! Don't destroy me like this. You can fix it, if you want. I'm begging you! Please! If this ever gets out, I'll be ruined socially in this community."

"That really means a lot to you, doesn't it, Mr. Roth?"

"It's everything I've worked for all my life—money, respectability, and a place in society. If I lose that, I might as well be dead."

"Look, this is the Taylors' affair, and their guest list. I'm just a participant, so I'd suggest you call Mr. Taylor and talk to him if you want forgiveness. I'm not about to leave here for anyone or anything, and that's my final word on the subject. So if you'll be kind enough to leave. . . ."

"You gotta help me, Irish. He'll listen to you; you're the only one who can help me now."

"You should have thought about that when you were doing all your conniving and scheming and before you sent your punkyass kid in there to buy me off. As far as I'm concerned, you're just getting paid back in the same kind of coins you have been paying out all these years. Now, get the hell out of here, and go tell your wife and kid just what an asshole you really are."

"You won't help me then?"

"How many times do I have to tell you?—No. You made your own bed, now sleep in it."

"Well, I'm going to bring my wife and son anyway and just take my chances then."

"Fine. If you want to be refused entrance at the door with your wife at your side, go ahead. See if I care what a fool you make of yourself."

"We'll see who's the fool. I'm not through with you yet, Irish. I'll get you if it takes me the rest of my life."

"Fine, and I'm sure Mr. Taylor will be overjoyed to know you were here this morning making idle threats."

"I'll get you, Irish. You can bet on that."

"I can hardly wait," I shouted at him as he was leaving. He jumped in his car and burned rubber for half a block.

I sat down, still not quite believing what had just happened. But I figured I had better dismiss it from my mind and concentrate on the wedding. Father Thomas came in and greeted me. He asked me if I was ready for my big day. I assured him I was as ready as I'd ever be. I waited in there with him until he got all his vestments on and we were joined by the altar boys.

The time had arrived for me to take my place, so I walked out through the sanctuary and took my place at the head of the aisle to await the love of my life. Father Thomas and the altar boys took their places on the altar and the stage was all set.

The church was filled to capacity. I was finding it hard to find a familiar face in the crowd. I spotted Mrs. Taylor in the front pew, conveying her love and good wishes to me through her beautiful smile. Then the organist began to play and the ceremony was under way.

The doors at the rear of the church were opened by the ushers, exposing the wedding party waiting to enter from the vestibule. The procession started with the two little flower girls leading the way, followed by Pam and her father, with the maid of honor and my best man close behind, followed by the remainder of the wedding party.

I stood there proud and erect. I could feel a smile breaking out over my face while my overactive tear glands were busy producing tears of joy that I was having trouble containing. It was almost as if this beautiful experience were happening to someone else, and I was just an overjoyed spectator.

I was spellbound as the little flower girls passed me and Pam and her father approached. She looked so magnificent and beautiful that there was no doubt in my mind that she was one of God's beautiful little angels sent to earth to love and be loved by me.

They stopped in front of me. Mr. Taylor, with his voice just above a whisper, said, "I'm entrusting the care and welfare of this beautiful child to you, Irish. Look after her and love her always, and she'll make you very happy."

I replied that I would love her always and see to her every need. I shook his hand and could detect a tear in his eye, as I held out my arm for Pam. He turned away and walked the short distance to the pew to join Mrs. Taylor while Pam and I walked through the altar railing gate, making our way up to the altar.

Everything went perfectly and no one missed a cue. It seemed I had lived my whole life anticipating this moment. As I slipped the ring on Pam's sweet little finger, I could feel one of the tears I had been fighting back trickle down my cheek. I don't believe any man on earth had ever been any happier than I was at that moment. When Father Thomas told me, "You may kiss the bride," my hands were trembling slightly as I lifted the veil, exposing her truly radiant beauty in all its glory. She closed her eyes as our lips tenderly met; I felt as if I were drifting on a cloud. I never knew I was capable of loving anyone as much as I loved her at that moment.

It was only a matter of moments before Father Thomas concluded the mass and we were walking, arm in arm down the aisle as Mr. and Mrs. Bryan O'Malley. It was the most exhilarating feeling in the world to me, and I was completely oblivious to everyone in the church. I had the feeling my only reason for being alive was to make my new bride happy and to love her with all my heart.

We made it out into the vestibule and were standing there to await the onslaught of well-wishers. I asked Pam how she was feeling. "I have no feelings at this moment, Irish. I'm truly in heaven, and so much in love with you that I'm not aware of anything else on this earth but you, darling."

"I feel the same way, sweetheart."

Mr. and Mrs. Taylor were the first of the well-wishers to reach us. Mr. Taylor shook my hand and congratulated me and then was the first to kiss the bride. Mrs. Taylor, her eyes a little red from crying, stepped up. And I threw my arms around her and hugged her tightly. I couldn't hold back the tears of joy any longer.

"Thank you, Mrs. Taylor, for being your sweet, warm, beautiful, and understanding self." I let her go after giving her a tender kiss, and she offered me a tissue, and said, "Thank you, Irish." She gave Pam a hug and told her she was the happiest woman on earth.

It must have taken fifteen minutes to receive all the congratulations before we ventured down the church steps through a shower of rice, to the waiting cars that whisked us away to the wedding breakfast.

When we arrived at the country club there were still more reporters and more photos to pose for. We made it through the door and to the dining room. We were all seated and I think I finally began breathing for the first time since the wedding procession started down the aisle back at the church.

Helen Jenkins asked us how we were feeling now. Pam and I both told her our feelings were indescribable at the moment. "We just want to remain this happy for the rest of our lives." She reassured us that we would.

Mr. and Mrs. Taylor were having the time of their lives; they both looked simply radiant. I leaned over and whispered to Mrs. Taylor not to leave us alone for even a moment because I wouldn't be able to see it through without her by our side. She smiled and said, "You'll do just fine, son."

As soon as I saw Mr. Taylor making his way to the men's room, I excused myself and joined him there. "How's it going, Irish? Bet you're glad it's finally over, aren't you? All that waiting and all?"

"I am, Mr. Taylor, and I've never been happier in my life. Say, there is one thing you should know about. I hate to bring it up; but I feel I must."

"What is it, Irish?"

"Mr. Roth paid me a visit before the wedding this morning and practically demanded that I intercede for him with you. He was even generous enough to tell me I could keep the check if I did."

"And if you didn't?"

"He threatened to have me arrested for assault and battery on his son."

"What did you tell him, Irish?"

"To go to hell."

"Good for you, Irish. Don't worry about him; he's just a big blowhard."

"Well, I think it goes a little deeper than that, Mr. Taylor. He seemed extremely desperate. Like he was in big, big trouble and his whole world was about to fall apart. I think he was distraught enough to commit suicide."

"Do you really think so, Irish?"

"Yes, I do, Mr. Taylor. To be so desperate as to try and pull what he pulled last night, and then to be desperate enough to show up at the church this morning—well, I think he deserves watching."

"Okay, Irish. Let me make a couple of phone calls and we'll find out where he's coming from."

"Thanks, Mr. Taylor. I'd hate to be responsible for him jumping off a bridge or something."

"Hell, he's not your responsibility, Irish. If he has himself in a jam, that's his problem, not yours."

"Of course, you're right, Mr. Taylor. I felt you would want to know what was going on. That's why I told you."

"I appreciate your telling me, Irish. Now you let me take care of it, will you?"

"You got it, Mr. Taylor. As far as I'm concerned, the whole thing never happened."

"That's my boy. Now, let's get back to the festivities and enjoy ourselves."

We rejoined the others and after drinking several toasts, we headed back to the Taylors' house to freshen up for the reception to be held at two o'clock that afternoon.

Mrs. Taylor took Pam and me off into the library and told us she had taken the liberty of having our suitcases packed in the trunk of Pam's car, so that if we wanted to sneak away during the reception, we wouldn't have to stop back at the house. Pam thanked her for her thoughtfulness, and I told her she was simply superhuman. "As for you, Pam darling, you are so breathtakingly beautiful in your wedding gown that I just cannot find words to describe how I feel about the new Mrs. O'Malley. You just wait until I get you alone, and I'll let my emotions do my talking for me."

"Oh, Irish, hold me and tell me it's really true. Tell me again that I'm really Mrs. Irish O'Malley."

I held her tightly and said, "I'm having trouble believing it myself; but it's true, darling." I kissed her ever so tenderly, and told her I loved her more than life itself.

"There is one other plus that came out of this heavenly bliss, honey."

"What's that, Irish?"

I put my arm around Mrs. Taylor and Pam and said, "This is OUR mother now. What do you think of that?"

"Oh, Irish, I couldn't be happier."

Mrs. Taylor told us we had better freshen up so that we would be ready for the reception.

After I freshened up, I went back to the living room and joined the other guests there. There was one very special person there that I wanted to thank personally—Helen Jenkins. I walked over and gave her a big hug and a kiss and then held her at arms length and told her she looked simply marvelous. She was smiling, and told me I was full of blarney. "Look, I haven't had much of a chance to talk to you these past few days; but I want you to know how grateful I am for all you've done for me. You helped me over some difficult periods when I was losing faith. Your undying devotion to me had as much to do with my walking as anything on this earth, and I want to thank you from the bottom of my heart. I'll always have a very special place in my heart for you, Helen, and if there is ever anything I can do for you, please don't hesitate to ask. Even if it's only to talk, I'll be glad to listen. I want us to be friends and see each other often —you know, over dinner or at the theater. And if you're interested, to help us when we start a family. We'll be needing a beautiful nurse to take care of our newborn and her mommy."

"Thank you again, Irish, and I'll be looking forward to the dinner dates and the theater, and so will John. He's grown kind of fond of you, also."

"Good! Good friends are hard to come by, and I certainly wouldn't want to lose the Jenkinses as my friends."

We were soon joined by Pam and her mother, who joined right in the conversation. Pam asked her if I was bending her ear. "Yes, he is; but I love it. He's so full of love and good cheer today."

"Well, isn't everyone?" I asked.

"You bet we are," added Mrs. Taylor. "Say, Mr. Taylor was looking for you, Irish. I believe he is in the library."

"Okay, if you three beautiful ladies will excuse me, I'll rejoin you as quickly as possible."

"Okay, love. Don't be too long."

"I won't."

I knocked on the library door and Mr. Taylor said, "Come in." I walked over to the desk where he was sitting. He had a concerned look on his face as he said, "Well, Irish, you hit the nail right on the head. Mr. Roth took an overdose of sleeping pills this morning and is now in the hospital."

"Will he be all right?"

"Yes. Fortunately, his wife found him in time."

"I'm very sorry to hear that, Mr. Taylor. Do you know of any reason why he might have done it?"

"Yes. I've made a few preliminary inquiries, and it would appear he's on the verge of bankruptcy. The SEC is after him for some illegal stock transactions; then the Justice Department is after him for a land swindle in Arizona he was involved in with some gangsters from Nevada. The IRS is also going over his books, and God knows what all he's been involved in, in his quest for fame and fortune."

"I hate to see a man destroy himself with greed, gall, and a lust for power. I guess he figured if Junior was engaged to or married to Pam, you'd bail him out. What other motive could he have had?"

"I don't know, Irish. But I don't want you feeling badly about it. You had nothing to do with his problems, and I'm only telling you now, so you won't worry or have to read about it on your honeymoon."

"Thanks, Mr. Taylor. I do feel better knowing that I was only his last desperate attempt to keep from drowning. He had already tied the millstone around his neck long before I ever made the scene."

"You're right, Irish. And if you like, I'll just hold on to that check. If he goes to jail, his wife will need it to live on."

"You're absolutely right, Mr. Taylor, there is no need for her to suffer any more than she already has. I agree with you one hundred percent. In fact, I'll endorse it for you right now."

"Yes, that would be a good idea, Irish. For if they impound his assets, we may have a little difficulty converting it to cash."

I signed the check and handed it back to him.

"Okay, Irish, I'll get it cashed first thing Monday morning

and just hold the money until we see how this thing turns out."

"Whatever you say, Mr. Taylor. I trust your judgment."

"Well, Irish, I'm glad to hear that. And believe me, I'll never doubt your judgment of people. I don't know how you do it, but you can tell where they're coming from just by talking to them. We'll have to sit down one of these days and perhaps you can tell me how you're able to do that."

"Mr. Taylor, no one can be right one hundred percent of the time, but I guess I have an exceptionally long antenna for trouble, and am able to pick up the vibrations a little better because of it. I believe it comes from being on the defensive most of my life, and trying to put myself in the other guy's shoes and asking why they do and say things they do. Enough of this for now. We have a wedding party going on, so let's enjoy ourselves, shall we?"

"You bet, Irish."

We wandered back into the living room and found Mrs. Taylor and my lovely new bride. Mr. Taylor asked Pam and me how we would like to go to Hawaii for our honeymoon with his and Mrs. Taylor's compliments.

Pam thanked him kindly for being so thoughtful, but told him we would have to decline his generous offer. "Perhaps we could have a rain check on the trip, Daddy. We could go next year. Right now, Irish and I just want to go to San Francisco for a couple of days, get right back here, and get our married life off on the right foot. I hope you're not disappointed, Daddy. We really do appreciate the offer."

I reiterated our thanks and added, "Perhaps next year we could all go together. Pam and I would enjoy it more if you were with us to share the good times."

"Well, I can't argue with that logic, can you, Paula?"

"No way, George. And Irish told us he's rather anxious to start working, so you had better start looking for a place for him."

"Don't worry about that. There is only one place for Irish, and that is in public relations. I intend to respect his wishes for a nine-to-five schedule, with no exceptions. I don't want these two going through what we did, and this old dog has learned his new tricks well."

We all laughed while Mr. Taylor flagged down Arnold, who was making his way around the room with a tray full of drinks. When we each had a glass in hand, he proposed a toast to a happy and healthy marriage for Pam and me. We all drank in honor of the toast—or I should say I sipped it and watered a potted plant with it when no one was looking.

Time was really flying by, and before we knew it, we were back at the country club standing at the head of the reception line receiving the guests who all came bearing gifts. Everyone was gracious and wished us the best of everything. Occasionally I would get a bad vibration as I sensed the pent-up hostility of someone who still couldn't believe Pam would marry the likes of me, a poor boy from back east, with no formal education and not much to boast about, other than my love for Pam, and a medal that Uncle Sam gave me. But I didn't let it bother me, for by now, my inferiority complex was a thing of the past, and I felt I was as good as any of these bastards. And I wasn't interested in matching checkbook balances with them anyway. I figured if they liked me, fine. And if not, they could just leave me alone. I had nothing to prove, and I sure as hell wasn't in show business to show them a damned thing.

Finally, the last of the guests arrived, and the festivities began. The champagne fountain was bubbling over and everyone was getting their fill. The band was playing beautiful dance music; things were really moving along nicely. It wasn't long before Pam and I were to do the honors of cutting the wedding cake, with her feeding me the first piece, and then turning the knife over to Maggie, who had volunteered to help out. We began opening presents and putting them on display. God, I never knew there were that many gifts in the world. I had no idea what we would ever do with all of them. Perhaps we could open a store or something to dispose of them.

We managed to finish that task and thank one and all for being so thoughtful. I took Pam to the dance floor and the band began playing the "Anniversary Song." We were about halfway through when Mr. and Mrs. Taylor cut in on us, and we all waltzed off in different directions. Then, it was a steady succession of cutting in—the ladies with me, and the gentlemen with Pam. They kept us going nonstop for the next twenty minutes. We finally got a chance to sit down and catch our breath.

The major asked me how I was doing. "I'm going to make it, Major. And look, if I don't get another chance to tell you before Pam and I leave, we both want to thank you for coming out and being my best man."

"It was my pleasure, Irish, and you're both very welcome."

"Well, Major, I want you to keep in touch with me now and keep me posted on where you are and what you're doing. Will you do that?"

"I sure will, Irish."

The bandleader asked for quiet and told everyone about my exceptional talent for singing. (This was the same band that had played for the Taylors' anniversary party.) He suggested, "Perhaps if we prompt him a little, he'll sing a song or two for us on his wedding day. What do you say, folks?" Everyone clapped and cheered until I had no choice but to go up on stage just to quiet them down. I took Pam in tow and made her go with me, telling her I could not face it alone.

On behalf of Pam and me, I thanked all in attendance for being there and for all their lovely gifts. I told them we sincerely appreciated each and every one of them. "I especially want to thank Mr. and Mrs. Taylor, not only for the hand of their beautiful daughter in marriage, but also for opening their home and their hearts to me. I will love them always and would like to thank them in the only way I know how, by dedicating this song to them."

I turned to the bandleader and said, "Mrs. Taylor's favorite, please—'I'll Take You Home Again, Kathleen.'" I sang on and on, with the band doing a marvelous job of keeping up with me; the overall effect of the song was just great.

After the warm applause died down, I asked for special requests. It wasn't long before I had everyone in the ballroom singing along with Pam and me. We kept it up for a while, and then I asked the bandleader if they would play "True Love" for Pam and me. As they started playing, Pam and I faced each other. I handed her the mike and clasped my hands around hers and sang while gazing into her beautiful eyes. On the second chorus, she joined in, and we sang only to each other, oblivious to the crowd surrounding us. Our voices blended beautifully; we sang as if we had rehearsed it for months. There was such a warm and loving atmosphere permeating the air around us that it was almost as if we were floating on air, and the music and words were coming from afar.

When we concluded, I said, "I love you, Mrs. O'Malley." She responded with, "And I love you, Mr. O'Malley." We embraced and kissed as everyone in the room cheered and applauded us. I handed the mike to the bandleader and thanked him for being so patient with us and for making us look good with his wonderful musicians. He told us we were very welcome and to look him up if I was ever looking for a job. I shook his hand, smiled, and thanked him.

We made our way back over to the table. It really felt good to sit down. I asked Pam how she was holding up, and she admitted she was beginning to tire a little. We went into conference with Mr. and Mrs. Taylor and asked them when it would be appropriate for us to slip away. They told us we could leave any time we liked.

Mr. Taylor gave me the key to his locker in the men's lounge and said there was a change of clothes in there for me. Meanwhile Mrs. Taylor took Pam to the ladies' lounge to help her out of her gown and into her traveling clothes. We agreed to meet back at the table and then say good-bye to everyone and be on our way.

We arrived back all attired in our travel clothes and were about to make our departure when Mrs. Taylor said, "Just one more thing, Irish. You have to take the garter off Pam before you can leave." Everyone gathered around, while I knelt down and slipped her skirt gently up over her left knee.

Pam said, "The other leg, Irish."

"Given two choices, I'll make the wrong one every time."

Everyone laughed while I proceeded to take the garter off her right leg. I stood up, held it above my head, and flung it into the crowd of single men while everyone cheered.

We made our way to the entrance and up the four steps leading out into the lobby. We turned around and thanked everyone again and announced that Pam was about to throw her bridal bouquet. All the single young ladies flocked to the front, and Pam let it fly. While they were scrambling for it, we hurried out front to our waiting car. I shook Henry's hand and thanked him for his help. After helping Pam in and closing her door, I slid behind the steering wheel, pulled it into gear, and we were on our way to San Francisco.

22

The Honeymoon and the New House

We drove nonstop to the hotel in downtown San Francisco, checked in, and were escorted to the bridal suite by a bellhop. After he set our luggage down, I handed him a five-dollar bill and told him we'd see him in about a month. After he departed, I went over and locked the door behind him, and walked over and took my new bride in my arms and carried her over to the bed and gently placed her down on it. I kissed her as I asked her how she was feeling.

"Oh, Irish, words can't describe how I feel. Come lay beside me and let us catch our breath and drift off into the universe."

"You bet, sweetheart! Here, let me make you comfortable." I slipped off her shoes and took off her pearl necklace and earrings and her tiny little hat. While I arranged her things over on the dresser, I told her to lie back and relax. I took off my jacket and tie and laid them on a chair. I then sat on the edge of the bed and took off my shoes. I lay down beside Pam and took her hand, and we both drifted in silence for several moments. Both of us were still trying to bring ourselves to the realization that we were finally married. All the waiting, longing, anticipation, setbacks, and hard work was behind us. Even the wedding and the reception were now part of our past. Here we were in the bridal suite as husband and wife. It was such a wonderful feeling that we just could not put it into words.

I raised up on one elbow and kissed my new bride and asked, "How's the new Mrs. O'Malley feeling now?"

"Ecstatic, Mr. O'Malley, simply ecstatic."

"Shall we partake of the fruits of our marriage, my precious little baby doll?"

"Oh, yes, darling! Let's make love forever and ever."

We got up and quickly undressed and pulled the bedding down. I turned off all the lights and snuggled up as close as I could to her warm body. As our lips tenderly met, our love making began, and I swear it was even more sensuous than the first time. Pam was absolutely right when she had assured me that our premarital affair would not detract from our wedding night in the slightest. This was nothing less than heaven on earth for both of us. We did little sleeping that night. All our hopes and dreams were finally being realized. It was completely engulfed by her voluptuous charms and was absolutely unaware of everything else on this earth. Her every touch, her every movement, her every sigh and tender kiss only excited me more and only served to make me want to please her in every way I possibly could. Our love for one another kept us locked in sensual excesses until we drifted off to sleep just as the sun was beginning to peek through the window at us.

I was awakened around noon by a tender kiss. As I opened my eyes and looked into her beautiful brown eyes, I still thought for an instant that it was all a dream. I held her in my arms and said, "Good-morning, beautiful. How's the most precious lover in the world this morning?"

"I'm even more in love with you this morning than I was last night, lover, and I'm still having trouble bringing myself to the realization that we are finally man and wife. Oh, Irish, it is all I'd hoped it would be, and, oh, so much more. I know we'll never have another night like last night if we live to be one hundred. But we'll use last night for our guidepost in our quest for a long, healthy and love-filled marriage."

"I couldn't agree with you more, Pam, darling. You've expressed my sentiments exactly. I love you, Pam Taylor. . . . I mean, Pam O'Malley. See, I still have trouble believing someone as lovely as you could marry the likes of me."

"Oh, Irish, I'm the lucky one to have you fall in love with me as you did. You'll never know how lonely it was, growing up the way I did, wanting someone to hold me and kiss me good-night and tuck me in. And even when I grew up and was in college, I was still a very lonely person and had almost resigned myself to the fact that I'd wind up being an old maid. I was sure, because of Daddy's wealth, I'd never find anyone sincere enough to fall in love with me just for little ole me, without being taken in by his influence. I told Carol the first night after we dropped you and Moose off that you were the one I had waited all my life for. I hoped more than anything that you wouldn't be scared off when you found out about Daddy."

"Oh, darling, I know what it's like to be lonely, too. Like I've told you, our marriage was made in heaven, and all the money, influence, or even all the evil forces on this earth won't stop us from being happy and in love until the day we die."

"I know, Irish O'Malley. And Mrs. Irish O'Malley will be the proudest woman on this earth to make the journey through life with you."

We sealed our love with a kiss, and just naturally began making love to each other. We came back to earth after another lovely episode. Pam jumped up and said, "Come on, Irish, I'll race you to the shower." I jumped up and ran for the bathroom, but she beat me by a step or two. "Didn't think I could move that quickly, did you?"

"No, I didn't, but I'm proud of you."

We showered quickly and she kidded me about having someone to wash her back from now on, and I said I hoped she'd extend me the same courtesy.

"I might if you're nice to me."

"Well, I guess I'll get my back scrubbed all the time then, for I could never be anything but nice to you."

"Thanks, Irish, and if I'm ever anything but nice to you, I want you to tell me about it."

"I might, or I might just pout about it."

"Well, if I see you pouting, I'll know." "Okay, darling, okay."

After we got dressed, we made our way to the elevator and down to the lobby. We headed for the dining room with the sudden realization that it had been almost twenty-four hours since we had put any solid food in our stomachs. We stuffed ourselves at lunch, and wandered out in the sunshine. It was a beautifully clear day, with just a little white cloud here and there to break up the oceans of heavenly blue skies overhead.

I asked Pam what she wanted to do. "Ride the cablecars, Irish." "You've got it, sweetheart!" And that is just what we did for the next two hours, up and down the hill, joking and laughing and having a wonderful time.

After we tired of that, I made a suggestion that we go back to the beach. We grabbed a cab and were there in no time. I took her to the same spot where I had first kissed her and kissed her again. I held her ever so tightly and told her, "This place brings back wonderful memories, Pam. This is the exact spot where the magic of love really touched me with that first kiss."

"Same here, Irish. That was the most beautiful moment of my life."

We sat down on the sand, and I took Pam's shoes off and then my own shoes and socks. We kissed and made small talk for a while and then got up and went wandering down the beach hand in hand, letting the waves lick at our feet. Finally we came upon the little out-of-the-way cove where I had first made my declaration of love to Pam. We lay down on the sand, and as I held her in my arms, I told her again how very much I loved her.

"And I love you, Irish, with every fiber of my being. I'm so glad you brought me back here, Irish. The only thing I'm sorry for is that I didn't confess my love for you that first evening."

"Hush, darling. To paraphrase Shakespeare, the world is our stage and we are but actors upon it. And you played your part in our sweet and tender love story with all the warmth and emotions any actor ever put into a performance. Just look at this happy beginning of a beautiful marriage. I only pray I can play my part and make you half as happy as you make me."

"Oh, Irish, I couldn't be happier. And I know you'll always make me happy."

We lingered on there for the next hour, just relaxing and watching the water. It was so right, our being there in the warmth of each other's arms protected by the overhang of the ledge above us.

Pam asked if I thought Moose and Carol could see us now. "I'm as sure of that as I am of my love for you, darling. And I'm equally sure they're both very happy for us."

"You know, Irish, it's comforting to know that."

We decided to go back to the hotel when we suddenly discovered we had left our shoes about a half mile down the beach. "Five will get you ten they're not there any longer, honey." "Well, let's walk back down and see, shall we?"

"Okay."

We headed back down the beach. Sure enough, someone had lifted them. I laughed and asked, "How are we going to get back into the hotel with no shoes on?"

Pam said, "Well, I guess we'll just have to walk in."

"Good thinking, sweetheart. I knew you would figure something out."

"Wise guy, I bet you no one even notices we're not wearing shoes when we get there."

"How much?"

"Five kisses and a big hug."

"I like that. Either way, I'm a winner."

We caught another cab. No sooner had we stepped out of the cab at the hotel than the doorman said, "Pardon me, miss, you must have left your shoes in the cab." I laughed and said, "No, this is the latest fad."

We walked into the lobby and over to the desk to pick up the key and then walked over and pressed the button for the elevator. While we were waiting for it, we turned around to discover about twenty people in the lobby staring at us.

Pam, a little embarrassed and red-faced, asked, "What do we do now, Irish?"

I answered, "Smile and wave to the nice people." We did, and just that quickly they all turned away from us and went back to what they were doing before they took up watching us.

Finally, the elevator arrived, and we made it back to our room. Pam sat down at the dressing table while I flopped down on the bed, and propped myself up on my elbows to watch her. She was truly magnificent with that long and silky light brown hair.

I broke the silence by calling her name, "Pam, honey."

"Yes, Irish."

"Can I ask you a favor? You can say no, if you want to. I mean —I don't want you to get upset or anything like that."

"What is it, Irish?"

"Well, would you be offended if I asked you if I could brush your pretty hair for you?"

"Is that all, Irish?"

"Yes,

Why were you afraid to ask? Should that upset me?"

"I don't know, I heard somewhere, or perhaps I read it, that girls don't like men brushing their hair, and I was afraid you'd be offended if I asked you if I could."

"Not in the least, darling. I love for someone to brush my hair," she said, throwing the brush to me. I jumped off the bed and pulled a chair up behind her and began ever so delicately running the brush through what to me was the most beautiful head of hair in the world.

She threw her head way back, and I leaned forward and kissed her, and said, "Thanks, honey. I've wanted to do this ever since we first met. You're so neat, petite, and absolutely meticulous about yourself and everything you do. Even your pretty little toenails are painted to perfection, and I love you for it, sweetheart. I know I'm somewhat of a slob myself, but I promise I'll try to be every bit as neat and particular about myself and our home as you are."

"Well, thank you for those lovely compliments, Irish O'Malley. But I don't want to change a thing about you. I love you just as you are, and if you want to throw your clothes around the house, do it. I'll love picking up after you. I think that is where a lot of newlyweds make their biggest mistake. They figure once they're married they have every right in the world to change their partner to conform to their way of thinking and doing things."

"Well, I, for one, Pam, darling, wouldn't want to change a hair on your pretty little head. I married you for what you are and not what I expect you to turn into."

"I feel the same, Irish. You just be your sweet, lovable self, and we'll do just fine. You can brush my hair any time you like, too."

"Thanks, honey. I guess subconsciously I was afraid of messing it up or something. But for some reason ever since we first met I have always had this secret desire to run a brush through your magnificently beautiful hair. Does that sound crazy to you?"

"No, honey. I've always been proud of my long hair and try to keep it as neat as possible."

"You've done a magnificent job, too, honey," I said, as I kissed her on top of the head. I kept brushing her hair for the next fifteen minutes and finally handed her back the brush, telling her to finish it to perfection, as she always does. She looked at herself in the mirror, and commented, "I like it just the way you have it." She lay the brush on the dresser and we stood up and locked ourselves in a tender embrace.

"Say, you lost our bet, Pam. You owe me five kisses and a big hug."

"That's one bet I'll be happy to pay off right now." She hugged me for all she was worth, and planted five big ones right dead on my lips.

As we both hoped it would, one thing led to another, and before we knew it—and I might add to our delight—we were back in bed, making love to each other until our hearts were content.

Along about eight in the evening, I suggested a little food and nourishment, and my beautiful bride agreed wholeheartedly. She suggested we find a nice, quiet restaurant with a small dance floor.

"Candlelight and soft music, my dear."

"Oh, yes, darling, it sounds so romantic."

"Well, then, let's do it, my dear."

We were up, showered, dressed and out of there in record time. We asked the desk clerk if he knew of a romantic place and he suggested a perfect, little restaurant up on a hill, overlooking the bridge and the bay.

It was even more than we bargained for. A little Italian restaurant with red checkered tableclothes, candles stuck in empty wine bottles, and three violins playing soft melodic music. We had the place practically to ourselves. The food was out of this world, and we danced the night away until two in the morning, when they were getting ready to close the place down. I slipped the violin players a twenty-dollar bill, and asked them if they would play, "I Left My Heart in San Francisco" for us one more time. They played and we danced. I told Pam that song really had a very special meaning for me, and it still brings a tear to my eye every time I hear it.

"I know, Irish, and I love it, also. It will always be our song."

We were soon back at the hotel enjoying our marital bliss. We spent the next day and night there and decided to head back for Sacramento on Tuesday to start looking for a house of our very own so we could set up housekeeping and really get down to this business of playing house.

We arrived back at the Taylors' at two o'clock in the afternoon and quietly let ourselves in through the side door. We walked into the living room where Mrs. Taylor was sitting with another woman, and we yelled, "Surprise! We're home!"

She jumped up and ran over to greet us, throwing her arms around both of us. After she let us go, I grabbed her around the waist and spun her around again before releasing her. "Did you miss us, Mrs. Taylor?"

"Did I ever! Did you both have a good time, and did everything go all right?"

Pam told her it couldn't have been any better. Just perfect.

"Oh, I'm sorry, let me introduce you to Mrs. Phillips. She's a real estate agent, and she might have a listing that is just what you kids have in mind."

After the introductions, she showed us a picture of a beautiful little Cape Cod bungalow down by the river, surrounded by trees and a beautiful lawn. Pam and I looked at the picture and then at each other. We both knew instantly that it was just what we had in mind. "Could you take us over to see it this afternoon?"

"Yes, I can take you now, if you'd like."

"Do you have time, Mrs. Taylor?"

"Of course, Irish. Just give me a minute or two to get ready."

It was no time at all before we were pulling into the driveway of what Pam and I immediately knew was going to be our new home. After the real estate agent unlocked the door, I picked Pam up in my arms and carried her across the threshold and put her down in the living room. Hand in hand we rambled through the house, not saying a word. We let ourselves out into the backyard and went running all the way to the fence at the rear of the grounds to get an overall view of our little dream house. Pam looked at me and said, "What do you think, Irish?"

"I think it's perfect, and if you like it, we'll buy it."

"I love it, Irish. It's everything I dreamed it would be."

We ran hand in hand back to the house and announced with delight that we would take it.

"Just show us where to sign."

Mrs. Phillips, the real estate agent, was a little dumbfounded at our impetuosity. She fumbled in her handbag for a sales contract.

Mrs. Taylor said, "I can just feel the love being generated in this beautiful little house. I'm sure you'll both be very happy here."

While Mrs. Phillips was preparing the sales contract, Mrs. Taylor, Pam, and I inspected it a little closer. They were already making plans for what was to go where and where they could get this and that. They would ask what I thought, and I told them interior decorating was way out of my line. As far as I was concerned, I told them, they had a free hand to furnish it any way they chose, and I would be simply delighted with whatever they came up with.

Mrs. Taylor asked us if we would be kind enough to let her and Mr. Taylor pay for the house as a wedding present. We both thanked her very much but told her we would appreciate it more if we paid for it ourselves and hoped she would not be offended.

"Not in the least. You'll let us help you furnish it, though, won't you?"

"Of course, Mother," said Pam, throwing her arms around her and giving her a big kiss. "Thank you for finding our dream house for us."

"That goes for me, too, Mrs. Taylor," I said, stepping up to kiss what I considered to be one of the most beautiful women in the world.

"Oh, all I did was make a few inquiries for you. That's all."

"Oh, is that all? Well, you got us exactly what we wanted, and we appreciate it."

We signed the sales agreement and asked how soon we could move in.

"You can stay now if you like, but it will take about thirty days until closing. However, for all intents and purposes, it's your house right now."

"Great, honey, we'll start bright and early in the morning to get it ready to move in."

"Whatever you say, darling. You're going to be the lady of the house."

"Yes, and you're going to be the man of the house, Irish. It's going to be so much fun. I know we'll be very happy here. Our love can only grow in this beautiful atmosphere."

Mrs. Phillips drove us back to the Taylors', still not quite believing how easy the sale had been. She dropped us off and quickly departed. We went on into the house and sat down in the living room. Pam said, "I can't believe it. It all happened so suddenly. We've only been home for two hours and already we own a house of our own."

I couldn't believe it was all luck. "Tell me the truth, Mrs. Taylor, how many houses did you look at while we were gone, before you found that one?"

"Oh, Irish!"

"Come on, Mrs. Taylor."

"Well, perhaps twenty."

"You're incredible! You'll always be dear, sweet, precious Mrs. Taylor to me. Say, listen, Mrs. Taylor, Pam and I felt kind of badly about running out and leaving you with that crowd and all the work at the reception and would like to make it up to you in some way if we can."

"Nonsense. I loved it, what with all the beautiful compliments everyone was giving you kids, and how marvelously everything went. It was a dream come true for me. Speaking of that, I had all your gifts put in the game room. Would you like to go down and look them over now?"

"I'd love to. To tell you the truth, I was in such a trance at the reception that I couldn't even tell you what my name was."

We walked in to a room simply loaded with gifts. Mrs. Taylor said she took the liberty of separating them and putting all the duplicates to one side. She said she figured we would have little use for fifteen toasters and twelve electric skillets. "You must have enough linens and towel sets here to last you for the next twenty years." I said, "That's good. This way Pam won't have to wash them. When one gets dirty she can throw it away and get a new one out." They both laughed at me.

Pam wanted to know what we were going to do with all the duplicates. Mrs. Taylor, always one step ahead of us, told us she had made arrangements with a local department store to take them back and give us credit on furniture or anything else in the store that we might want to buy.

"You're terrific, Mrs. Taylor. Gee, looking at all of these presents, I guess we'll be busy for weeks writing thank-you notes, honey."

"Yes, I guess we will, Irish."

Mrs. Taylor again beat us to the punch. "I don't see why. All you have to do is sign the cards. The envelopes are already addressed and stamped. Perhaps one afternoon this week you can take care of that."

"You know, Mrs. Taylor, we never get done thanking you.

What would we ever do without you? Thanks again." She just smiled her loving smile at us.

We examined the gifts for the next forty-five minutes or so, with Pam chattering on about how we can use this or that, and with me agreeing right down the line.

Mrs. Taylor mentioned that she had had my things moved into Pam's room, and she hoped that would be all right. She added that she had sent back the hospital bed and all the other paraphernalia that went with it.

"You've been a busy little beaver, haven't you, Mother!" said Pam.

"Well, I didn't think we needed all those reminders around here. Remember what Irish told us: Look forward, not backward."

I gave her a big hug and a kiss and told her, "I'm going to love being your son. I know we are all going to be very happy from now on. I really feel like somebody here; it's the most secure feeling I've ever had in my life. I just feel warm and loved and only want to return that warm and loving feeling any way I can."

"Oh, Irish, just knowing you feel that way makes us all very happy. And you don't have to prove you love us; we already know that. Shall we go inspect the new living arrangements Mother has provided for us?"

Arm in arm, all three of us went to Pam's room. We entered the room that Mrs. Taylor had done up to perfection. It almost took my breath away, and I exclaimed that I felt like a stranger in paradise. Pam reiterated the same feeling.

"Well, I'll leave you two strangers in paradise, while I go wash up for dinner. I'll see you two downstairs."

"Okay, thanks again, Mrs. Taylor."

Pam and I surveyed our new kingdom. I asked her how it felt to be sharing her beautiful room with a man.

"Not just any man, Irish; but the most beautiful human being in the world. I'm sure God will look kindly on our love and see that we are always happy. I love you, Irish O'Malley."

"And I love you, Pamela O'Malley."

"I simply love the sound of that name, Irish. Oh, I feel we are completely in tune with the whole universe."

"Do you really think so, Pam? The universe is a mighty big and beautiful place."

"Yes, I know, Irish. To me this universe we live in is like a precision timepiece. I cannot imagine this fine instrument not having a master craftsman as its creator, and that creator is looking favorably upon us at this very moment."

I took her in my arms and kissed her, telling her she saw love and beauty in everything, and the world was a much better place now that she graced it with her warmth and beauty.

The grandfather clock in the hallway rang six times, bringing us back to reality. "Say, we had better get washed up; it's dinnertime."

We made it just as the Taylors were sitting down. Mr. Taylor came over and put his arms around us and welcomed us home. He urged me to sit down and tell him and Mrs. Taylor all about our trip. We filled them in on our trip and even told them about losing our shoes on the beach and trying to sneak back into the hotel in our bare feet. They really got a kick out of that.

Mr. Taylor asked if we had had a chance to see the Sunday paper and read the nice write-up they gave me on winning the medal and the beautiful story of our wedding, along with pictures and all. We confessed we hadn't had a chance to see it yet, but would look at it after dinner. "We were too busy buying a house this afternoon."

"You bought a house this afternoon?"

"Yes, Daddy. Mother found us our dream house, down by the river. If you have time after dinner, perhaps you and Mother would like to go over with Irish and me and take a look at it."

"I'd love to, honey. Tell me all about it."

"Well, to tell you the truth, Daddy, we can't."

"You can't; why not?"

"Well, Irish and I just knew the moment he carried me across the threshold that it was built just for us, and we were so anxious to see everything that in our excitement, we didn't see anything. Does that make sense to you, Daddy?"

"Yes. In a way, I guess it does."

"Gee, Mr. Taylor, I couldn't even tell you if the bathroom has fixtures in it or if the kitchen has a sink. Wouldn't it be something if we had bought a house with four rooms and a path?" We all laughed and Mrs. Taylor assured us that it had all the modern conveniences.

We drove over directly after dinner. This time we examined it from stem to stern and had the Taylors walk every inch of ground with us and give us their opinion on what should go where and what to do about this and that. I really believe they were enjoying it every bit as much as Pam and I. We stayed until after dark, and Pam and I offered to treat them to a hamburger and a Coke at a drive-in. It was hard to believe it, but this was their first trip to a drive-in restaurant, and they loved it. On the way home Mr. Taylor asked me when I wanted to start working.

I told him, "The sooner the better. Now that we're big property owners, with a mortgage and all, I have to get to work and start paying for it."

"A mortgage?" he asked quizzically. "Didn't Mrs. Taylor tell you kids we wanted to buy it for you as a wedding present?"

"I told them, George, but they insisted they would appreciate it a lot more if they paid for it themselves. They are going to let us help them furnish it for them, though, and I think they're right in wanting to pay for their first house themselves, don't you?"

"I'm sure they're right," Mr. Taylor agreed. "Tell you what, Irish, there is a joint board meeting in the morning and everyone who is anyone will be there. It's so seldom that we all get together in one place that I would like to take you with me and introduce you to everyone."

"Pam and Mrs. Taylor are going shopping in the morning for furniture, rugs, drapes, and so forth. I'm sure I would only confuse things for them, so if it's all right with them, I'd love to go with you."

"It's perfectly all right with us, Irish, if you're sure you can rely on our judgment as to color, style, and design."

I laughed and said, "Would you listen to that? You two have

to be the neatest, most meticulous perfectionists in the world. And you're asking me if I can rely on your judgment? Let me assure you both that there is no way in the world you could ever disappoint me. Whatever you decide on will be perfectly acceptable to me."

"Okay, then it's all settled. I'll have him home to you around one tomorrow afternoon, honey. Will that be all right?"

"Fine, Daddy, and I'm sure Irish will prove to be one of your most worthy assets."

"I've been convinced of that for a long time, honey. And if I catch you there after five in the evening, Irish, I'll fire you."

"You have a deal, Mr. Taylor."

We spent the evening catching up on the newspaper articles, belated wedding greetings, and gifts, and still savoring all that had happened to us in the past few days. It was really the first chance the Taylors or Pam and I had to catch our breath and unwind, and I related these feelings to them. They agreed and added it was a time of their lives that they would never forget.

Mrs. Taylor could not resist the chance to pay me another compliment. "You know, Irish, when I first laid eyes on a somewhat insecure and uncomfortable little Irishman nicknamed Irish, I knew you were very special. But I never dreamed you would bring so much joy and happiness into our lives. Mr. Taylor and I both bless the day Pam first brought you home, Irish, and we'll be thankful for the remainder of our lives."

"No, Mrs. Taylor, it is I who am grateful to all of you for your undying love and understanding. You have all had a hand in letting me see how warm and loving life can really be. It is I who will be thankful for the remainder of my life."

"Okay, Irish, we just want you to know we love you. Now, how about some coffee and a piece of Maggie's custard pie, before we retire for the night."

"You talked me into it."

After we finished our coffee and pie, Pam and I excused ourselves, but not before I asked Mr. Taylor what time we were leaving in the morning.

"Oh, about eight o'clock will be fine, Irish."

"Okay, I'll be ready."

Pam and I no sooner closed the bedroom door than we both did a striptease act in record time and soon were standing under a nice, warm shower, kissing and lathering each other with soap. After drying off, we headed for another night of heavenly bliss. For some reason, Pam told me our lovemaking kept getting better for her, and I felt the same way. We made love in every conceivable position until the wee small hours of the morning and finally fell asleep locked in each other's arms. Pam woke me about seven in the morning with a tender little kiss. She announced it was a brand new day, and she wasn't sure now if she wanted to let me go with her father or not. "No, I'm just kidding you, Irish; but would you make love to me once more before you go?"

"Darling, I couldn't think of a sweeter way to start off any day, and when we can, we should start off each day by making love. Do you think that's a good idea?"

"Wonderful, Irish," she sighed, as we two became one once again. I was on top of her and in her and the warmth of her vagina excited me. It was unbelievable how much pleasure I derived from being inside her body. Our bodies were in perfect accord, and we made our lovemaking last for a good fifteen minutes before we both felt that heavenly feeling of a climax.

I was a little behind schedule now, so I quickly showered, and while I shaved, Pam laid out my blue suit, white shirt, and a striped tie. I quickly dressed, and we both went downstairs to wait for Mr. Taylor. Maggie spotted us and insisted we have breakfast, saying, "Man does not live on love alone."

"Okay, Maggie, bring on the other, then."

We were soon joined by Mr. and Mrs. Taylor, and Maggie fed us all. Mr. Taylor asked me how I was feeling this morning. I confessed to being a bit nervous and hoped I wouldn't be a disappointment to him today.

"Don't worry about that, Irish. You just be yourself, and I'm sure everything will be just fine."

We kissed the ladies good-bye, and they wished us well. We told them I'd be home around one and departed.

23

Irish is Introduced to the Business World

We arrived at the Taylor office building and went directly to the conference room, where everyone was already assembled. Mr. Taylor directed me to a seat behind and to the side of the head of the table. The meeting was called to order, and they went through their ritual of reports, reading of minutes, prospects for the future, and the whole number.

There was a knock on the door, and the doorkeeper answered it. It was a delivery boy with a bundle of magazines. The doorkeeper signed for them and brought the bundle directly to Mr. Taylor. He opened them and examined the first copy, saying, "Ah, yes, this is what I've been waiting for." (It was a bundle of news magazines with the article about me and the Taylors in it). Mr. Taylor had a copy handed out to all in attendance, telling them they were seeing it for the first time, the same as he.

"The young gentleman I'm about to introduce to you is there on the cover. I take great pleasure in introducing my son-in-law, Irish O'Malley, as the newest member of the Taylor organization. Needless to say, he has some impressive credentials, as this article will point out to you."

I stood up and walked to the head of the table and stood beside

Mr. Taylor. Everyone applauded—I imagine to be polite, for I was sure they were not impressed with the likes of me joining their ranks. I guess they were a little jealous, and perhaps rightly so. Most of them had worked their way to the top and figured I just married my way into their ranks. In a very real sense, they were right.

I thanked them for their warm welcome and started in by saying, "Mr. Taylor here has the notion that he can make something out of me; but let me assure you he has his work cut out for him. I'm not naive enough to believe he has all the powerful and high-priced help gathered around this table for that express purpose. No, he is calling on a much higher authority. I caught him praying on his rosary on the way over here this morning and heard him saying under his breath, 'Deliver me, oh, Lord, for I know not what I'm going to do with him.' " Everyone laughed and got a big kick out of it.

I went on to tell them that he was about to cut me loose on them and let me roam at will throughout the organization. "I guess he figures that will keep me out of his hair and spread the burden around a little more equally." Still more laughter. I told them that I had heard some of the work performed in the Taylor industrial plants was advanced, but I never imagined I'd see what I saw over at the nut and bolt factory the other day. "I saw a bolt chasing a nut up and down the aisles, with the nut hollering, 'No, no, not without a washer' ". The roof almost came off the building, and everyone applauded again.

I told them I had always thought asphalt was rectum trouble until Mr. Taylor pointed out to me that he owned an asphalt plant and he explained what it really was. "So you see, I really do have a lot to learn, but I learn fast. I remember when I was eight years old, my mother took me upon her knee and told me it was about time we had a talk about the birds and the bees. I said, 'Okay, maw, what do you want to know?' But enough of this foolishness now. I've taken up enough of your valuable time. I'll be looking forward to meeting each and every one of you individually, and hope I don't drive any of you crazy. Thanks again for your warm welcome."

I retreated to my chair and let Mr. Taylor get on with the meeting. My little speech pretty well broke the meeting up so he simply closed the formal meeting and the whole affair degenerated into a big bullshit session.

Everyone was coming up to Mr. Taylor and myself to be introduced and commenting on the article and congratulating me on winning the Congressional Medal of Honor. I had my antennae tuned in to discover any undercurrent of hostility. As I shook hands and was introduced to people, I would make a conscious character analysis of them. If they gave me a warm, friendly handshake, I would get the feeling they were all right. On the other hand, if they gave me a limp handshake, I made a special mental note of it, for I felt they deserved watching and could not be trusted, as far as I was concerned.

It was time to break for lunch. I asked Mr. Taylor if he would mind terribly if I skipped it and went back home to give Pam and Mrs. Taylor a hand. "No, no, not in the least, Irish. It's past noon already, and I promised I'd have you back by one."

"Thanks, Mr. Taylor. I'll just grab a cab out front."

"Okay, Irish, and I want to tell you that you made quite an impression on everyone here today."

"Thanks, Mr. Taylor. We should have things pretty well in hand, and perhaps I can start full time by next Monday; would that be all right with you?"

"Fine, Irish. If you need more time, just take it."

"Thanks, Mr. Taylor. I'll see you this evening."

I arrived back at the Taylors' just as Mrs. Taylor was pulling up in Pam's car. I paid the cab driver and walked over to greet her.

"Hi, Mrs. Taylor. Where's Pam?"

"Hi, Irish. She's over at the new house instructing the painters and waiting for the lady to measure for the new drapes. I came over to pick you up and fix us all a little lunch to take back over."

"Fine, let me get out of this suit, and into some work clothes, and I'll be ready to go in no time."

"Okay, Irish, take your time."

I changed my clothes and hurried back to the kitchen where Maggie and Mrs. Taylor were busy packing a picnic basket and filling a big thermos jug. "Hi, Maggie," I said. "How have you been? Haven't had much chance to talk to you lately."

"Oh, fine, Mr. Irish, and how have you been doing?"

"Need you ask, you silly girl, you." She and Mrs. Taylor both laughed.

"Mr. Irish, you're something else."

"I'll take that as a compliment, Maggie."

"That's what I intended it to be, Irish."

"Well, I guess that just about does it, Irish. Shall we head back to your little love nest?"

"With all speed, my dear lady. See you later, Maggie."

We drove back over to the new house, walked in, and hollered for Pam. She came running out, threw her arms around me and gave me a big kiss. Mrs. Taylor observed, "It would appear you were missed, Irish."

"Yes, I'll say, and if this is any indication of the reception I'll be getting upon my return from work, I'll never be late coming home, I can assure you of that."

"Okay, you two," said Pam, "where is the grub basket? I'm starved."

"Oh, we forgot it. I knew there was something we were forgetting, Mrs. Taylor."

"Oh, it's all right," Pam said.

"Gee, we can't get an argument out of her anyway, so I guess I'll go bring it in."

"Ha, ha, I knew you were just kidding me. Well, I'll get you next time."

We ate our lunch out in the backyard under a big oak tree, while the ladies filled me in on all their activities. It seems they had everything under control. The painters were busy with instructions to stay at it until the job was complete. The carpet people were due there at seven o'clock in the morning, and the drapes were to be delivered along with the furniture the following afternoon.

Mrs. Taylor was having her gardener come over in the morning to cut the grass and prune the trees and shrubs. As if all that were not enough, some guy showed up, saying he had instructions to resurface the driveway and wanting to know when he could start. "Who called you?"

"Some guy named Mr. Taylor. Do you folks know him?"

Mrs. Taylor said, "We've met, and you can start any time you like."

"Okay. Thanks, lady. I'll call the boys and we'll get it done this afternoon."

After he left, we all sat there and roared with laughter at the preceding conversation. "Some guy named Mr. Taylor. Do you folks know him?"

"Yeah, we've met!"

"How did your meeting go this morning, Irish?"

"Fine. By the way, John Jenkins' article hit the newsstands today. Mr. Taylor had fifty copies sent directly to him and gave one to everybody at the meeting."

"Oh, I'd love to see it. Did you bring a copy home with you?"

"No, but I can run out and get a copy for us, if you like."

"Would you, Irish?"

"Sure. Do you want to go with me?"

"Go ahead, Pam. I'll look after things here."

"All right, we'll be right back."

We drove to a shopping center about two miles down the road, walked into a drugstore, and went right to the magazine rack. Sure enough there we were, as big as life, on the cover. We bought three copies and quickly returned to show them to Mrs. Taylor. We all sat down with our own copy, read the story and glanced at the pictures. Pam and Mrs. Taylor were ecstatic, and I must admit it was quite a thrill for me too.

"How does it feel to be a celebrity, Mrs. Taylor, with your picture on the cover of over two million magazines?"

"I don't know, Irish. It's kind of scary, to tell you the truth. Wonder how Sister Margaret and her students are reacting about now?"

Pam said, "I'll bet school is out for the day back there in Pennsylvania."

"I'll bet you're right. We'll have to give her a call this evening and tease her about being a cover girl. She really looks precious with that beautiful smile of hers, doesn't she?"

"Yes, she does, Irish. And you look simply marvelous standing there, so proud and erect."

"Surrounded by all that warmth and beauty and with you two lovelies on either arm, I couldn't be anything but proud."

"Oh, Irish, there is no doubt in anyone's mind you were the star of that show."

Our mutual admiration society was broken up by three ladies making their way across the lawn to where we were sitting.

We stood up as they approached. They introduced themselves as our neighbors and said they would like to welcome us to the neighborhood. I did the honors and introduced Pam, her mother, and myself.

The one lady who looked about thirty-five said, "Taylor, O'-Malley. My goodness, don't tell me you're the young couple married last Saturday and your husband here is the Congressional Medal of Honor winner."

Pam said, "Guilty on both counts."

"Well, we certainly are proud to have you for neighbors, and we promise to respect your privacy."

I said, "Don't worry about that. In another week or two, no one will even remember our names. We just want to blend in with, and become part of, the community. We simply fell in love with the house and the neighborhood, and we just hope we can be good neighbors to you all. We would invite you in for a cup of coffee, but the painters are busy in there, and they ran us out too."

"Look, I have a fresh pot on over at my house. Would you like to come over there for a cup?"

"I'd love it. How about you, Pam? Mrs. Taylor?"

"Lead the way, dear lady; I've been simply dying for a cup of coffee all day."

So we all went next door for coffee. They were extremely gracious and gave us an orientation to the neighborhood as to the stores, churches, recreation facilities, and what have you. They told us everyone in the community was big on picnics, little get-togethers and backdoor barbecues, and hoped we'd share in them. They asked us when we were planning on moving in, and Pam told them Saturday, if everything went according to schedule.

"Good. We are really looking forward to having you for neighbors." Pam told them we were looking forward to it too. We spent the next two hours getting acquainted, and finally had to take our leave to return to the Taylors' for dinner.

Things kept up at a whirlwind pace for us. We were settled in our new home right on schedule, and I started to work for Taylor Industries the following Monday.

Just as I knew it would, all the fanfare died down, and Pam and I became just another newlywed couple in a middle-class neighborhood. We became close friends with some of the neighbors.

Pam and I grew closer and our love stronger as time moved along. After four months Pam announced that she was pregnant, and we celebrated the occasion with a night of dinner and dancing with the Taylors and the Jenkinses. Outside of the Taylors, the Jenkinses became our most frequent visitors, although it seemed we always had someone over on weekends to play cards, or go to the theater with us, or do something else. Mrs. Taylor bought me a piano for my birthday. We would spend hours hammering away on it and having old-fashioned sing-alongs. Life couldn't have been richer or more rewarding for both of us.

Mrs. Taylor and I kept up our affair, but very discreetly, I might add, and only once or twice a month. It was a warm, loving, and rewarding affair for both of us. Somehow, Pam always knew when I had been with her mother, even though I would never announce when I was going over to see her. I would always ask her how she knew, and she would never tell me until one day she confessed. "After you've been with Mother, you come home to me with a special twinkle in your eye, like Peck's bad boy, trying to hide something from me. And Mother, she goes around for days afterwards with a radiant glow on her face that only appears after she's had a tryst with you."

"You're too much, you precious doll baby. Just when I think I could not possibly love you more than I do, I find myself falling deeper and deeper in love with you."

"I'm glad, Irish, and I hope our love never stops growing."

"How are things going at work, honey?"

"Oh, just fine, honey."

"Come on, Irish, I have noticed you in deep thought lately. Is something wrong?"

"I can't deceive you, honey. Something is wrong. But believe me, I don't know yet just what it is."

"Well, do you have any idea, Irish?"

"I get real bad vibrations when I'm around any one of three of your father's closest cohorts. It's as if they are planning something really evil, and I get the feeling that your father is the target of their plot."

"Have you discussed it with Daddy yet?"

"No, honey, and I wish you wouldn't say anything to him just yet—or to anyone, for that matter. I promise to let you know as soon as I get to the bottom of it."

"Well, Irish, I'm sure you must have something to go on or you wouldn't be this upset about it."

"I do, honey, but I can't prove anything. When your father is around, those three avoid each other like the plague. And as soon as he's out of town they spend every minute together in secret conferences. I sure would like to know what they talk about in there."

"I don't want to press you, Irish; but I wish you would let me help you carry the load."

"Okay, honey. I do need you to help me, if only to listen. I believe that there is a conspiracy to capture control of Taylor Industries and that those three are right at the heart of it. I've been picking up bits and pieces of information here and there and keeping a secret diary of interviews I've conducted and things I've overheard. Right now I have about a thousand pieces to the puzzle, and I'm trying to put it all together before I approach your father with it."

"For instance, we have lost seven out of the last eight major defense contracts this year. That's never happened before. Southern Corporation has been underbidding us each time, and that's never happened before. I know your father is concerned. That's why he has been spending so much time in Washington, trying to find out what's going on. I believe the problem lies with those three right there under his nose. I overheard them in the lounge yesterday discussing the latest contract loss and they were not overly disturbed. One would think they would have really been concerned, since they made the final bids themselves. I heard one of them say something about the computer came through again. I suspect they are rigging the bids, and the only reason for doing that is that they must have some kind of a secret deal worked out with Southern."

"Why would they want to do that, Irish? They're all wealthy, and they enjoy prominent positions in society. I don't understand."

"I couldn't, either, at first. But after you have all the money you want, then there is nothing left to strive for but power and prestige. This is what they're after, and by controlling the conglomerate, they would occupy a very powerful and prestigious position. If they were to succeed, I'm sure they would cut each other's throats until one of them emerged as king of the hill. That's how the game is played."

"Oh, Irish, I do hope that you're wrong and that there is a reasonable explanation for all this."

"I do, too, honey. But if there is a conspiracy, it would kill your father to lose control of all he's worked all his life for. I'm going to pursue this matter carefully and deliberately and bring it to a conclusion one way or another. Your dad is the closest thing I've ever had to an old man, and I can't sit back and see him destroyed when I'm in a position to do something about it."

"Irish, don't they audit those contracts?"

"Sure, to see if the arithmetic is correct, but a lost bid holds about as much appeal as last week's newspaper, and there is neither the time nor the money to go back over them. They just go on to preparing the next one, and the lost ones are forgotten. Simple as that. I have copies of the last eight here at the house, and I was able to get copies of the bids of Southern too. I want to compare them to see where the differences are. I'm going to convert all the figures to percentages of the total bid and see if that sheds any light on things."

"Can I do that for you, Irish? I don't have much to do during the day, and I would imagine you wouldn't want anyone at the office to know what you're doing."

"I sure could use the help, honey. I'll bring home one of our new adding machines that will make it a lot easier. In the meantime, I'm going to have to start taking my personal calls at home here. I've hired a couple of unsavory characters to do some snooping for me and I gave them specific instructions not to try and contact me at the office."

"Isn't that a little dangerous, Irish?"

"No, I just want them to tail these guys and let me know who they see and when and if their activities conflict with the best interest of Taylor Industries. I have to be able to prove a connection between them and Southern Corporation before I can go to your dad about any of this."

"Oh, Irish, please be careful. Why can't you tell Daddy now? He could get to the bottom of it, I'm sure."

"True, honey, and I've thought of that. But verifying this would take a complete audit of the whole business, and that takes about two years. By that time they could have destroyed him and all he's worked for. Your father is really a trusting person and doesn't always follow his own advice."

"What do you mean, Irish?"

"Do you remember how Mr. Roth was able to take advantage of your father's friendship and trust? Well, these three characters, I'm afraid, have discovered the same flaw in his character. They're so close to him that they are above suspicion in his eyes."

"Oh, Irish, this is terrible, and I hope you get to the bottom of it quickly."

"I'll try, honey, and I thank you for wanting to help. I have some charts and graphs I've set up. I'll bring them home tomorrow, and if you like, you can help me with them. As I pick up the bits and pieces, we'll chart them and try to get an overall picture of what is happening."

"I'll help in any way I possibly can, Irish."

"Thanks, sweet pea. I was beginning to get a little weary, carrying the load alone."

"I wish you had come to me sooner, Irish. That's what I'm here for."

"I know, honey, but I didn't want to worry you. And there is still an outside chance that I'm all wet. I hope it turns out that way. But my gut instinct tells me differently. Oh, enough of this for tonight. What did the Doc have to say today, honey?"

"Everything is just fine, Irish, and I will be making you a proud papa after the first of the year."

"Oh, that's simply wonderful, honey," I said, as I lay my hand on her stomach. "Has little Paula started moving yet?"

"How do you know it's going to be a girl, Irish?"

"Well, I promised your mother."

Pam laughed and said, "You're too much, Irish. And what are you going to do if it's a boy?"

"Well, I guess we'll have to send him back and get him altered, for I wouldn't want to disappoint your mother."

"Okay, I'll have twins then, a girl for mother and me and a boy for daddy and you."

"Okay. Would you do that for me, Pam?"

"Sure, why not?"

"Great. I'll order two cribs and double of everything else then. And, we'll get an extension built on the house to accommodate the children. And let's see, we'll need two nurses. Do you suppose Helen Jenkins could find us another one?"

"Oh, stop, Irish, you big nut, you, and take me in your arms and love me like you've never loved me before."

I took her in my arms and passionately kissed her. We locked in an embrace and one thing led to another. After it was all over, we wound up lying on our big bearskin rug in front of the fireplace with the fire flickering in the background.

"Oh, Irish, every time we make love is better than the previous time. I love you, Irish O'Malley," she said, as she cuddled

430

into me, and I kissed her pretty hair and ran my fingers through it.

"You know, Irish, this is the first time we couldn't wait until we were in the bedroom."

"Yes, I know, honey, and we'll have to be careful outside for fear we won't make it to the house." She giggled her girlish little laugh and said, "Oh, Irish."

We lay there for the next several hours, dreaming of what the future had in store for us, and wondering what our firstborn was going to look like, and if he or she would grow up to become President of the United States. We finally drifted off to sleep, right there on the rug.

The next six weeks were really productive as far as our endeavor to uncover the ills of Taylor Industries. The more we dug, the more evident it became that something was very wrong. I would bring my bits and pieces of financial information home to Pam, and she would place them on the appropriate chart or graph.

I would continue my role as the stupid son-in-law and wander through all the departments talking to people. They were very loose with information and had no idea what I was doing. They figured I was trying to learn the business to impress the old man, and all were very helpful.

After it became evident that my suspicions were correct, I took matters into my own hands and started a clandestine operation of my own. At my own expense, so that there was no record, I hired, an ex-con who was a terrific black bag man. I had him masquerade as a telephone repairman while he opened and photographed the contents of the three top conspirators' safes.

I hired an electronic expert to bug their phones and record their conversations. I even called our competitors and got a lot of valuable information from them as to materials and component costs. It's really amazing how much information you can pick up just by asking.

We had thirty-seven subsidiaries down in southern California set up specifically to supply us with components for our defense projects. After the graphs and charts began to take shape, I discovered that ninety percent of their production was going someplace else and not to Taylor Industries. Very unusual, I thought, so I sent my black bag man down to southern California to find out just where the production was going. When he reported back that it was all going to one wholesale outfit, I only had to carry it a step further to find out that the wholesale outfit was owned by our chief competitor, Southern. What was even more revealing on the graphs was that these components were being purchased at a fraction of what it cost us to manufacture them.

Pam felt we had enough to go to her father with by now, but I still didn't have the goods on the bastards behind the whole thing. So I sent the black bag man to their homes to look for and photograph bank statements or savings deposits, books, or any other financial records or scrap of paper from Southern. I really didn't know what I was looking for, but I had to have something to tie it all together with.

He hit pay dirt at two of the three houses: Swiss bank accounts for one million dollars each, and a secret letter revealing the details of their agreement with Southern Corporation to seize control of Taylor Industries and describing what their positions and rewards would be for their efforts.

I still didn't know how they were rigging the bids, so I called a salesman from BIM and led him to believe we were thinking of making a change and getting rid of our Sparrow Rim Computers. I quizzed him for hours on the advantages of their equipment as opposed to ours. I asked him specifically if it were possible to tamper with his equipment. He told me everything I needed to know about the flaws in our computers and how it was possible to change results by adding additional punch cards. He explained how to go about it, and he even elaborated on how one person in a strategic location could change the end results by simply running a handful of cards through the computer, thereby changing the figures and totals.

I thanked him very much for coming in and told him I would definitely bring the subject up at the next meeting of the board of directors.

DONALD R. WAGNER

He no sooner cleared the door than I headed for the personnel office, figuring that their accomplice in the computer room was probably scared and afraid to take any time off for fear of being discovered if someone else took over his duties for even one day. My search was soon rewarded with the name of a guy who hadn't taken a day off in the last eighteen months. He even forfeited his vacation time. I figured this was my man, so off I went to get a look at him firsthand.

Sure enough, he was extremely standoffish, and his answers to my general questions were very vague. This only confirmed my suspicions of him. I broke my own cardinal rule and stayed after work that night. With the help of my black bag man, I broke into the computer room and into this computer operator's desk. Sure enough, we found four sets of cards. I ran them through the duplicator, which only took a matter of minutes, and then put his cards back in the desk, exactly as we had found them. We locked up, and for all intents and purposes no one ever knew we were there.

I arrived a little early the following day and went back to the computer room. I went to one of the computer operators and asked her how long it would take to get a printout of about twelve hundred cards. "Ten minutes or so."

"Well, I have a special project I'm working on for Mr. Taylor, and it's very hush-hush. Can I trust you to be quiet about it and run some cards off for me?"

"Certainly, Mr. O'Malley."

I gave her the cards out of my briefcase, and she ran them off for me. I took the printout and the cards and put them back in my briefcase and hurried back to my office, telling this pretty computer operator I wouldn't forget her and reminding her not to mention a word about it to anyone. She promised she wouldn't. But even if she did, no one knew what I had printed out anyway.

I took the rest of the day off and went home where Pam and I compared the printout to the old bids that she had converted into percentages. Sure enough, they matched perfectly. What was throwing us off the track was we were losing by a different

433

percentage on each bid—sometimes three, five, eight, or ten percent. This was the reason for four sets of punch cards.

Pam said, "Well, I guess we have enough to go to Daddy with now, don't we?"

"Oh, we have more than enough, sweetheart. I'm just wondering what effect this will have on him and how he will react. What he's going to do about it is the big thing that's got me worried. If he goes off on one of his rampages and starts firing people and shutting down subsidiaries and the like, he'll get so tangled up in lawsuits, sabotage, name-calling, and what have you, that he'll be destroyed anyway. There has to be another way out of this, but damned if I know what it is."

Pam suggested we go to our neighbor Jerry, who was a CPA, and ask his advice. "I'm sure we can trust him, and he may be able to offer an alternative before we talk to Daddy."

"Good idea, honey. Let me call him at his office and see if I can get him to come back here, and we'll go from there."

I had little trouble getting Jerry to come to the house with me. I told him it was extremely urgent. We showed him everything we had and let him digest it all. We even set up the whole Taylor conglomerate on the pool table, with the use of Monopoly markers, along with Southern Corporation's operations as we knew them.

We explained to Jerry how far-reaching this thing was and our anticipated reactions from Mr. Taylor. We asked him to look for alternatives to offer Mr. Taylor. Jerry spent the next two days at our house going over everything—financial statements, our charts and graphs, and the whole bit. He worked out several plans of action for Mr. Taylor to take, all of which would have him come out of it smelling like a rose while totally destroying those who were trying to do him in.

I asked Jerry how long he figured it would take to present the whole picture to Mr. Taylor. "Perhaps three hours," he said.

"Okay. I'll call him now and have him stop here on his way home from work. That way if he goes off on a tangent he won't be able to do anything about it until tomorrow."

I called him at his office and told him Mrs. Taylor was at our house and wanted him to stop by and pick her up. I'm sure he thought it kind of strange that we didn't take her home or have Henry pick her up, but he didn't question it, and he said he would be there as soon as possible.

I then called Mrs. Taylor and asked her to come over as quickly as possible, figuring she could help restrain him, should the need arise. We were about to destroy his faith in human nature and wanted to be prepared for the worst, while hoping for the best.

Mrs. Taylor arrived first and we briefly described what was going on, and then Mr. Taylor arrived. Pam let him in. After I introduced him to Jerry, he asked Mrs. Taylor if she was ready to go. "No, George, I think you had better stay and hear the kids and Jerry out. I want you to promise me you won't get mad and fly off the handle like you usually do when you get bad news. Promise me you'll stay and hear them out until the end."

"Well, I don't even know what I'm agreeing to, but I agree." He added with a little laugh, "I'll bet it's one of Irish's practical jokes, isn't it?"

"I wish it were, Mr. Taylor, but I'm afraid it's dead serious business."

"Well, it couldn't be that bad, Irish."

"You're right, Mr. Taylor. It's worse. I'm afraid I'll have to ask you again to promise to hear us out until the very end and not go out of here tonight half-cocked."

"Okay, okay, Irish! Get to the point."

"Let's go into the rec room. We have some charts and graphs we want to show you. They will reveal the whole picture of what is happening to you."

I started in by telling him there was a conspiracy to take over Taylor Industries and that I would not reveal the individuals involved until after we had presented all the facts to him.

"I'm sure you must have proof of this, Irish. Otherwise you wouldn't make such a rash statement."

"I do, Mr. Taylor. Enough to send some people to prison for years and years, should they be prosecuted." I went on to explain all the charts and graphs we had assembled, with Jerry filling him in on how they were able to cleverly disguise the losses from the subsidiaries in southern California against the profits of our San Jose plants that were to be taking one hundred percent of their production. I went on to explain how they were rigging the bids and showed him the printout and the punch cards used in the operation. Then we showed him the comparison of our bids with Southern's and showed him how they matched perfectly with the printout as to percentages of key items in the bids.

The more we revealed to him, the madder he got, and he insisted on knowing who was behind all this. We cautioned him that a false move at this time could be fatal and that we had a plan worked out that not only would get him the revenge he sought but also would be very profitable to him. We begged him to hear us out.

"Okay, that's the least I can do after all the trouble you've gone to on my behalf. I'm curious about one thing, though. Why did you do it? I mean, why did you go to all this trouble? I don't understand."

"I'm sorry you had to ask, Mr. Taylor, and I'm a little hurt, I might add."

"No, Irish, I didn't mean anything cynical by my inquiries. But you must admit, it is a bit unorthodox, to say the least."

"Well, Mr. Taylor, let's just say I'm repaying you for an old debt. If it hadn't been for you, I wouldn't be here today. Besides that, you're the closest thing I've ever had to an old man, and I certainly couldn't stand by while someone was trying to destroy my old man, now could I? As for Jerry here, he's doing it as a favor to Pam and me and expects nothing in return. Money is not important to him. He has a successful business and is perfectly happy, the same as Pam and I. I'm sure when the smoke all clears, you'll find some way to reward him for his efforts, though."

"Well, how about you, Irish? You certainly deserve a lot of credit for uncovering this mess, and I intend to see that the culprits know it was you who exposed them and put an end to their little charade."

"Like hell, Mr. Taylor, you wouldn't do that to me, would you? I mean, if they knew I was responsible for exposing them and uncovering their little scheme they might get the impression that I was able to think for myself and get things done. I wouldn't want them to think that. It would destroy me. I would be completely useless to you from then on. No, when the time comes to confront them with the truth, you must take all the credit yourself, and never, never let anyone know that Pam, Jerry and I had anything to do with it. I like playing the role of the stupid son-in-law. No one makes any demands on my time. It gives me the freedom I need to be creative, and I'm not pressed with deadlines and the like. You wouldn't take all that away from me, would you?"

He laughed for the first time since we began and said, "Any way you want it, Irish. Say, Pam, I could use a good stiff drink. Do you have anything around here?"

"Sure, Daddy. I'll be right back."

"Well, Irish, what have you and Jerry come up with to combat this conspiracy?"

"First, let me let you listen to some tape recordings and show you some other interesting facts before we make any proposals."

"Recordings of what?"

"Some facinating telephone conversations of your three closest associates."

"What?"

"Yes, Mr. Taylor. They're the ones who are pulling the strings, and they were so close to you that they were above suspicion."

"Why, I ought to go to their houses tonight and fire them on the spot."

"No! no! Mr. Taylor, you promised to hear us out, remember?"

"Well, all right, then, let's get on with it."

We began playing the tapes which revealed how they were conspiring to drive Mr. Taylor into financial ruin and step in and buy him out for next-to-nothing with the financial backing of Southern Corporation. Some of the tapes were rather amusing. I came up in the conversation several times, and each time I was dismissed as absolutely no threat to any of them. In one tape they referred to me as a world beater and a perpetual motion machine with no beginning and no end. They said I was just trying to put on a show for Mr. Taylor and didn't know my ass from a hole in the ground. According to them, I could search for twenty years and never know what was going on. They laughed because they were convinced that a high school dropout couldn't possibly outwit them.

The tapes revealed to Mr. Taylor that they had been steering him to Washington to look for the trouble with the lost contracts. The tapes also mentioned their many trips to Southern California when they were booked to go to New York. I'm sure they had no idea their phones were tapped. The thought probably never entered their minds; they were so sure of themselves.

After the tapes, I opened my briefcase and showed him the secret agreement they had made with Southern, along with photographs of their Swiss bank accounts.

Mr. Taylor was flabbergasted and wanted to know how I was able to gather all this information in such a relatively short time. I told him there was no way I could let him know that. "What you don't know, you can't testify to, Mr. Taylor. We had a rule in the army and only gave out information on a need to know basis. It would not help you to know who the shadows were or the phone man or even the bag man. They have all been paid off and are long gone looking for their next jobs."

"I believe you're right, Irish. It would do me no good to know. But how did you pay them off?"

"I borrowed fifty thousand dollars on the house here and paid them in cash, so there are no records anywhere."

"How about the phone? Surely you had to contact them."

"Yes, sir, on a pay phone. And I paid for the calls on the spot, so there is no record at the office or here at the house."

"Damn, Irish, you've thought of everything, haven't you?"

"Well, you knew I was resourceful and had an inexhaustible curiosity. When I set my mind to something, I keep asking why. The results are right here before you."

"Whatever made you zero in on these three?"

"You won't believe it, Mr. Taylor, if I told you."

"At this point, Irish, I'd believe anything you told me. What put you on their tail?"

"A handshake."

"A handshake?"

"That's right. Remember when you took me to that board meeting and introduced me to everyone there?"

"Yes. They still talk about the little speech you gave that day."

"Well, as you introduced me to each one and I shook their hand, I made a conscious character analysis of them."

"You lost me, Irish." Jerry, Pam, and Mrs. Taylor all admitted they were lost too.

"I consciously tried to pick up their vibrations—good or bad —by how they shook my hand. If they gave me a nice, firm handshake, I got good vibes. And I did, from everyone there, except those three. They gave me a limp handshake, and I got really bad vibes. I made a mental note that they were not to be trusted and deserved watching."

"Well, I'll go to hell. Pardon my language, but that is fantastic. Still that doesn't explain how you were able to get the goods on them."

"I soon noticed that they would avoid contact with each other when you were around. But as soon as you would go out of town or were out of the building, they would go into conference for hours on end. Then I heard them discussing a lost bid and they were not overly concerned about it, which I felt they should be, and one thing led to another, with Pam converting all the figures on the lost contracts into percentages and keeping the graphs and charts for me as I would pick up bits and pieces. We were going to come to you sooner, but we wanted to be sure of everything before we did. We knew an audit would take two years and probably would not have uncovered half of what we got. It certainly wouldn't have revealed their secret agreements and Swiss bank accounts, nor would it have permitted the wiretaps and the black bag jobs. I'm not sure what their timetable is, but in two years—at the rate they're moving now—they could have you on the verge of bankruptcy. So that's why we went all out, pulled out all the stops, and played the game their way."

"Well, Irish, just the three of them couldn't have pulled this off. They had to have help."

"They did, Mr. Taylor. Perhaps hundreds of people helped them in one way or another, either willingly or unwillingly. These three were dictating policy and pulling the strings and everyone under them felt compelled to go along for fear of losing their jobs or they felt it was none of their business. But really, only those three had the overall picture until now, and they figured that no one would suspect them or figure out their scheme until it was all over. Then it wouldn't matter if they were caught or not."

"The operation is so big and so spread out. Even your accounting, the very heart of your business, is spread out over several buildings, with accounts receivable in one and accounts payable in still another. All your cost accounting is done in San Jose, and the only one who had the whole picture is one of the conspirators, your comptroller, who gathers all the pieces and dictates how everything is to be arranged on the financial statements. The only other paid and willing participant was the supervisor in the computer room. I don't know what they gave him or what they promised him, but we can beat him at his own game, as Jerry will explain later."

"Look, Irish, you have my mind reeling right now, and I need some time to absorb all that you've told me tonight. Although I'm anxious to hear what you've come up with to combat all this, I'm afraid I couldn't absorb another bit of information tonight."

"Anything you say, Mr. Taylor. And believe me, I wish we hadn't had to be the bearers of such bad news. Please do me a personal favor, will you?"

"What is it, Irish?"

"Well, Jerry and I both agree at this point that the difference between making the right move and an almost right move would be the same as the difference between a lightning bug and lightning itself."

"I agree with both of you, and I promise to do or say nothing until we go over your proposals and recommendations. I'm very perplexed tonight. Those three SOBs destroyed my faith in human nature; and just as quickly, you, Jerry, and Pam have restored it. The most gratifying thing that has come out of all this tonight was to hear Irish refer to me as his old man and I just want you to know I appreciate that, Irish. Now, Paula, if you will, I would like to go home and do some serious thinking and try to absorb all this."

"Surely, George. Let me get our coats."

We all walked them out to their car and were saying good-night. I kissed Mrs. Taylor on the cheek. It didn't go unnoticed by Mr. Taylor. He smiled and remarked, "You really love Mrs. Taylor, don't you, Irish?"

"You bet, I do, Mr. Taylor. She's pretty to walk with and witty to talk with. To me she can laugh away the darkness and smile away the snow. One little kiss on the cheek and all my problems melt into nothingness. She'll never want for someone to love her as long as I'm alive. I'll see to that."

"I'm glad to hear that, Irish, and I'm kind of fond of her myself. Well, good-night. I'll see you at the office in the morning, Irish. Business as usual, and I promise not to tip our hand."

"Fine, Mr. Taylor; see you then."

They departed and we returned to the house. I asked Jerry what he thought of the situation now and what he thought Mr. Taylor might do.

"Well, Irish, he can't dispute the facts presented to him tonight, and he's much too smart a businessman to do anything foolish at this point."

We sat there for another two hours going over all of Jerry's proposals and discussing which one we thought Mr. Taylor might go for and made plans to meet here again tomorrow night with Mr. Taylor and lay out the proposals for him. Jerry said good-night, and Pam and I saw him to the door. After he was gone, Pam and I hit the shower and settled down in bed to talk about us.

I placed my hand on her stomach and I felt the baby move for the first time. I was really amazed and expressed my amazement to Pam. "She moved, honey! She moved!"

"I know, Irish, she is getting quite active here lately. I guess she's getting kind of anxious to see her handsome daddy."

"You mean her beautiful mother."

"Oh, Irish, I'm the one who is getting anxious to see her. I can hardly wait. I know she will be a beautiful baby."

"I notice you're referring to the baby as 'she' now honey. What made you change your mind or, rather, make up your mind?"

"You did, Irish. You want a little girl, so I'll see that you have a little girl."

"You're precious, darling. You'd do that for me?"

She laughed and said, "Sure, Irish, why not? I told you I wanted to make you happy so . . . . ."

"You're too, too much, you little baby doll, you."

"Oh, Pam, you'll never know how I enjoy these quiet nights with you, not to mention the peaceful days. If I told you you had a nice body would you hold it against me?"

She giggled and said, "I'd love to, but our little bundle of joy is coming between us."

"No, she is just bringing us closer together, if that's possible."

"Irish, you're really worried about all this business with my father, aren't you?"

"Well, I was, honey, but now that your father knows what is going on, he'll take charge and straighten things out in a hurry. I have all the faith in the world in your dad. He didn't get to where he is today by being a fool, I can guarantee you that. I just feel badly that I had to be the bearer of such bad news; but I'm sure he appreciates finding out now when he can still do something about it. It just goes against my grain to think those three could be that deceitful and downright corrupt. And after all he's done for them! I bet they'll wind up like Mr. Roth."

"Do you think so, Irish? They are pretty well-off and even if

Daddy fires them, they'll still have all that money Southern Corporation gave them."

"True, but from what I've discovered about their character, they'll not have it long. Someone just as crooked as they are will con them out of it before long. Ah, but here we are letting them interrupt our quiet time, and we shouldn't do that. So, let's just talk about you, shall we?"

"No, I want to talk about you."

"Okay, we'll talk about each other. Bet I love you more than you love me."

"No, you don't."

"Well, how much do you love me?"

"More than you love me, I'll bet."

"Honey, do you realize that we have just gone full circle and we still don't know who loves who the most?"

"True, Irish. We love each other equally."

"I'll buy that as long as you love me more every day, for I love you more every day."

"Hold me, Irish, and tell me not to worry. I hope Daddy gets things back under control really soon."

"He will, honey; in the meantime let me give you something to think about."

> That the birds of worry and care fly
> above your head.
> This you cannot change, but that they
> build nests in your hair
> This you can prevent.
> Lao-tse—Chinese Philospher

"Okay, Irish. I don't want any birds building nests in my hair, so I won't worry. The only thing I know about money matters is that it does."

I shook with laughter. "That has to be one of the most profound statements ever made, honey. Forgive me for laughing, but you caught me completely offguard with that pun."

"I'm glad, Irish, I love to hear you laugh. And when you laugh, I know you're happy, and that's what it's all about, isn't it?"

"It sure is, honey, and never stop being your sweet, kind, gentle and precious self. And I agree, money matters."

I started to chuckle again and said, "Wait 'til I tell your dad that one. He'll get a big kick out of it."

I put my arms around her. She snuggled close to me and before long we both drifted off to sleep.

24

Irish Gains Control of Taylor Industries

It was three days before Mr. Taylor got together with Jerry, Pam, and me at our house. When he did, he brought with him his attorney, the president of a large bank in California, and the president of one of the largest security firms in the country.

We all went into the rec room where Pam gave everyone something to drink. After introducing his associates to us, Mr. Taylor floored me by asking how would I like to be the owner of Taylor Industries.

"You have to be kidding, Mr. Taylor. I would be as lost with it as you would be without it."

"Nevertheless, Irish, that is what we are here for, to make you the sole owner of Taylor Industries. I have the papers that have to be signed to make it official. All you have to do is sign here."

"Well, I'm sure you have a logical explanation, Mr. Taylor, and I can hardly wait to hear it. What makes you think I can run Taylor Industries? I'd probably run it into the ground in less than a year. Christ, that's like taking me out to the airport and putting me at the controls of an airliner and telling me to take off and land it."

"Irish, if it will put your mind at ease, it will only be for sixty days. You see, what you and Jerry and Pam uncovered was only the tip of the iceberg. There is so much fraud, embezzlement, and espionage going on that it is going to take someone who doesn't have the personal interest in the business that I have to straighten it out and get it running again."

"I don't understand, Mr. Taylor. What makes you think I can handle the job or that I would want to?"

"You don't have to, Irish, that's for sure, but you're the only one on this earth that I trust enough to give this authority and responsibility to. You won't be alone. My attorney and his associates will help you with the legal end of things. Mr. Anderson here will handle all the financing for you, and Mr. Clements will provide the security. Between you and Jerry here, you can make all the decisions as to what has to be done and these gentlemen will follow through and see that it is taken care of."

"Well, what are you going to be doing while all this is going on, Mr. Taylor? Don't you even want to hear what Jerry and I have come up with?"

"Irish, whatever you decide will be perfectly all right with me. For all intents and purposes, it will be the same as if I had died and willed the business to you."

"But, I don't know a contract from a bank account, Mr. Taylor. I think you're making a big mistake thinking I can handle it."

"Irish, you have it all laid out here for you on your pool table, and with your charts and graphs combined with all this help— the finest that money can buy, I might add—you'll do just fine. I have Mrs. Taylor's personal guarantee on that."

"Blind faith, you mean, don't you, Mr. Taylor?"

"Look at it this way, Irish. I'm not risking a damned thing. If it weren't for your efforts, I would have lost it all by hook or by crook anyway. Besides, I know you can do it."

"Well, I would feel better if you at least heard us out and let us show you what we had in mind. You are probably going to be mad as hell when you come back if you don't take the time to listen now. I can guarantee that it will neither be nor even resemble the Taylor Industries as you know it now."

"Irish, the reason we are all here tonight is because of the way the business is now. I just want you to sign the papers, and I'll be on my way."

"On your way where?"

"Mrs. Taylor and I are taking a sixty-day cruise around the world. We have always wanted to, and we both feel we should go now before we are too old to enjoy it. We are going to take a page out of your book and live like there is no tomorrow."

"Well, I'm happy for both of you, Mr. Taylor, and I won't deny you both that pleasure. I also agree wholeheartedly that you both deserve the time off. But I want you to understand that this whole thing could conceivably blow up. If that happens, you could be broke when you return."

He laughed and said, "Not if I'm any judge of human nature. I'm not even going to think about what might happen. I'm going on vacation, and you can fill me in upon my return."

"Well, Mr. Taylor, I told you months ago that I don't make any important decisions without the advice of my confidante, and we both know who that is."

"I anticipated you, Irish. She should be here at any moment now. All you have to do is agree, and Mrs. Taylor and I will be on our way tomorrow afternoon—right after the board meeting where I plan to make a formal announcement so that there will be no misunderstandings."

Ten minutes later Mrs. Taylor arrived. We immediately took her into the bedroom for a private conference. Pam asked her mother if she was aware of what her father had in mind, and she said that she was.

"Well, what do you think, Mrs. Taylor? Personally, I think he has taken leave of his senses to entrust a lifetime's work to an unproven, untried, and untrained little SOB such as me. Mr. Taylor's decision is completely beyond my comprehension, and quite frankly I'm at a loss for something to say at this moment."

"Well, don't say anything, Irish. Just sign the papers, be your own man like you always are, and things will work out just fine. There is absolutely no doubt in my mind that you will be fair and just and bring everything to an amicable solution for all concerned."

"My God, Mrs. Taylor, do you realize you are placing the

weight of the world on my shoulders? I'll probably wind up with a hernia."

She and Pam both laughed and said, "We doubt that, Irish."

"Well, Mrs. Taylor, I just don't want us to have a falling out over this. I would rather go pick strawberries for a living than do anything to endanger our relationship."

"We know that, Irish. But believe it or not, Mr. Taylor is only forty-five years old, and believe me, the years have taken their toll on him. He can't be as objective about things as you can. He would have a tendency to be too conservative, making all the wrong decisions, and he'd wind up in the hospital with a nervous breakdown. If he has learned anything from being around you, Irish, he's learned that life is too short to let that happen. You would be doing us both a great favor if you would undertake this project. Believe me, Irish, no matter how it turns out, our friendship and our love will still be intact. There is no one else in the world we love enough or trust enough to place such power and confidence in."

"Then you feel he hasn't taken leave of his senses? And you think that I would be doing him a service by undertaking this project?"

"Most emphatically yes, Irish."

"Well, then, all we need is Pam and Jerry's approval to go along with it. I'll do my best, Mrs. Taylor, and I just pray to God it all works out for the best. What do you say, Pam?"

"I think you can do it, Irish, and I'm with you one hundred percent of the way."

"I'm sure you will be, honey. I love you all for having so much faith in me, but believe me, Taylor Industries will never be the same."

We rejoined the others in the rec room. I asked Jerry if he could spend the next two months with me without putting his accounting firm in any jeopardy. He assured me that, other than a few hours a week, his associates could run the business without any foreseeable problems.

"Good then, I want you as a special consultant to Taylor Industries, and you can name your own fee. You know the nuts and bolts of the corporate structure and can keep me in line, should I wander into the never-never land."

We signed all the necessary documents and they were notarized on the spot; I was the sole owner of Taylor Industries. It was a closed corporation with only three stockholders, Mr. Taylor who owned ninety percent; his wife, who owned five percent; and his attorney, who owned five percent.

We spent the rest of the evening making small talk. Mr. Taylor steadfastly refused to discuss business or even hear any of our plans. It was finally time for everyone to leave. Jerry and I told our new associates that we would be in touch with them tomorrow afternoon to get things started. We said good-night to everyone, including Jerry, leaving only Mr. and Mrs. Taylor, Pam and me there. I implored them to leave us an itinerary of their travel plans in case of an emergency. Mr. Taylor said he would leave it with his attorney so that, should a personal family problem arise, we could get in touch with them through him. As far as business matters, he emphasized that he would be unable to be reached.

"I guess we're going to have to swim or drown, Pam. They are leaving us to our own devices, honey. I just wish it were sixty days from now and we were welcoming you folks home instead of saying good-bye."

"Oh, Irish," said Mrs. Taylor, "you're turning into an old worrywart like me; everything will be just fine. Now, we really must be saying good-night."

We walked them to their car, and I shook Mr. Taylor's hand and thanked him for his faith and confidence in me. I then gave Mrs. Taylor a big hug and a kiss and told her I would miss her terribly. "I've become so attached to you, Mrs. Taylor, that I almost feel as if I can't function without you in my life."

"I know, Irish, and perhaps that is not such a good thing. We all need this time away from each other. As long as you have Pam here to look after you, you'll do all right, I'm sure."

Pam kissed them both good-night and told them we would drive them to the airport tomorrow, and then they were gone.

Pam and I settled down for the night. I took her in my arms

and held onto her for all I was worth. I confided, "I am probably more frightened right now than I have ever been in my life. Just the thought of what transpired here this evening boggles my mind, honey, and I just don't know. Do you have any idea why your parents would do this to me? Gee, I thought your mother loved me. And I was quite certain your dad and I had a real good relationship built up. But, to do something like this, it's just beyond my comprehension."

"Oh, Irish, let me try to put your mind at ease, if I can. Mother discussed all this with me this afternoon, so perhaps I can shed a little light on the subject for you. Daddy has wanted to revamp Taylor Industries for some time now. He has a lot of losers along with all his winners. For one reason or another—perhaps through friendships, associations, favors, or what have you—he has been unable to look at the business objectively for some time now. That is the reason why the vultures are moving in and trying to pick him apart. They have found out he is vulnerable. Then, too, it's rather difficult to tear apart and rebuild something you put a lifetime of work into. That is why it is going to take someone like yourself to get the job done. You owe no one anything—no favors, not even the time of day. You have such a keen sense of human nature that, as Daddy always says, you know where they're coming from by just shaking their hands and talking to them. If you are worried about breaking Daddy or driving him into bankruptcy, you can forget it. I wasn't supposed to tell you, but we can't keep things from each other. The truth is, it would be virtually impossible to bankrupt Taylor Industries in sixty days, regardless of what you might do."

"Well, I thank you for telling me that, honey. And please, please don't let me become hard and callous. Please remind me I'm dealing with human beings with all their faults and imperfections. God only knows I'm not perfect myself! I only pray that God gives me the wisdom to make the right decisions and the strength to see them through."

"He will, Irish," she said, as she caressed my face and tenderly kissed me. It wasn't long before we were completely lost in our marital bliss and had not even the slightest notion that there were other people in the world beyond one another.

The following morning we were all gathered in the board room when Mr. Taylor passed out the mimeographed copies of our agreements, excluding the sixty-day clause. He announced that he was getting out of the business and retiring, turning the controls over to his son-in-law, and that this was his last official act as head of Taylor Industries. The look of sheer astonishment on their faces was really something to behold.

I took the gavel and announced that the meeting was officially closed and that I would expect them all back there at nine in the morning for another meeting. Mr. Taylor and I both quickly left the building. Pam and her mother were waiting for us. We drove them to the airport and I really felt like crying when I saw Mrs. Taylor walk up the steps of the airplane and disappear inside. Pam expressed my own sentiments when she said, "It won't be the same without calling her for advice and having her drop in on us, will it, Irish?"

"It certainly won't, honey. I think mommy bird has released her little birdies to give them a chance to try out their wings. Let's not disappoint her. Let's show her we can fly and catch worms on our own."

"That will make both of them happy, Irish, and we can do it. I know we can."

Pam took me back to the office, kissed me, and wished me good luck. I thanked her and told her I would need it. I told her to have supper—excuse, me, I mean dinner—ready at the usual time for I'd be there. She smiled and drove off.

I no sooner got off the elevator than I was surrounded by everyone and his brother all wanting to know what the hell was going on. I told them, "All in good time." I made my way into Mr. Taylor's office and told his secretary to call the painter to remove his name from the door and put mine in its place.

"What will Mr. Taylor say when he returns?"

"He won't be returning, so it's perfectly all right. I'll take full responsibility for everything that happens from here on out." I went on into the office where Jerry, the attorney, the banker, and the security man were waiting.

"Well, Jerry, how about Plan A, with no holds barred?"

"That's the quickest and the best way, Irish."

"Okay, Plan A it is."

We described the plan thoroughly and in great detail. Ostensibly what we planned to do was get Taylor Industries out of the defense contracting business and set up in other fields that we felt were growing and would be more lucrative, if that were possible. There was absolutely too much bullshit connected with defense contracts; there were too many factions to pay off and satisfy. Jerry and I both felt it was not worth the headache, the aggravation, the backbiting, and the cutthroat tactics to pursue defense contracting and try to make it respectable.

The basic thrust of our program was to declare a thirty-day moratorium on all accounts payable and to stop all purchasing for the same period.

We then arranged to close down the thirty subsidiaries in southern California. We requested a security man to be placed at each plant in the morning and to permit no one to enter under any circumstances. Thirty-seven accountants were instructed to give each and every employee two months' severance pay and just explain that the companies were up for sale and perhaps the new owner would want to hire the employees back as soon as the sales were completed.

We then instructed the bank president to put a freeze on all Taylor Industries accounts. No one would be authorized to write a check, make a withdrawal, or conduct any other financial transactions without first consulting Jerry or me.

We checked with the attorney on the feasibility of transferring all excess funds into the small foundation Mr. Taylor had set up to take care of his pet charities. He advised us that this was perfectly proper. With this knowledge, we instructed the banker to make the necessary arrangements to have all the cash reserves and accounts that had been padded with hundreds of thousands of dollars reduced to their original amounts and the excess transferred to the foundation fund.

It seemed these three conspirators had forged Mr. Taylor's name on documents authorizing these accounts to exceed their original limits. They kept it a secret from Mr. Taylor through phony financial statements. Then, once they were able to force Mr. Taylor to sell by making him believe he was going broke, they would be in clover, with all these hidden funds.

There was one more big obstacle we had to eliminate, and that was a huge two and one-half billion dollar multiyear defense contract due in Washington by the end of the week. I had my new secretary call in one of the conspirators who was our chief contract negotiator. I advised him that I wanted every copy of that bid in my office immediately. In return, I was greeted with inconsequential drivel as to why that was not possible and that Mr. Taylor always let him handle it. I hung up. After being reassured by the security man and the banker that they would follow our instructions to the letter, with no exceptions, Jerry, the lawyer, and I proceeded to his office and walked right in. He was belligerent as hell and I had to remind him he was working for me now and not Mr. Taylor.

"Now, I want those bids," I demanded. I lied to him, telling him I was going to personally take them to Washington and submit them in person. I went on to explain that if we didn't get this contract, we might as well close up shop. He calmed down and apologized, saying he was used to doing all that himself. He then reassured us that there was no way we could lose this one.

I asked him how he could be so confident after losing seven out of the last eight. He said he had some inside information. I asked him to share it with us, but he said he couldn't.

I reminded him again that he was working for me now, and that if he knew anything, he had best tell us.

"Well, I heard from a guy at Southern that their bid will be approximately three percent higher than ours, so we can't lose. We are the only two in the country big enough to bid on it anyway."

I thanked him and we returned to my office with the understanding that the bids would be sent in to my office right away.

After closing the door, I told the attorney and Jerry, "That SOB is lying through his teeth. They want to stick us with this monster. I'll bet anything you want that this bid is supposed to be the straw that breaks the camel's back. Who makes the final check on these things before they are signed?"

"The gentleman we just left."

"Okay then, am I correct in assuming I have to sign them before they are submitted?"

"Right."

"All right, there isn't time to redo them, so we'll go along with his plan right up to the point of where I deliver them myself. The only change is I'll never submit them. I'll just get on the plane and take off Friday morning and submit nothing but a package of blank papers. Then Southern will be stuck with the contract and will think these three bastards double-crossed them. As for us, we'll just let the chips fall where they may. I figure by next Monday morning those three will be suffering from humilation and defeat and then we can approach them about all the money they have embezzled through those phony engineering firms and insurance kickbacks. In my opinion, we can recover most of that money without too much difficulty."

"Well, Jerry, I guess that is enough hell-raising for one day, so why don't we go home and get a good night's rest. We are going to have a very rough day tomorrow when the shit hits the fan down south and at the bank."

By the time Jerry and I walked into the meeting room in the morning, the place was really buzzing. We waited for the security man, the attorney, and the banker before calling the meeting to order.

Everyone wanted to be the first to talk. Rumors, accusations, and denials were circulating around the room like wildfire. I finally managed to restore some semblance of order and told them the next one who spoke out of turn would be dismissed from the room. I admonished them, "Stop acting like a bunch of children, and start conducting yourselves like grown, responsible men." Man, if looks could kill, I would have been killed on the spot.

I summarized our action thus far and told them there would be more changes to follow. I assured them that I would keep them advised every step of the way. They all questioned my authority and were downright nasty, accusing me of trying to ruin all Mr. Taylor had built up over the years. I listened until I heard all I wanted and then simply closed the meeting.

When I returned to my office, my secretary handed me a resignation she had already typed up. I called her into the office and told her I was giving her two months off with full pay, and that she would be recalled at that time, if she wanted to come back. I told her I could tell her no more at this time, but that I knew how she felt. She agreed, and I immediately called my old secretary to take her place.

I spent the rest of the morning receiving phone calls and reiterating different aspects of Plan A to those directly involved while having my secretary ward off all those trying to gain an audience with me. The situation became so chaotic that I had to place a guard outside her door to stop anyone from entering.

Jerry and I continued to work out of my office, closing smaller companies that were not making a profit and providing the employees with two months' severance pay to relieve the financial burden on them. We immediately listed the business for sale in the hopes that it would be purchased by some larger firm with similar interests. What we were trying to accomplish was to divert all the paying interests and holdings into the Taylor Foundation while eliminating all the losing investments. As far as we were concerned the biggest losers were the defense contracts, and they were going to be the biggest challenge to get rid of.

I signed the big defense contract for two and one-half billion dollars on Thursday afternoon with a little ceremony in the board room. I even made a dramatic speech, pointing out that although they might not agree with all I was doing, winning the lucrative contract would keep us all in bread and butter for the next four years. The chief contract negotiator wanted a signed copy for his files. I declined, giving the excuse that it would be bad luck, but promising that I would give him a copy upon my triumphant return from Washington the next day.

The three conspirators were even brazen enough to ask me when I was going to permit the southern California subsidiary to be reopened. I told them the matter was under advisement, and I was not ready to make a decision at this time.

Jerry suggested that we have our chief suspects tailed. One quick phone call put tails on all their asses. We beefed up security there at headquarters and gave instructions that once everyone was out on Friday evening, no one, but no one, would be permitted in the building until it opened on Monday morning.

I took Pam with me to Washington, figuring we'd stay lost until Monday morning. I took the precaution of having an inconspicuous guard placed at our house and at the Taylors', for at this point, I wasn't sure if they had figured out my plan, or just what they might try in their efforts to stop me.

We submitted our bid and only had two hours to wait until the bids were to be opened. We met the chief contract negotiator for Southern there and even took him to lunch. After lunch he went back for the opening. Pam and I begged off, saying we would be there shortly. Instead we went to the airport, and I phoned in for the results. Of course, the results were already known to us. Southern was unopposed and was awarded the contract.

We then boarded a plane for Denver, Colorado. Mr. Taylor had been working on a deal to sell all his plant equipment, office furniture, and even the vehicles and company owned-aircraft to a leasing firm in Denver and then lease it all back from them at a yearly rate. His associates kept trying to talk him out of it, for various reasons, and they managed to postpone and delay implementing the purchase and lease agreements. I had had our attorney make all the final arrangements, and was to sign the papers in Denver on Saturday morning.

When we arrived in Denver, I called Jerry at the office. He was there, along with his hand-picked crew of twenty-five accountants and my black bag man. Their project for the weekend was to open all the safes in the building and go over all the records in the purchasing department, accounts payable and receivable. They were to uncover the proof we needed to confront those responsible and demand retribution and their resignations.

I told him all went well in Washington, and that I was in Denver to close the sale and lease-back deal. He told me they had already discovered one and three-quarter million dollars in cash in the comptroller's safe, along with a ledger revealing how he was diverting funds from one account to another, as well as the true financial picture of Taylor Industries. I told him to keep looking for more evidence of improprieties. I explained that as soon as I was through in Denver, I was going on to Los Angeles to talk to a group of investors about the sale of the plants in San Jose, and that I would call him from Los Angeles.

Pam and I attended the meeting in Denver the following morning where we hit a slight snag. They offered us ten million dollars less than what they had agreed upon. I countered with a proposal that we would agree to that sum if they would release us from a guaranteed leasing period. It was too tempting a proposal; they couldn't refuse. They figured, like everyone else, that we would be in the defense contracting business forever, and that clause was really meaningless. I'm sure they thought I was crazy, giving up ten million dollars without a fight; but I didn't care much what they thought.

We arrived in Los Angeles and went directly to our meeting there. We worked out the same sort of agreement with them buying the plants and property and then giving us long-term leases on them. We made our offer extremely attractive to them, also, by agreeing to sell, at below-market value, if they would give us an escape clause in our lease, saying we could withdraw at any time. They readily agreed, figuring we would be in business for years to come.

I called Jerry to find out how things were going. He told me that what they were unearthing was absolutely incredible. Everyone, it seemed, had their finger in the pie, and they were working around the clock to put all the pieces together. He promised to construct a comprehensive picture of just what was going on in time for my meeting with him at nine o'clock on Monday morning.

I called the attorney to describe what had transpired and told him the sale of the plants and the property would be ready by Wednesday. I asked him to contact the president of Southern, let him know we were thinking of selling out, and see if he wanted to make us an offer. I figured this should really infuriate Southern after being double-crossed and stuck with that two and one-half billion dollar contract that they just had to lose money on. Their plants were booked to capacity, which meant that they would have to come to us for help anyway. Unless they wanted to build new plants and equip them, there were no facilities in the country, other than ours, that were large enough or that had the proper equipment to perform on the contract.

We knew they couldn't afford to build new plants on a contract they were losing money on, so our position at this point was enviable. Then, to rub salt on the wounds, they were going to find it very, very difficult to perform on their present contracts without the production of the thirty-seven subsidiaries in southern California that they had based their previous bids on and from whom they had been getting their production for next-to-nothing. Jerry and I figured it would be cheaper for them to try and buy them outright from us rather than look for alternate sources. In fact, some of the instruments and other parts we were manufacturing were not available from any other source.

If we were able to sell our facilities to them, it would not only be a very large capital investment for them, but their original cost estimates based on the conspirator's help would be under by some five hundred percent, causing them to lose even more money on their present contracts. There was no way they could back out of their obligations to perform unless they went out of business. They were not about to walk away from what they felt was an open door to the U.S. Treasury, and, consequently, they would perform at any cost. Jerry and I figured we would, at least, make it expensive for them, by diverting some of their huge reserves into Taylor Industries and ultimately into the tax-free Taylor Foundation.

Pam confessed that she was a little bewildered by all this, and I admitted, "I am too; but as long as I don't think of it in terms of dollars and cents and visualize it in my mind as a big Monopoly game then I should be able to see it through. This next week will be the roughest, and after that, it will all be downhill, I'm sure."

We checked into a hotel for the night, and just spent the evening relaxing and trying to catch our breath. We wondered out loud where the Taylors were, and I wondered if her father would approve of all that was transpiring. Pam imagined them in Paris or Rome having the time of their lives. If he knew what Jerry and I were doing, I imagined Mr. Taylor pulling his hair out and ranting and raving like a madman. Pam reassured me that was why he didn't want to know and had placed all the responsibility on my shoulders. "I'm sure it will all work out, Irish, and he'll be a very happy man when they return."

"I hope you're right, honey."

We headed back to Sacramento the following day, arriving at the airport around nine in the evening. We went directly to the Taylor house, figuring some asshole would be waiting at our house to talk business or some other asinine thing. We were stopped at the driveway by the security guard I had requested. I identified myself, and he let us pass. Pam was a bit surprised. I told her it was just a precaution I had taken because when the stakes are this high, there was no end to what a competitor might do to get an edge or locate information.

I arrived at the office at nine in the morning and went directly to my office. A seemingly endless number of people were waiting to get in to see me. I didn't even acknowledge their greetings, but kept right on walking. Jerry and the attorney were already in there waiting for me.

They laid out what they had uncovered over the weekend—everything from payroll padding to kickbacks for the purchasing agents. We decided it was time to start weeding out the bad seeds and started with the comptroller. I had my secretary call him into the office and had the attorney confront him with all we had on him, including the secret agreement he had signed with Southern. He became a completely broken man and started to cry and beg for another chance. I told him there was only one way to resolve his present dilemma and that was to sign a full statement as to his part in the conspiracy and agree to make restitution. For this, we would let him resign and simply let the record show he resigned without cause. This was our one and only offer—take it or leave it. He decided to take it.

After he had dictated his statement to the stenographer, we had it typed for him to sign. We informed him that we had already taken the liberty of removing the money from his safe, and it was in the bank for safekeeping. He confessed it wasn't all his; that half a million of it belonged to his coconspirators. We thanked him and had him escorted from the building.

We called in the other two kingpins and gave them the same ultimatum. They were belligerent as hell and denied any knowledge of anything. We presented them with the signed statement of their buddy and also showed them the copy of their agreement with Southern. We told them we would accept retribution in the amount of one million dollars apiece by Wednesday morning. They both claimed they didn't have it. I gave them the numbers of their Swiss bank accounts and told them to make a withdrawal from them; "Anything you stole over a million, you can keep. Right now, we want a signed statement and your resignation—without cause, of course. I don't intend to destroy you. I just want what's due to Taylor Industries. That's our best offer, gentlemen, and I would suggest you snap it up." They asked what we would do if they didn't.

"Well, there are federal funds involved here, and of course, the IRS might be interested—not to mention charges of fraud and embezzlement. Shall I go on, gentlemen?" They came across with the resignations, the statements, and a promise to have the money returned by Wednesday morning, at the latest. I thanked them and cautioned them not to talk to anyone about what had just transpired; otherwise our deal was off. We had them escorted from the premises also. They were crushed by defeat. They never knew what hit them; only that all their plans had gone awry.

My secretary interrupted me, saying she had Mr. Phillips on the phone, and he said it was of paramount importance that he speak to me immediately.

"Who's Mr. Phillips?"

"He's chairman of the board of Southern Corporation."

"Well, things are happening faster than I had hoped. Listen, Jerry, while I talk to him, how about getting that paymaster in here, so we can find out what he knows about this payroll padding?"

"Okay, you got it, Irish."

"Mr. Phillips, congratulations on winning that contract on Friday." There was dead silence on the other end of the phone.

"Mr. Phillips, are you there?"

He cleared his throat and said, "Yes."

"What can I do for you today?"

"Well, I hear you closed your manufacturing subsidiaries down here and I was wondering how come."

"Why, are you interested in buying them? They're for sale, you know."

"Well, not exactly. I was curious as to when you were going to reopen them."

"I'm not."

"Why?"

"I don't need them, especially now that you beat me on that last big bid."

"Well, what are your plans, if you can't sell them?"

"I'll liquidate them and sell the property. They're too far away for us to keep an eye on, anyway. Anything we need we can manufacture over in San Jose, so we really don't need them."

"Well, it was my understanding you were selling ninety percent of your production to a wholesale outfit down here. Don't you have a contractual obligation to them?"

"Gee, Mr. Phillips, I don't know where you get your information, but they were set up to supply us exclusively, and we have no contract to supply anyone. In fact, if I don't sell them by the end of the week, I'm turning them over to the liquidators for disposal or perhaps I'll sell the machinery to that outfit in Denver and the property to a land investment outfit there in Los Angeles. I don't know yet, but they should be out of my hair by the end of the week. In fact, I'm not bidding on any more defense contracts, and I plan to dispose of our whole San Jose operation also. You wouldn't be interested in buying that, would you?"

"Look, Mr. O'Malley. Something is very wrong here, and I would like to come up and talk to you this afternoon. Will you have time to see me?"

"Well, I'll be pretty busy the rest of today, but you can come, if you like. We'll have dinner over at the Taylors' house and can spend the evening talking. I would suggest you bring your lawyer with you and perhaps we can work something out. I'll let you talk to my secretary and she can give you the address and all."

"All right, Mr. O'Malley. I'll see you then."

I switched his call over to my secretary, turned to my attorney and said, "What do you think?"

"I think you've got him backed into a corner, and you can practically name your own price."

"Good. Oh, hell! I'm sorry, I should have asked you if you had other plans for this evening. I'm always getting ahead of myself, and I apoligize."

"No, no, Irish. It's perfectly all right. I'm adequately compensated for my time, so don't worry about it. It just does my old heart good to see you and Jerry take charge and clean out this rats' nest. That's my greatest reward."

I called Pam who was still at the Taylors', told her what I had planned for tonight, and asked her if she minded terribly.

"Not in the least, Irish; I'll have Maggie cook up one of her specials."

"Thanks, honey, I love you."

"I love you, too, Irish."

462

Jerry returned with the paymaster, whom we confronted with what Jerry and his boys had uncovered over the weekend. With his face white as a ghost, he told us he knew they were going to get caught sooner or later. He confessed he never took a penny himself but was covering up for others who were having phony payroll checks made up. He said it started about three months ago and every week they kept demanding more.

"Well, why didn't you say something to someone?"

"I was afraid of losing my job. I have a wife who is terminally ill with cancer and a son who is in college. I'm fifty-six years old. Where else can I get a job that pays me what Mr. Taylor was paying me here? I've been with him for over twenty years now."

"Well, look, Mr. Epstein, we're not interested in destroying you. In fact, if you help us, I'll see that you keep your job, and we'll pick up the tab for your wife's illness and your son's education. That is, of course, if you're telling the truth about not taking a penny for yourself."

"It's true. I swear it, and I can prove it."

"Okay, okay. Jerry, why don't you assign a couple of your boys to Mr. Epstein here and see if we can get those phony checks out of the system today? Now, Mr. Epstein, I presume you have records of all the phonies issued to date and the names of all those who received them?"

"Yes, I do, Mr. O'Malley. And don't worry, I'll cooperate in any way I can."

"I'm sure you will. Just don't say anything to anyone yet, okay?"

"Okay, Mr. O'Malley."

I asked the lawyer for the best way to handle it, and he suggested a standard form which they could sign in order to make restitution and a standard letter of resignation.

"Okay, as soon as we get the list, can you have someone prepare the necessary papers?"

"Sure, Irish."

"Well, where do we go from here?"

"Well, why don't we get those purchasing agents out of the way before lunch?"

"Okay." I had Janice, my secretary, call them front-and-center immediately. We confronted them with what we had uncovered —the phony invoices for goods that were never delivered and the whole package. We demanded statements concerning their involvement and the amounts they received for their efforts. We had them sign letters of resignation—without cause, of course —in return for their testimony, should we have to bring the suppliers to court for restitution. We figured it would be a waste of time to try to make them pay back their share, so we told them their statement and testimony would be payment enough. Armed with these statements, the lawyers had letters drafted to the various suppliers demanding repayment or a court action.

We went to lunch with Jerry in the executives' dining room and things sure were buzzing in there until we walked in. Then you could have heard a pin drop. Jerry said, "I don't think we're too popular in here."

I laughed and said, "Well, I'm sure they all have something to hide and are just wondering if they have been discovered yet."

Jerry laughed and said, "That's closer to the truth than you might think."

"Yes, I know."

We sat down at a table. Seated at the very next table was our next target, the executive in charge of insurance and logistics. I invited him to join us at our table, which he did—very nervously, I might add.

I introduced Jerry and the attorney and started questioning him on how he could so absentmindedly permit ninety percent of the production from our subsidiaries in California to be sold to our chief competitor. He had a look of sheer astonishment on his face, and could not speak a word.

I said, "Well, never mind that. Now what's more intriguing to me is we paid out one quarter of a million dollars' worth of insurance premiums to an agency and we have no policies to back them up. Perhaps you could tell us how that could have happened. Do you think possibly you mislaid the policies, or they haven't delivered them yet? Maybe the agency just decided to keep the money, hoping we wouldn't have to use the insurance. What do you think?"

He said, "I think I'm going to be sick."

"Look, why don't you drop by my office after lunch and we'll take your statement and letter of resignation without cause, in return for your testimony, should we have to sue for recovery of that money. You can even keep your cut. How's that for a deal?"

"I think I'd better take it."

"Good. You look like a smart man to me and one who knows a good deal when he hears one. We'll see you in my office in a few minutes. Okay?"

"Okay."

Jerry looked at me and asked, "What made them think they could get away with it?"

"Greed, pure and simple. Once the seed is planted in them it grows and festers until they get caught or destroy themselves. Damned shame, too. They're all good men, and to think they have to start all over again. It's incredible."

After lunch we took care of the young executive who had lunch with us and then finished up the payroll fraud business without a hitch. All the accomplices signed the necessary papers without too much fuss. I signed all the letters demanding repayment from the suppliers and our insurance agent. It was quite a day.

We had an even bigger evening ahead of us, so I had Jerry and Mr. Jacobs, the attorney, call their wives and have them join us there at the Taylors.' We arrived around five thirty and were soon joined by the wives. We sat in the living room with everyone getting acquainted when the doorbell rang.

Arnold showed Mr. Phillips, his attorney, and two associates into the living room. After introductions all around, I had Arnold fix everyone a drink. We made the usual small talk until dinner was served. During dinner Mr. Phillips kept asking pointed questions, which I fielded to my advantage. Then I got the distinct impression that he was getting irritated, so I said, "Gentlemen, let's have our coffee in the library where we can get down to business. Will you ladies please excuse us? We'll join you in the living room as soon as possible."

We went into the library and closed the door. Mr. Phillips seized the initiative and started a blistering attack on us. "Nobody is going to shove a deal like this down my throat and get away with it. Where is Mr. Taylor? I can talk to him. I don't even know this punk kid here. Who the hell does he think he is?" On and on he went, until he finally got it all out of his system. I asked him if he was quite through. "For the time being."

"Well, that goddamned door swings both ways, and if you don't settle down, it might hit you in the ass on your way out. You're in my house now, Mr. Phillips. Besides that, if God had intended you to do more talking than listening he would have given you two mouths and only one ear."

"I don't have to take that from you, O'Malley, or whatever your name is."

"It's Mr. O'Malley to you, and you can leave any time you like. You need me. I sure as hell can get along without you, and don't you forget it."

His associates advised him to settle down and hear what we had to say.

A hush came over the room, and I broke the silence with a question. "Shall we talk this over like human beings or terminate the meeting right now? What's it going to be?"

"Okay, we'll hear you out."

"Well, first of all, let me assure you, I am Taylor Industries, and I'm calling all the shots. Is that understood?" They agreed.

"Now then, as of last Friday when we lost that last bid, we are officially pulling out of defense contracts. We will be bidding on no more of them. So, you see, we are no longer a threat to you in that respect."

Mr. Phillips interrupted and asked me if I had lost my mind.

"Perhaps. Several of my top executives must have thought so for they resigned today, along with several dozen middle-management personnel. I can't say for sure, but someone sabotoged my bid and gave me the wrong envelope to submit last Friday, and I'm not mentioning any names because I can't prove anything. Nevertheless that is why we're getting out of this cut-throat business."

"Do you want to sell the plants and the property they are sitting on?"

"We already have."

"Well, why didn't you give us a shot at them? We would have given you a fair price for them."

"Well, I still have those thirty-seven subsidiaries down your way; I'm looking for a buyer. Would you be interested in them?"

"Let's stop pussyfooting around, O'Malley, and take the gloves off, shall we?"

"Be my guest, Mr. Phillips. You have the floor."

"You're on to that crooked little scheme that three of my associates cooked up with three of your top executives, aren't you?"

"I have no idea what you're talking about, Mr. Phillips. Perhaps you could elaborate."

"They talked Taylor into opening up those subsidiaries to supply your San Jose plants, and then they diverted ninety percent of the production to a wholesale firm owned by us. That was one of the reasons we were making such fantastic profits—the material was only costing us peanuts. Now, you figure you have us over a barrel, don't you?"

"Are you sure you have covered everything, Mr. Phillips?"

"Yes. They told me about it after I talked to you this morning. Now you're trying to hold a gun to my head, figuring I have to buy in order to be able to perform on my contracts."

I feigned innocence.

"Such devious employees we get nowadays, Mr. Phillips! They actually did that to poor old Mr. Taylor? Who were they? I'll see that they are dismissed first thing in the morning."

"They no longer work for you, O'Malley. You fired them this morning."

"Well, so that is the reason they resigned. I was wondering what got into them. Now I know. Their little scheme backfired and they were afraid of being found out. You don't suppose it went any deeper, do you, Mr. Phillips? I mean, they

467

wouldn't go so far as to rig bids or try to force Taylor Industries into what looked like bankruptcy on paper, so they could buy it up for next-to-nothing do you? That would take some big backing. I don't think they could swing a deal that big by themselves."

"I haven't the slightest idea what you're talking about, O'Malley. Now I've had those plants down south appraised and they're only worth ninety million—equipment, building, and property combined. Do we have a deal?"

"Well, what about retribution for all that your associates stole from us? Somewhere in the neighborhood of twenty million."

"You can't prove that."

"Perhaps not, but an audit will reveal it, and I'm sure Uncle Sam would be interested. He must have a dozen different agencies that would like to get their teeth into something like that. How would you like GSA sitting in your offices for the next two years? What do you suppose that would cost you?"

"Okay, ten million more; but that is it."

"Not quite. We have the papers drawn up for one hundred twenty million and not a penny less. Now, do we have a deal?"

He looked at his attorney and his associates, and they advised him to take it without hesitation. We signed the papers right there on the spot, and Jerry, being a notary public, notarized them.

Mr. Phillips said, "Now, I want you to get your goon squads away from my plants."

"Certainly, Mr. Phillips, just as you say. As soon as I receive a call from my banker that the one hundred twenty million is deposited in my account, I'll have them vacate the premises immediately."

"Okay, okay, it will be transferred in the morning."

"Now then, about this other business, O'Malley." "You mean there is more, Mr. Phillips?"

"You know damned well there is. Who did you sell the San Jose operation to? I'll have to buy them in order to perform on the two and one-half billion dollar piece of shit my cohorts got me into. Incidentally, are you planning to forfeit on your remaining contracts?"

468

"No, indeed, we plan to finish them all. It's only six months' work. I'm afraid you'll have trouble buying them from the new owners. You see, we sold the plants and the equipment to two different sources on a lease-back arrangement."

"You're crazy, O'Malley, why would you want to do that? The lease payments will eat you up, and they don't make the lease that you can wiggle out of on a deal that large. You just leased back a whole huge white elephant. You're not as smart as we thought you were. Ha, ha."

"Tell you what, O'Malley, out of respect for Mr. Taylor, perhaps we can work something out to sublease the facilities from you for perhaps the next five years. That will get you off the hook on those lease payments for that long anyway. Then I'm afraid you'll have to suffer with them from there on out."

"Jesus Christ, Mr. Phillips, your generosity overwhelms me. You'd do that for me? I'm truly touched, and I appreciate the gesture on your part. But we had something else in mind. Mr. Jacobs, my attorney here, has drawn up all the details of our plan and we have it here on paper for you to take back with you tonight. You can look it over and perhaps you'll want to make a counteroffer or whatever. Your attorney and Mr. Jacobs can work out the details. Maybe we can get together on Thursday morning at my office and reach an agreement then."

Mr. Phillips took a deep breath and blew hard. "Okay, O'Malley, we'll look it over; but I can almost guarantee you we won't agree."

"Of that I'm sure, Mr. Phillips, but I don't know much about these things. Mr. Jacobs here keeps me out of trouble on them, though."

We escorted them to the door. Mr. Phillips' attorney asked Mr. Jacobs if it would be all right if he called him in the morning. He agreed and at that, they all departed.

We rejoined the ladies in the living room. I apologized to them for keeping their husbands away from them with these long hours, but promised that things were slowly getting back to normal and that they would have the pleasure of their company for dinner from now on. They were very understanding and said they didn't feel slighted or put upon in the least.

"Well, how do you feel about the way things went in there, Mr. Jacobs?"

"I'm still trying to digest it all, Irish. At times I thought you were blowing the whole thing, and at other times I wanted to laugh because you had him going so bad. Your steel nerves kept the meeting right on course, you accomplished everything you set out to accomplish, and you didn't have to use your ace in the hole. I was absolutely amazed at how you waltzed him around and got that extra ten million without so much as a 'go to hell' out of him. The part I liked best was when you told him if God had intended for him to do more talking than listening, he would have given him two mouths and only one ear. (Everyone started laughing.) I don't think anyone has ever talked to him like that in his life, and he was dumbfounded."

"Well, what do you think our chances are of closing the San Jose deal with him on Thursday? It is a bit unreasonable and might be more than he can take."

"Well, Irish, I honestly believe he doesn't know about the contract rigging of the secret three-million-dollar deal, and you can always bring that up to him if you like. You're definitely in the driver's seat right now, and he doesn't have much choice but to go along."

"Well, let's hope so. We'll know for sure on Thursday."

We spent the next hour just talking in general before Jerry and Mr. Jacobs said good-night at the door.

Pam and I decided to spend another night there at the Taylors' and settled down in our old room. We were both really starting to miss Mrs. Taylor, and tried to reassure ourselves that the time would pass quickly until she returned.

Pam said, "If only they would call and let us know where they are."

"I know how you feel, honey; I'd give anything to hear your mother's voice again. When they get back we'll have to be sure they don't do something like this ever again."

"We'll see to it, Irish."

I'm sure there could never be another situation like this ever again."

Pam snuggled her pretty little head under my chin and fell fast asleep, while I stroked her beautiful long brown hair. It wasn't long before I dropped off myself.

When I arrived at the office in the morning, I was greeted by our friendly banker who was very nervous and a little apprehensive. I asked him what the trouble was, and he confessed he was really starting to feel the strain.

"In what way?" I asked.

"Jesus, Irish, when we got into this thing, I had no idea you and Jerry were going to do what you're doing. I'm worried about this huge amount of money that is gathering in the Taylor Foundation account. Do you realize there is already over seven hundred seventy-five million dollars in there, with more coming in every day?"

"Well, why should that bother you? I don't understand."

"Do you realize, at six percent simple interest, what that amounts to over a year's time?"

"No, but I'm sure you're about to tell me. Right?"

"Well, at sixty thousand on a million, that times seven hundred seventy-five, it would be enough to break our bank. As soon as the directors find out about it, they're going to raise hell with me for letting it happen."

"Well, what do you suggest? I'm expecting another three hundred thirty million, not to mention a two million dollar retribution tomorrow. And then, if Southern agrees to buy us out, that involves another sixty million. What the hell am I supposed to do with the money? Bury it or something? I'm not asking you to put it in interest-bearing accounts, am I? I merely want you to be custodian of it until we get everything settled. Then we'll get most of it back in circulation. I can assure you of that. By the way, I hope it is understood that your board of directors is not to use any of that money for loans or anything else. That money is on demand deposit and subject to be withdrawn at any time."

"Yes, that is in the agreement, Irish; but it still makes me nervous."

"Relax, I have some more good news for you. We sold those

subsidiaries in southern California last night and there is one hundred twenty million being transferred to your bank this morning. Now I wish you would get back there and call me when it arrives."

"Okay."

He got up and headed for the door, just shaking his head in bewilderment.

I had Janice run over to the cafeteria to get us some coffee. In the meantime Jerry and Mr. Jacobs arrived, and I told them of my visit from the nervous bank president. They both said they never realized we had raised that amount to date. Jerry told us the figures were changing hourly, and he had assigned four guys to try to keep up with them.

Jerry informed me that some of the vendors were starting to press for payment.

"Oh, shit, that's right; we did shut their water off, didn't we? What do you suggest, Jerry?"

"Well, if Mr. Jacobs can give me ten attorneys, I'll have ten of my boys work with them, plus a team of gophers. With this staff we'll handle their claims as they present them and upon proof of delivery or services rendered. If we find a discrepancy in their claim we'll turn it over to the lawyers for settlement. We can also use fraudulent bills for grounds to get out from under some of these long-term supply contracts we have."

"You guys know more about that than I do, so if you can get him the lawyers, Mr. Jacobs, and . . . . what the fuck is a gopher, Jerry?"

He laughed and said, "If the lawyer or the accountant needs any information, the gopher goes for it."

I laughed and said, "Well, get all the gophers you need, Jerry."

I was finally alone, so I shed my coat and tie and was rolling up my sleeves when Janice returned with the coffee. I invited her to join me and asked her what her salary was. She told me, and I told her that as of last week, her salary was going to be the same as Mr. Taylor's secretary, with all the fringe benefits she enjoyed, too. She thanked me kindly. I told her she deserved it since she was doing a hell of a job under some trying conditions, and I appreciated the fact that I could trust her and depend on her. "Most of all, you can keep your mouth buttoned, and that is very important for this next week or so. By then the shit will have hit the fan, and everyone will pretty much have the complete picture of what we have done here, so then it won't matter."

"Well, Mr. O'Malley . . . " "Hold it right there, Janice; you call me 'Irish.' Hell, I get so tired of people calling me 'Mr. O'Malley.' I always have to stop and think to realize it's me they're talking to."

"Okay, Irish. Anyway, I just do my job and pay no attention to all the gossip."

"Good girl."

Just then the phone rang and I answered it. It was the president of the insurance company requesting an urgent meeting with me. I told him to come right on over.

Janice finished her coffee and got back to her secretarial duties. Twenty minutes later, the insurance president was in my office.

He was very apologetic. I assured him I understood that these things sometimes happened; but I was more interested in what they planned to do about it.

He told me that the executive who was responsible was forced to resign his position this morning and was to make restitution to avoid prosecution. In the meantime, he had a cashier's check for two hundred fifty thousand to reimburse us for our loss. He asked me to sign a release form for him, which I did. He said he hoped we would be kind enough to keep it quiet, because if the papers ever got hold of something like this, it could ruin their business. I told him I understood, and considered the matter closed. He also put in a plug for renewals, and I assured him if we were still in business that we would be glad to let him personally handle our insurance needs. He thanked me and was on his way.

I spent the rest of the morning bringing all our charts and graphs up to date. Things were really looking very good at this point.

473

After lunch, we held a meeting with all the plant managers and production supervisors. Our goal was to reduce the six months' work we had left on our remaining government contracts to thirty days. We planned to do that by going on a crash program of seven days a week, twenty-four hours a day, until they were complete.

The plant managers assured us we would have trouble with the unions if we implemented our plans. I told him, "Let me worry about that. As of tomorrow, it's three shifts, seven days a week. Understood?"

"Understood."

"Make all the necessary arrangements for the additional personnel, materials, and the like. If any of you gentlemen feel you can't handle it or want out, speak now or forever hold your peace." There were no objections, so we adjourned the meeting.

I had Mr. Jacobs get in touch with the union officials and set up a meeting with them for the following afternoon.

In the meantime the nervous banker called and told us he had received the one hundred twenty million draft from Southern. We promptly called our security man and instructed him to let Southern take over all the subsidiaries. I personally called Mr. Phillips and told him what we had done and offered to let our accountants stay there for a few days to help them get started by recalling the personnel we had laid off. He thanked me and said he had men ready to take over the management this very afternoon. He also told me that our proposal on the San Jose deal was extremely unreasonable. I told him we could work out the differences on Thursday when we met. He thanked me again and hung up.

Jerry and Mr. Jacobs were rather surprised and asked, "Why are you being so nice to that big blowhard?"

"Well, gentlemen, it has something to do with saving face. His face. He has all those stockholders to answer to and we did get what we want so far. Besides that, it doesn't cost any more to be nice. The price of the phone call is the same." They both agreed.

"What next, gentlemen? Oh, I had a call from one of our

lobbyists in Washington this afternoon. I told him and his associate we would no longer need their services since we were going out of the defense contract business. I guess that will start a chain reaction in the Department of Defense, won't it?"

"You bet it will. Be prepared for all those bastards to be around with their hands out, expecting payment for past favors."

Janice came in and told me there were four vendors waiting to see me. "Well, Janice, start them in, one at a time."

We handled them all alike with no exceptions and no deals. We showed them the signed statements, the promises to testify, the phony invoices, and the whole bit. We told them we would accept nothing less than one hundred percent reimbursement by Friday or we would sue and bring criminal charges where appropriate. We dispensed with them in less than forty-five minutes.

"Well, gentlemen, I promised your wives that you would be home for dinner tonight, so let's get the hell out of here before something else breaks loose." They both agreed, and we left by the side door to avoid any further confrontations.

I hurried back to the Taylor house and told Pam we had better stay there for the rest of the week to avoid anyone who might want to discuss business at night. She agreed. We insisted Maggie have dinner with us, and we talked and laughed as we relived what were now the good old days when I first came back from Japan.

After dinner, I suggested to Pam that we take Paula for a swim in the pool. Pam was really starting to show and was worried about losing her figure. I reassured her that the glow on her face from pregnancy more than made up for her temporary loss of figure. "Now, how about that swim?"

"Okay, Irish, let's go."

"Maggie, we're going skinny-dipping so see that we are not disturbed, will you please?"

"You got it, Irish."

Pam giggled. "Irish, you shouldn't say things like that."

"Did I embarrass you, honey?"

"Well, I forgive you, okay?"

"Okay."

It sure felt good there in the pool without a care in the world. We just relaxed and swam until our hearts were content. I was really beat, and so was Pam, and we retired around eight o'clock that evening for a good night's sleep.

Our meeting with the investment group from Los Angeles got started at nine o'clock on the dot. Everything went smoothly, and all the papers and contracts for the lease-back agreement were signed and notarized on the spot. When it came time to give us the money, they presented us with ten different bank drafts which I handed to our nervous banker, who quickly began to add them up. We all laughed at him, and they assured him it was all there—all three hundred thirty million dollars of it. He was very businesslike, though, and double-checked it anyway.

They suggested we have lunch together to celebrate closing the deal. I begged off, saying we had some delicate union negotiation coming up. Instead of us, I told them we had our two top public relations men standing by to show them the town and not to spare the expenses. We shook hands and we turned them over to the PR men, who took them in tow.

We went back to my office where Mr. Peters and Mr. Warren were waiting for me. I told them to come right on in. They both put their certified checks for a million dollars apiece on my desk and asked me if I was satisfied.

"Look, gentlemen, I hold no animosity toward either one of you. I wish you both the best of luck in your new endeavors."

"Do you really mean that, or are you just trying to make us feel better?"

"Hell, no, I mean it. I never judge a man's future by his past. I gotta believe he learned something and won't make the same mistakes again. There are a couple of things that are still bothering me that perhaps you could clear up before you go. Number one, what made you do it? I mean, Mr. Taylor treated you guys like kings."

"Well, I guess we got greedy and figured it was our last chance to make the big, big times like he did."

"You mean, you were jealous of him?"

"Perhaps that was it. All we know is that it was the worst mistake of our lives."

"One other thing, strictly off the record, of course. How much did you actually take him for, over and above this million?"

"Well, off the record, it was more than the amount of those two checks. And off the record, Irish, why did Taylor ever pull a trick like leaving the business in the first place? Did he lose his mind or what?"

"No, he was just weary and wanted to get away and enjoy life before it passed him by completely. Is that so hard to understand? Hell, he had been working himself into an early grave."

"Well, when he comes back and sees how you have literally destroyed all he worked so hard all his life for, he'll probably drop dead anyway."

"Perhaps, but that is my problem now, isn't it? Good day, gentlemen. And again, lots of luck in your new endeavors."

After they were gone, Mr. Jacobs spoke up. "You really amaze me, Irish! By all that's good and holy, those two should hate your guts, but I have a feeling that they have nothing but respect and admiration for you. I don't know how you do it, or why it works, but don't change what you're doing."

"It's simple enough, Mr. Jacobs. If you were in their shoes and got caught doing what they did, wouldn't you want a chance to save face and start over again, without being destroyed? What good would it do any of us if they were put in jail? They'll be paying for this the rest of their lives anyway, so who am I to throw rocks at them? I'll bet they'll sleep better tonight than they have for a long time, knowing their nightmare of being caught is finally over, once and for all."

"Well, Mr. Taylor told me you had a keen sense of human nature. According to him, you could walk with kings. To tell you the truth, when this whole thing started, I advised him against putting you in charge. But now I see his decision as a stroke of genius on his part—fantastic, simply fantastic."

"How about lunch, fellows? We have that union business after lunch and I want to be well fortified for that. Could you lend me five dollars, Jerry? I'm broke and hate to charge lunch up there in the cafeteria."

They laughed like hell and reminded me, "You have two million dollars laying there on the desk and you don't want to charge lunch."

"Well, I was afraid that little cashier might not have change for a million, and I wouldn't want to embarrass her by asking her to put it on the cuff."

"Come on, Irish; we'll buy your lunch for you."

"Good. Maybe tomorrow I'll have Pam pack one for me."

Over lunch, I asked Jerry if he would call that investment expert he'd been telling me about and get him started on some proposals for us. "Our good banker friend is getting very nervous with all that money building up in the Taylor Foundation account and I'd hate to see him have a heart attack."

When we returned to the office the union representatives were there in full battle gear. I ushered them right into the office, and we sat down for some serious negotiating. I took the first five minutes to describe in detail exactly what we had in mind. In their rebuttal, which took about forty-five minutes, they pointed out that we had contractual obligations and our contract only called for a forty-hour work week. They also mentioned their right to strike, and so forth. I just sat there and let them have their say. They finally summed it all up by telling me that a contribution of fifty thousand dollars by me to their pension fund could perhaps avert a strike.

I told them that was damned decent of them, but that they just were not paying attention to me when the meeting started. "For all intents and purposes, there is no more Taylor Industries. We're not bidding any more work; we're simply finishing up our present contracts. We have already sold all the equipment and the plants."

"You can't do that," they insisted.

I interrupted by saying, "Gentlemen, I sat here and patiently listened to you for forty-five minutes. Now I wish you would show me the same courtesy."

Once they shut up, I continued. "Now, then, we want to

finish up our contracts and go out of business very quietly, and we have no intention of putting anyone out of work. We are negotiating with Southern Corporation to lease our facilities to work on their contracts, and we have stipulated that they hire all our employees at least to get started. Then, it will be up to you gentlemen to keep them there. Is that fair enough? If not, we'll close the doors tonight and never reopen them again, and you'll have thirty-two thousand members walking the streets. Is that what you want? I'm not threatening you; I'm telling you the truth, like it really is. We already have our money, but what about those thirty-two thousand employees? The decision is on your shoulders now. So, what's it going to be?"

"You wouldn't be bluffing now, would you, O'Malley?"

"I don't have to bluff. And if you would do your homework, you should have known what was happening before you came in here mouthing off. You didn't even know what you were talking about. So, what's it going to be? It's your move now."

"Well, what about our contracts?"

"What about them? They're your contracts, and if you had read them, you'd know that we have escape clauses in there that you agreed to. These exempt us from any and all damages or payments should we go out of business. So, that's it, gentlemen, and as far as I'm concerned, this meeting is now adjourned."

"Well, our lawyers will be in touch with you."

"Fine. Have them contact Mr. Jacobs here; he's our legal counselor. But, just keep in mind that if you shut us down tonight, Southern will break off negotiations, and we'll simply forfeit the rest of our contracts. If that happens, the door will never open to defense contracting again." They got up and left in a huff.

I asked Mr. Jacobs what he thought, and he gave us his honest appraisal. "At this point, they really don't have any choice. But you should be aware that they have been known to do stupider things, so we will really have to wait and see if they carry out their threat."

We spent the rest of the day meeting with various department heads to prepare for negotiations with Southern in the morning.

We figured we were really going to have a fight on our hands, even though we held all the trump cards.

Around a quarter to five we got a call from the president of the union, saying that they would go along with us if we would let them be represented at the negotiations with Southern in the morning. I agreed to allow their lawyer to sit in on the negotiations, but only as an observer with no say whatsoever in the negotiations. When they objected, I told them, "Take it or leave it. In fact, if your guy opens his mouth once, he'll be expelled from the meeting."

He finally agreed—reluctantly, I might add. At that, we called it a day and headed home.

Pam and I retired early again and I stayed awake until the wee hours of the morning dreaming up ways to make our task easier tomorrow. I tried to place myself in Mr. Phillips' shoes and anticipate what he would say and do and how he would react to this and that. I knew I had him over a barrel, but I still wanted to close the deal as painlessly as possible, and with the least amount of bullshit.

I went into the office early the following morning and had Janice type all the proposals and counterproposals I had dreamed up, so that I wouldn't forget any of them.

The negotiations were to begin at ten o'clock. Southern's representatives began arriving as early as nine o'clock. We had them ushered into the board room set up for the occasion. I asked to be notified the minute Mr. Phillips came into the building. It wasn't long before I got a call from the guard at the main entrance that Mr. Phillips had just entered the building.

I walked to the elevator, personally greeted him, and asked if he would spend a few minutes with me in private before the meeting started. I mentioned that I had some alternate proposals he might be interested in. We stepped into a little office off the main corridor, and I let him read my proposals. After he was through, he turned to me and remarked, "There are some very generous offers here, O'Malley. Do you mind if I ask you why you're being so generous?"

"Look, I know you like it with the gloves off, so let me tell you

our position as opposed to yours and perhaps then you'll understand better. First off, I know there has never been any love lost
between Southern and Taylor Industries and that you have been
trying for years to gain control of Taylor. I know everyone was
trying to force George to go public with his stock. I also know
that every other conceivable scheme to undermine him was
afoot. There was even a secret agreement with our comptroller
and two of our top executives to make George think he was
going broke and then force him to sell out for peanuts. The price
you paid for that was three million. There was also contract
rigging, and you stole seven of the last eight contracts by having
our computer rigged. Then, the last one that you won was really
a gift from me. I was on to the scheme and knew it was the straw
that was supposed to break the camel's back. That's why we
crammed it down your throat to make you come to us. Of
course, there is no need rehashing the subsidiaries in southern
California again, so we'll skip over that chapter. Anyway, I tried
to put myself in your shoes and to figure out what you could
successfully sell to your board of directors. I figured you could
sell them on a leasing arrangement a lot easier than you could
sell them on such a tremendous cash outlay. That is why we sold
the plants and equipment and leased them back on a long-term
lease."

"I follow you so far, O'Malley, but you fucked up on your
leases and you'll pay dearly for that."

"Well, I don't think so. We have escape clauses in both agreements and plan to exercise them as soon as we have completed
our contracts."

His face turned white and he exhaled very hard as if he had
just lost his ace in the hole. "How in the fuck did you ever
manage that?"

"Money, Mr. Phillips. Money talks. It cost me ten million
dollars for the escape clause on the equipment and machinery
and almost twenty-two million for the one on the plants and
property. But I have them, and we plan to exercise them."

"You've thought of everything, O'Malley, haven't you?"

"Well, I figure you can't use any more trouble than you al-

481

ready have with that two and one-half billion dollar contract, so I want to make it as easy as possible for you. I know you wouldn't want to get tangled up with the Department of Justice in a bunch of lawsuits for price-fixing, fraud, and what have you. I know you are an extremely proud man and don't want to lose face, and what I'm offering you here is a chance to return to southern California as a conquering hero. You can boast that you accomplished all you set out to do, and oh, so much more. You can boast that you put us out of business and even wound up with our office building. And you can even change the name of it, to prove it to the world. I'm sure you will have no trouble selling the whole package to your board of directors since you'll be accomplishing their goals also."

"Most of all, Mr. Phillips, I'm agreeing to let you save face for humanitarian purposes. I don't want to see a whole lot of people get their lives all fucked up because you and I don't happen to agree. I want to avert a bloodbath when you take over; that is why I stipulated you must keep our employees on for at least one year. As far as the financial world goes, everyone will simply think I couldn't handle the job and you forced me out. It will be years, and perhaps never, before anyone is able to piece together the whole story, and I can assure you that they will get no help from me. You see, I'm not a proud or vain man, and I don't give a damn what people think about me. If they like me, fine; if not, they can leave me alone."

"Got any coffee around here, O'Malley? I need a few minutes to digest all this."

"Sure."

I picked up the phone and asked Janice to bring us a pot of coffee as quickly as possible. Mr. Phillips kept pacing around the room pounding his fist into his open hand while he contemplated his alternatives.

Janice knocked on the door and entered with a tray of coffee and donuts. She smiled her lovely smile as I introduced her to Mr. Phillips. He shook her hand and asked me if she went with the deal.

"No, sir, she is my right arm, and I couldn't function without her."

Janice spoke up and said she hated to mention it, but everyone was waiting for us to start the meeting.

"All right, Janice; tell them we will be there shortly."

Mr. Phillips poured himself a cup of coffee and sat down. While stirring his coffee he looked up at me and said, "You know, O'Malley, those leases were my strong suit this morning and now they're gone. We were also going to con you out of your remaining government contract, but Uncle Sam squalled like a stuck pig, so we'll have to figure on getting the contracts out of the way so we can get started on our contracts. Six months is too long, perhaps, you'll have to forfeit on some of them."

"Well, we wanted you to have them also, but we ran into the same opposition you did. So we have accelerated to a twenty-four hour-seven-day-a-week schedule and should have them out of the way in approximately thirty days. That won't cause you any serious delays. I mean, you can have your plant engineers move in tomorrow and start getting all the preliminaries out of the way if you like."

"Yes, we can live with that. But suppose we can't pick up the leases after you drop them?"

"There is no way you won't be able to do that. They made those leases and purchases with the expectation of Taylor Industries being in business forever. They will kiss your ass to pick up those leases if they have to—of that I am certain. In fact, the terms are exorbitant the way they're set up, and I wouldn't be surprised in the least to hear that you were able to negotiate a better price than I got on them."

"Well, okay, O'Malley. It looks like we have a deal. Shall we go to the meeting and have these changes read into the record?"

"Sounds good to me, but why don't you take them and have them read into the record as your own ideas? That will make it a little easier for you to sell to your board of directors and more plausible to the negotiators you brought with you today. You know, it's a matter of pride and saving face. Like I say, I just want to get things done. I'm not interested in getting credit for it or any pats on the back. I get my satisfaction from getting things done. Let someone else have the spotlight."

"Goddamn, O'Malley, you're all right. I must confess, I wouldn't be this generous if I were in your position, but you got a deal. Someday you'll have to tell me what the hell makes you tick. I have never dealt with anyone like you in my life, and I must say, it has been an experience I won't soon forget."

"Well, the others are waiting. Shall we join them?"

We walked in the board room and took our places. I called the meeting to order and gave the floor to Mr. Phillips. You could see the fierce look of determination on the faces of all the negotiators on both sides of the table. They were braced for a long and hard battle, determined not to give an inch one way or the other.

Mr. Phillips soon dispelled those notions, however, by announcing Southern was accepting our offer as presented, with certain exceptions and changes. He went on to spell out the changes, which he had recorded and entered in the agreements, including the provision that they would lease back to us two floors of the Taylor Building at the cost of one dollar a year. One floor for all the government agencies like contract analysis, navy, army, and what have you; and one floor for us to conduct and wrap up our loose ends, such as taking care of claims. There was also some law stipulating that we had to keep an office open for one year after going out of business.

I agreed with all the changes, much to the amazement of everyone sitting at the table, including Jerry and Mr. Jacobs. We initialed the changes and gave the package to the stenographers to type up for our signatures. We concluded the whole affair within one and one-half hours and were through in time for lunch. I told the typists to work right through lunch so we could sign them and get these gentlemen on their way home in time for dinner with their wives and sweethearts. Everyone laughed.

After lunch we signed the final agreements, with Mr. Phillips assuring me he would have no trouble selling it to his board of directors and have the sixty-six-million-dollar draft transferred by ten o'clock in the morning. We all shook hands and I adjourned the meeting.

Jerry, Mr. Jacobs, and I returned to my office. Mr. Jacobs said, "Well, Irish, I don't know how, but you did it again."

"Did what, Mr. Jacobs? It was all Mr. Phillips' doing, not mine. He wanted to avoid a confrontation as much as we did, and that is why he suggested the compromise agreement. Which reminds me, we went and negotiated ourselves out of an office building. What do you know about that?"

Jerry was fumbling around through the papers on my desk and picked up a copy of the proposals that Janice had typed for me that morning. He began reading them and then interrupted, saying, "Mr. Phillips' idea, my ass. Look at this, Mr. Jacobs."

Mr. Jacobs glanced at them, then laid them down and said, "I would have bet money on that. Why did you let him take all the credit, Irish? You didn't have to do that. We had him dead to right."

"True, but this way he saved face and can return to southern California as the conquering hero. We got everything we wanted, and more, so why not?"

Mr. Jacobs shook his head and said, "You are truly amazing, Irish. I don't know of another human being who could have pulled it off as smoothly. I figured we'd be negotiating until this time next week. I envisioned all kinds of name-calling, charges, and countercharges. I'm sure we would have eventually won, but there would have been a bloodbath during their takeover of the San Jose plants and the offices here. There could have been hatreds built up that would have lasted a lifetime; but you managed to avert all that. I can see no reason why the takeover shouldn't be smooth and orderly and, of course, after they have had a year to get to know our employees, I'm sure they will have no trouble holding on to their jobs."

"Well, that's what I was shooting for, Mr. Jacobs, and we have a good start in that direction. Let's just keep our fingers crossed and hope it all works out."

We spent the rest of the afternoon bringing the charts and graphs up to date. The overall picture was beginning to shape up just the way we had planned it. We were completely out of the manufacturing business, with the exception of a few small manufacturing plants we had up for sale, and we decided that if we didn't sell them by the end of next week, we would turn them over to the liquidators to dispose of them for us.

25

Rebuilding the Taylor Fortunes

The following morning we met with the financial whiz kid whom Jerry had recommended. We spent the morning going over what he had come up with. We were interrupted only by a phone call from Mr. Phillips who informed us he had no trouble getting his board of directors to buy the whole package, and the sixty-six-million-dollar draft was on its way. I thanked him and told him that whenever he wanted to move in any of his key personnel, our people would cooperate in every way possible to make the transition as smooth as possible.

After I hung up, I had Janice get the banker on the phone, and I informed him that the draft was on its way. I asked him if he could join us there in my office, because we were ready to disburse some of the funds that had been accumulating in his bank. He told me he would be there in record time.

We agreed to disburse almost three-quarters of the funds and invest them in government bonds and other treasury securities. We bought over three hundred million dollars' worth of municipal bonds and invested heavily in blue chip stocks such as IT&T and IBM.

After our banker friend departed hastily to fulfill our wishes, we took care of several other loose ends and decided to leave the office about four that afternoon. I asked Jerry and Mr. Jacobs how they thought we were doing in our first two weeks. "You mean, how are you doing, don't you, Irish? We think you're doing just great."

"Come on, fellows, I couldn't make a move without you two to back me up. It's all your planning and thinking that is making everything so successful."

"Well, think what you want, Irish, but you are the catalyst who has put it all together. And I must admit I never thought it was possible—two weeks ago I had my doubts as to whether anyone on this earth could pull off a project of this magnitude in a year, let alone two short weeks. It is nothing short of a miracle in my book."

"We got all the right breaks, that's all. Gentlemen, have a good weekend. First thing Monday morning we are going to have to look for a new office building to house the Taylor Foundation. So enjoy yourselves until then."

After they were gone, I called Janice into my office and told her she could take the rest of the day off also, if she wanted. She declined, saying she would stay in case I needed anything. "Well, in that case, why don't you bring us a couple cups of coffee and we'll just sit here and talk. How will that be?"

She returned in nothing flat. After pouring the coffee, I asked her to tell me all about herself.

"There is not much to tell, Irish. I'm twenty-six years old, divorced with no dependents. I have my own apartment and no roommates. I like my job and have no great ambitions or expectations out of life. I only want to live it to the fullest and enjoy every day; I feel every chance for pleasure should be seized as if you'll never have another chance at it."

"Don't you have a boyfriend or expect to get married again someday?"

"I don't believe I'll ever get married again, Irish, and I have no steady boyfriend. I don't know; I have a different point of view on life than most people do. You probably wouldn't agree or approve of it, so I won't tell you."

"Oh, don't be so sure. I'm as liberal as they come and when I talk to a beautiful girl such as yourself, I listen mostly to what they say with their eyes."

"What are my eyes saying to you, Irish?"

"Well, please stop me if I'm wrong or if you think I'm getting out of line, for I wouldn't want you to think badly of me. I think your eyes are telling me you are very lonely and that you feel we could share a beautiful, brief interlude together with no hang-ups, no promises, and no obligations. Just two ships passing in the night, sharing warmth and affection culminating in a sensually rewarding experience for both of us. How far off base am I?"

"You're right on base, Irish, and we still have forty-five minutes before I have to go home to that lonely apartment. It certainly would make the weekend a lot easier to face, and it will never get any further than this office, I promise you that."

I set my coffee cup down and stood up, taking her hand and helping her to her feet. I took her in my arms and kissed her. She whispered that there was a bed in the ladies' lounge and after she locked the office doors, no one would bother us there. I agreed. After she had locked everything up, she returned and we went into the ladies' lounge. I helped her out of her clothes, and the anticipation was driving me wild. I had undressed her in my mind many times already, and to think I was actually doing it for real was almost inconceivable.

After she was undressed, I quickly shed my clothes and lay down beside her. I began kissing her and running my hands over her beautiful naked body. I could wait no longer and got into position. My penis slid into her warm vagina and I began making love to her with all the passion I could muster. She responded in kind and moved her body in delirious ecstasy as if it were going to be the last opportunity she ever had as long as she lived. After I climaxed, she wrapped her legs around me and held me tightly with her arms to make it last even longer. I kissed her tenderly and suggested we rest a little and do it again before we had to go. She agreed and had me roll over on my back.

While I was resting, she began to experiment on me with her tongue and her hands, finding the soft, sensitive areas of my body and stimulating me anew. I finally cuddled into her breasts and began nursing them. She had never experienced that before and confessed that it felt wonderful. I had another erection and made love to her again. It felt so good and we were now both physically satisfied, so we showered, got dressed and walked back into my office where I poured her another cup of coffee. She sat there sipping it, deep in thought. I asked her if she felt better now and she confessed she felt marvelous.

"Irish, I don't want you to think I'm some old whore who goes around throwing herself at her boss all the time. I'm not, and believe it or not, that was the first time I've had intercourse since my marriage broke up, when I was only nineteen."

"I don't think anything like that, Janice. And you don't have to explain or tell me any of this, if you don't want to."

"No, I want to, Irish. I think you're the one person on this earth who could understand. I even went to a shrink for three years after my divorce, but all that SOB wanted to do was get my clothes off me, so I stopped going to him and tried to work things out for myself."

"Janice, would it surprise you to hear that I know exactly how you felt? Many of the same things you're going through right now, I have experienced myself. I was literally dying of loneliness with hundreds of people all around me, and I was too afraid to reach out to anyone for help. I can remember times in my life when I would have given anything on this earth just for a woman to take me in her arms and tell me she cared even if she was lying to me. I needed to touch another human being to let me know I was not alone in this world. Is that how you felt, Janice?"

"Oh, yes, Irish; I felt I was being consumed by loneliness. My husband was very young, and had a real drinking problem. He promised he would stop once we were married, and he did for the first thirty days. Then he was right back on booze again. He would beat me if I would refuse to have sex with him when he had been drinking. He would literally rape me and make me perform all kinds of unnatural sex acts with him. If I wouldn't, he would beat me all the more. After that tragic marriage, I felt for years that I was incapable of ever loving a man again."

"Well, Janice, you made the classic mistake when you married him. You married him for what you thought you could turn him into, not for what he was. Marriage has never changed anyone. If they drink before they're married, they will continue after they're married. Same with any bad habit, or what have you. When choosing someone to spend the rest of your life with, you have to accept him for what he is—faults and all. You have to be prepared to accept a person's shortcomings and never, never compare that person with another. Everyone is different, Janice, and I suppose that is why we have give-and-take in marriages. This fifty-fifty business is a lot of bullshit. There are times in married life when you have to go all the way for your partner and there will be times when your partner will have to go all the way for you."

"I could see the hurt and longing in your eyes, Janice. I knew you needed to be touched by another human being. I knew how it must have been for you and my heart cried out to help you. And if I was helpful in any way, I'm glad I was able to. I don't think any less of you either, Janice. In fact, I only think more of you for having the courage to reach out for my extended hand."

"Thank you, Irish. I needed our little affair. I really feel for the first time since my divorce that I am capable of loving another man. Who knows, I may even call a girlfriend and go out dancing this weekend, or something. I may even get lucky and meet some nice guy. I feel like I want to live again and not merely exist."

"I'm happy for you, Janice. It sounds like you have it all together again. If you do get lucky and want a chaperone, my wife and I would enjoy the pleasure of your company, of that, I'm sure."

"Thanks, Irish. But let me get lucky first."

"Just remember, Janice, happiness is a state of mind, not a place, and love is something to do, someone to love, and something to hope for."

"I'll remember, Irish, and I'll always remember you."

"I hope so, Janice, and have a very nice weekend. See you bright and early Monday morning. Okay?"

"Okay. Good-bye, Irish."

She gave me a tender kiss and a warm embrace and was on her way. I sat back in my chair and reflected on what had just taken place. I thought to myself, "If anyone had told me this morning that this was going to happen today, I would have laughed at them." Then I thought, "Well, if our affair will help her to cope with her loneliness, why not? Besides, it was a very pleasant experience for me, also. A fantasy fulfilled."

I picked up my briefcase and headed for the elevator. Within the hour I was at the Taylors' house being greeted by my beautiful little wife. She was full of her usual good cheer and gave me a big hug and a big kiss. "How did it go today, sweetheart?"

"Fantastic, Pam, my darling. Simply fantastic. The sale to Southern was finalized today, and we have a pretty good start of building a new portfolio for the Taylor Foundation. Then last, but not least, I finally found out what has been bothering Janice. I'll tell you about it over dinner; I'm starved."

"Oh, you precious little baby doll, let me see if Maggie has your dinner ready for you." I stuck my lower lips out as if to sulk and said, "I'll cry if it's not ready." She laughed, took my hand and hurried us to the dinner table.

"I don't understand a thing about business, so why don't you tell me about Janice first. I know you have been worried about her."

"Well, only if you promise not to get jealous of my talking to another woman."

"Why should I, when you come home to me every night and love me like I'm the only woman on this earth?"

"You are first and foremost in my mind, darling, and there would be no life for me without you. That you can believe. As for Janice, we finally had a chance to sit down and have a long talk, and I finally got her to open up and tell me what has been bothering her. It seems her problem was a lot like ours before we met. She was dying of loneliness with hundreds of people all around her. I know you know the feeling, for you've told me so."

"I know it all too well, Irish. Poor girl. But she's young and beautiful and shouldn't have any trouble attracting a man. It must go a lot deeper then."

"It does, honey. She had a disastrous marriage when she was nineteen years old. Her husband was an alcoholic and would beat her and literally rape her every time she refused him when he was drinking. After her divorce she simply withdrew from life and even went to a shrink for three years to learn to cope with her feelings and emotions. I guess that, in itself, was a bad experience for her, for she told me all he wanted to do was get her clothes off her. So she quit going to him and has been trying to work things out for herself for the last four years. She lives alone in a little apartment. She seldom, if ever, goes out on dates and never has any friends over. She told me she felt incapable of love and thought perhaps she would never fall in love again."

"How sad, Irish. I know that lonesome feeling, and so do you. Were you able to help her?"

"Well, I don't know. I pointed out to her why her first marriage failed, by telling her what you told me about not trying to change your partner once you're married. I reminded her that each person is the same after marriage as before, and I gave her all your good advice on marital bliss that has worked so well for us. Incidentally, where did you get all that good advice in the first place?"

"From Mother, who else?"

"I should have known that. I sure do miss her, don't you?"

"I do too, Irish. But tell me about Janice."

"Well, that's about it, although I think I managed to talk her into going out with her girlfriend this weekend. I told her that perhaps she would get lucky and meet a nice guy and that if she did, you and I would chaperone them. What do you think of that?"

"I think she'll take your advice, and I think she'll get lucky and we'll help her in any way we can, Irish. It truly amazes me with all you have on your mind—all these big business deals and all—that you could find time to listen to her problems. I shouldn't be surprised, though. You're a superhuman person and no matter how far you go in life, you'll always be sweet, lovable Irish O'Malley to all who have the pleasure of meeting you."

"Oh, you flatter me too much, my dear. But I must confess I'm vain enough to enjoy it, so please don't stop. Not to change the subject, but where in the world do you suppose your parents are? I mean I'm really getting homesick for them, especially your mother. I wish they would at least call us to let us know they're all right."

"I know exactly how you feel, Irish, and I would give anything at this point to hear her voice on that old telephone. I keep getting this feeling that they are lurking in the background, not too far out of sight, keeping a close eye on us so that no harm comes to us."

"I know. I get the same vibrations and have a feeling Mr. Jacobs talks to them every day, although he steadfastly denies it. He claims he's only to contact them in an emergency. Well, if we don't hear from them soon, I'm going to be tempted to create an emergency, just to talk to them."

Pam smiled and said, "I know how you feel, Irish. But we'll survive, and they know it. I'm sure they're not too far away, especially with me being pregnant. You know how mother feels about that."

"I know. I thought a team of wild horses couldn't drive her away at this point. And I'm positive your father could have accomplished everything we've done, and probably more efficiently. He gave all those reasons for putting me in charge; but I guess we'll never know the real reasons until they return."

The next thirty days went by very quickly, and we accomplished almost everything we had set out to do. We performed on our remaining contracts and finished ahead of the schedule we had set up for ourselves. The transition from Taylor Industries to Southern was accomplished rather smoothly considering the magnitude of the transition. Things could have been much worse, but everyone cooperated fully and ironed out all the little problems that came up.

By now we had turned Mr. Taylor's portfolio inside out and had completely rebuilt it. We sold all the small manufacturing companies with the exception of three real dogs, which we turned over to the liquidators and disposed of them for whatever we could get for them. We even sold his interest in several other corporations with poor financial prospects and converted the proceeds into blue chip stocks.

By now word had spread all over the country about the strange goings-on in Sacramento. For one reason or another everyone wanted to know what the inside story was. We didn't tell anyone anything and just let them speculate. All calls and inquiries were referred to our public relations department, which was instructed to issue a statement to one and all that we were going out of the manufacturing business.

One story in a national trade journal reported that I had sold a billion dollar conglomerate to Southern Corporation for the paltry sum of sixty million dollars. They had it billed as the greatest bargain of all times for Southern. Jerry, Mr. Jacobs, and I got a good laugh out of that story.

We managed to reduce our affairs of Taylor Industries to one floor of the old Taylor office building, and we had all the government offices consolidated onto another floor, leaving everything else, personnel included, intact for Southern to take over. There were very few resignations and everyone concerned seemed to accept their new employer with expectations of a long and productive future with them. I was extremely happy for that.

As a gesture of good will, we had the Taylor sign removed from the top of the building and replaced with one approved by Southern.

We were settling our claims with lightning speed and only had to bring suit in six or seven cases. We expected to settle those out of court. They were really of no concern to us, other than to show everyone we meant business and would sue for our just due.

We acquired a new office building in Sacramento that was less than a year old. They were having trouble selling all the leases on it. We converted the top two floors into a luxurious suite of offices and conference rooms to house the Taylor Foundation. We installed every conceivable luxury that money could buy. I remember commenting to Mr. Jacobs that it was a vulgar display of wealth. He reassured me that Mr. Taylor wouldn't mind.

"I know, Mr. Jacobs. But it's my conscience that bothers me. However, this is one of those times when I feel completely justified in treating my conscience with total contempt. Let's face it, out of all the things I started with my conscience has caused me more trouble and bother than everything else combined."

He laughed and said, "I never heard it put quite that way before, but I'm sure it gives you a great deal of satisfaction."

"It really does, Mr. Jacobs."

Even Janice had come completely out of her shell and was really starting to enjoy life again. She was dating on a regular basis, kind of playing the field while looking for Mr. Right. She would tell me of her impending dates. I would always manage to have tickets to one affair or another and would suggest she double-date with Pam and me. She would accept more often than not, and she and Pam would confide in one another about all their girl problems and men in general. It was really great to see her so happy.

I kept on Mr. Jacobs' tail relentlessly, urging him to call the Taylors and tell them to come home. Pam was well into the eighth month of her pregnancy, and I was afraid the baby would be born without Mrs. Taylor there to hold my hand. I was sure I couldn't face it alone. I considered myself somewhat of a coward when it came to things like that.

Pam was so big by now that I would kid her that if she got any bigger we would have to get a wheelbarrow to carry the baby around in. She was a good sport about it all and never complained once, although the doctor told me she was having troubles. Nothing serious, but it was quite uncomfortable for her since she was so small.

I insisted that Mr. Jacobs have all the papers ready for Mr. Taylor to sign the minute he arrived back in town. I informed him, "I want this burden off my shoulders with all due speed. I am as uncomfortable with all of the responsibility as Mr. Taylor must be without it." I reminded him that we had accomplished everything we had set out to do and there was no reason for them to stay away any longer. He kept telling me to be patient and time would pass quickly.

26

The Taylors Return

Pam and I had long since moved back into our little dream house and were enjoying life to the fullest. Our love grew by leaps and bounds, and we really seemed to prosper in our love. We were extremely dependent on one another now that the Taylors were temporarily out of the picture. We were actually learning we could function without them. Perhaps Mrs. Taylor wasn't so heartless after all, leaving us to our own devices like this. She knew sooner or later that we would have to sink or swim and just wanted to make sure we knew how to swim.

We went walking down by the river one evening and hadn't been gone too long when Pam began to feel faint. We sat down for a short time and then decided we had better head back to the house in case we had to call the doctor if she started into labor. I tried not to show my anxiety, but Pam sensed it anyway, and said, "Stop worrying, Irish. You'd make a good midwife."

I cried, "Oh, my God, please hurry, Pam. Just the thought scares the hell out of me."

She laughed at me and said, "That's the first time I've heard you cuss for weeks. It seems you only cuss now when you get nervous or excited."

"Well, I'm both of them now, honey, and as soon as we get to the house I'm calling the doctor and Helen Jenkins to come over and check you out. Perhaps Helen could start staying with us now, in case you have trouble during the day or at night."

"What about all the other times, Irish?"

"Well, them, too. I mean, hell, you're going to have a baby, how can you be so calm about it, Pam? I mean, I'm going to be a father and you're going to be a mother, and damn, not ever being a mother before . . . I mean, a father . . . oh, well, you know what I mean, don't you, I hope."

Pam just kept laughing at me, and the more I continued to babble nervously the more she continued to laugh. We soon arrived at the back door of our little Cape Cod house. I opened the door for her and said, "Ladies first." We walked through the kitchen and into the living room, where we got the surprise of our lives. There stood Mr. and Mrs. Taylor, smiling broadly from ear to ear. We were both stunned and stood there with our mouths wide open in absolute shock.

Mrs. Taylor yelled, "Surprise!" As she did, I lunged for her and hugged her as tightly as my strength allowed. Mr. Taylor put his arms around Pam and, concerned, asked her how she was doing. "Fine, Daddy. Why didn't you warn us you were coming so we could have been ready for you?"

"Well, we wanted to surprise you two."

I was finally able to release my hold on Mrs. Taylor long enough to shake Mr. Taylor's hand and welcome him home. I put my arm around Pam, and we both stood there, still numb from the shock, with tears running down our cheeks. I looked at Pam and called her "crybaby," to which she replied, "You, too, Irish."

I again took Mrs. Taylor in my arms and said, "Welcome home, dear, sweet, precious, Mrs. Taylor. You'll never know how we've missed you both."

"Well, we must confess, we missed you both terribly ourselves."

"Come on, sit down and tell us all about your trip."

"Oh, forget the trip. How's everything going here?"

Pam spoke up and said, "Oh, great, but Irish is a little nervous about becoming a new mother and all." She laughed, and so did the Taylors. I explained, "I was just a bit upset because she was feeling faint while we were walking down by the river. I guess I got our prospective roles reversed."

Mrs. Taylor was laughing. "Sure you did, Irish."

"All right, Pam, I'll tell them what you did if you're not careful."

"Irish, you wouldn't, would you?"

"Come on, Irish, tell us," urged the Taylors.

"Well, I guess I'm going to have to, now that I have their curiosity aroused."

"Okay then, I'll just hide my head." I put my arm around her and said, "I think it's funny myself, but if you don't want me to tell them then, I won't."

She laughed and said, "Well, go ahead."

"Pam called me at work one afternoon and told me the car was full of water. I asked her where the car was, and she told me in the river. She had left it in gear and didn't set the handbrake. The car had rolled down the driveway, across the road, and into the river."

We sat there and laughed with Pam remarking, "Now we're even, Irish."

"It certainly is great to have you two back home. Life just wasn't the same without you. And now that you're home, Mrs. Taylor, perhaps you can help me keep Pam in line."

"Has she been misbehaving on you, Irish?"

"Well, no, but she insists on doing everything she used to do before she started carrying Paula around with her. I keep telling her to take it easy and let me do more, but she insists on doing the housework, shopping, and what have you."

"What makes you so sure it's going to be a little girl, Irish?"

"I promised you, Mrs. Taylor, and you know I wouldn't disappoint you."

"Well, tell you kids what. Why don't you get a few things together and come stay with us tonight. Between Maggie and me—and Helen starting next week—we'll see that she doesn't overdo it, Irish."

"I'm all for that. How about you, honey?"

"Do I have a choice?"

"Sure, you can walk out the door with us or your dad and I will carry you. What's it going to be?"

She smiled her knowing smile and said, "At least, he's giving me a choice. I believe I'll walk, though."

"Okay, you sit still and your mother and I will grab a few things."

Mrs. Taylor and I gathered up enough things to last a few days with Mrs. Taylor saying she would come back tomorrow and get us whatever else we needed.

"Look, Mrs. Taylor, for what it's worth, I just could not have stood another minute of a day without you in it. I've never been so homesick for anyone in my whole life."

"I feel the same about you, too, Irish. It truly is a warm and tender feeling to know you're loved and wanted, Irish. I cannot find the words to describe how Mr. Taylor and I love you and Pam. It is almost as if we were reborn again and given a second chance at life and happiness. We intend not to lose these good feelings. There is an old saying, Irish, that teachers learn from their students. Well, I, for one, don't mind telling you that Mr. Taylor and I have learned from you and Pam more about life and living in a relatively short time than most people learn in a lifetime."

"Thank you, Mrs. Taylor; but it is not so one-sided, you know. Pam and I have matured a lot and can face life, due in no small measure to your kindness and your prescription for marital bliss—which we follow to the letter, by the way. It's knowing that you love us and that you care that gives us confidence. Nothing is any good unless you have someone you love to do it for. Pam and I are very lucky. We have you and Mr. Taylor to do it for. How does it go now? Happiness is something to do, something to love, and something to hope for. Pam and I are very fortunate; we have all three ingredients for happiness."

Pam walked in and asked us if we were about ready to leave.

She smiled and hugged her mother again and said, "I still can't believe you're home, Mother."

Mrs. Taylor asked her why she was so agreeable about going to stay at their place until the baby is born.

"Well, you see, Mother, I have a little game I play with Irish. I let him think he's getting his own way, and then I let him have it."

I laughed, gave her a big kiss, and said, "Don't you let her fool you for a moment, Mrs. Taylor. She just couldn't wait for you to invite us over, and I've heard tell a girl needs her mother at a time like this more than anything in the world. All I can do is stand around and wring my hands and worry for her."

We all returned to the living room where Mr. Taylor was closing the windows and turning out lights. "Do we have everything?" he asked.

"Yes, I think so; but if we don't we can come back tomorrow for it."

"Don't forget to water my roses when you come over tomorrow, Irish."

"I won't, darling, and I'll bring you one of them every day, to prove I've been taking care of them for you."

She smiled and said, "Isn't he sweet, mother?"

"Of course he is, honey; now let's get on our way. We have so much to talk about and so much catching up to do."

"Okay, Pam, why don't you ride with your parents and I'll follow in our car. Now that we have retrieved it from the river I think it will make the trip." We all laughed and were on our way.

After we were settled in at the Taylors' house, we all sat down in the living room to get reacquainted. Pam and I were both ecstatic that they were finally home and told them so. I finally asked Mr. Taylor if he wanted to hear how we drove him into bankruptcy while he was away.

He laughed with a smile of confidence and said, "There will be plenty of time to tell me tomorrow. To tell you the truth, I can hardly wait to see the new office building. I mean, well. . . ."

"See there, Pam, we were right."

"Yes, indeed, Irish."

Mrs. Taylor asked us what we were talking about.

"Well, your husband just gave it away. You see, when you and Mr. Taylor got on that plane, Pam and I had the feeling you were kicking us out of the nest to see if we could fly on our own and survive without your influence on our lives. Well, we vowed we would not disappoint you. But we had the feeling all along that you were not far away and were looking over our shoulders every step of the way. Don't misunderstand. We loved it. It was comforting to know you were there if we needed you; it was just that we were both so homesick for you we could have died. So now that the cat is out of the bag, so to speak, how did we do?"

Mr. Taylor spoke up and said, "Marvelous, kids; simply marvelous. There was no way in the world I could have accomplished what you did. It was just impossible for me to do. I don't want you to think I influenced any of the decisions you made, Irish. It was all on the up-and-up, and everything you did you did on your own. That was the deal. Win, lose, or draw. Mr. Jacobs would call me, worried to death about some of your deals, and he'd want me to intervene, but I told him to have as much faith in you and your ability to deal with people as I did and his worries would quickly be dispelled. Well, after the first two weeks, he didn't call much. You made a believer out of him, Irish."

"I can't take all that credit, Mr. Taylor. I had the finest brains in the country giving me advice and telling me what was what, so the lion's share of the credit must go to them."

"True, Irish, they made a lot of bullets for you. But it was you who had to stand up there on the firing line and fire them. Mr. Jacobs told me about your nerves of steel and how you were strong when you had to be and compassionate when you felt the need to be. He told me his fee for the whole project would be absolutely nothing. He said it was really something to marvel at, just to see how skillfully you put the principles of human nature to work and how you manipulated people to your way of thinking and got them to agree to your terms while making them appear to be their own terms. He told me there was no way he could keep up with your mind, because it works with the speed of a computer. You would be closing one deal and already have analyzed how it would benefit you and how you could use the results to clinch the next, and the next, deal. He claims this has been the most rewarding and facinating two months of his life."

"Well, I'm glad he enjoyed it. And I really enjoyed working with him, also. To be perfectly frank with you, though, Mr. Taylor, the only way I could see the overall operation through and keep my sanity was by visualizing it in my mind as a big Monopoly game and keeping in mind that the people I was dealing with were only other players in the game. I felt I couldn't lose, since Mr. Jacobs and Jerry and I were the only ones who had the complete picture. Thus, we were able to more or less con Southern Corporation and all the other players into playing the game our way. If I had thought of it in terms of actual dollars and cents, I probably would have panicked and run for cover."

"I kind of doubt that, Irish. You're too much in control to ever panic. And when someone finally figures out just what you accomplished, I have a feeling you will emerge as a giant in the financial world."

"Then, let's hope no one ever finds out. But enough of this business talk. You still haven't told Pam and me about your trip. Where did you disappear to?"

"Well, first we flew to New York and spent two weeks there. We went sightseeing, to the theater, the finest restaurants—you name it, we tried it. Then, after it became apparent to Mr. Jacobs that Irish had everything under control, including himself, we flew on to Europe and spent the next two weeks touring the major cities before we became homesick. We have been in San Francisco since then, just dying to return home. And today we could not take it any longer and decided to return early."

"Oh, and we are so happy you did. You should have let us know you were in San Francisco, and we could have joined you there last weekend, at least."

504

"No, we said sixty days, and we were determined to see it through until it simply got to be too much for us today."

"Well, we know how you felt. And if we had had any inclination you were in San Francisco, you would have had us on your doorstep. We missed you both that much."

"We were planning a gala homecoming for you, but I think this is so much nicer because we don't have to share you with everyone else. We have you all to ourselves."

"How sweet, Irish! I believe that is what I missed the most—your charm and wit."

"Well, what I missed the most was the sound of your melodious voice. I was so homesick to hear one of your cheery greetings that I would have given a million dollars just to hear you say 'Good morning, Irish, and how are you today? I had a million dollars to give, too, didn't I, Mr. Taylor?"

He chuckled and agreed, "Yes, you did, Irish. And I got a kick out of Mr. Jacobs' telling me, with two million dollars lying on your desk, you tried to borrow five dollars for lunch so you wouldn't have to embarrass the little girl up at the checkout by asking her to put it on the cuff. I believe that's the way he phrased it. Oh yes, and I would have given a million dollars myself to see the expression on old man Phillips' face when you told him, 'If God had intended you to do more talking than listening, he would have given you two mouths and only one ear.'"

We all laughed. "Perhaps that is why you were so successful, Irish. You let everyone know right from the start that you were in complete control. You knew exactly where you stood; you were not afraid to take chances, and you were not impressed or intimidated by either wealth and power. You were completely foreign to them—an outsider, a stranger. They figured they could take advantage of your youth and inexperience. That is why the leasing outfit in Denver finally knocked your price down by ten million dollars and the people in L.A. who bought the plants and the ground they were sitting on knocked your price down by twenty-five million. They both thought you were crazy settling for those amounts. But little did they know that those escape clauses you had them put in the lease-back agreements were going to cost them twice that amount. Little did they know you were using them to close your deal with Southern. They really thought they had made the leasing deal of the century and were really going to get fat at your expense. I understand Southern has brought them back in line now."

"Well, that's good. But I want to thank you for having those sales contracts and lease-back agreements all worked out, Mr. Taylor. They were really the keystone to the whole operation. If we had had to negotiate them from scratch, the whole arch of the Taylor Industries could have come crashing down on our heads. So, you were really the genius behind the whole operation. Mr. Jacobs and Jerry and I simply put your plans into action, after which everything just fell into place."

"Tell me something, Irish. How in the world did you know I wanted to get out of the manufacturing and the defense contracting business? I never indicated that to you, I'm sure."

"Oh, yes, you did, Mr. Taylor. I picked up bad vibrations every time we would talk about them. And I also know why you stepped aside and let me rearrange your fortunes for you."

"Well, this should be interesting, Irish, for I have never told another living soul, not even my wife, what my motives were and why I couldn't handle it myself."

"Well, correct me if I'm wrong, Mr. Taylor, but after Jerry revealed our plans, if we had been doing anything contrary to your wishes, I'm sure Mr. Jacobs would have at least tried to steer us in another direction, right?"

"Right on the money so far, Irish. Although I must admit that if you had simply cleaned up the mess and stayed in the manufacturing business I would have gone along with it. It was strictly your choice. Now, for the second part, Irish, I'm dying to know your thoughts on that."

"Well, Mr. Taylor, I'll have to be perfectly candid with you, so perhaps if you would like, we could discuss it at another time."

"No, no, Irish. I think I know what you're getting at, and it's about time my wife and daughter found out that I'm not the knight in shining armor they always thought I was. In fact, I'll feel better with it all out in the open anyway. It needs to be told and I'll spare you that, Irish, by telling it myself."

"It's not necessary, Mr. Taylor, seeing as how you're not associated with that conniving bunch of animals anymore. Why don't you just forget it and we'll go on from here?"

"Well, Irish, it's great to be considered great; but it's even greater to be considered human. That's what I want to be from now on—human. You see, Paula and Pam, what Irish was so reluctant to talk about is the fact that Taylor Industries had become so corrupt and so out-and-out dishonest that it was actually running me. I had made so many crooked deals and accepted so many favors and paid so many people off up and down the line that everyone and his brother figured I was fair game, and there was very little I could do about it. I'm talking about big, big people in Washington, as well as manufacturing suppliers and so on. I had people on the payroll I couldn't fire if I wanted to because they were friends of someone I owed a favor to, or because they were covering up something we had done that wasn't quite kosher. It had gotten to the point where I was going out of my mind. Then, along came Irish, picking up all his bad vibrations as he puts it, and without my even knowing it, he uncovered it all. He pulled things out from under the rug that I thought were buried forever. I never figured on the comptroller and those other two birds conspiring to sell me out to Southern, though. That was really the straw that broke the camel's back."

"Still, I was in no position to fire them, for they had enough on me to tell me to go to hell if I confronted them. Of course, I could have stopped their little scheme, but it would only have been a matter of time before they would have figured some other way to dethrone me. The only thing I had going for me was the fact that I had kept it all together in a closed corporation, and there was no way they could keep me from selling it or giving it away."

"This is where you came in, Irish. You were as pure as the newly driven snow. Since you owed no one anything, there was no way for any of them to blackmail you. All the past favors, deals, swindles, and what have you didn't hold water as far as you were concerned, and they knew it. All they could do was make the best deal possible for themselves and try to get away without being prosecuted for theft, embezzlement and whatever. I must commend you on the way you handled the resignations and how you were able to make them pay retribution. It could have been a real bloodbath, Irish, and even I could have been hurt very badly."

"I know, Mr. Taylor. I meant what I told every one of them. It was not my intention to destroy them, and I sincerely hope they are successful in their new endeavors. Hell, I'm not God. Who am I to judge anyone? They were all smart men and could see a good deal when I offered it to them. That's why they all took it, and their lips are sealed forever. That is, if they intend to ever work again, and I'm sure they all have a long way to go before they can retire. So it worked out best for all concerned."

"Well, Paula and Pam, that is about the sum and substance of it without going into all the details. I was just another crooked defense contractor. But that is all behind me now, and I feel as if the weight of the world has been lifted off my shoulders. I want to thank you, Irish, for being considerate enough to want to spare my family from hearing this, but I'm glad they know now. Maybe, with a little luck, they will forgive me. Paula, Pam, I want you to know that all those times when I was impossible to get along with were caused by my guilty conscience getting the better of me. I'm truly sorry for all the hell I put you two through over the years. I hope you can forgive me."

They both walked over to his chair and put their arms around him. Mrs. Taylor told him that it takes a big man to admit when he's been wrong, and she was proud of him for owning up to his past mistakes. Pam concurred.

"Say, why don't we open a bottle of champagne to launch the Taylor Foundation this evening. After all, it's a whole new way of life and that doesn't happen every day."

"Great idea, Irish," said Mr. Taylor, as he got up and went to the bar to pick out a bottle.

We gathered around the bar while Mr. Taylor put the bottle on ice to cool it. He asked Pam how she was feeling. "Just great, Daddy, now that you and Mother are home."

"She's such a love, Mr. Taylor. She wouldn't even know how to complain if she were in mortal agony. I know she has to be uncomfortable, but she has never once admitted it. She has to be the most loving and giving little angel God ever gave the breath of life to. Of course, I must confess I caught her standing in front of a full-length mirror the other day singing, 'I should have danced all night.' "

"Oh, Irish, I was not."

"I know, honey, I'm just teasing you." I took her in my arms and kissed her. "Happy, honey?"

"You bet, Irish. Happiness is something to do, something to love, and something to hope for, and we have all three, don't we?"

"We sure do, honey, and happiness is not an action; it is a feeling—one of the nicest feelings in the world."

Mrs. Taylor said, "Will you listen to the philosophers. Where did you two pick up all these little pearls of wisdom?"

"Well, if you promise not to laugh or tell anyone, Mrs. Taylor, we'll tell you."

"Okay, I promise not to breathe a word of it to anyone."

"Pam reads poetry to me every night before we go to sleep and sometimes she even lays the heavy stuff on me, like philosophy or prose. She is really a wealth of information and I learn something new from her every day. She devotes a lot of energy to making our lives interesting and happy. She puts love into everything she does, and I love her for it. Just this morning she hit me with a profound statement that, nothing is either good or bad, except by comparison. You know, I've thought about it all day, and I believe she is absolutely right."

"I just like to keep him on his toes, Mother, you know."

"Yes, and speaking of keeping me on my toes, I'll bet those guys that went to work for Southern will be on their toes."

"Why is that, Irish?"

"They raised the urinals in the men's room by a foot."

"Oh, Irish, you big nut, you."

Mr. Taylor, who had been chilling the champagne, stopped rolling it in the ice and popped the cork. He poured us all a glass and proposed a toast.

"Here's to my granddaughter, her mother and father and her grandmother."

"Don't forget grandfather, Mr. Taylor." We all drank to the new baby.

I proposed a toast, "To love, touch not, taste not, feel not, want not—and you'll never know the wonders of love." We all drank to that. Then I proposed a toast to the new Taylor Foundation and to a long and successful life for it.

27

Pam Becomes Critically Ill

Pam clutched my arm. I sat my glass down, put my arm around her for support, took her glass, and asked her if she was all right. "I'm just a little light-headed, Irish. Too much excitement, I guess."

"Well, we had better get you to bed so you can rest."

"No, no, I'll be all right."

"Nonsense," I said, as I picked her up in my arms and headed for the stairs. Mrs. Taylor ran on ahead with Mr. Taylor following close behind. Mrs. Taylor had the bed pulled down by the time I got there and I lay Pam down on the bed and took her shoes off.

She was white as a ghost. I asked Mrs. Taylor if we should call the doctor. After feeling Pam's forehead she agreed. I ran back downstairs and called and told him to hurry over because Pam was having trouble. I went back upstairs where Mr. and Mrs. Taylor were attending Pam.

"How is she, Mrs. Taylor?"

"Irish, she's unconscious. Call the doctor back and tell him to meet us at the hospital."

"Mr. Taylor, will you see if you can find Henry to drive us."

I raced back downstairs and caught the doctor just as he was leaving. I told him we were taking her directly to the hospital, and he should meet us in the emergency room.

I picked Pam back up in my arms, blankets and all, and hurried downstairs. Mrs. Taylor opened the door, and we stood in the driveway for what seemed like an eternity before Henry and Mr. Taylor finally pulled up with the car. We placed Pam inside and instructed Henry to proceed to the hospital as fast as possible.

Poor Pam was white and Mrs. Taylor could hardly find a pulse.

We arrived at the hospital about ten minutes later. Mr. Taylor ran in and had them come out with a stretcher. After we got Pam out of the car and onto the stretcher, they hurriedly took her to an emergency room where they began administering oxygen to her while taking her blood pressure and all the other preliminaries.

The doctor arrived and went right to work. He had them take blood samples which they rushed to the lab. He listened to her heart and pulse and seemed unable to explain what was happening. He was with her for about fifteen minutes before he came out to talk to us.

"What's wrong, Doc?" I asked in a very nervous voice.

"I'm not certain at this point. Did this come on suddenly?"

"Yes, it did, without warning. We were talking and laughing and she just got sick. I carried her to bed and by the time I went downstairs to call you and got back to her room she was unconscious. We brought her directly here. What could it be, Doc?"

"I suspect uremic poisoning or toxemia. We may have to take the baby."

"Oh, God, is it that serious?"

"Yes, I'm afraid it is, Irish. I'll call and have an operating room ready just in case. Every minute counts."

"Well, how soon will you know?"

"Just as soon as I get the lab report. Perhaps ten minutes." He made his way to the phone to make the arrangements.

DONALD R. WAGNER

I looked at the Taylors and could feel the tears running down my cheeks. Mrs. Taylor put her arms around me and tried to reassure me that everything was going to be all right.

"Oh, my God, Mrs. Taylor, if anything happens to Pam or the baby, I don't know what I'll do. I had no idea she was sick, or believe me, I would have personally dragged her to the doctors."

"We know, Irish. Just try to relax and bear with us. We'll see it through together."

The doctor returned, saying he had made all the necessary arrangements and should have his answer in a few minutes.

"What are her chances of carrying the baby full term, Doc?"

"At this point, Irish, not very good at all. If she has either one of the illnesses I mentioned, it could affect the fetus and the sooner we remove it the better off they both will be." Just then the technician came running down the hall and handed the doctor the report. "Toxemia. We'll have to move quickly."

They immediately wheeled Pam down the hall to a waiting elevator. We went with them as far as the operating floor. Pam was still unconscious and her skin had taken on a pale ashen tone. I held her hand all the way and was praying aloud to God to please let her and the baby be all right. When we reached the operating room, they directed us to a waiting room, and assured us they would keep us advised.

We wandered into the waiting room and sat down, still in a daze. No one spoke a word for the longest time. I began to weep and Mrs. Taylor came over to comfort me. I put my head on her shoulder and asked her how this could possibly happen. "Just an hour ago we were all so happy, and now this. I don't understand how God can be so cruel, Mrs. Taylor."

"Irish, I wish I had the words to soothe you and to explain it to you; but I'm just as puzzled as you are. All I can tell you is don't give up hope and keep on praying, Irish. God will listen to your prayers, I'm sure. Mr. Taylor and I will be praying right along with you. You have to believe, Irish, with all your heart and soul that it is going to turn out all right."

"I want to believe, Mrs. Taylor. Oh, God! How I want to believe. If I could I'd give my life to save Pam and the baby."

"There is no doubt about that, Irish, but right now, it's in the hands of God, and we have to keep the faith."

We tried to console each other and finally an intern came in and announced that Pam had given birth to twins.

"Twins?"

"Yes, a boy and a girl."

"How is she?"

"Well, her condition is very grave at this point and the next twenty-four hours will be critical."

"The babies?"

"They're perfect. A little underweight, but simply perfect."

"Were they affected by the toxemia?"

"Well, it's too early to tell: but at this point it appears that they were not."

"How soon can we see Pam?"

"She is still in the operating room. The doctor sent me out to tell you the news. She should be out in another half an hour and then in recovery for at least a day. She is a very sick girl and if you have any special prayers, I would suggest you pray them. She's going to need all the help she can get."

"Oh, yes."

"Look, why don't you go down to the nursery and see the twins. They're in incubators, but perhaps it will help take your mind off things."

"Oh, yes. Let's go down right now."

We tapped on the window of the nursery at the nurse, and she pointed them out to us. There they were, less than an hour old and screaming their heads off. We stood there in utter amazement. We all had tears streaming down our faces. I finally was able to speak. "Pam would kid me about having twins. One for you, Mrs. Taylor, and one for you, Mr. Taylor. So I guess we won't have any problem with a name for my son. George O'Malley. I like it. Paula and George O'Malley. How does that sound?"

"Wonderful, Irish, simply wonderful."

"Look, why don't you two stay here and watch our babies? I want to go back to the waiting room in case there is any news about Pam."

DONALD R. WAGNER

"Let us go with you, Irish."

"Okay, if you like."

After arriving back at the waiting room, I suggested we call Helen and let her know what was happening. Mrs. Taylor called her, and she joined us there at the hospital within twenty minutes. We filled her in on all the details as we knew them and asked her what she knew about toxic plasmosis.

She told us it was usually associated with pregnancy. They didn't know what caused it and there was little they could do in the way of treatment. In most cases, though, once the pregnancy was terminated, the disease and the symptoms would clear themselves up and go away. We asked her what the chances were of the babies' being affected and she told us quite honestly that she didn't know, but the fact that the doctor had terminated Pam's pregnancy and that the babies were reacting so normally was a very good indication they were not affected.

"Oh, that's good news. Now if they would just tell us Pam is going to be all right. Oh, God, Helen, I had no indication Pam was sick. She never complained, and other than being tired most of the time, there was just no way to tell. If anything happens to her, I'll never forgive myself. She missed her doctor's appointment last week. I should have insisted she make another. She assured me that she would see him again this week anyway, and that it wasn't necessary."

"Oh, Irish, stop blaming yourself. You couldn't have possibly known what was wrong. I'm sure God and our faith will see us through this. We have to believe."

After what seemed like an eternity, the doctor joined us there in the waiting room. He sat down and told us, "The prognosis at the moment doesn't look good at all. We have her on life-support systems now. She suffered two cardiac arrests during the operation along with massive hemorrhaging. We managed to stop the bleeding, but due to her weakened condition and the toxemia, her chances of survival are very grave indeed. It's in the hands of God now. We've done all we can do for her."

"Well, tell me, doctor, what you're saying is that her system is poisoned. Is that correct?"

515

"Yes."

"Well, can't you get rid of poison? I've read about an artificial kidney machine. Would that help clear up the poisoning?"

"Yes, it would, Irish. But in her present condition, I hesitate to subject her system to the additional shock."

"What chance does she have without it?"

"Almost none."

"Then, it's clear to me that we should take the chance and put her on the machine."

"Well, Irish, you'll have to take full responsibility."

"I'll take that responsibility if it will improve her chances."

"Oh, if it is successful, it will improve her chances a hundred-fold."

"Okay, you have your answer there, Doc. Get to work and get her on that machine." He got up without a word and headed back to the operating room.

I turned to Mrs. Taylor and said, "Oh, God! I hope I've made the right decision."

Mrs. Taylor put her arms around me, while Mr. Taylor and Helen put their hands on my shoulders. "You did, Irish, you did. And you have to believe Pam will pull through this."

"Oh, I do believe, I do, I do."

The following twenty-four hours crawled by at a snail's pace. We spent most of our time in the waiting room, dozing off from time to time, or walking down to the nursery to check on the twins. We even tried to consume some food. We just didn't have any appetite and kept praying everything would turn out all right. I insisted the doctor cancel all his other appointments and stay there at the hospital in case he was needed. He reluctantly consented to do so. It was about midnight the following day when he came in and told us they had taken Pam off the kidney machine and that she appeared to be holding her own. They intended to keep her on the respirator for another twenty-four hours, as a precautionary measure, until she had a chance to regain some of her strength. He told us her prognosis at the moment was very good. The toxic levels in her blood were reduced by seventy-five percent and they were administering a new medication that should help clear up the remainder.

We asked him if he had had a chance to consult with the pediatrician about the twins. He smiled and said, "Yes. They were totally unaffected, and are perfect in every respect. Of course, they only weigh a little over four pounds each, so they will have to remain in the incubators for a while longer, or at least until they gain a little more weight."

"Oh, that's great, Doc. And Pam is out of the woods now, too, right?"

"Well, not quite, Irish. But her chances have improved by one hundred percent since this time last night. God must have answered your prayers, for to tell you the truth, I didn't think she had a chance of surviving. Your decision to put her on the dialysis machine turned the tide for her, Irish. I was afraid the shock to her system would be too much for her. But, as it turned out, it saved her life."

"Oh, thanks, Doc. When can we see her?"

"She is still unconscious, Irish, but perhaps you will be able to visit her tomorrow evening for a few minutes. I'm sure she'll be awake by then. Why don't you all go home and get a good night's rest before I have to admit you, too."

"Okay, Doc, thanks again. Look, Helen, why don't you take Mr. and Mrs. Taylor home. I'll just lay down here on the couch and catch a few hours' sleep."

"Oh, Irish, why don't you come with us?"

"Please, Mrs. Taylor. I'll be better off here."

"All right, Irish. Are you sure you'll be all right? Do you want me to stay with you?"

"I'll be fine, now, Mrs. Taylor, and Pam is going to pull through. Don't you worry. I have it straight from the Man himself. He reassured me in the Chapel this evening, as I was praying my rosary, that all was well with the O'Malley family. I took that to mean that Pam will be fully recovered in no time at all. So you run along now and rest assured that the crisis has passed. It's simply the recovery process we have to go through now."

She put her arms around me and I began to cry on her shoulder. I regained my composure and gave her a kiss on the cheek and thanked her, Mr. Taylor, and Helen for being so kind and supportive. "I couldn't have made it without you three by my side. Now run along and get a good night's sleep."

"All right, Irish, and you try to get some sleep yourself. I'll bring you a change of clothes in the morning."

After they departed, I lay down on the couch comforted by the thought that Pam was going to survive and be all right. I drifted into a deep, deep sleep. I was awakened the following morning by the touch of Mrs. Taylor's tender hand on my face. As I opened my eyes, I could see her beautiful face beaming at me, with Mr. Taylor standing beside her.

I instinctively smiled back at them and asked if there was any further word on Pam this morning.

"Yes, Irish. We just spoke to the intern who told us she spent a very restful night, and that her vital signs are back to normal. Barring any further complication she should be coming around this morning."

"Thank God. Our prayers have been answered. Have you had a chance to check on George and Paula this morning?"

"Yes, they're doing just great."

"Have they gained any weight? When will Pam be able to see them? You know, she is going to be so anxious to hold them. She's been like a child in wild anticipation waiting for them to be born. I just hope we can restrain her. Poor little darling never knew what hit her, and I'm sure when she wakes she is going to have a million and one questions that will have to be answered on the spot."

"When she awakens, Irish, we'll reassure her that everything is just fine."

"I would like you to be with her when she first wakes up, Mrs. Taylor. I'm sure you can comfort her better than anyone else on this earth. She might get the impression that I was trying to protect her and not tell her everything if I spoke to her first. She has undying faith and trust in you and knows you could never lie to her under any circumstances. I think it's important she suffer not even a moment of anxiety, don't you?"

"Yes, I do, Irish, and I thank you for your faith and trust in me also. I'll be only too happy to be with Pam when she wakes.

Listen, Mr. Taylor has a change of clothes for you and your shaving things. There is a shower down the hall if you would like to get cleaned up."

"I sure would. I must look awful and I wouldn't want to frighten Pam when I see her. Tell you what I'll do. I feel so good this morning that as soon as I get cleaned up, I'll buy breakfast for you two. How does that sound?"

"Great, Irish. Now you run along and we'll wait for you here."

After I showered and shaved, I felt like a new man. I rejoined the Taylors and before we went to the cafeteria for breakfast, we left word at the nurses' station where we would be in case Pam regained consciousness.

Over breakfast we talked about how surprised Pam was going to be when she found out she had given birth to twins. We speculated on how she was going to manage with two of them to look after. The smiles had returned to our faces as we discussed the future, and all the fear and apprehension was gone from our voices. We were all certain at this point that the crisis had passed and it was just a matter of time now until things were back to normal. Of course, none of us knew what normal would be with twins. Although it was never mentioned, we all knew that as little as they were, they would be dictating our comings and goings from now on and that our lives would be centered around them. It was a good feeling, though. It was as if all of us could hardly wait to get them home and start caring for them ourselves.

Helen and her husband, John, joined us there in the cafeteria. Helen had cleared through the hospital that she could look after Pam and keep an eye on the babies. We talked for a few minutes and then made our way back to the waiting room, stopping by the nursery to check on our new arrivals. They were doing just fine, picking up weight and really starting to take on their own personalities. There was no doubt about it. They were both going to have blond, curly hair and be just as good-looking as their mother.

Our next stop was at the nurses' station where we checked on

Pam. She still hadn't come around. With the doctor's permission, Mrs. Taylor joined Helen at her bedside to keep the vigil while Mr. Taylor and I returned to the waiting room. John asked if there was anything he could do. We assured him everything that could possibly be done was being done and it was just a matter of waiting now. "Well, if you're sure there is nothing I can do, I may as well go on to work then, but I'll stop back this afternoon."

"Thanks, John. We really appreciate your concern, but everything is under control, especially now that your dear wife is on the job. We have every reason to believe everything will be fine, so you run along now. We'll see you later."

After John was gone, I asked Mr. Taylor if it would be possible to have Mr. Jacobs bring the papers over to the hospital so that we could transfer ownership back to him.

"Oh, Irish, don't worry about such things now. There will be plenty of time to do all that later."

"I know, Mr. Taylor, but the thought of all that money and power scares the hell out of me and makes me very uncomfortable. The sooner you're back at the helm the better I'll feel."

He put his hand on my shoulder and confided, "Sometimes it scares the hell out of me, also, Irish. But I'm sure under the new arrangements things will be a whole lot better for all of us."

We sat there and bullshitted for the next three hours. I filled him in on all of our exploits. He was simply fascinated to hear how we backed Southern into a corner and eliminated all their counterproposals and how we were able to close the final deal without a word of dissent. He was truly amazed.

Finally Mrs. Taylor came in with the news we had been waiting so long for. Pam was awake and asking for us. Without a word we raced to Pam's bedside. The doctors and nurses were busy removing the life-support systems from her, saying she no longer needed them. They told us her progress to this point was no less than a miracle. We stood patiently by and as soon as they were through, I walked up to the head of the bed and ever so gently leaned into Pam's outstretched arms. "Oh, love, you're going to be just fine. And did your mother tell you about the beautiful babies you gave birth to?"

"Yes, Irish, but I already knew it."

"You did?" I asked, in utter amazement.

"It's difficult to explain, Irish. I died on the operating table and actually left my body. I was hovering above the operating table and watched the whole procedure. They're beautiful babies, Irish, and they will make us all very happy."

"Oh, Pam, darling, I never doubted for a moment that there was a God and your experience only goes to strengthen that belief."

"Oh, there is so much more I have to tell you, Irish. I can't find the words to describe the feelings of comfort and love that I experienced."

"There will be plenty of time, darling. Right now, let's just concentrate on getting you well again. Okay?"

"Okay, Irish. Just one thing though. I agree wholeheartedly with your names for our children. George and Paula O'Malley sound great to me."

The doctor tapped me on the shoulder and told me he thought it best to let her rest now. I reluctantly agreed and told Pam we would be right outside the door if she wanted us. I kissed her and said, "Thank you for our beautiful son and daughter, honey."

She smiled and said, "I'm charged with making you happy and raising our children, so don't worry about a thing, Irish. All is well with the world today."

Mr. and Mrs. Taylor and I walked out into the hall. Mr. and Mrs. Taylor looked at me in astonishment. "Irish, I never mentioned a word about calling your son 'George.' How do you suppose she knew? And what is even more amazing is what she was saying about watching the operation while out of her body."

"It's true, Mrs. Taylor. Death is not the end, but only the beginning of something warm and beautiful. I know, because I've gone through a similar experience but have been reluctant to talk about it for fear people would think I was crazy or was having hallucinations. But let me assure you that what Pam experienced was very real. There are no words on this earth to describe what happens or the feeling you get—the peace and tranquillity, the warmth and the love. All I can tell you is that there is a God, and he has given us all a purpose in this life. We will not die until that purpose has been fulfilled. The only problem I encountered with my experience is that I became perplexed. I became anxious to leave this life, knowing what was on the other side, and at the same time felt I was obligated to stay and fulfill my purpose in life."

"When did you experience this phenomena, Irish?"

"When I had malaria overseas. That was before I ever knew Pam even existed. Since then I have felt many, many times that marrying Pam and raising a family was what God had intended for me in this life. When it's over, I'll go willingly and with great expectations. I have absolutely no fear at all of dying. If God had chosen to take Pam from us, I would have had great difficulty understanding his reasoning; but with faith and time, I'm sure I would have been able to accept it as his will."

"Oh, Irish, how beautiful! I've never heard an expression of faith to even come close to that. I know now why you look at life as you do; why wealth and power mean nothing to you. If Mr. Taylor and I could only firmly believe what you're telling us, Irish."

"You can, Mrs. Taylor. If you ever have any doubt in your mind, just think of your daughter and your grandchildren and remember this day."

Helen came out into the hall and told us Pam was sleeping restfully. She suggested that we go have lunch and she would stay with Pam. We agreed and were feeling so relieved we ventured out of the hospital and across the street to a nice little restaurant for lunch. The Taylors were fascinated by what Pam had told them and kept pressing me for more details of my experience with this phenomenon.

I tried to explain as best I could, but there are really no words in the English language to describe the surrealistic feeling and the surroundings. I began, "I am only able to reconstruct the time elements from conversations with Moose, my buddy, while we were in the hospital in Japan. The experience happened after we were there for about a week. I had been running a temperature of up to 105° F all that time and was unconscious. Then, all of a sudden I was awake, but I wasn't in my body. I was hovering over the bed close to the ceiling looking down while my body was burning up with fever. I could see Moose sitting next to the bed with tears in his eyes, cussing a blue streak and begging me to come to. I remember asking myself, 'Why is Moose so concerned about me? I'm perfectly fine and have never felt better in my life.'

I then started to hear loud buzzing sounds and wondered what they were. They subsided and were replaced by a loud bell, like a fire bell. The ringing was really intense in volume and then there was a long dark tunnel. I remember traveling through it at a terrific rate of speed. I wasn't frightened by this and could see a light at the end of the tunnel. The further into the tunnel I got, the faster I would go and the brighter the light became, until I was suddenly out of the tunnel and facing this brilliant light. It didn't hurt my eyes, and I could look directly into it. It was almost transparent and had no physical shape to it. It was like a cloud of brillant white smoke that was communicating with me. It wouldn't speak words to me, and I didn't speak to it; it was more of a thought transfer. And yet there was no mistaking what it was telling me, and it knew exactly what my responses were, although I never uttered a sound."

"Like I said, there was never a word exchanged between us, but for the purposes of an explanation, I'll convert our thoughts, into words. Can you understand any of this so far?"

"Please go on, Irish. I'm sure when you've told us the complete story, we'll understand perfectly."

"Well, this image, we'll call it, asked me what I had done with my life that I wanted to talk about. I was completely at a loss, although I wasn't frightened in the least. There was such an aura of love of affection emanating from this image that I wanted to get closer and become consumed by it. It was such a magnificent feeling; there are no words to describe it."

"Then the image said, 'Come with me; I want to show you something.' We went a little further and I saw my whole life in sequence, like slides on a projector, only the scenes were very real and went all the way back to the first things I could remember in life. Even when some bad things would come up, the image didn't give the impression of scorn or contempt but simply left me wondering, 'was it worth it?' The whole process only took a matter of a few seconds, but I can remember it now just as vividly as if it had happened yesterday. Even now, to describe the highlights of what I saw would probably take an hour or more, but in that few seconds I could see and comprehend every last detail of what I saw."

"The image directed my attention to a valley of lush green grass with a beautiful river flowing through it. I could see my brother and my father. Although I had never laid eyes on him while on this earth, I knew immediately it was my father. I also saw a lot of guys I knew who had been killed in the Korean war. It was as if they were transparent, yet they were exactly the same as you and me. Somehow the image conveyed to me that someday I would return to that valley and cross that river, but not just yet. I only knew that I had to be patient and wait a little while longer."

"I remember pleading for permission to stay, but the image assured me that it would return for me later, and that I must go back now. Within an instant the image disappeared and I felt myself being sucked back through this long black tunnel and ended up in my body, which was still lying there on the bed. From what I could gather from Moose, the doctor told him I was gone and had even pulled the sheet up over my face. As soon as the doctor left the room, Moose pulled the sheet down, grabbed my arms, and began shaking me, demanding that I wake up. According to Moose, I started breathing again, and I regained consciousness the following day. That's the whole story as best as I can relate it to you. Like I told you, it's almost impossible to believe, and there are no words to describe the beauty and serenity of the experience. But, believe me, it happened, just as surely as we're all sitting here right now."

"Oh, Irish, I do believe you, especially after what we just experienced with Pam. And I can see why you were so reluctant to tell anyone about it. It's not the sort of thing people would readily accept, and you would only subject yourself to ridicule or scorn from people. People are so skeptical and so unwilling to believe in things their minds cannot comprehend or understand."

Mr. Taylor said, "It will be interesting to hear what Pam experienced and how it compares to what happened to you, Irish."

"Look," I decided, "just so there are no doubts or misunderstandings, tell you what we'll do. You two are the first people I have ever breathed a word of this experience to. When we visit Pam this afternoon, we'll encourage her to talk about her experience and see how it compares. Okay?"

"Sure, Irish, but we don't need any further proof. We believe you."

"I know you do. But it's as much for me as it is for you. Even though there is no doubt in my mind that it happened to me, it will strengthen my convictions and eliminate the possibility of any future doubts from my mind. Is it a deal?"

"Of course, Irish. Just one thing has me curious, though, and I hope you don't mind my prying like this. I'm thoroughly fascinated, and you're the first person I've ever met who could describe an experience like this. I've read about people experiencing unexplained phenomena in their lives, like their lives flashing before their eyes and the like, but I've never met anyone who could give such a vivid recollection."

"I understand, Mrs. Taylor. You can ask me anything you like, and I'll answer as best I can."

"Well, didn't this image give you any indication of what your purpose in life would be or give you any hint or impression as to how long you would be here?"

"As best I can describe my impressions, Mrs. Taylor, there was nothing to imply a specific purpose in life or absolutely no indication of how long I would live. My impressions were of a more general nature. In other words, I was not charged with getting married and raising X number of children to start a holy crusade. No, nothing quite so specific. Instead, I was left with the impression that my work on earth was not finished and that as the tasks presented themselves I would know what to do and would do it. The image conveyed to me that I must help people and perhaps make them laugh—anything to help ease their burden and make life more bearable for them. Even though I was forbidden at that time to enter the lush green valley and cross that beautiful river, I was left with the impression that we are living in hell by comparison to what awaits us in the hereafter. To try to sum it all up, Mrs. Taylor, I would probably say I came away with a new love and understanding of my fellow human beings: Of their needs, and not their wants, because there is a vast difference between what we need and what we want. Does that help you to understand any better what I'm trying to say?"

Mr. Taylor said, "It certainly does, Irish. It explains a lot of things for me personally. For instance, I could never understand how you could be so compassionate to Mr. Roth when he was trying to do you in. You didn't hate him; you only hated what he was trying to do. Then, a little closer to home, you hated what I was doing—being in the defense contracting business and all the crooked dealing I was involved in; but you didn't let it interfere with what you thought of me personally, or at least, that is the impression you gave me. I could never understand your rationale before, but I do now."

"Well, thank you, Mr. Taylor, and I'm glad you understand. There was no way I could have told you that. You would have had every right in the world to tell me to go to hell and mind my own business. By every standard we use to judge things in this world, you would have been perfectly justified in doing so. Another thought just came to mind, Mr. Taylor. You've been given a second chance, also. Perhaps not as dramatic as Pam's or my experiences, but a second chance, just the same."

"What do you mean, Irish?"

"Well, now that all your fortunes are wrapped up in one neat, little bundle in the Taylor Foundation, you're in a position to use your wealth and influence for the good of the multitudes, and not just to make yourself and a few others rich. Let me explain. The very nature of a foundation is primarily as a tax shelter, correct?"

"That's right, Irish."

"Well, that's what Jerry, Mr. Jacobs, and I had in mind when we channeled all the proceeds from the sales and what have you into the foundation fund you had set up to take care of your pet charities. Simply a tax shelter, so we would not have to give Uncle Sam ninety percent of the proceeds. This was all we had in mind. However, now that we can look at it from a different angle, perhaps it was intended to be that way from the beginning."

"I don't quite follow you, Irish."

"Well, now that the Taylor Foundation is established, the only way you can keep your tax-exempt status is by making contributions to universities, charitable organizations, research, and so forth. Just think of the tremendous amount of good you can do with your money now. You're in a position to do things that will help millions of people by financing research to help eliminate cancer or providing funds for a multitude of other problems that need solving. The beautiful part is that you can do all this without having to even touch the principal. As close as we can figure—and our figures are conservative, I'm sure—with the interest, bonds, and dividends, you'll be showing a net increase yearly of over ninety million dollars. That will buy an awful lot of research, or finance a lot of summer camps for city kids, or perhaps even build a hospital or two. The beautiful part is that it will be self-perpetuating and the good deeds you can do will go on long after you have gone to your final reward. You have an opportunity to become one of the greatest philanthropists of all times, Mr. Taylor. How does that make you feel?"

He was really at a loss for words and looked stunned. He finally said, "I don't know what to say, Irish. This is the first time I can remember when I've been at a loss for words. I feel very complacent. Let's give this notion of me as a philanthropist some time to sink into this thick skull of mine."

"Surely, Mr. Taylor. Do you think we should be getting back to the hospital now? I can hardly wait to hear of Pam's experience. If I could only love that girl more; but I swear, I don't know how."

"Oh, Irish, you have enough love in your heart for the whole world, and I'm sure no girl was ever loved more than you love Pam. Mrs. Taylor and I feel very fortunate, indeed, that you and Pam found each other, for we are really the biggest benefactors of your love."

They had moved Pam from the recovery room to her private room by the time we got back, eliminating what they figured would be a long time in the intensive care unit. We walked in and were greeted by Helen, who asked us what we thought of the remarkable recovery being made by our little sweetheart.

We smiled, and Mrs. Taylor said, "We were not surprised that anyone with so much love in her heart was doing so well." We stood there admiring the radiant glow on her face as she lay sleeping. It was still hard to imagine that I was married to such a beautiful princess.

It wasn't long before Pam was awake and bubbling over with love and good cheer. She just kept talking incessantly. I told her to slow down because we were having trouble keeping up with her. We talked for another twenty minutes and then I asked her to tell us more about her surrealistic experience.

Her face took on a special glow as she recalled it. "I hope I can find the words to describe it. I know I was not dreaming or hallucinating. It was very real, and I just ask you to believe me, for it really and truly happened to me."

"We'll believe you, darling, but you did leave us up in the air. Naturally, we are a little bewildered and are wondering if you are feeling well enough to fill us in on the details."

"Well, all right, I'll do my best. But I'm sure I won't even come close to describing the actual experience for there is nothing that I know of to compare it with. I remember regaining consciousness on the operating table and thinking, 'I'm going to die. Oh, poor Irish, how will he ever manage with the baby.' I then started drifting right out of my body and took up a position close to the ceiling. I had no particular thoughts at this time. I remember watching the delivery of the twins and thinking how precious they were, and how happy Irish would be when he saw them. I then saw a whole flurry of activity around the table. My heart had stopped and they were trying to revive me. Everything suddenly went dark. It was so dark you could see absolutely nothing. I wasn't scared, simply curious as to why it suddenly got so dark. I began to move, slowly at first and then very rapidly."

Mrs. Taylor asked her if she was frightened by this experience.

"Oh, no. I had absolutely no fear at all. I felt I was traveling faster than the speed of light, and then suddenly the darkness ended and I saw a brilliant light. It was so beautiful, so bright, so warm, and so loving. I felt compelled to get closer to it; the closer I would move the better I felt. I can't describe the sensation I experienced. All I can say is that it was simply heavenly. Perhaps I shouldn't be telling you all this; you'll think it's just hallucinations I was having."

"Oh, no, honey, I implore you to go on talking about it. Please tell us what happened then."

"Well, Irish, it's kind of weird. We talked—and yet we didn't talk like you and I are talking. This beautiful light seemed to know what I was thinking and I knew what it was telling me, even though we never uttered a sound to each other."

"Did it have any particular shape to it? What did it tell you?"

"Well, it had no physical shape that I could detect, although I had the feeling it was a man and his shape was obscured by the brilliance emanating from his body. He asked me if I thought I had completed my life's work. I remember thinking, 'No, I have those new babies and Irish to look after. They need me, and I can't go just now.' He knew exactly what I was thinking and told me not to be afraid. He told me he would permit me to return and would come for me later. He was gone just that quickly and then I felt a superhuman force drawing me back through the darkness and back into my body. Oh, Irish, Mother, Daddy, Helen! Please don't dismiss what I just told you as hallucinations or dreams. It was real, very, very real and it actually happened to me."

"We know it did, sweetheart, and we believe you. Every word you spoke is the truth. Would it surprise you to know I had a similar experience when I had malaria and was in the hospital over in Japan? I had just related that experience to your mother and father over lunch and the similarities are so striking that there can be no doubt in our minds, honey, that what you experienced was real."

"Irish, why didn't you ever tell me about it?"

"For the same reason you were reluctant to talk about it. First of all, there were no words to describe it, and secondly, for fear it would be dismissed as just a dream or some other trick the mind plays on you at times like that. Like your mother pointed out, people are not willing to accept things they cannot understand or have no firsthand knowledge of, so there is no need to subject ourselves to ridicule and scorn by making these experiences public knowledge. As long as we know, and we all believe, this is what is important. Right, Mrs. Taylor?"

"Right you are, Irish, and your experiences are so much alike that there can never be any doubt that they were real."

"Hold me, Irish, please hold me." I took her in my arms and held her as tightly as I possibly could. "I love you, darling, and I'll never be afraid again as long as I live." "That's good, honey. Perhaps God was just testing us to make sure we were worthy of raising George and Paula. They're pretty special kids, you know."

"Oh, with such a wonderful daddy they're also the luckiest kids in the world. When do you suppose I will be able to hold them in my arms and shower them with my love and affection?"

"Perhaps Helen could answer that for us. What do you think, Helen?"

"Well, I can't say for sure, but they are coming along so well that it shouldn't be much longer."

"Oh, I hope not."

"You just relax, honey, and time will pass quickly now that you're making such a remarkable recovery. In no time at all we'll all be at home enjoying our newfound loves together."

"Oh, thank you, Irish, just for being your sweet, wonderful self and for loving me like you do."

"I can only love in proportion to how you love me, darling, and my cup runneth over again and again."

"Irish, I keep telling you not to fill it so full." She started to laugh and clutched her stomach. I asked if she was all right. She answered, "Yes, but I'll have to try not to laugh for a while."

"Okay, love, we'll keep the jokes to a minimum. Is there anything we can get for you or do for you, honey, to make you more comfortable?"

"No, not a thing right now. Just having you all here is all I need at the moment."

"Well, we'll be here for the duration, sweetheart. You can make book on that."

"Make a book? What do you mean, Irish?"

"You can bet on it."

Just as I promised Pam, the next five days went by swiftly and the twins were out of their incubators now and ready to meet their parents face to face. We were all standing around the bed, waiting for Helen and another nurse to return with them, and the anticipation had reached a state of intense and eager expectation. The moment arrived with Helen making a grand entrance with little Paula, followed closely by the other nurse carrying little George.

Pam was all propped up and had tears streaming from her eyes as she reached for her first precious bundle of joy. Mrs. Taylor reached for little George and was as excited as if she had given birth to him herself. Mr. Taylor and I stepped to the foot of the bed and watched with joyous hearts while Pam and her mother inspected the new arrivals from head to foot, commenting on how beautiful and well-developed they were. There was absolutely no descriptive adjective in the dictionary that they didn't use in their praise of the babies. After several minutes of savoring their new loves they chanced to remember Mr. Taylor and me at the foot of the bed. They apologized for not sharing with us and asked us if we would like to hold them.

Mr. Taylor took George from Mrs. Taylor, and I ever so cautiously took Paula from Pam's arms. I was bombarding Pam and Mrs. Taylor with questions on how to hold her and what I was to do once I held her in my arms.

They assured me she was not all that fragile and would be content if I held her to my shoulder and got acquainted with her. She was so tiny and precious. I was overwhelmed as I pressed her gently to my shoulder, holding her with as much care as if I had the crown jewels of England in my arms. Through my tears I could see how happy and pleased Pam was and how anxious she was to get her back. Mr. Taylor handed little George to her and said, "Thank you for the beautiful grandson, honey." She smiled and started making baby talk to him while I handed Paula to him, asking him what he thought of his new granddaughter.

"I've never been happier in my life, Irish." Poor Mrs. Taylor was so overcome by this extraordinary occasion that she had to sit down and try to regain her composure. I asked Pam if I might hold little George just for a few seconds.

"Sure, Irish," she said as I reached for him. While I held him, I told him a story. "Now, little George, let me clue you in about your mother and your grandparents. You're the luckiest guy ever to be born and smart as a whip, too. Just think, of all the parents and grandparents on this earth, you and your beautiful sister chose the most precious mommy and grandparents in the world. Of course, I must warn you and your sister. They will be your uncompromising taskmasters and your quiet inspiration. And best of all, they will love you always. So will I, son. You know, I was a pretty lucky guy myself. Your mommy could have had any guy on this earth she wanted, and she chose me. In the bargain, she threw in her wonderful mother and father. Now that you and your sister have joined the family, we are all going to be very, very happy for the rest of our lives."

While we were oohing and aahing over our beautiful babies, in came the doctor making his rounds. I asked him point-blank if the twins were strong enough to come home. "Yes, they are,

Irish. They are perfect in every respect and can be discharged any time now."

"Good, and Pam has recovered to the point where she can come home with them, Doc."

"Wait a minute, Irish. Not so fast. I want to keep Pam for a few more days. Perhaps you don't realize that we almost lost her on the operating table. It takes a while to get over what she has been through. I absolutely forbid it."

"Well, you are going to have to reconsider, Doc. I hate going over your head, but we have it from the highest authority that Pam is going to be perfectly all right, and we want her discharged this afternoon at the latest."

Mrs. Taylor expressed concern. "Do you think that's wise, Irish? I mean, the doctor has handled many cases like Pam's and you wouldn't want to take any chances, would you?"

"There is absolutely no risk involved, Mrs. Taylor, especially with you and Helen looking after her. Besides that, Mrs. Taylor, with the babies at home, how do you suppose that would affect Pam? No, I'm sure it's the right thing to do. Don't you agree, Pam?"

"Mother, I can't stay here with my little angels at home. Irish is right. I want to come home today."

"Okay, then, it's all settled, and if it will make you feel any better, Doc, we'll take her home in an ambulance so you won't have to worry about her pulling her incisions or anything."

"Well, of course, I can't force you to stay, Pam. And if that's what you want, I'll discharge you this afternoon, providing they take you home in an ambulance and you stay off your feet for a few more days anyway."

I clapped my hands in glee. "Thanks, Doc. Now, if you'll get the papers in order, I'll call for a private ambulance to be here at one this afternoon." He just shook his head and walked out of the room.

Pam was jubilant and threw her free arm around me as I leaned over to kiss her. "I couldn't be so cruel as to leave you here and take the babies home, honey. You'll have to pay close attention to your mother and Helen, though."

"Oh, Irish, I love you, and I'll do whatever you tell me to. My heart jumped up in my throat when he said he would discharge the babies and keep me here."

"I know, honey, and we're not taking any chances either. What the Doc doesn't know is that we have some divine help, and I'm sure we're doing the right thing."

Helen and the other nurse finally persuaded us to give up the babies so they could return them to the nursery for their bottles and get them ready for the trip home.

"Oh, my God, Mrs. Taylor; we have to find another crib real quick. I've been so preoccupied I never gave it a thought."

She laughed at me and said, "Settle down, Irish. We have a nursery all set up with accommodations for both Paula and George."

"At your house?"

"Of course, Irish, and we ordered another crib for your place also."

"Oh, my goodness, Mrs. Taylor. You never cease to amaze me. As worried and busy as you've been this past week, you still found time to do all that? It's no wonder Pam and I love you like we do. I took special notice of how Paula and George cuddled up to you also. Little as they are, they know when they're loved."

"Thank you, Irish. Now, you had better go call for that ambulance, don't you think?"

"You bet, my dear, sweet, precious Mrs. Taylor. I'll be back before you know I've been gone."

28

Pam and the Twins Come Home

The trip to the Taylors' house came off beautifully. Mrs. Taylor had really outdone herself in furnishing the nursery and making all the preparations for the arrival of the newborns. There was such a feeling of love and contentment in the air that I wished out loud that it would last forever.

After Pam was settled in bed with Mrs. Taylor, Helen, and me hovering around her, anticipating her every need, I commented that it was my turn to take just as good care of her as she did of me when I was laid up, and I intended to be at her bedside until she was completely recovered. She thanked me for being so loving and caring. She asked for her babies and Mrs. Taylor and Helen went to get them. When they returned, they put one in either arm for her. She looked just like an angel there, with those two snuggled into her.

"Oh, Irish, Mother, Helen, if I could just find the words to tell you how I feel at this moment. I have never experienced such a warm, loving and tender moment as this." I told her it was motherly love that she was experiencing, and to savor every luscious moment of it, for that's exactly how God intended it to be. "Thank you, Irish, for allowing me to come home today with my little angels. I don't think I could have taken being left behind in that hospital."

"We know, honey, and we'll take every bit as good care of you here as they did in the hospital. Love is all you need right now, and you'll be up and back to your vibrant and vivacious self in no time at all. You just take advantage of this opportunity to rest now, for I have a feeling George and Paula are going to keep us very busy from now on."

"Oh, I know, Irish, and won't it be fun watching them grow and teaching them to walk and to talk?"

"Right, honey, and it will be a great opportunity for me to tell them all my old stories."

"I'll bet you will, too, won't you, Irish?"

"Well, maybe just a few."

Helen left for a moment and returned with their bottles. "It's time for the youngsters to be fed. Do you want to feed one of them, Irish?"

"Oh, my goodness. Maybe I had better observe this time. You know, so I can get the hang of it. I wouldn't know where to start."

"Okay, you big chicken, you!" cried Mrs. Taylor. "Let me have George, Pam, and I'll show Irish how it's done." She sat down with George and stuck the nipple in his mouth. He took it from there and was really sucking it up. I watched with utter amazement, as Paula was doing the same for Pam. I kept alternating my gaze between Pam and her mother. I began to ask pointed questions. "How do they know what to do? No one told them, I'm sure. And how do you know when they have had enough since they can't tell you?"

They laughed at me and said, "You'll learn soon enough, Irish."

Helen commented, "All you have to remember, Irish, is to keep one end full and the other end dry. Then, you'll have perfectly happy and contented babies."

Maggie came in with a tray of coffee and cakes. "Hi, Maggie, what do you think of our sweet little Miss Pam giving us twins?"

"Oh, Mr. Irish, I couldn't be happier for all of us. There is so much love and happiness in this house, I wouldn't take a job for a million dollars if it meant I had to leave here."

"Well, thank you, Maggie. I'm even learning how to feed them now."

"You are? Then, why aren't you holding one of them and doing the feeding now?"

"Well, I'm observing this time. Perhaps the next time I'll get the hang of it. They're so tiny and all, you know."

Mrs. Taylor told me to sit down, which I did, and she handed George to me. After I had him securely in my arms, she held the bottle out for me.

"I need a third hand, Mrs. Taylor. I'm afraid to let go of him."

"Just cuddle him in your left arm and reach for the bottle with your right hand." I did, and then asked what to do next.

"Just put the nipple in his mouth, and he'll take it from there." I did, and sure enough, he dug right in. They were all laughing and smiling at me while I commented with fatherly pride that my son was a fast learner.After George finished his bottle, I asked, "What do I do now?"

"Burp him, Irish."

"I beg your pardon?"

Mrs. Taylor took the bottle from me and told me to put him on my shoulder and pat his little back until he burped.

I laughed in disbelief. "You have got to be kidding!"

"Just watch how Pam does it."

She held little Paula up to her shoulder and patted her lightly on the back. I followed suit and did the same with George. George let out a belch. I commented, "Not bad manners, just good whiskey. Right, George?"

I felt his bottom and it was wet. "Quick, Mrs. Taylor, we'll have to send George back. He leaks."

They all laughed at me. Helen took him and asked me if I would like to learn how to change a diaper. 'This should be good," I said, as I followed her into the nursery. She changed him in nothing flat and handed him back to me. We returned to Pam's bedside and I said, "See there, nothing to it."

"You changed him, Irish?"

"Well, no, but I observed, and there is nothing to it."

"Well good then. I believe your daughter is in dire need of a change, also."

"Helen, Mrs. Taylor, she's picking on me."

"Fight your own battles, Irish," they hollered at me.

I traded Georgie for little Paula and headed for the nursery. I stood there by the table wondering what to do next when I looked over my shoulder and spied Mrs. Taylor and Helen observing me from the doorway.

"Okay, you got me. Perhaps I had better observe another time or two before I solo." They laughed and came to my rescue. After they changed her, I reached for her and marched right back to Pam and said, "See there, you didn't think I could do it, did you?"

"Well, no, Irish."

"Well, I didn't; your mother did."

She smiled her loving smile and said, "That's woman's work anyway, honey, so don't worry about it."

"Oh, no, I want to learn, so I can help you. It's just that they're so little now, and I'm afraid of hurting them."

I asked her how she was feeling now and she confessed she was a little tired. Helen and Mrs. Taylor took the babies from us, saying it was time for their nap. They returned after putting the babies in their bassinets and urged Pam to try to take a nap herself. I promised I would stay right there by her side until she woke up.

"Oh, Irish, I love you, and I thank you for being so good to me. Mother told me you never left the hospital the whole time I was in there, so why don't you take a nice long walk, or go for a swim or something while I'm sleeping."

"It's all right, honey. I love being with you and there will be plenty of time for walking and swimming as soon as you're up and around. So you just try to get some rest now and stop worrying about me, okay?"

"Okay, Irish." She closed her eyes and after a few minutes drifted off to sleep.

Life was really beautiful for the next six months. Pam fully recovered within two weeks, and we were back in our little Cape Cod house within a month. Of course, it took a lot of gentle persuasion to convince Mrs. Taylor to let us go. If she had had her way, we would have been there until the twins were grown up and married. She finally agreed that it would be the best thing to do and made us promise never to hire a babysitter. She considered that her sole responsibility and wouldn't hear of anyone else staying with Paula and George.

I finally cornered Mr. Taylor and got all the papers signed and got him reinstated as captain of the ship—the Taylor Foundation. Mr. Jacobs suggested that I retain ownership of the Taylor Industries until all the final audits were completed and government bureaucrats were satisfied that everything was on the up-and-up. We encountered a few minor waves from the SEC and IRS, but Mr. Jacobs and his battery of lawyers, along with Jerry's help, were able to handle them without too much difficulty. We had settled all our lawsuits out of court and there was very little for me to do except be there and let Taylor Industries die a slow and peaceful death.

We couldn't talk Jerry into going to work for us full-time, but did manage to have him sign us on as one of his accounts. We were lucky enough to hire the whiz kid Jerry had introduced us to, the one who had helped us set up the Taylor Foundation. Mr. Taylor was really impressed with him. He was an expert at manipulating the stocks and bonds to our best advantage. We were making money faster than we could count it. Also, all of this took the pressure off Mr. Taylor, so that he could devote most of his time to his philanthropic activities. He was really a changed man. We were able to convince his old secretary to come to work at the Taylor Foundation and he explained to her why it had been for the best that I had acted as I did. After all, she knew of all the shady deals and all the corruption and would have felt obligated to try to protect Mr. Taylor at all costs. And that would have only hindered our plans to dismantle the Taylor Industries.

I kept Janice on as my secretary. She was really doing exceptionally well in all areas. She had a boyfriend now, and things were looking like wedding bells might be in her future. She was extremely happy.

The twins were growing by leaps and bounds. Needless to say, their grandparents were spoiling them rotten, but we didn't mind, really. They brought so much joy and contentment into all of our lives that they could do no wrong. Even Mr. Taylor was completely taken by them. He would get right down on the living room rug and play with them, making faces and doing his darnedest to get them to laugh for him. He would greet each new success with "Did you see that? Look how bright they are. I think they are trying to talk to me." I'm sure Mr. and Mrs. Taylor loved the twins every bit as much as Pam and I did. It was as if we had found a utopia and everything and everyone was there to add to our enjoyment of life.

Pam and I were well into our second year of marriage by now, and our love just seemed to keep growing. We were sitting in the living room over at the Taylors' one evening, talking to Mrs. Taylor, when she commented on our love for one another.

"You know," she said, "usually after the first few months of marriage, people more or less tend to take one another for granted, but that is not the case with you and Pam. It is really remarkable how loving and caring you two are for one another. Little things that Irish does for you, like opening the car door, holding your chair until you sit down, or touching your hair when he passes you; all the courtesies that go with a courtship have carried over into your marriage, and I think it's simply beautiful the marvelous rapport you two have."

"Well, Mrs. Taylor, at the start we had a lot of good times together, and they helped us to endure the inevitable disillusionments and disappointments that you have in any long-term relationship. First we lost Moose and Carol. Then we had to overcome all the objections to our relationship because we were from two different worlds. Then, of course, I had to report back to the army and almost lost my life and had given up on life itself. Add to that the long, long process of getting me over my paralysis. It has been a growing experience for both of us, combining a bit of mystery, a lot of intensity and enjoyment, a good

540

measure of determination to overcome the rough spots, plus a willingness to laugh off the setbacks that you find when you are very close to someone whom you love very dearly. Is it any wonder our love grows day by day?"

"I would also like to add, Mrs. Taylor, that in no small way are you responsible for our relationship being what it is. You have helped us to grow, have given us a broader perspective, and have made us feel good because you love us. That really makes a difference. We feel you are the one person we can talk to, who we can tell everything to and feel confident that we will be listened to. And even if we are terribly unreasonable, it's all right. You help us to see things from a different point of view."

"Our love allows for differences from what might be considered the norm. One of them being the tender love affair of you and me, Mrs. Taylor. Pam and I have experienced it in a loving way. We were both totally blind to its real benefits at first, but in our evolving love for one another, we have been able to identify and realize that your love for me and my love for you has helped us understand and love one another even more. It's not only okay; it's beautiful."

"Because we have you and Mr. Taylor to help us work things out and to have good times with, we have a certain optimism about life. Your love adds to our enjoyment and trust of other people and helps us in developing other relationships. Having you and Mr. Taylor to love us and look after us is a nurturing experience that allows us to go forth and face life courageously."

"To sum up my love for my very dear wife here, let me just say this. God grant if I'm allowed to carry one possession from this earth, it is the memory of my love for her. And let me say, I love you both very dearly, and you have both been my bridge over troubled waters many, many times. Thank you and I love you."

I put my arms around Pam and kissed her tenderly. She looked longingly into my eyes and said, "I love you, Irish." We looked over at Mrs. Taylor, who had a tear in her eye. I went to her and knelt beside her chair. "Gee, I'm sorry, Mrs. Taylor, I'm always making you cry." She put her arms around me and kissed me on top of the head and said, "Don't ever stop, Irish. They are tears of joy."

Even the babies playing on the floor seemed to approve and showed their approval by laughing out loud for us. I crawled over to them on my hands and knees, rolled over on my back, and held Paula up in the air while making baby talk to her. George wanted to be included and crawled up on my stomach and began jabbering away. I set Paula down beside me and asked George what I could do for him. He lunged forward and started patting my face. I held him up and shook him. He loved it and was giggling his little head off. Just then the telephone rang. Mrs. Taylor got up to answer it.

29

Irish Inherits the Taylor
Foundation

She returned rather quickly and her voice trembled as she said, "Pam, it's your father. He's had a heart attack and is in the hospital." I jumped up and called for Maggie. Maggie came running in, wanting to know what the trouble was. "Maggie, will you watch the twins for us? Mr. Taylor has had a heart attack, and we must rush over to the hospital."

"Certainly, Irish. You go on ahead and don't worry about a thing. Call me, and let me know how things are after you get there."

"I will, Maggie," I said as we hurried out the door and got into the car.

Mrs. Taylor filled us in on what she had been told over the phone. It seemed that Mr. Taylor had been attending a meeting and had suddenly clutched his chest and fell to the floor. They called an ambulance and rushed him to the hospital.

I let Pam and her mother out by the door and went on to park the car. I joined them as quickly as I could in the emergency waiting room. They still had no word on him and were really worried about the outcome at this point. Pam and I comforted Mrs. Taylor as best we could, but there was little we could do to ease the shock and the sadness with which it hit all of us.

About twenty minutes later the doctor appeared at the door and asked, "Is anyone named Irish out there?" I told him I was Irish. "Mr. Taylor won't quiet down until he talks to you. Would you please make it as quickly as possible?"

"Okay, Doc. And would you fill Mrs. Taylor and her daughter in on what is going on while I'm talking to him?"

"Surely."

I walked over to the table where Mr. Taylor lay and took his hand. "Hi, Mr. Taylor. What are you trying to do to us here?"

"Hi, Irish. I'm so glad you're here. Irish, I'm getting ready to die and I have to talk to you."

"Don't talk like that, Mr. Taylor. You'll pull through this thing all right."

"No, Irish. I know this is it. There is no sense trying to console me. I don't have much time, Irish, so please don't interrupt until I'm through."

"Okay, Mr. Taylor."

"I'm turning the Taylor Foundation over to you, Irish—lock, stock, and barrel. I want you to take good care of it, and when it's your turn to join me, I want you to give it to my grandson. Will you do that for me?"

"What about Mrs. Taylor?"

"Irish, I know Mrs. Taylor loves you and has been having an affair with you. I realize how emotionally involved she became with you when you were recuperating, and I also realize how much you are in love with her. It's okay, Irish. I never minded, for you made her extremely happy and by doing so made me extremely happy too. The last two years of our marriage were definitely the best years, and we attribute them to your coming into our lives. I want you to look after Mrs. Taylor and protect her from all the gold diggers and con artists who would prey on her loneliness and need for companionship. If she really falls in love again and wants to get married, it's all right, Irish. I just don't want to see her get hurt."

"I understand, Mr. Taylor, and I'll do my best."

"I know you will, Irish, and this will make a prediction of mine come true."

"What is that, Mr. Taylor?"

"I once said that you could be the richest and the happiest man on this earth, and now you have a chance at becoming the richest man on earth if the Taylor Foundation continues to prosper as it has been doing. Just don't let go of your basic values, Irish, and you'll also be the happiest."

"Look, Mr. Taylor, would you like to see Pam and Mrs. Taylor? They're right outside the door."

"Yes, Irish, I would like that."

I walked over to the door and asked them to come in. The doctor blocked the door and said he would not permit it. I grabbed his arm firmly and squeezed it, and told him to stand aside.

"He's a very sick man and can't stand the strain," the doctor insisted.

"He's a dying man who wants to see his wife and daughter: now *I* must insist *you* stand aside," I said.

He gave me the weirdest look, and I stared right back at him. He knew I meant it and so he stepped aside.

We walked over to the table, Mrs. Taylor and Pam took up positions on either side of him, while I stood at the foot of the table. They took his hands and were remarkably composed, fully comprehending what was happening. He smiled at them and said he was one of the luckiest men ever to be born and had no regrets now that it was almost time to call it quits. "I appointed Irish the man of the family now, and he'll look after you both. Irish has more than enough love in his heart for both of you and my grandchildren. I want to thank you, Paula, for sticking with me all these years. I can only hope it's been worthwhile for you."

"Oh, George, it has been. We had some rough and lonely years, but the good years more than made up for the bad ones. I have no regrets and would do it all over again with you."

"Thanks, Paula. My lovely daughter, Pam, who was smart

enough to pick out the happy, homey philosopher named Irish who has no price tag. My little baby who gave me some of the happiest moments of my life, especially little Paula and George. Thank you, honey." Pam leaned over and kissed him. He closed his eyes and said, "I'll be waiting for you, Paula, when it's your turn to join me."

I looked up at the monitor, and it went flat. The doctor and the nurses moved in and asked us to please leave the room. They were going to try to revive him. We walked out in the hall and stood in total silence for the next ten minutes. Finally the doctor appeared and told us they had failed. "Don't blame yourself, Doctor, you did everything you could. Come on, Mrs. Taylor, let Pam and me take you back home." She was softly sobbing into her handkerchief. Pam and I supported her arms and helped her through the door. I had them wait while I got the car and drove up front to pick them up. We were all overcome with grief and spoke very little on the way home. I told Pam to stay with her mother and that I would start notifying everyone and call the undertaker and make all the necessary arrangements.

I called Helen first, and she and John came right over. I called Mr. Jacobs and Jerry. I then called the mortician and told him we would be over in the morning to make all the arrangements for the funeral. I was on the phone calling everyone I could think of, informing them of the sad news.

Mrs. Taylor appeared at the library door with a tray of coffee and rolls. I stood up to greet her and took the tray from her and set it down on the desk. I took her in my arms and just held her tightly for the longest time. I asked her if she would like to sit down and talk.

"I'd like that, Irish." She was pretty well composed by now, although she had big tears in her eyes.

"Oh, Mrs. Taylor, I wish I had the words to comfort you. Death is as much a part of living as being born, but it strikes with such suddenness sometimes that it takes us completely off guard and we are unable to cope with it. It is times like this when we have to draw upon our faith in God and try to accept it as his will. He alone has the Master Plan and he alone can answer the question 'why.' We just have to accept his wisdom and knowledge and believe that everything happens for a reason, even though the reason may never be known to us. Pam and I both experienced the other side of life, Mrs. Taylor, and I can tell you right now, Mr. Taylor is in the hands of the Lord and completely consumed by that brilliant light of warmth and love both Pam and I spoke of. We just have to believe his work here on earth was completed, and he has gone to his final reward, as you, I, Pam, and everyone alive will do one day."

"Would you like me to tell you what Mr. Taylor and I spoke of before you and Pam came in, Mrs. Taylor?"

"Yes, Irish. I would like that."

"His main concern was for your well-being, Mrs. Taylor, and he charged me with ensuring your happiness. He knew of our affair and told me it was perfectly all right. He was convinced that your loving me only made you love him more. He told me the last two years with you were the happiest ones of his life and he even tried to attribute that to my coming into the picture. Of course, I dismissed all that as nonsense and told him that you and he had many, many years of happiness before I ever came upon the scene."

"He claims to have left the entire Taylor Foundation to me —lock, stock, and barrel. I questioned the wisdom of this and suggested it belonged to you, not me. He insisted this was the best solution in case you were to find another love and want to get married again. It would eliminate charlatans, con artists, or others who might try to take advantage of a lonely widow with millions of dollars. He claims this way you can be sure they will only want you for you, and not for your money. However, Mrs. Taylor, I don't want the slightest bit of friction or resentment between us, so if it's true, I want to go on record right this very minute as stating I will give it all back to you, every single penny, if you want. Your love means more to me than all the money in the world. As for being lonely, you'll never be lonely or want for anything as long as Pam and I are alive. Please let me assure you of that."

"Is that all he told you, Irish?"

"No, Mrs. Taylor. He spoke of Pam and wished he had raised her differently. I assured him he did just fine by her. If he had raised her any other way, she and I might never have met, and he might have been denied his grandchildren. He thanked me, and told me that was a very consoling thought. He also said that when I died, he wants the Taylor Foundation to go to little George. His main concern was for your happiness, Mrs. Taylor, and he told me he felt I had more than enough love in my heart for both you and Pam. It relieved him to know that you would always have someone to love you as long as I was alive. At this point I could see he was fading fast and I asked him if he would like to see you and Pam. He said that would make him very happy. You know the remainder, Mrs. Taylor."

"Oh, Irish, I feel so relieved he knew about you and me. That somehow takes the guilt away, if you know what I mean."

"I do, Mrs. Taylor."

"As far as his leaving the Taylor Foundation to you, Irish, I couldn't agree more with him. You're the only person on this earth to guide the foundation in the direction it should go. I doubt if I'll ever have another romantic encounter in my life, Irish, except you. You're all I'll ever need to keep me from being lonely. Even if we never have another physical encounter, just knowing you love me will be enough."

"Thank you, Mrs. Taylor. Would you like a cup of coffee now?"

"I sure would, Irish."

I fixed her a cup of coffee and then went to the door and called Pam in. She went directly to her mother and asked if she was feeling all right.

"Yes, honey. I'm okay now that I've talked it over with Irish. I think I'll be able to accept it and with time—that's the big thing now—get used to the idea that your father is really gone."

"Oh, mother, would it help if Irish and I and the twins moved back in for a month or two to help you over the rough spots?"

"I'd love that, darling, but you two have your lives to live, and I wouldn't want to interfere with them."

"Now, enough of that, Mrs. Taylor. It's all settled. We'll be here for as long as you need us, or until you get sick of us and throw us out."

She smiled and even managed a little laugh and said, "I can hardly imagine that ever happening, you two. If it were up to me, I'd have you sell your house and move back here permanently: then I could really spoil the twins right, couldn't I?"

"Don't discount the idea, Mrs. Taylor. We may get used to living here and not want to move out."

She smiled again and said, "Let's just play it by ear for a while, shall we?"

"You bet, Mother."

Arnold knocked on the door and said there were quite a few people out there and wanted to know if we wanted to see anyone.

"We'll be there shortly, Arnold."

"Are you sure you're up to this, Mrs. Taylor?"

"Yes, Irish, I'll have to face it sooner or later, so why don't we all go out there now and be as gracious as possible?"

There must have been twenty-five or thirty people there to express their condolences and we mingled with them freely. I happened to notice that one guy had Mrs. Taylor cornered, and she seemed quite irritated by him. I asked Pam who he was. She looked and said, "Oh, no. He's one of daddy's old business associates. Mother despises the ground he walks on. He was always trying to get her to leave Daddy and go out with him. He can't keep his hands to himself. I guess now that he found out Daddy is gone, he thinks the door is open to him."

"Are you sure, honey?"

"Yes, I'm sure, Irish."

I walked over toward them. He kept putting his arm around her, and she kept putting it down and moving aside. "Who's this gentleman, Mrs. Taylor?"

"This is Mr. Evans, Irish."

"Say, Mrs. Taylor, I believe Pam wants to talk to you." She heaved a sigh of relief and started walking across the room. Mr. Evans started in hot pursuit. I tripped him and apologized saying, "I'm truly sorry." He gave me a dirty look as I helped him up. I said, "I would like to talk to you for a moment, if you don't mind."

"I don't have time right now. Mrs. Taylor needs me to comfort her. Don't you realize she just lost her husband and needs me?"

"Don't flatter yourself, Mr. Evans. She loathes you, and the sooner you get your ass out of this house the better she'll like it."

"No punk kid is going to tell me what to do. I'm staying right in this house until she tells me to leave."

"I'm saving her the trouble by telling you for her. Arnold, would you get Mr. Evans' coat. He's leaving right now."

"Arnold, forget the coat, and prepare the guest room for me. I'll be spending the night." I grabbed his hand, quickly put my arm inside his and had him in such a position that by applying pressure on his hand I could have broken his wrist. I told him to keep his mouth shut and start walking, or I would break his wrist. I escorted him outside, with Arnold right behind me. Arnold had summoned Henry, the chauffeur, and the four of us stood there in the driveway.

"Now, that we're outside, Mr. Evans, I can speak a little more freely. You're just like a goddamned vulture, trying to swoop down and pick up the pieces. You're not worthy to lick Mrs. Taylor's shoes."

"Well, who in the hell do you think you are to tell me? Mrs. Taylor can make up her own mind, I guess."

"She has. She hates the sight of you, and always has. I'm her son-in-law and am now custodian of the Taylor fortunes. Mr. Taylor left Mrs. Taylor penniless and totally dependent on me, so your dreams of winning her over for her money are all gone, Mr. Son of a bitch. Now get the hell out of here before I break both your legs and you have to crawl out. Henry, Arnold, if you ever see him around here again, sic the dogs on him. Call the police and have him arrested for trespassing."

He turned and walked to his car and left in a cloud of smoke. I just shook my head at Arnold and Henry and muttered, "Some people are just too much, aren't they?" They both agreed, and we all went back inside.

Mrs. Taylor came over and thanked me for getting rid of Mr. Evans. "That was all I needed on a night like this."

"I'm sorry I didn't see him sooner, Mrs. Taylor. And you just let me know if he so much as calls you on the phone, will you?"

"I certainly will, Irish. George was right, wasn't he? It didn't take the parasites long to start moving in."

"It sure didn't. He was brazen enough to think he was going to take over the guest room and be your constant companion. To see you through this thing, he said. I never wanted to hit anyone so much in all my life."

"Thanks again, Irish. I feel safe and secure, knowing you're around."

I smiled at her and said, "Be assured that Pam and I will let no harm come to you, Mrs. Taylor."

"I know that, Irish, and thanks again."

Helen and John came over to me and asked if there was anything they could do. "Oh, Helen, if you could stay and look after the twins for us, it would be a great relief to us all."

"Certainly, Irish. John, will you run back home and get my things for me?"

"Certainly, and I'm sorry, Irish."

"Thank you, John. Helen, what in the world would we ever do without you? I certainly appreciate this."

She smiled and said, "It's nothing, Irish."

"Yes, it is, Helen, and I want you to know we cherish your and John's friendship more than anything on this earth. Even money couldn't buy your friendship; that's what makes it so priceless to us, Helen."

"Thank you, Irish, and we feel the same about you, Pam, and Mrs. Taylor."

Speaking of Mrs. Taylor, Helen, how do you feel she's holding up?"

"Remarkably well, Irish. However, I'm sure the full impact of what has happened has not caught up with her yet."

"I'm sure you're right, Helen, and we'll stay close by her for the next few days."

Pam walked over to us and told us she had just checked on the twins and they were sleeping. I put my arms around her and asked her how she was holding up. "I'm all right, Irish; it's Mother I'm worried about. She is remarkably calm, and I'm afraid it is going to hit her all at once."

"Yes, honey. Helen and I were just talking about that, and we'll all have to stay close by her for the next few days. Helen is going to stay over and watch the twins for us while we make the arrangements and all in the morning." Pam gave her a hug and thanked her. "You're precious, Helen, and Irish and I both love you." She smiled and said, "Thanks, you two. Now let's go talk to your mother and see if we can get her to go to bed early tonight. She is going to need all the strength she can muster."

We walked over to her and she even managed a smile for us. "Helen is going to stay over and help us with the twins, Mrs. Taylor." "Oh, thank you, Helen, we certainly do appreciate it."

"It's my pleasure, Mrs. Taylor. Now how about you? Don't you think it would be a good idea for you to retire early tonight?"

"No, Helen, I strongly believe I can face it with my son and daughter here to support me and see me over the rough places. They have both experienced death, and I must draw upon their faith for reassurance that it was meant to be this way. As Irish pointed out, only God has the Master Plan and only he knows why; we simply have to accept Mr. Taylor's death as God's divine will. They both assured me that George is in the hands of the Lord now and would want me to get on with the business of living. I guess tonight proves, beyond a doubt, that none of us knows where or when death will strike us. We must live as if each day will be our last day, for it may very well be. Now, as long as I have Pam and Irish to draw my strength from, I'll be just fine."

We were up early the following morning after a fairly good night's sleep. We sat at the table in silence and picked at our breakfast. We were soon on our way to make arrangements for the funeral.

We stopped first at the funeral home. We then went to the cemetery to choose a lot. It was extremely painful for all of us because the lot Mrs. Taylor chose was only a few yards from where Carol was buried. We went on to the church and talked to Father Thomas for over an hour. With the arrangements all made, we decided to go back home.

There were a great many people there at the house to give their condolences and offer help of one sort or another. There was even one investment broker who somehow made his way into the house and tried to corner Mrs. Taylor. What a heartless son of a bitch! I saw him talking to Mrs. Taylor and had no idea who he was, but I kept my eye on him. Suddenly Mrs. Taylor motioned for me to come over.

"Irish, this gentleman is leaving. Will you please show him out?"

"Certainly, Mrs. Taylor. This way, my friend."

"Wait a minute. Did I say something to offend you? Someone is going to have to look after your affairs for you, Mrs. Taylor, and I just thought I could help."

Mrs. Taylor just kept walking. I motioned for him to follow me and started for the door. He chose not to follow me and decided to take another crack at Mrs. Taylor, figuring he had nothing to lose at this point, I guess. I turned and when I saw him approaching her again I saw red. I rushed over and said, "This way, buddy. Don't make the same mistake twice." I went outside with him and told him he had better never show his face around there again.

"Well, all I did was present my credentials and tell her we would be only too happy to manage her affairs for her."

"Right, you fuckin' parasite. You guys don't even give the body a chance to get cold before you start moving in. Now get your ass off this property before I have you locked up for trespassing." He turned and walked away, thoroughly convinced that he had done nothing wrong. To him, it was strictly business, I guess.

I went back inside and found Mrs. Taylor and told her I was sorry that had to happen to her. "It's all right, Irish, as long as I have you to look after me, I won't let things like that bother me."

"Well, if anyone else tries anything like that, I'm going to make an example of him for all the world to see, so they will all leave you alone."

She smiled and touched my face. "Thanks, Irish. I think I'm going to like having you look after me as you look after Pam. Mr. Taylor sure knew what he was doing when he left you in charge. I'll always be grateful to him for doing that, Irish, for I could never manage alone."

"Oh, Mrs. Taylor, you'll never know how happy that makes me to hear you say that. I want to take care of your every want and need for as long as you live. To tell the truth, I didn't sleep much last night. I kept having this terrible thought that you might resent what Mr. Taylor did, and in turn resent me. I couldn't bear that, Mrs. Taylor. I want you to know that any decision you make regarding the Taylor Foundation will be my command and will be carried out without hesitation or question."

Pam joined us and asked if everything was all right.

"Yes, honey," said Mrs. Taylor, putting her arms around her. "Some men are born into greatness while others have to work all their lives to attain it. The vast majority never come close. Then there is Irish, who has had it thrust upon him. I know he will carry it well, and on Irish, it looks simply wonderful."

"I know, Mother. By the way, we've decided to sell our house and have the twins help raise you. How does that sound?"

"I'm overwhelmed. I'm sure we'll all be very happy for all the days of our lives."

30

Life is All But Over for Irish

After the funeral, we arranged to have our things moved back to Mrs. Taylor's house. But instead of selling our house we decided to lease it out. It just meant too much to us and held too many fond memories for us to sell.

Things went along at a whirlwind pace for the next six months. We were all pretty well adjusted to the idea that Mr. Taylor was actually gone, and we were learning to get along without him. It was extremely difficult and trying at times, but we were all learning to cope with it.

The twins, Paula and George, were beginning to walk now. They were getting into everything, but they could do no wrong as far as Mrs. Taylor was concerned. They seemed to fill the void left in her life by Mr. Taylor's death and she cherished them. Of course, Pam and I were rather fond of them ourselves.

I was sitting in the living room one evening when Pam joined me. She looked a little pale, which worried me. "Are you feeling all right, honey?"

"Fine, Irish, I'm just a little tired. I seem to tire awfully easy lately."

"Perhaps you had better make an appointment to see the doctor."

555

"Oh, it's nothing, Irish, I'm sure. Do you feel up to playing the piano tonight, Irish? I'd like to sing with you."

"Sure, why not? Are you sure we won't disturb the children?"

"No, they're fast asleep. And once they're asleep you couldn't wake them if you played the piano right beside them. They get their good sleeping habits from you, I'm sure."

"Oh, yeah! Well, what would you like me to play for you?"

"You know, Irish."

"Okay."

I started playing "Danny Boy" for her as I had done perhaps a hundred times in the past. Sure enough, by the time I got to the second verse, the tears were flowing down her cheeks like a sparkling waterfall. I would usually get caught up in the emotions of the moment and after I was through playing we would wind up in each other's arms sobbing away and just holding on for dear life. It was a very sad song, but it seemed unnatural that it should stir our emotions as it did.

We were soon joined by Mrs. Taylor, who had heard us at the piano and had decided to join us. She wanted to hear her favorite "I'll Take You Home Again, Kathleen." After I finished she leaned over and gave me a hug and a kiss.

"Mrs. Taylor, would you do me a favor?"

"Sure, Irish, what is it?"

"Would you call the doctor and make an appointment for Pam? She tires awfully easy lately, and I'm concerned about her."

"Oh, Irish, I'm all right. He's just an old worrywart, Mother. I'm just fine."

"Well, honey, it wouldn't hurt to get the doctor's opinion. And if he tells us you're just fine, then my mind will be at ease. Will you do it for me, please?"

"All right. I'll do it tomorrow, if it will put your mind at ease."

"Thanks, sweet pea. I love you, and wouldn't want anything to happen to you."

She gave me a real strange look and put her arms around me and hugged me as tightly as she possibly could.

I jokingly said, "I don't know what I said to deserve this, but I sure like it." As I sat there holding her in my arms, she was softly crying on my shoulder. "Ah, what's the matter, honey? Did I do something to upset you?"

"No, Irish, I'm okay. I just feel sentimental tonight. It's really all right."

"Say, I don't mind, honey. That's what my shoulders are for —for you to cry on, anytime you like."

"Thanks, Irish. I love you more than life itself."

"And I love you, too, sweetheart."

"Okay, Mrs. Taylor, you can call the doctor in the morning, if you will."

"Consider it done, Irish. But I'm sure Pam is right, and there is absolutely nothing to worry about."

"Well, if I wasn't absolutely certain of that myself, I'd take her to the doctor tonight. But it won't hurt to be sure. Right?"

"Right, Irish."

Pam and I retired early that night. After we were in bed Pam suddenly asked me if I would read some poetry to her.

"What would you like to hear, lover?"

"Oh, Irish, would you please read to me the last verses of *Sonnets from the Portuguese?* They seem to stir all the emotions I have been feeling lately, Irish. I guess I'm getting sentimental in my old age."

"Oh, listen to you now. I don't think you're ready for a rocking chair just yet. Let's see, now.

> *I thank all who have loved me in their hearts*
> *With thanks and love from mine. Deep thanks to all*
> *Who paused a little near the prison-wall*
> *To hear my music in its louder parts*
> *Ere they went onward, each one to the mart's*
> *Or temple's occupation, beyond call.*
> *But thou, who in my voice's sink and fall*
> *When the sob took it, thy divinest Art's*
> *Own instrument didst drop down at thy foot*
> *To hearken what I said between my tears . . .*
> *Instruct me how to thank thee! Oh, to shoot*
> *My soul's full meaning into future years,*

557

That they *should lend it utterance, and salute*
Love that endures, from life that disappears!"

"How do I love thee? Let me count the ways.
I love thee to the depth and breadth and height
My soul can reach, when feeling out of sight
For the ends of Being and ideal Grace.
I love thee to the level of everyday's
Most quiet need, by sun and candle-light.
I love thee freely, as men strive for Right.
I love thee purely, as they turn from Praise.
I love thee with the passion put to use
In my old griefs, and with my childhood's faith.
I love thee with a love I seemed to lose
With my lost saints—I love thee with the breath,
Smiles, tears, of all my life! and, if God choose,
I shall but love thee better after death."

"Beloved, thou hast brought me many flowers
Plucked in the garden, all the summer through
And winter, and it seemed as if they grew
In this closed room, nor missed the sun and showers.
So, in the like name of that love of ours,
Take back these thoughts which here unfolded too,
And which on warm and cold days I withdrew
From my hearts ground, indeed, those beds and bowers
Be overgrown with bitter weeds and rue,
And wait thy weeding; yet here's eglantine,
Here's Ivy! take them, as I used to do
Thy flowers, and keep them where they shall not pine.
Instruct thine eyes to keep their colours true,
And tell thy soul, their roots are left in mine.

ELIZABETH BARRETT BROWNING

"Oh, thank you, Irish. I'm sorry I cry so much lately. I guess I'm turning into a big baby on you."

"Nonsense, honey. I love it when you get sentimental like this. You're so kind and loving to me that I should read to you every night."

"Irish, what would you do if I died?"

"I don't even want to think about it."

"No, seriously, Irish. Would you be able to let me go without putting up a struggle should the time ever come?"

"Oh, Pam, darling, let's not talk about such things. I can't bring myself around to thinking about it. Please, let's just drop the subject and talk about something more pleasant."

"Okay, Irish. I love you, Irish, and don't ever want to leave you. Please make love to me like you've never made love to me before, Irish. I'll do my best to return your love, darling, with my every breath, smile, and tear, just like in that beautiful piece of poetry you just read to me."

True to her word she couldn't have loved me more. I could feel all the sweet warm vibration from every inch of her beautiful body. She was simply radiant and all aglow with warmth and affection, the likes of which I never experienced in my life. I tried my very best to be as warm and loving to her, but I'm sure I didn't even come close.

"I love you, Irish. Oh, God, how I love you! Promise me you'll never forget me, Irish, as long as you live. Please promise, Irish, please."

She was crying openly by now as I tried to calm her. "Hey, of course, I promise, darling. What is all this? You're breaking my heart with all these tears. What are you trying to tell me, sweetheart? You're being very enigmatic, and I can't for the life of me imagine what you're getting at."

"Hold me, Irish. Please hold me."

I took her in my arms and held her tightly to me until she had cried it all out of her system. "Feel better now, honey?" "Yes, Irish. I'll be all right now."

I decided not to pursue the subject any further, thinking she would tell me in her own good time and in her own good way.

The following morning I was up and off to the Taylor Foundation as usual. After an uneventful morning, I had a surprise visitor. My dear, sweet wife dropped in and offered to take me to lunch. How could I refuse such an offer?

During lunch I asked her if she had seen the doctor.

"Yes, Irish, I have. He took some blood and wants to run some tests on it. I don't know what he hopes to find or what he's trying to prove. I'm perfectly all right. In fact, I'm taking the twins for their swimming lessons right after lunch."

"Well, that's great, honey. I'm sure there is nothing to worry about. How are the twins doing with their lessons, by the way?"

"Oh, great, Irish. They take to the water like a couple of fish. Who knows, maybe we'll have a couple of Olympic swimming stars on our hands in a few years."

"Well, time will tell, love. But if they have any athletic talent, it will have to have come from the Taylors. We O'Malleys are not athletically inclined."

"Oh, come on, Irish, I've seen you swimming when you were paralyzed from the waist down, so you can't tell me you're not a super swimmer."

"Well, I had to, or you and your mother and Helen would have beat the hell out of me. And that's the truth."

She laughed and said, "Irish, I'm gonna bop you on your nose."

I leaned close to her and dared her to do it. Instead of hitting me she caressed my face and gave me a tender little kiss.

"Wow! Pam, you'd better be careful. Remember what happened that night on the big bear rug in front of the fireplace?"

"I remember, Irish, and I'll try to restrain myself."

"Please, not on my account." I laughed, and so did she. "I love you, Pamela."

"I love you, too, Irish, and much as I hate to leave such good company, I have to hurry home and get the twins so we're not late for their lessons."

"Okay, love, and thanks for lunch."

"My pleasure, Irish. Any time at all."

It was three days later when Mrs. Taylor called me at the office one morning. It seems the doctor had called her and set up an appointment for Pam, her and me for that afternoon. I asked what the trouble was. She told me the doctor had been very cryptic and had only said that he would fill us in on the details when we got there this afternoon. I made arrangements to meet them there at the doctor's office at one o'clock and spent the remainder of the morning wondering what in the world was going on.

One o'clock finally arrived, with Mrs. Taylor, Pam and me

560

sitting in the doctor's office waiting for him to put in an appearance. We didn't have to wait long before we were ushered right into his office.

I was the first to speak and asked him why all the secrecy.

He sat down behind his desk and opened a file folder he had been carrying with him. His voice was solemn as he spoke. "I wish I didn't have to tell you what I'm about to tell you."

"What is it, Doc?"

"Pam has infectious hepatitis, and there is nothing we can do for her."

"What are you saying, Doctor? There has to be some mistake. Surely there is something you can do to fight it. I just will not accept this. It is simply out of the question. Come on, Pam, Mrs. Taylor. We'll go to another doctor or perhaps I'll take you to Baltimore to Johns Hopkins, or some other medical school, where they'll be able to treat you and get you all better. I'm sorry, Doc, but you're fired."

"Irish, please, sit down. We have run every conceivable test known to man, and there is nothing that can be done. Irish, you know me well enough to know if there was the slightest chance, I'd say take it; but there is no chance she'll survive."

Pam and her mother were sitting there dumbfounded. The full shock of what we had been told had not quite registered with any of us yet.

"Would you please leave us alone for a little while, Doctor?"

"Certainly, Irish. Take as much time as you want. I'll be in the other room."

"Oh, God! Mrs. Taylor . . . tell me I'm not really here. Tell me that this is all an illusion and not real. Tell me I'm dreaming and will wake up shortly. Pam, I love you. I refuse to believe God would do this to us. How can he? Why you, love? Why not me, instead? Oh! Sweet Mother of Christ, why are you doing this to us? Why?"

I walked over to where Pam was sitting and reached for her hand. She stood up, and I threw my arms around her and began to cry openly. "Oh, God! I love you, darling, and I can't give you up. I just can't."

"Oh, dear, dear, Irish, please, let's not talk about it now. Just let me hold you. We have now. We have today and we'll make the most of what time we have left, Irish. Please don't do this to yourself, Irish."

I held on to her for what seemed like an eternity. Mrs. Taylor came over and put her hand on my shoulder and asked if we would like to go home. "Yes, Mrs. Taylor, we had better go home. Come Pam, darling, let's go home with your mother."

It was well into the evening before I could even regain my composure enough to talk intelligently. I was completely depressed. "What a way to get it," I thought, "right between the eyes, no warning, no nothing. Bam! there it is. Oh, Pam, darling, I'm so sorry. I only pray God will take me with you. I can't bear the thought of going on living without you."

"Irish, don't talk like that. We must be brave and accept this as God's will."

"You know he told me he would be back for me some day. We should be thankful for the year of heavenly bliss he gave us, Irish. He didn't have to do that, you know. He could have kept me when he had me before, but he let me come back to you, Irish."

"I know the Lord works in strange ways, honey, and that he has the Master Plan, and only he can answer why or how. I'm trying to accept what's happening, but I'll never stop praying and begging, if that will help, for God not to take you from me."

"Oh, Irish, I love you, and I wish things were not as they are; but I'm trying with all my heart and soul to accept this as God's will. Please bear with me, darling, and help me see it through. I'm going to have to draw upon your inner peace and strength, Irish. I'll never be able to face it alone; but together, just as we faced everything else in life, we'll see it through and manage to accept whatever God has in store for us."

"Pam, darling, I'm so sorry. Here I am only thinking of myself, as usual. Of course I'll help you, sweetheart, and I'll never utter another word of dissent. We'll see it through together, and I promise to accept whatever happens as God's will. I love you, sweet pea, with all my heart and soul."

She put her arms around me and hugged me for all she was worth. She suddenly said "Come on, Irish. Let's go skinny-dipping."

"You got it, sweetheart," I said, as I returned her smile.

We hurried down to the pool and quickly shed our clothing and dove in the pool. We had a terrific time for about fifteen minutes and then Pam became very fatigued. I helped her out of the pool and we lay there, reminiscing the past while she tried to regain her strength. Somehow it seemed more comfortable talking about the past and all the good times. It was as if we didn't even dare speak of the future or that we were afraid to.

We made love there by the pool and spent the remainder of the evening there before retiring to our own room. Before she fell asleep, Pam asked me if it would be possible for us to get our little house back.

"I'll see to it first thing in the morning, honey. I'll have our tenants put up in a nice hotel for a while, or perhaps send them on a vacation, but I'll get our house back for you."

"Thanks, Irish. If I have to die, I want to die there where all the warmth and love of my life lies in the very fibers of that little love nest of ours."

I could contain my tears no longer and tried to bury my head in my pillow so Pam wouldn't see me crying. I had promised to be strong for her sake. She put her arm around me to comfort me. "I'm so sorry, Irish, I shouldn't have said that. I was just thinking out loud."

I quickly regained my composure and told her if it helped to talk about it that I was more than willing to listen and would try to control my emotions.

"Thanks, Irish, I knew I could count on you to help me, darling. I love you, Irish. I know it sounds like a broken record, but I don't know how else to say it. I love you! I love you!"

"I know I won't have to worry about Georgie and Paulie. Between you and Mother, they'll be just fine. Please don't let them forget me, Irish. Promise?"

I promised her through my tears that I would perpetuate her

memory for all times—not only to our children, but to the world.

"Thanks, Irish, but my touch of immortality lies with God in heaven and I'll have you all with me again someday so we can share eternity together."

"Oh, that sounds so wonderful, Pam, darling. If we only could just make it happen without going through this long drawnout process of living and dying. But then, it wouldn't be worth having if it were not worth working and suffering for now, would it?"

I continued to hold Pam close to me and weep myself to sleep while praying. "Lord, I am not worthy that thou should come under my roof. Speak but the word and my soul shall be healed. Lord Jesus, please forgive me a sinner. Show me the light and the way. Give me the strength to bear up under this heavy load you have laid upon my back. Help me not to falter for Pam's sake. Help me to be strong. Give me the wisdom to say all the right things and the courage to accept your will. If it be thy will, then it shall be done. Lord, you are greater than any problem I could ever have. Lord, I hurt; Lord, I hunger; Lord, I thirst. I know I'll never be worthy of your love, Lord, but if you would but speak the word, then my hunger and thirst would be satisfied and my hurt would be soothed."

I woke up the following morning and eased out of bed so as not to wake Pam. I went out into the hall to use the phone. I called the people who were leasing the little house from us and told them I would like to talk to them this morning and that it was very urgent. I then went on down to the kitchen and got Maggie to fix Pam her special breakfast of soft-boiled eggs and toast and a pot of tea. Poor Maggie was sure taking it hard, but was trying to be brave for my sake. I reassured her that it wasn't easy for any of us, and we would all have to place our faith in the Lord and accept this as his will.

She had big tears in her eyes as she handed me the tray. "Thanks, Maggie, I'm gonna need you to be strong for me. Will you do it for me?"

"Sure, Mr. Irish."

I returned to the bedroom and set the tray down on the nightstand. I sat on the edge of the bed while I gazed at my lovely wife sleeping there. She had such a peaceful contented look on her face that it would have been a sin to wake her. As I sat there, she reached over to my side of the bed and began feeling around while saying, "Irish, where are you?"

"I'm over here, love." She opened her eyes and smiled her beautiful smile at me. It simply turned me inside out. She reached for me, and I fell into her arms.

"I love you, Irish."

"And I love you, Pam darling."

There was a little tap on the door, and I went over to answer it. It was Georgie. I picked him up and carried him over to the bed and sat him on his mother's lap.

"How did you get out of your crib, young man?" He just smiled and cooed and wanted to play. It wasn't long before Mrs. Taylor came looking for him.

"How in the world did he get out of his crib?"

"I don't know, he must have heard his daddy up and crawled out over the top. Paula is still sleeping."

"Well, she's an old sleepyhead like her mamma here. George and I are the early birds, and we catch all the worms, don't we, Georgie?" He smiled and began to clap his hands for me.

Mrs. Taylor reached for him, saying, "Come on, big guy, it's time for your bath and then we'll get you some breakfast." He put his arms around her and gave her a big hug.

"I think he likes you, Mrs. Taylor."

"I know he does, Irish."

After they were gone, I told Pam I had her breakfast for her.

"Oh, aren't you sweet." She sat up and I got her all comfortable and put her tray on her lap for her. I sat there and chatted with her until she finished. "Look, love, I have something very important to take care of this morning, so if you will let me get away for about an hour, I'll have a big, big surprise for you, okay?"

"Sure, Irish, I love surprises. What are you up to, and what is my surprise?"

"You're also very curious, and if I told you it would not be a surprise, now would it?"

"Can you give me a hint?"

"No, no, no."

"Just let me get dressed and I'll be back as soon as possible."

"Okay, Irish. Are you sure you don't want to tell me what it is?"

"I'm sure, sweet pea."

After I dressed and kissed Pam good-bye, I hurried down to the river and told our tenants just what I had in mind. They were more than happy to go along with the arrangements. They began packing their things immediately while I called for a mover and some extra help. I also had them send a truck and several men to the Taylors' to pick up our things there and bring them back to the cottage.

I called the Taylors' house and got Mrs. Taylor on the phone. "Oh, Mrs. Taylor, can you get away for a few minutes? I have to talk to you alone."

"Sure, Irish, where can I meet you?"

"How about that little restaurant down by the river? Don't tell Pam where you're going, all right?"

"Sure, Irish. I'll see you there in about twenty minutes."

I got there first and was sitting at a table over in the corner when Mrs. Taylor came in. I stood up and motioned for her to join me. I took her coat for her and held her chair as she sat down.

"You're still the perfect gentleman, Irish."

"Thank you, Mrs. Taylor. You and Pam make it so easy for me to want to be a gentleman."

I sat down and reached across the table for her hand. "Oh, Mrs. Taylor."

"Irish, I wish I had the words to comfort you or knew what to say, but I don't."

"I know, Mrs. Taylor. And I'm sure it is just as hard on you as it is on me. I just wanted to talk it over with you alone. I don't have any idea of how I'll ever learn to cope with it. I'm going to need you more than ever, Mrs. Taylor."

"Yes, and I'll need you, Irish. We'll see it through together just as we have with the other tragedies and setbacks we've experienced. We'll make it, Irish. Paula and Georgie are counting on us to make it. Pam is sure we'll make it, and we promised to raise those children in such a manner as to make her proud and perpetuate her memory."

"We will, Mrs. Taylor. I hate to ask this next question, but I have to know."

"Don't ask, Irish. Pam has less than two weeks. Once the infection starts spreading, she'll go very quickly."

"Will she suffer much, Mrs. Taylor?"

"No, Irish, the medicine and drugs will ease her pain considerably. Our love and understanding will make it bearable for her. We'll have to be strong for her sake, Irish. We have no choice."

"I know, Mrs. Taylor. She made a special request last night, and I am getting it taken care of right now."

"What's that, Irish?"

"She wants to move back into the little house, so I've made arrangements to have our tenants move into a hotel for a while and put their things in storage. I have a van coming to your house to have her things moved back into the little house. Will it be all right with you, Mrs. Taylor? She told me if she has to die, she wants to die in the warmth and comfort of our first little home. She loved that little house with her whole heart and soul and it holds so many fond memories for us. Our children were conceived there, and oh, the countless happy hours we spent together there—the walks down by the river, the barbecues with you over, and the sing-alongs at the piano. Just everything, Mrs. Taylor."

"Of course. You're right, Irish, and I'll do whatever I can to help."

"Thanks, Mrs. Taylor; I knew I could count on you. It seems I'm always counting on you."

"I wouldn't have it any other way, Irish. Now I had better get back before I'm missed."

"Okay, Mrs. Taylor, and I'll be along shortly. Don't tell Pam about the arrangements for the house yet. It's going to be a surprise."

"You've got it, Irish."

I waited for a respectable interval and then drove back to the Taylors' house and swept Pam off her feet and rushed her out to her car and drove off. I didn't want her there when the movers showed up.

"Where are we going, Irish?" "To the moon, sweetheart, and then to the top of the universe, and then beyond."

She laughed and said, "We've been there before, Irish. Take me some place different this time."

"Well, will you settle for a trip to the mountains for the afternoon?"

"Okay, I'm sure you'll find some way to keep me amused up there."

"Oh, you bet I will, love, you bet I will."

We spent the afternoon high up in the mountains enjoying the pleasure of each other's company, just relaxing the way only we could do with each other. It was almost impossible to believe the repose Pam and I had. I never could remember a time when she ever spoke an angry word to me, or I to her. Our love was like something you only dream about. We complemented each other in every respect, beautifully and perfectly. There was no way we could have been better matched, even if it had been done with a computer.

We were on our way home when she asked me what my surprise was.

"Patience, my dear, patience."

"Oh, come on, Irish, you can tell me now. The day is almost all gone anyway."

"Well, okay then, how about if I just take you and show you?"

"Good, I love surprises. How long will it take to get to our little dream house on the river? Oops. I goofed, didn't I?"

"How did you know?" I asked after I stopped laughing.

"Oh, Irish, you have always gotten me everything I ever wanted, and I asked you to get our little house back last night, and I just guessed, that's all."

"Oh, love, you're so precious and beautiful." I stopped short while trying to contain the tears that were rolling down my cheeks.

"Come on now, Irish. You promised."

"I know, Pam, and I'm truly sorry. Please forgive me and try not to pay any attention to me when I cry. Just keep in mind that they are tears of joy I'm shedding because I'm so happy God sent you into my life. Just think of them as tears of joy because of all the happy times we spent together. Oh, God! How I love you, darling."

"Thank you, Irish. No girl was ever loved more than you have loved me. I thank God for what we had, Irish, and I want you to be happy for me when I go. Please don't be sad or weep for me. You have experienced the hereafter, Irish, the same as I have, and you know I'll be happy with God and all our loved ones who went before me. We'll be waiting for you all to join us, Irish. Promise you won't be sad."

"Oh, Pam, I can't promise you that. My heart is aching for you, honey, and I don't ever want to get over you. I'll constantly think of you for as long as I live, Pam. As for being sad, I'll do my best to try and only think of the good times, and when I do I'll smile, and I couldn't possibly be sad when I remember your precious smiling face."

She snuggled into me as we drove on and on trying to get to our little house before dark. The sun was just beginning to set as we pulled into the driveway. Mrs. Taylor was just coming out the front door, and she had the twins with her.

"Hi, Mother!" "Hi, Mrs. Taylor!" We greeted her as we got out of the car.

"Look, Mrs. Taylor, I'm sorry we ran off like we did, but I wanted to surprise Pam. I couldn't fool her, though. She guessed it."

"No, no, everything is all set. I don't mind a bit. I'll take Paula and Georgie home with me tonight so you can be alone."

"Thanks for everything, Mrs. Taylor." "You're quite welcome, both of you."

We kissed her and the twins good-night and waved to them as they drove off.

We decided to take a walk down by the river before going in

the house. We didn't walk very long because Pam tired rather easily. Upon returning to the house, I picked her up and carried her through the doorway. Mrs. Taylor had all our things arranged exactly the same as Pam had originally arranged them before we had moved into the big house with Mrs. Taylor.

"Do you like it, honey?"

"Oh, Irish, you and Mother are too much. It's just perfect, and just the way I wanted it to be. I'm glad I said yes when you asked me to dance that night in San Francisco."

"I'm kinda glad you said yes, too."

"Do you want me to build a fire, honey?"

"I'd love a fire, Irish, and I'll fix us a snack and something to drink. We'll eat on the bear rug in front of the fire, okay?"

"Okay, but as soon as we're through eating, I can't guarantee what will happen next."

"I'll take my chances, Irish."

We spent a beautiful evening together, reminiscing by the fireplace. We cherished every waking moment of every day. Pam would continue to tire very easily, and by the end of the first week she started to run a high temperature. The doctor checked her daily and wanted to put her back in the hospital where they could monitor her condition closely.

Pam refused, and I backed her to the hilt. I told the doctor not even to suggest it again. "Pam wants it this way, and that's the way it is going to be. You either treat her here, or not at all."

"All right, Irish, I'm sorry. I just thought it would be easier on all concerned if Pam were in the hospital. It can't be easy knowing what's happening and living with it twenty-four hours a day."

"What about Pam? How do you think she feels? It's the least we can do to be with her and hold her hand for as long as she wants us to."

"I know, Irish, and I'm sorry. I apologize for interfering."

"It's okay, Doc. We understand each other now and shouldn't have to discuss it ever again. Consider the subject closed."

Pam continued to fade quickly, and I finally consented for Mrs. Taylor to call the priest to give Pam the last rites of the church. It broke my heart to see Father Thomas going into her room. There seemed to be an air of finality about it. The stupid clock on the wall kept ticking away and in a fit of despair I walked over, took it from the wall, walked to the door, and threw it out into the yard. I don't know why. Perhaps I thought if I stopped the clock, somehow all time would stop, and I wouldn't have to face the inevitable task of giving up Pam.

Helen and John were there, and Helen came over and put her arms around me and began to cry on my shoulder. She didn't have to speak a word. I knew how she felt and could feel her heart breaking as she held me even tighter. "Oh, God, why does it have to be this way?"

Father Thomas came to the door and asked us all to come in. Pam was calling for us. Maggie kept the twins out in the living room while Mrs. Taylor, Helen, John and I, along with Father Thomas, gathered around Pam's bed.

She had a truly radiant smile on her face, more radiant than any smile I had ever seen on her face before. She looked at us and thanked us all for being there.

"Oh, Irish, take my hand. It's time, Irish, and they have come for me. Remember you told me you would let me go without too much of a fuss."

I couldn't speak a word. It took all my powers of concentration to hold back the tears.

"Mother, Helen, John, where are my babies?"

Mrs. Taylor went to the door and motioned for Maggie to bring the twins in.

We held them for her one at a time. She kissed them and told them to be good for their daddy and grandmother. Maggie took them back out of the room and Pam looked at me and said, "I'll be seeing you in heaven, love." She closed her eyes and was gone.

I looked at everyone in the room, told them she was gone, and asked them if they would please give me a few minutes alone with her. They departed, closing the door behind them.

All the pent-up fears and emotions were finally released. I was weeping openly as I leaned over and kissed her beautiful face. "Oh, dear God, please take good care of her. I don't know why you chose to take her from us and perhaps I'll never know or understand why. But I'm sure you must have your reasons for wanting this beautiful angel in heaven with you. It was Pam's wish that I thank you for what time we had together on this earth, and I do, Lord. Please give me the strength and courage to carry on."

I kissed her again and slowly drew the sheet over her lovely face. I turned and walked slowly out the door. My eyes were so full of tears that I could hardly see where I was walking and I tripped over the coffee table. I barely caught myself before I fell. I then asked Mrs. Taylor if she would take me away for a little while.

"Surely, Irish. Helen, help Irish to my car, and I'll be out in just a minute."

Helen walked me to the car. Neither one of us spoke. We just stood by the car in silence, letting the tears flow like water. There was simply nothing any one could say or do. It was God's will and it was being carried out. All we could do was stand by and watch, as time and fate carried out their duties.

Mrs. Taylor came out shortly and I gave Helen a hug and a kiss and got in the car with Mrs. Taylor, and we drove off.

Somehow, perhaps through the grace of God, we made it through the funeral and even survived for two weeks beyond. I was trying to learn how to live without my heart and soul, for they were buried with Pam. I was only a shell of a man. I would go for long walks, and all I would see were faceless people. I would listen without hearing. I would look without seeing. I would touch without feeling. I was stripped of my heart and soul. Nothing was real any more, everything was just an illusion to me. I was truly walking through the worst storm of my life and felt sure it would never end. I was certain I was losing my mind.

I would go over to the cemetery and sit by Pam's grave for hours on end, just reminiscing and praying to God for the strength to go on without her.

DONALD R. WAGNER

As if in a trance-like state, lyrical rhymes would pop in and
out of my head.
Despair would set in

> My heart is a sad and lonely affair
> It's cold and lonely, but who's to care
> I cannot see or hear or feel
> I'm so numb, so pitiful, so unreal
> I possess no heart with which to feel
> Just empty illusions with which to appeal
> My case to the Lord and with life to deal.
> It's as if I'm lost on some distant shore
> Just sitting and listening to the ocean's roar
> Oh, must I be lost forever more
> Nothing more than a wreck upon the shore
> Just the wretched shadow of a man am I
> Oh, why must I live while my wife had to die
> Please dear Lord, please hear my cries
> For it is with you and my wife that I must abide
> Unlike a ship that struggles on a stormy sea
> There are no ports to comfort me
> It is only in heaven where I'll be free
> To love my wife as she loved me
> Oh, how I long for worship and adore
> Just to be with my wife forever more

Then I would cry out in desperation

> Oh, angel of death, is there no appeal
> It's my lonely fate you also seal
> Like a thief in the night, so brazen and bold
> You stole her life, my heart, my very soul
> For as I lie in my cold, lonely bed
> After all is done and all is said
> With aching heart the words are read
> My dear sweet precious wife is dead.

I would remember her smile

> How rare and captivating was her smile
> Complimenting her uniqueness so tame, yet wild
> A rare, rich, kind and loving smile
> Oh Lord, can you tell me of her status now?

I would remember her love

IRISH

> God created with love—my wife saw with love
> She lived with love—she gave with love
> Beautiful, rare and rich—her gift of love
> She gave with the highest compliments of love
> Captured in the warmth of her loving affections
> To all whom she knew—she gave love's perfections.

I was sitting by her grave one bright, warm evening when Mrs. Taylor walked up behind me. She put her hands on my shoulders and asked if I was all right. I stood up and acknowledged her presence with a smile and a kiss.

"I'm all right, Mrs. Taylor. It doesn't seem to hurt as badly today as it did yesterday, and perhaps tomorrow it will hurt a little less, until I may even be able to finally start living again."

"Oh, dear, dear, Irish, it's been such a short time. You take all the time you need, Irish. Everyone understands, and we are all here for you if you need us."

"Thanks, Mrs. Taylor. I want to be fair to you and the children, and I'm afraid I haven't been worth living with since Pam has gone. But I'll make it up to you and the twins. I promise."

"We know you will, Irish. Listen, I found this letter from Pam in her nightstand, Irish. It's addressed to you. Would you like to be alone to read it?"

"No, no, dear Mrs. Taylor. We never kept anything from you, and I'm afraid I wouldn't be able to read it through my tears. Would you please read it to me?"

My dear, sweet, precious Irish:
God's will has been done, and life has come full cycle once more. I am now in heaven with the Lord and await you, my love. God will come for you when your work on earth is through. You must believe, love, and keep the faith.

Oh, dear, Irish, I wish I had the gift of words to express all that I felt for you on earth and how I wish to spend eternity with you. Please indulge me, sweetheart, while I borrow from the songs and poetry we loved so much to feebly attempt to tell you how very much I love you once and for all.

You remember 'Danny Boy,' don't you?

The words flashed through my mind and the tears welled up inside my eyes as I recalled the words. I fell to my knees, and Mrs. Taylor asked if she should continue. I nodded my head yes.

> "You've come back when all my flowers are dying
> I've gone to rest but dead I'll never be.

DONALD R. WAGNER

You've come and found the place where I am lying
    Please kneel and say a special prayer for me
And, I shall hear though soft you speak above me
    And Oh, my grave will warmer, sweeter be
For as you pray, you'll tell me that you love me
    And, I shall sleep in peace until you come to me."

I fell down on her grave and was sobbing my heart out. Mrs.
Taylor knelt down beside me and stroked my head. "Irish, I had
better not go on just now."
"Oh, please do, Mrs. Taylor, maybe I can get all the hurt out
of my system. If you will, please finish."
"All right, Irish."

Oh, dear, dear, Irish, it will seem an eternity, but time will pass quickly, and
one day you, too, will escape the bounds and bondage of earth and together
we'll fly aimlessly through God's heavens, through paradise, enjoying all the
magnificent beauties and the magnificent splendors too numerous to mention.
All the pleasures set forth for us by God himself. Never ending, ever changing,
never wanting, never caring. Only peace, sweet, sweet peace, my darling.
Sweet peace and tranquillity; and we will be uninhibited, unafraid, and unashamed to express our love and devotion for one another for all eternity, with
God and our loved ones.

Weep not for me, my love, for I am in the hands of the Lord. We both await
your smiling face, Irish.

". . . I love thee with the breath,
Smiles, tears of all my life! and, if God choose,
I shall but love thee better after death."

All my love, Pam